Democratic Miners

SUNY Series in American Labor History

Robert Asher and Amy Kesselman, Editors

Other books in this series include:

DEMOCRATIC MINERS

Work and Labor Relations
in the
Anthracite Coal Industry, 1875–1925

PERRY K. BLATZ

State University of New York Press

Published by
State University of New York Press, Albany

©1994 State University of New York

For information, address the State University of New York Press,
State University Plaza, Albany, NY 12246

Production by Christine Lynch
Marketing by Dana E. Yanulavich

Library of Congress Cataloging-in Publication Data

Blatz, Perry K.
    Democratic miners : work and labor relations in the anthracite
coal industry, 1875-1925 / Perry K. Blatz
        p.   cm. — (SUNY series in American labor history)
    Includes bibliographical references and index.
    ISBN 0-7914-1819-7 (alk. paper). — ISBN 0-7914-1820-0 (pbk. :
alk. paper)
    1. Coal miners—United States—History.   2. Anthracite coal
industry—United States—History.   3. Trade-unions—Coal miners-
-United States—History.   4. United Mine Workers of America-
-History.   I. Title. II. Series.
HD8039.M62U6148 1994
331.88'122335'0973—dc20   93-843
                                                              CIP

10 9 8 7 6 5 4 3 2 1

to
Warren D. Blatz and William A. Shaughnessy

Two gentlemen with whom I have been privileged to share
my preoccupation with the past

Source of Map:
United States Geological Survey, *Twenty-Second Annual Report to the
Secretary of the Interior, 1900–1901*. Part III, *Coal, Oil, Cement*.
(Washington: Government Printing Office, 1902).

The WYOMING FIELD is the northernmost. Its principal cities are Carbondale, Scranton, Pittston, Wilkes-Barre, and Nanticoke. To the south is the LEHIGH FIELD, in and around Hazleton and from Tamaqua east to Mauch Chunk. To the south and west is the SCHUYLKILL FIELD, comprising the cities of Mahanoy City, Shenandoah, Shamokin, and their vicinity, and also extending west from Tamaqua past Pottsville into Dauphin County north of Harrisburg.

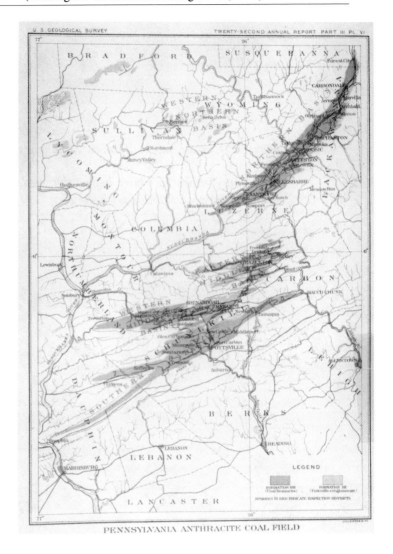

PENNSYLVANIA ANTHRACITE COAL FIELD

CONTENTS

List of Figures

List of Tables

PREFACE

I was drawn to this topic by a fascination with work. Industrial work has long held a great deal of interest for me, perhaps because I have so little firsthand knowledge of it. Because of its complexity, the work process in the anthracite coal industry in the late nineteenth and early twentieth centuries has been especially intriguing. I acknowledge that work is only one facet of the experience of workers, but one that is just as important as life away from the job. More than a decade ago, David Brody suggested that historians might well find the workplace to be "the common ground applying to all American workers."[1] While this is not the place to undertake a full bibliographical treatment of American labor history in the 1980s—or, as it is increasingly called, "working-class history"—I believe that too few historians have taken Brody's advice. While not focusing on the workplace, John Bodnar has labeled it as one of three arenas, along with the family and the neighborhood, in which workers "could actually exert some power and influence."[2] I have chosen only one arena for this study because I believe that, for this industry at least, that arena needed detailed treatment.

This book is also about unions, in particular the United Mine Workers of America (UMWA). As a graduate student in the latter half of the 1970s and early 1980s, I fully absorbed the dominant ethos of those years, that the lives of American workers must be told "from the bottom up." Labor unions were generally considered not to be a central part of this story, at least labor unions that had success in organizing and collective bargaining like the UMWA. But I found, as my interest in work in the anthracite industry developed, that I could only do justice to the topic by devoting a growing amount of attention to the union. In trying to tell that story, I have worked not so much "from the bottom up" but "from the top down," as far as I could go. For example, newspapers and district union convention proceedings are relatively traditional historical sources, but in using them I have sought to dig deep enough to get at what a rank-and-file worker or a rank-and-file delegate might have thought.

Thus this book describes a great many little known workplace disputes and internal union quarrels. In many ways it is a "local history" of the workplace and the anthracite districts of the UMWA. Without such detailed treatment, a great many of the historical actors on these pages would never have a chance to appear. Still, I have delved into this industry, not to bring a number of hitherto ignored individuals and events to light, but to tell the story of the experience of work and the unionization of the anthracite coal industry. I have done my best to go beyond well-known labor disputes like the anthracite strike of 1902. While not ignoring that epic struggle, I have tried to place it in the context of numerous workplace disputes to reconstruct how individual mine workers might have related to that strike. I have also sought to go beyond what took place at the national level of the UMWA to reach the district level and, when possible, even the local level. It would be much easier for the reader and, to be sure, for the author, if that could have been done through broad generalization. But, for such an approach to succeed, the historian would have to view individual workers in much the same way that the operators of the coal mines viewed them. The operators dismissed the specific, detailed grievances of workers by pointing out that any changes in the work regime would necessitate a higher price for coal that the market could in no way bear. In dealing with the union, they wanted to negotiate with as few leaders as possible and over only the broadest issues. As I note below, such an approach makes the experience of the individual worker irrelevant.

It is a pleasure to have the opportunity to thank those who have helped with a project such as this, especially when it has consumed some fifteen years, from the beginning of my research on this topic to publication. At the dissertation stage, three fellow graduate students long ago at Princeton University—Christine A. Lunardini, Michael S. Mayer, and Leonard N. Rosenband—provided useful criticism as well as camaraderie. I'm afraid I've lost track of them, but I attribute that to my struggle to complete this work. That means that now that I have the time to try to get back in touch with them, I had better do so. The readers of the dissertation from which this work has eventually emerged, Michael A. Bernstein of the University of California at San Diego and Daniel T. Rodgers of Princeton University, offered numerous helpful criticisms. I also had the very special opportunity of working with Arthur S. Link of Princeton University as my advisor. Melvyn F. Dubofsky of the State University of New York at Binghamton provided helpful comments and advice on the dissertation as its outside reader. More recently, he took the trouble to mention my unpublished work along with other published works in a keynote address to a conference on the anthracite industry. That encouraged me in my labors toward publication. Joe Gowaskie of Rider College has read portions of my work at various times and offered helpful commentary. Although my conclusions have differed somewhat from his, my work has been improved by what he had already done.

Throughout my research, I have been assisted by capable and courteous professionals at a number of archives. Over the years, Lance E. Metz of the Center for Canal History and Technology in Easton, Pennsylvania, has consistently aided me above and beyond the call of duty. Mary Ann Landis, formerly of the Anthracite Museum Complex, has helped me on a number of occasions. Years ago when he was executive director of the Wyoming Historical and Geological Society in Wilkes-Barre, Pennsylvania, William H. Siener extended considerable assistance and hopitality. So did June Wech and the late William P. Lewis of the Lackawanna Historical Society in Scranton. In the early stages of my research, Matthew Magda and Carl Oblinger were kind enough to introduce me to oral history. Several veterans of the anthracite coal industry—Roger J. Howell, E. Stewart Milner, Russell Jones, and Joseph and Michael Seliga—allowed me to take advantage of their years of experience by consenting to be interviewed.

Anthony Zito of Catholic University of America not only kept me entertained during a delightful visit to the archives there recently, but he also showed sufficient faith in me to grant access to the unmicrofilmed portion of the John Mitchell Papers. Denise Conklin of Historical Collections and Labor Archives at Pennsylvania State University has been most helpful, as has Christopher Baer of the Hagley Library. The staff of the George Arents Research Library at Syracuse University always rendered courteous, professional assistance during my visits there. I also appreciate the cooperation I've received in obtaining photographs to illustrate this work from Michael Knies of the Center for Canal History and Technology, Chester J. Kulesa of the Anthracite Museum Complex, and Wendy Franklin of the Wyoming Historical and Geological Society. In addition, Jule Znaniecki of Nanticoke, Pennsylvania, graciously agreed to let me copy several photographs from her personal collection without ever having met me face to face. I especially appreciate her help.

A number of people at Duquesne University have assisted me on this project. Sally Lutz has kept things running smoothly in the history department despite my practically incessant requests for xeroxing. One of our student aides, Christopher Hyde, has handled most of those requests in his own inimitable manner, and he also brought a number of his Macintosh skills to bear in setting up a particularly complex table for me. Three graduate assistants provided invaluable help. David Janssen scanned most of my dissertation, and Christine Scafidi "cleaned up" the scanned text. Aimee Robertson saved me from a number of errors by her careful proofreading. Denisa Gloster of the Duquesne University Library assisted me in processing numerous interlibrary loan requests. Also, the University provided support through grants from the Noble J. Dick Faculty Development Fund and the Westinghouse Computer Literacy Fund.

Two portions of this work have appeared in print previously. Part of chapter 2 served as my contribution to the proceedings of a most pleasant conference in April 1989, which has become *The Early Coal Miner,* edited by Dennis F. Brestensky of Pennsylvania State University, Fayette Campus. Also, part of chapter 4 became "Local Leadership and Local Militancy: The Nanticoke Strike of 1899 and the Roots of Unionization in the Northern Anthracite Fields," *Pennsylvania History* 58 (October 1991): 278–97, through the efforts of its most able editor, Michael J. Birkner of Gettysburg College. I would like to thank the Pennsylvania Historical Association for giving me permission to reprint it. In bringing this work into print, I've benefited greatly from the assistance of Christine M. Lynch and Clay Morgan of SUNY Press.

In recent years, I have come to realize just how difficult it is to find time to critique the work of others while trying to pursue your own. Thus I especially appreciate the efforts of two friends, Joseph F. Rishel of Duquesne University and Howard Harris of Pennsylvania State University, who have given me considerable help on several chapters of this book. I also appreciate the occasional prodding and persistent encouragement of the chairman of my department, Bernard J. Weiss, who helped me put into perspective the significance of Rinaldo Cappellini. In addition, I would like to thank Michael P. Weber of Duquesne for reading the dissertation on which this work is based, making helpful suggestions for revision, and commenting on various revisions. He not only found time to do this in a most busy schedule as Academic Vice-President and Provost, but he has consistently provided encouragement and support.

My deepest professional debt is to the editor of this series at SUNY Press, Robert Asher of the University of Connecticut. When I first spoke to him about this work, I had come to believe that this material, however much confidence I retained in it, had little appeal to others. He not only showed interest in it, but gave me the kind of guidance I needed to turn it into a book. While I should be ashamed to make such an admission, I must say that he led me to the major themes of this work. Without his effort and insight, I'm afraid it might never have reached print.

If personal thanks are expressed in the depth with which they are meant, they would seem inappropriate in a place like this. Still, I am happy to take this opportunity to thank a number of people whose help and understanding has been all the more valuable since they never experienced the kind of professional pressures under which this work was produced. My father, Warren D. Blatz, is not here to see the final product, but I hope he is aware of it in some way beyond our ken. His love for a good story first sparked my interest in history. With this work out of the way, I hope to visit my mother, Helen F. Wilbert, more frequently. She has given me support and encouragement for more years than I care to enumerate. Her husband, John Wilbert, gave me a striking objet d'art that reminds me of the struggles of mine workers daily when I look at it in my office. My wife's family has provided a great deal of encouragement and understanding over the years, especially her parents, Mary E. and William A. Shaughnessy. I was most fortunate in receiving some especially useful suggestions on revising my dissertation from the latter. But, more important, his quiet courage and unfailing good humor in the midst of the most severe trials have served as an inspiration to me. My boys, Billy and Kevin, may have been just as happy to have their father out of their hair at the office, but I have missed them. Finally, and most important, my wife Kathleen has had to bear much of the burden of this work without the fulfillment of authorship. I only hope that I can make it up to her.

INTRODUCTION

This is a study of working-class militancy, of unionization, and, more generally, of democracy. Two very different episodes of working-class militancy in the anthracite coal industry have been subjected to considerable study—the notorious exploits of the Molly Maguires and the anthracite coal strike of 1902. The Molly Maguires have been examined so often by scholars and other writers that this author could add little to their work.[1] Indeed, focusing on the crimes and punishment of the Mollies fails to tell us much about a far more significant issue at the center of the mythic aura that surrounds them—how and why workers take the initiative to address their own grievances. That issue is central to this study but, unfortunately, it has been largely ignored in examining the industry's other most notable episode, the anthracite coal strike of 1902. While it too has received a great deal of scholarly attention, much of that has been conditioned by the implications of the strike for national politics. The drama of the strike has drawn scholars to it, as President Theodore Roosevelt finally decided to settle the five-and-a-half-month-long walkout by sending Secretary of War Elihu Root to negotiate with the ultimate robber baron, financier J. P. Morgan. As Robert H. Wiebe has noted, the history of the strike has often been presented as a kind of Progressive "morality play." In that drama John Mitchell, the plucky, youthful leader to the United Mine Workers of America (UMWA), gallantly organized and defended the long-suffering multitudes who toiled in the mines against an intransigent set of coal operators led by George F. "Divine Right" Baer. But even the arrogant coal barons cold not ignore the power of the President who, backed by an aroused, progressive public, forced them to accept arbitration.[2]

That tale is a significant one in American history, but it is so significant that it needs to be explored at a much deeper level. Why did the 150,000 men and boys who worked in and around the anthracite mines in 1902 strike for nearly six months against some of the most powerful railroad corporations in the nation? Why did they join the UMWA? Why did that union succeed where others had failed? What happened to the men of anthracite and the union after the epic strike? These are the questions this study will address.

Like so many other industrial pursuits between the years 1875 and 1925, mining anthracite coal was no easy way to make a living. Overall, the hard-

1

ships workers experienced during the long nonunion era from 1875 to 1899 differed only marginally from those they confronted from 1868 to 1875, when the Workingmen's Benevolent Association (WBA), a pioneering industrial union, exerted considerable power in the industry prior to its demise in the latter year. Nor did their struggles for material well-being lessen substantially from 1897 through 1911, when the UMWA managed to establish and maintain a foothold in the hard coal industry. Only when the severe underemployment that had traditionally beset the industry abated from 1912 through 1925 did most workers experience a significant improvement in their standard of living. During each of these periods, the forces that divided workers remained powerful—ethnic rivalry, a labor force atomized into numerous jobs performed by workers of vastly differing age and skill, regional rivalry among the three major fields where anthracite was mined, and the staunch opposition of employers. But, most anthracite mine workers also had to face low, insecure earnings and numerous injustices in the workplace. These shared experiences encouraged solidarity.

The wrenching day-to-day insecurity that American workers faced served as a necessary, but by no means sufficient cause for unionization. The mere existence of low wages and workplace injustices helps to explain the presence of worker discontent and some interest in labor organization.[3] But, like their counterparts throughout an industrializing America, anthracite mine workers faced an exceedingly difficult struggle to accomplish the organized, institutional solidarity that a union represented. Success could be achieved only in conjunction with the periodically rising tide of union fortunes nationwide, coinciding as it did with long-term economic upswings. Still, those had in no way guaranteed permanent unionization in anthracite, as the failure to establish a viable union there during the rapid growth of the Knights of Labor across the nation in 1885 and 1886 showed. Regardless of national trends, unionization, at least in a major industry like anthracite coal, could not be achieved in any significant way without another critical element: a union organization that had competent leaders, a timely sense of militancy, and a willingness—despite occasional radical pronouncements—to accommodate itself to capitalism.

Always weighing in the balance against the many forces that discouraged unionization and divided workers is that evanescent one that constituted the primary impulse toward unionization—rank-and-file militancy. While it necessarily grew out of worker discontent, no clear relationship between the two can be discerned. Especially given the limitations of sources for studying the attitudes of turn-of-the-century workers, efforts that aim to determine the level of discontent they felt from one day to another are likely to reflect our own reactions to the conditions they faced. Similarly, any understanding of how that discontent accumulated and resulted in protest, resignation, or moving away from a particular mine or from the industry altogether hinges on matters of individual personality, which we are all too prone to examine through our own very different frames of reference. What the historian can do is to look at the militant action that occurred in the form of strikes, whether they affected the entire industry for months or individual mines for days. These latter brief, localized job actions, which have received little or no attention from scholars, occurred with and without a union, in prosperous and not-so-prosperous times, and generally resulted from worker antipathy to specific work rules and working conditions. Militancy persisted sporadically during the lengthy nonunion era between the decline of the WBA and the rise of the UMWA, but it did not result in a stable union organization. Nonetheless, mine worker militancy burgeoned into an almost irresistible force that functioned symbiotically with the organizing efforts of the UMWA to unionize the anthracite fields from 1899 to 1902.

The failure of unions in the anthracite industry from 1875 to 1899 and the UMWA's success thereafter arise from a basically similar industrial setting. So do the erosion of the union from 1903 to 1911 and its rebirth from 1912 to 1925. The sources of fragmentation and the roots of solidarity must be found, not just in the all-too-obvious hardships that confronted workers, but in the never-ending day-to-day conflict between worker and foreman in the workplace, and between union and corporate leaders in the larger arenas beyond.[4] Those struggles reflected an ever-shifting balance of forces in which any success or failure, no matter how significant, could only be transitory. The intensity of these conflicts insured that they would serve as a profound learning experience for managers as well as workers. As a general rule, failure spurred learning more vigorously than success.

The men who ran the coal mines, whether they held top management posts in railroad corporations, were independent entrepreneurs, or worked well down the chain of command, displayed an implacable conservatism in seeking to maintain the basic structure of the work regime. Since large-scale anthracite mining had begun in the 1820s, those businessmen had presided over the accumulation of a congeries of ad hoc work load and payment arrangements that, given the complexity that characterized mining, had developed differently from region to region, town to town, company to company, mine to mine, and frequently even from one place to another in the same mine. Those ad hoc arrangements allowed bosses the flexibility they desired to control a workplace whose physical dimensions changed continually, but whose relatively low level of technological change did little to enforce uniformity.[5] Retaining such arrangements as long as possible matched the innate conservatism of men who had grown up with the industry, but, more importantly, such a strategy was quite simply convenient for them.

Workers, of course, had a very different perspective. What their bosses saw as reasonable arrangements, they tended to view as an interminable series of capricious impositions that cheated them while making their lives profoundly insecure. While they undoubtedly wanted to earn more money, the level of their compensation was less likely to arouse the sense of personalized injustice at the workplace that would result in militant action than did the morass of work rules they confronted. For example, anthracite miners could not understand why, at most mines, they were paid not according to the weight of the coal they produced, but according to the number of cars of coal they filled. Those cars differed so much from one location to another that miners came to see the system of payment by car as little more than another way to rob them of the full value of their labor. In a related grievance, miners might accept in principle a company's decision to penalize or "dock" them for loading too much slate or other refuse in a car or for not filling the car full enough. But they had little faith in the fairness of the decision-making process far above them at the surface—a process that consistently levied what the miners believed to be inordinate penalties. Those workers who performed other tasks in and around the mines and were paid by the day faced a very different problem that arose from the same source. They could not understand the utter lack of uniformity in job categories and rates of payment. By speaking about such longtime ad hoc arrangements in terms of veneration, managers merely made workers more generally suspicious of the work regime.

For many years, the perception of injustice fostered by so many aspects of work in the anthracite industry had spurred workers to undertake job actions from time to time, regardless of whether any union was in place. However, that perception could also make workers receptive to a message of unionization, especially when it was delivered by a workers' organization that was growing and had already demonstrated considerable staying power: the UMWA at the turn of the century. As a result of a lengthy strike in the bituminous coal industry in 1897 and chaotic competitive conditions there, the UMWA had successfully negotiated a pathbreaking collective bargaining contract in 1898. Armed with that contract, moderate leaders like John Mitchell had gained for the union a reputation as a responsible labor organization, one that progressive business elements and an increasingly progressive public opinion could accept and even praise.[6]

The UMWA, with Mitchell at its helm, deserves considerable credit for organizing the anthracite mine workers. It was one of all-too-few unions at the turn of the century that eagerly sought to enroll members from the growing number of immigrants from eastern and southern Europe, organizing them on an industrial rather than craft basis. If, like so many other unions, it had hesitated to use immigrant workers' countrymen to approach them in their own languages, it could have had no success at all.[7] But the anthracite mine workers did not join the union merely because John Mitchell and his organizers told them to do so. Many joined because they had recently been or were still engaged in localized job actions that provided a propitious opportunity for the union to send them an organizer. Others undertook walkouts soon after they were initially organized, much to the chagrin of district and national leaders. Such militancy, whether workers participated in it, witnessed it, or merely heard about it, demonstrated to workers that they could challenge the work regime. When it took place concurrently with a well-financed organizing drive by the nation's most powerful union, the fragmentation that had characterized the work force was submerged beneath a rising wave of solidarity. In anthracite, the union gradually became a powerful vehicle for militancy, frequently against the wishes of its leaders. Protected by a strong national union, broad-based local militancy was expressed in a gathering wave of localized walkouts from 1899 up to the eve of the industrywide strike of 1902. That tide of local militancy, as much as the organizing skills of John Mitchell and other UMWA leaders, engendered the marvelous solidarity that kept the industry's 150,000 workers on strike for five-and-a-half months from May through October 1902.

The increased militancy and the unionization of anthracite mine workers proceeded hand in hand with the growth of labor organization nationwide arising out of the economic recovery that followed the depression of 1893–1896. But the railroads that dominated the anthracite coal industry also benefited from that prosperity by finding ways to jettison the competition that had made life difficult for them in the previous two decades. Until 1898 they had experienced little consistent success in their efforts to apportion the market for coal. Only after that year, following considerable maneuvering by J. P. Morgan and his associates to reorganize railroads and interlock directorates, did a lengthy period of price stability and profitability ensue.[8] But while a few of their confréres in big business circles had begun to see growing labor unions as organizations with which they might deal effectively, the men who ran the anthracite railroads could not accept such a progressive stance. They viewed unions as illegitimate institutions that sought to eliminate the employer's "freedom to control" employees and the workplace, generating in the process the most pernicious sort of disorder and challenging the most basic rights of property.[9]

From 1899 to 1902, the horrific vision of union-agitated disorder seemed to materialize for managers unable and unwilling to understand the sources of labor unrest. Workers from practically every segment of the highly differentiated work force rebelled against work rules that had long perplexed and oppressed them. The youngest workers, in their teens and even younger, showed an especially intense combination of militancy and solidarity. The one common element in the experience of anthracite mine workers was the capriciousness of the work regime that flowed from its complexity and the ad hoc way in which it had developed. Workers could unite behind their varied perceptions of unfairness to endorse the call of the UMWA to settle all these matters by meeting with the operators in a system of "joint conferences," like those in which the union had successfully negotiated since 1898 in the bituminous industry. By achieving a contract for mines in the Central Competitive Field from western Pennsylvania to Illinois that helped alleviate competitive pressures for the soft-coal operators there, the UMWA had gained the economic power and public influence it needed to confront the anthracite railroads. But since those railroads had moved effectively on their own, like so many other corporations in turn-of-the-century America, to reduce competition, they could find no positive role for the union. Because they could not bring themselves to see the injustice that riddled the work regime over which they presided, the railroad executives viewed the UMWA as nothing more than a harbinger of anarchy, agitating workers into militant action that, ironically, union leaders generally opposed.[10]

In the anthracite industry, the UMWA took advantage of the mine workers' militancy in mine after mine to organize. Yet, ever cognizant of its own institutional imperatives, it downplayed militant union action, hoping to persuade the men who ran the mines that the union could stabilize labor relations as it had in the bituminous fields. That was an impossible task. The leaders of the UMWA found in many instances that they could not prevent or control local strikes and, in any event, they could never have controlled them sufficiently to allay the suspicions of the railroad executives. Two concurrent but rather separate conflicts headed toward a climax in the epic strike of 1902—one between workers and managers over control of the workplace and another between the union and the railroad executives over establishing collective bargaining. However, the intervention of President Roosevelt in the strike prevented any final resolution. Anthracite coal was such an important commodity that he acted to restore coal production for the winter. But he did not coerce workers to return to their jobs, as Grover Cleveland had done in the Pullman Strike eight years before. Instead Roosevelt pressured the railroad executives, through a J. P. Morgan acutely sensitive to the President's powers to initiate antitrust prosecution, to accept binding arbitration, as John Mitchell had long been willing to do. That the President was willing to use the powers of his office to benefit the UMWA showed how successful Mitchell's strategy of carefully cultivating influential friends and maintaining a respectable public image could be. That public image, when compared to the arrogance displayed by the railroad executives, had weighed mightily in Roosevelt's decision to intervene. Still, to keep that image and those friends, the union would have to keep a tight rein on its members.

Up until this point, workers had learned that they could exert considerable power through rank-and-file militancy and through union organization. However, they had also learned that their power had only been gained through many arduous battles, large and small, with the strike of 1902 keeping them out of work for almost half a year. Their militancy and their allegiance to the union, however deeply rooted in perceptions in injustice, were directed toward pragmatic goals. This was especially true for immigrant mine workers from eastern and southern Europe and their children, who together comprised more than one-third of the work force by the turn of the century. Workers sought a fairer workplace, both for their own self-respect and to feel more confident about achieving the overarching goal of security for their families.[11] Most mine workers, like so many other American industrial workers, would continue to weigh the benefits of militancy along with its risks. They did not hesitate to assert themselves at the workplace, but did so in pursuit of the concrete goal of a fairer, and hence more secure, experience on the job, which would help them obtain greater security for their families. While assertiveness at the workplace undoubtedly petrified employers who saw their most basic rights to property threatened, the workers' actions constituted something far short of a larger vision of "workers' control."[12]

The leaders of the union learned that, with presidential intervention, they could obtain a form of recognition in anthracite. But they also knew that the survival of their organization was in no way guaranteed.[13] Mitchell above all realized just how important a public image of respectability had been to the union's success. The price the UMWA had to pay to keep that image was to stay within the carefully restricted role allotted to labor unions in America at the turn of the century. What the men who ran the union had much more difficulty understanding was just how much the need to maintain a positive image would limit their ability to address the most pressing concerns of workers. In settling the 1902 strike, the Anthracite Coal Strike Commission conveyed the nature of those limits. While it mandated some sizable concessions to the workers, the Coal Strike Commission sought in its award to disrupt the day-to-day operation of the industry as little as possible and thus scrupulously avoided thoroughgoing reform of most management practices. The Commission did little to address the workers' day-to-day perception of unjust dealing by their bosses; consequently the work regime would continue to frustrate workers for the rest of anthracite's life as a major American industry.

The events of the years from 1899 to 1902 had gone largely against the coal operators, but they learned from these years that they could not afford to let the public continue to perceive them as arrogant and avaricious, however accurate such a perception might be. Above all, the anthracite executives realized that they had to be willing to negotiate directly with union representatives. Just as important, from the award of the Commission, they learned that even when the public intervened it would not demand fundamental changes in the way they conducted their business. As they moved toward giving the appearance of being reasonable, the coal magnates also realized they need not go much further—that the appearance of reasonableness was enough.

The men who ran the union found the decade after 1902 to be a most sobering one. As events throughout the nation showed them that a putatively progressive America would not necessarily welcome unions, the leaders of the UMWA came to realize that even when anthracite executives met with them cordially, substantial concessions would not necessarily follow. What they could do was to involve themselves in bargaining locally whenever disputes arose, as they always did in the chaotic anthracite workplace. Gradually foremen and superintendents, as well as top executives, would become more comfortable dealing with the union.

Union leaders also learned that workers looked at them and their organization pragmatically and decided whether or not the accomplishments of the union were sufficient to merit the payment of dues. A growing proportion of workers thought it did not from 1906 to 1912, and the union lost patience with them over the amount of effort necessary to change their minds. Still, at most mines the union retained a presence, however small, and that enabled it in 1912 to take advantage once again of the buildup of grievances and transform it into a rebirth for the UMWA in anthracite. From its earliest days, the union had to deal with the eastern and southern European immigrants who increasingly came to dominate the anthracite workforce. But, after 1900, union leaders had a difficult time moving from encouraging their presence in the union to accepting their full participation in it. This tension, along with the never-ending stream of workplace disputes, helped feed an insurgent movement in the largest anthracite district, which would struggle from 1912 to 1920 before taking control and leaving a habit of insurgency in its wake.

From 1875 to 1925, anthracite mine workers showed a rather sophisticated understanding of two fundamental realities of American capitalism. First, they realized that they would have to plot their own strategies to achieve the dream of security for their families. Second, they appreciated, as labor leaders most assuredly did too, that the men who controlled capital and managed its institutions, however avaricious and arrogant they might be, had a firm grip on the resources that could make those dreams come true.

Still, if anthracite mine workers were too pragmatic to plot the course of their lives toward a vision of industrial democracy, they nevertheless demanded a voice in decisions that affected their earnings, their jobs, and their union. In 1902, the union had succeeded in establishing itself as an effective, if conservative challenger to unbridled corporate power in the anthracite fields. Because the UMWA had done so, workers had considerable freedom, even the freedom to avoid paying dues to the union, one of the few freedoms that coal operators sought to guarantee. Once large numbers of eastern and southern European workers returned to the union in 1912 or joined it for the first time, many would participate in it, whether union leaders liked it or not. By pursuing their right to be heard at the workplace and in the union, workers shaped their own understanding of the pitfalls and potential of democracy.

1

Capriciousness and Complexity: The Insecurity of Anthracite Mine Workers

The capricious character of the workplace regime in the anthracite coal industry in the closing decades of the nineteenth century made it exceedingly difficult for mine workers to achieve either physical or psychological security. In and around an anthracite coal mine—or colliery, as the entire physical plant was called—few workers could be secure in the knowledge that their work was steady, however high a daily wage they might earn. That lack of steady employment gave workers little assurance that they could rely on earning enough to support their families. Just as important, they could have little confidence that they received an amount for their labor similar to those who did such work in nearby mines, or sometimes even in the same mine. Moreover, working as they did in one of the most dangerous industries in the world, they could by no means be confident of surviving to work another day. Capping the reign of caprice was a management style best characterized as a shallow paternalism that offered little to workers but demanded their loyalty in return.

So much of this capricious character stems from the workplace itself, which for most mine workers changed continuously, since the industry's very purpose was to extract that material which constituted the boundaries of the workplace. The miner had to deal with his product as he found it, and the process of production consisted of excavating and removing the workplace itself. Further complicating the process, veins of anthracite coal ranged from essentially level, as was common for bituminous coal, to practically perpendicular. The incline of veins might even change as miners moved through them, and sometimes seams of coal could break off suddenly or double over on top of themselves. Conditions such as these dictated variation and complexity in every area of the work experience, which might vary from vein to vein in a single mine, and far more extensively from one mine to another. The mere fact of such extensive variation militated against security for mine workers in the anthracite region, which stretches more than 100 miles in a sort of crescent from east central to northeastern Pennsylvania through such cities as Pottsville, Wilkes-Barre, Scranton, and Carbondale.[1]

9

Still, variation in the workplace experience cannot be attributed solely, or even most importantly, to geology. That most capricious of human institutions, the market, made its own special imprint on the lives of anthracite mine workers. The anthracite industry's work force expanded significantly during the late nineteenth and early twentieth centuries, more than tripling from 35,600 workers in 1870 to 126,000 in 1890, and eventually moving to a peak of nearly 180,000 workers in 1914.[2] The opportunities for work, however arduous, that this growth provided brought thousands of immigrants from southern and eastern Europe, as did the growth of other American industries in the same period. While these immigrants made up only 5 percent of the anthracite work force in 1880, by 1890 they comprised, with their children, more than 20 percent, a figure which ten years later increased to approximately 40 percent.[3] These workers entered an industry in which ethnic conflict had already flared repeatedly between the Irish and their Welsh and English bosses and coworkers, displayed most memorably in the pursuit, prosecution, and execution of the Molly Maguires in the 1870s.[4] Thus, in the closing decades of the nineteenth century, ethnic fragmentation burgeoned for a work force already fragmented on the job by the many different tasks they performed and the wide variation in the amounts they earned.

EARNINGS, UNDEREMPLOYMENT, AND FRAGMENTATION

Perhaps the most capricious way in which the market shaped this industry is in the pervasive phenomenon of underemployment. Underemployment has long been endemic to the coal industry. When confronted by an economic downturn, coal operators seldom laid off employees for long periods of time, as did employers in other industries.[5] In the latter half of the nineteenth century, especially in the anthracite industry, coal mines were becoming deeper, more extensive, and consequently more expensive to open. Such mines would be ruined very quickly without extensive daily maintenance. Facing high overhead costs, most mine operators continued to produce some coal to maintain cash flow, however low the price of coal might fall. Also, maintaining a low level of production, rather than none at all, served to dissuade mine workers from leaving the area altogether. With some work available, they could hold on, hoping for a relatively rapid return to steadier production. This was essential for the operators, because anthracite production traditionally picked up in the late summer and fall to meet the coming winter's demand for home-heating fuel, anthracite's primary use. Operators needed to insure that a sufficient number of mine workers would be ready so that the mines could move quickly into full production when the need arose.[6] Profit to be made in meeting that peak demand encouraged a great deal of excess capacity in the industry. However, mine workers and their families had to eat each day of the year, and they often found it difficult to do so during months in which the mines might operate two or three days per week, or less.[7]

During 1889, when anthracite mines overall averaged 194 full ten-hour days of operation, about one-quarter of them were in operation for fewer than 150 days.[8] Some might lie idle for months to undergo extensive repairs and a number would be abandoned each year.[9] From 1881 through 1889, the anthracite mines averaged 209.2 full ten-hour days of work per year. The 1890s were much more difficult, however, as the mines averaged only 183.3 full days of operation at the same time that the nation's manufacturing industries averaged 285 days annually—this in a decade in which the nation experienced depression from 1893 to 1897.[10]

The hardship underemployment could bring was poignantly conveyed in 1890 by the Grand Master Workman of the Knights of Labor, Terence V. Powderly. Although he never worked in the mines, Powderly lived most of his life in the largest city in the anthracite region, Scranton, where he served as mayor from 1878 to 1884. When the mine workers of Scranton and vicinity faced one of their many bouts of underemployment that winter, Powderly reported on the distress in a series of letters published in the *New York World*. Among the many cases of distress he reported was that of one Thomas Daley, who had come from Wales to work in the mines of the Delaware, Lackawanna, and Western Railroad (DL & W) some eighteen months earlier. His wife and five children joined him eight months after he had arrived but, at the very time that his financial responsibilities grew, he found he had less opportunity to earn money. After his family's arrival, Daley worked barely half time; and in December 1889, he worked only ten days. January 1890 was even worse—in that month he worked less than seven full days. His earnings for January totaled only $13.10. Powderly told his readers: "Mr. Daley is not an intemperate man, he does not gamble, he is not addicted to any of the vices that reduce the incomes of other men, but he could not fatten his children on $13.10 a month." To add to Daley's already crushing burdens, his wife had died recently, after she gave birth to the couple's sixth child. As Powderly put it: "The hopes which animated Thomas Daley's breast when he came to America but eighteen short months ago are dead ashes on his lonely, poverty-stricken hearth tonight."[11]

Such a tale tells us only that disaster could befall anthracite mine workers and their families, as similar disasters befell many other industrial workers during these years. Unfortunately, the extensive fragmentation of the work force makes an investigation of the standard of living of anthracite mine workers in the 1880s and 1890s especially problematic. Not only did mine workers do a variety of jobs across a broad range of earning potential, but the needs of these workers varied from those of boys living at home to men supporting young families largely on their own to elderly men working out their days in jobs generally held by children.

Mining may prompt visions of a relatively undifferentiated work force but, while this may have been generally accurate for the bituminous coal industry, it was far less so for anthracite. In 1889 nearly 80 percent of mine workers in bituminous were "miners" engaged in the actual extraction of coal from the coal face. However, by the latter part of the nineteenth century anthracite was used primarily as a home-heating fuel, which had to be as clean as possible. Consequently, a much larger proportion of the anthracite work force helped to clean the coal and a much smaller proportion mined it. In anthracite, only 30 percent of the workers were "miners," while approximately 15 percent were "miner's laborers," who loaded coal for the miner. Thus, less than 50 percent of the workers performed the basic tasks of mining and loading coal, and those two jobs were frequently performed separately. Furthermore, approximately a third of the workers were employed outside the mines on the surface. The work force was further fragmented by age, with 37 percent of all surface workers, 6 percent of all underground workers, and more than 17 percent of the total anthracite labor force in 1890 under sixteen years of age.[12]

Anthracite coal was extracted almost universally by the "room-and-pillar" method, in which miners cut rectangular rooms, also called "breasts" or chambers, into seams of coal at regular intervals off the major passageways of the mines, called "gangways." Practically all "miners" were "contract miners" paid according to their production. Usually this meant that miners earned a standard rate for each car or ton of coal mined in a particular vein and were expected to pay their expenses for blasting powder, oil, fuses, and, of course, labor. From time to time, a substantial proportion of miners would become involved in extending the coal workings, driving gangways or airways in what was known as "narrow work," since the passageways created were narrower than mining chambers. As a general rule such work, which required greater skill since it concerned the basic ventilation and transportation system of the mine, was more lucrative than the usual run of work in chambers.[13] In addition, a much smaller number of truly independent contractors performed "development work," that is, major projects undertaken with their own crews of perhaps six to eight men. Such a project was described in the following advertisement in the *Wilkes-Barre Record* in 1886:

> Tunnel to let. Proposals will be received at the office of the Division Superintendent of the Lehigh and Wilkes-Barre Coal Co., First National Bank Building, Wilkes-Barre, Pa. until Saturday, October 23, 1886, for driving a tunnel from the Red Ash to the Ross vein at Nottingham Colliery, Plymouth. Said tunnel is to be driven 12 feet wide and 7 feet clear of the rail, and will

FIGURE 1.1
Miner drilling, circa 1900 (Courtesy of Hugh Moore
Historical Park and Museums).

be about 700 feet in length. Specifications may be seen at the colliery or at
the office of the company's engineer, Wilkes-Barre. Thomas H. Phillips,
Division Superintendent.[14]

Assignment to such relatively lucrative work depended on what could be the
most capricious factor of all, the judgment or whim of a supervisor.

Earnings and conditions could vary substantially, not only from one
mine to another but from one vein to another or even from one chamber to
another.[15] Thus, the work of miners themselves was differentiated in a variety

of ways, from the geological conditions individuals faced to the work assignments they received and, of course, the skill they displayed. This differentiation reflected the freedom of the miner, especially when compared to the growing regimentation most other industrial workers, including bituminous miners, experienced in the latter part of the nineteenth century. While systematic and scientific management proceeded rapidly through American manufacturing at the turn of the century, it moved rather fitfully into bituminous mining and hardly at all into anthracite.[16] Although anthracite workers undoubtedly appreciated the freedom from direct supervision that increasingly distinguished their work, the depth of their appreciation depended upon their prior experience with such regimentation. Their freedom stemmed more from the employer's inability to place production under tighter control than the workers' resistance to change. Those workers might have valued it less than the comparatively steady employment that often prevailed in more closely supervised industrial environments.

Practically all miners were paid according to their production, but that production was measured in very different ways. Most miners were paid for each car of coal they mined, with a variety of different rates and sizes of car in effect, sometimes even at the same mine or at different mines of the same company. Others were paid by weight, a so-called miner's ton, which was far heavier than a standard ton because it included a sizable allowance for impurities. This standard also differed from one mine to another, and whether paid by the car or the ton, miners could be penalized or "docked" if the coal they sent to the surface contained what the docking boss believed to be too much slate, dirt, or other waste. These two methods of payment prevailed in the northern or Wyoming field, where seams of coal were seldom inclined more than ten degrees. In the other method, which was far more common in the central or Lehigh and the southern or Schuylkill fields, workers were paid by the yard, i.e., the amount of distance they advanced in their chambers. Where seams pitched more than thirty degrees, the coal could not be loaded into cars as it was mined, but would be left in the chamber so the miner could stand on the coal he already had mined to enable him to reach the advancing coal face. Thus coal was left in the miner's chamber until he had mined as far as he could, then the company loaded it into cars from the gangway. The miner's rate of advance into the seam was measured as he progressed and he was paid accordingly. Where coal was mined in this way, miners worked in pairs as partners or "butties," because the company took responsibility for loading and the complexities of this method made it most useful to have another skilled man around.[17] Regardless of how the coal was mined, a mine worker was assumed to have at least some basic skills and experience before he started as a miner. The state of Pennsylvania sought to institutionalize this and to limit the entry of immigrants into mining in 1889 by enacting a law requiring new miners to pass an examination before a board of experienced miners in each district and prove they had worked as miner's laborers for at least two years.[18]

Although the miner was generally one of the better-paid mine workers, the complexity and variation found in the workplace resulted in considerable variation in earnings. During 1888, the Pennsylvania Bureau of Industrial Statistics performed an extensive study of miners' earnings. From forty-five anthracite collieries it compiled the net annual earnings of the ten miners at each mine who earned the most and the ten who earned the least of those who worked steadily throughout the year. As can be seen in table 1.1, the average earnings for all of the top ten earners equaled $736.30 for the 243.1 days of work that they averaged. For their slightly shorter work year of 230.6 days, the bottom ten earners received an average of $452.31. Both groups worked quite regularly, with those in the top ten and bottom ten working 98.8 percent and 93.7 percent of the days on which the collieries operated, respectively. The table displays the distribution of the average earnings of the top ten and the bottom ten for the forty-five collieries as well as the considerable differences between the two groups. Average annual earnings for the top ten at each colliery ranged from $942.94 to $440.89, and earnings for the bottom ten ranged from $277.84 to $654.29. However, since both groups worked steadily throughout the year at the same collieries, the number of days they worked differed only slightly. Consequently, the two groups' earnings per day varied considerably, and the distribution of daily earnings at the forty-five mines is presented in table 1.2. Average daily earnings ranged from $4.08 to $2.02 for the top ten and from $2.74 to $1.31 for the bottom ten. The overall average earnings per day for all of the top ten miners equaled $3.03, and for all of the bottom ten overall average earnings per day equaled $1.96.[19]

The leading miners earned an average of $890.62 over 245 days, or $3.65 a day. They worked 99.5 percent of the days that their collieries operated. Individual earnings in this group ranged from $1,327.52 to $537.01. Those anthracite miners who earned less than all other steadily employed miners at their collieries averaged only $381.24, or $1.72 per day for 221.1 days. They worked 89.2 percent of the time that their collieries operated. For this group, earnings ranged from $565.00 to $208.87.[20]

In 1889, the Bureau of Industrial Statistics surveyed all miners at eighteen anthracite collieries regarding frequency of employment. Since there is no way to determine how representative these collieries were, data from them can be labeled as no more than suggestive. Variation from one mine to another was considerable. At five collieries, no workers at all were listed as working less than 100 days. Perhaps significant is the fact that none of these collieries employed more than 100 miners. At five other mines, the percentage of miners who worked less than 100 days ranged from 1.7 to 7.3. At the

TABLE 1.1

Average Annual Earnings For The Top Ten and Bottom Ten Miners at Forty-Five Anthracite Collieries, 1888

	NUMBER OF COLLIERIES WHERE EARNINGS AVERAGED:									Overall Average Earned	Overall Days Worked
	$900–942.94	$800–899.99	$700–799.99	$600–699.99	$500–599.99	$400–499.99	$300–399.99	$277.84–299.99	Total		
Top Ten	3	12	17	6	6	1	0	0	45	$736.30	243.1
Bottom Ten	0	0	0	2	12	16	14	1	45	$452.31	230.6

TABLE 1.2

Average Earnings Per Day For The Top Ten and Bottom Ten Miners at Forty-Five Anthracite Collieries, 1888

	NUMBER OF COLLIERIES WHERE EARNINGS AVERAGED:								Overall Average
	$4.00– 4.08	$3.50– 3.99	$3.00– 3.49	$2.50– 2.99	$2.00– 2.49	$1.50– 1.99	$1.31– 1.49	Total	Daily Earnings
Top Ten	1	9	12	18	5	0	0	45	$3.03
Bottom Ten	0	0	0	7	14	17	7	45	$1.96

eight other mines, the percentage of miners working under 100 days ranged from 18.1 to 70.4. At three of the mines, more than half of the miners worked for less than 100 days, including at the largest mine surveyed, in which 55.8 percent, or 373 of the 668 miners, worked less than 100 days.[21]

Any effort to evaluate these data is complicated by the fact that some of the miners who worked only briefly at the collieries surveyed earned a very good daily average. Consider three miners at one of the collieries. One mined there for fifty-three days and earned $225.04 ($4.24 per day), another worked fifty-two days and earned $204.07 ($3.92 per day), and another worked forty days to earn $172.73 ($4.32 per day). Obviously, each of these miners would have found it difficult to survive if he earned no more money during the year. However, if each could work three other stints like the one cited above, he would have totaled from $690 to $816 in earnings while working from 160 to 208 days.

The search for such highly remunerative mining at various collieries could by no means have been easy. Because of the seasonal character of demand for its product, the anthracite industry could consistently provide full employment for its workers for only several months during the summer and fall.[22] Entire collieries or large parts of them would need to close from time to time for extensive repairs, and some might face abandonment. Since collieries often worked only two or three days a week outside of the peak season, a stint of sixty days of work might take half a year to complete. Although a highly skilled miner could earn a good income at almost any mine, operators gave the best work to their regular miners. A great many of those miners who moved from mine to mine may have begun their journeys out of frustration and ended them in desperation.

Miner's laborers worked for the miner and not for the company. Consequently, companies generally took no notice of them. However, the Lehigh and Wilkes-Barre Coal Company (L & W-B) did pay the laborers, subtracting their wages from the miner's earnings. An examination of that firm's payrolls, which survive for only a few scattered months in the 1890s, gives us some idea of what these workers earned. The payrolls do not indicate clearly the basis on which laborers were paid. In the industry some laborers, most notably many of those who worked for miners performing narrow work, received a set amount per day. But laborers who loaded coal for miners in chambers were generally paid according to the number of cars of coal they loaded. A certain number of cars had become established as an informal daily production standard for miners and laborers. This standard constituted a "shift," and while miners and laborers might occasionally exceed that level of production, more commonly they failed to attain it. At the Wanamie mine of the L & W-B, located near Nanticoke in the Wyoming field, the rate recorded for laborers was $1.55 or $1.65. Since for approximately one-half of the laborers the rate is multiplied by a figure containing a fraction, usually fifths, it appears that a shift of five cars prevailed at this mine.[23] Some found the standard too taxing, but frequently the company prevented workers from meeting their quota by failing to supply enough cars to miners and laborers or closing down the breaker early in the day due to lack of demand.

Not surprisingly, miner's laborers tended to earn substantially less than miners. In addition, they necessarily would have a more difficult time than miners finding steady work, inasmuch as their work schedule depended upon the miner. In the month of April 1890 at Wanamie, some 118 miners averaged earnings of $36.09, while 134 laborers averaged $19.24. For February 1893, 168 miners at Wanamie averaged $42.09 in earnings, while 167 laborers averaged $22.53. In December 1896, a month in which there was an especially small amount of work available, 170 miners earned an average of only $24.72, while 112 laborers averaged just $14.61. Conceivably, with so little work for miners during that month, quite a few may have decided to load their own coal. Finally, in March 1899, 153 miners at Wanamie earned an average of $42.43, while 93 miner's laborers averaged $26.59. Many miners loaded their own coal in that month, too.[24]

Data on employment from the Wanamie colliery indicates that miner's laborers were the most transient of all mine workers. Of those found on the payroll for April 1890, only 17 percent could be found again in February 1893. Of all those listed for that month, only 11 percent appeared on the payroll in December 1896. Finally, of the laborers listed for that month, only 23 percent could be fund on the payroll in March 1899. These rates of persistence are the lowest for all the occupations at Wanamie and substantially lower than the figures for miners. Forty-three percent of the miners on the payroll in April 1890 were still on in February 1893. Forty-one percent of the miners on the payroll that month could still be found in December 1896. Finally, 55 percent of the miners listed for December 1896 were still on the payroll in March 1899.[25]

The fragmentation of the work force is further reflected in the work and earnings of "company men," who earned a daily wage. This category covered a wide variety of jobs, and not surprisingly, little uniformity existed in the industry over the rates to be paid for similar kinds of work. In 1888, the Bureau of Industrial Statistics also surveyed some forty-six mines to determine daily wage rates for company men in forty-three different jobs underground and fifty-three surface jobs. Daily rates at the twenty-eight mines that reported rates for carpenters underground ranged from $1.50 to $2.50, and a total of eighteen different rates were listed. Forty-two collieries reported a total of nineteen different rates for blacksmith's helpers, ranging from $.90 to $1.87. Forty-three mines reported a total of nineteen different rates for barn bosses, ranging from $1.20 to $2.77 for managing the stables housing the mules who did so much of the work both above and below the surface. Some forty-two mines reported eighteen different rates for prop-men, from $1.00 to $2.66 for performing vital work in cutting and placing roof supports, or props.[26]

Part of the wide variation in wage rates for the same job can be explained by the possibility that a job with the same title might encompass very different kinds of work at different collieries. For example, a blacksmith's helper who earned $.90 a day was most likely an actual apprentice learning the trade, while one who received $1.87 a day may well have performed a significant part of the blacksmith's work. A carpenter earning $1.50 a day probably could not match the skill displayed by one who earned $2.50 a day at another colliery. Similarly, the responsibilities of the barn boss who received $2.77 a day surely exceeded those of the one who earned $1.20.

Furthermore, the wide differentials in rates certainly represented one means by which an operator could tailor his work force to the precise geological and economic requirements of his colliery. Indeed, for some positions, such as driver, slate picker, and laborer, most collieries had a scale of wages for different "classes" of workers in the position. Thus, the teenagers who dominated the job of mule driver could earn higher wages by driving more mules and thus transporting a bigger load of coal cars along the main roads of the mines. Similarly, slate pickers, usually younger than the drivers, earned more if they had the final responsibility for removing slate from coal as it slid down a chute past other, lesser-paid pickers above them in the massive industrial buildings—called "breakers"—where the coal was cleaned and broken into appropriate sizes for heating homes.[27]

It is unlikely that such wide variation only reflected the demand of anthracite coal operators for workers with a broad range of skills. Indeed, if the supply of labor in the industry had been elastic, that is, if it had responded effectively to changes and differences in wage rates, those rates would have tended toward uniformity. Since they did not, factors other than the differentials in wage rates must have intervened to dissuade mine workers from moving to mines that paid higher rates, thereby influencing low-paying collieries to raise their rates. An oversupply of labor and the underemployment it bred are the likely causes of this inelasticity. With the outlook for finding steady work elsewhere uncertain at best, there would be little positive incentive for workers to move.

The company men who had the steadiest work were the relatively small proportion of workers involved in the basic maintenance of the colliery— those who fed and monitored the boilers, ran the pumps, and operated the elevators in which men and matériel were transported into the depths of mines. Such workers were practically assured of as many days of work per month as the total number of days in the month. They commonly worked

FIGURE 1.2
Miner, driver, and mule, circa 1900 (Courtesy of Hugh Moore Historical
Park and Museums).

each day except every other Sunday. Since many of these posts had to be manned continuously, the men who held these jobs usually worked a twenty-four hour day on alternate Sundays to provide a day off per fortnight for themselves and their fellow workers. Generally they would be on the job ten hours a day on the busier day shift or fourteen hours a day on the night shift.[28] Although they might earn only $1.50 to $1.80 per day, less than many miners, they could easily earn more than $40 per month or approximately $500 or even $600 per year because of the burdensome steadiness of their tasks.[29]

Because of the opportunity for steady work they provided, these jobs were in considerable demand. Still, such work may well have been too steady at times for these men, especially since their responsibilities were so great. If boilers were not working properly, fans might malfunction, keeping explosive gas from being exhausted from a mine. Any failure of pumps would result in the rapid flooding of portions of a mine.

The most awesome responsibility was in the hands, literally, of the engineers who controlled the carriages that went up and down the shafts. On October 30, 1886, that responsibility weighed heavily indeed upon a veteran engineer at the W. G. Payne Colliery in Luzerne Borough, William Moses. He moved the carriage before a worker named William Brace had finished removing a mine car from it. That Brace and the mine car both plummeted down the shaft was horrifying indeed, but the reaction by Moses may supply some sense of the pressures that beset colliery engineers.

> The falling car made a terrible noise which was plainly audible in the engine room. Moses did not know what had happened and did not stop to inquire. . . . Realizing at once that he had made a terrible mistake in hoisting up the carriage he barely waited to stop his engines, when he drew a pistol from his pocket and placing the muzzle to his head, fired. . . . His employer regarded him as one of their most valued and trusty employees. He was 49 years of age and leaves a wife and family of grown-up children.[30]

Table 1.3 displays the variation in time worked among various jobs at the Wanamie colliery, while table 1.4 examines the average earnings of the company men, along with those for miners and miner's laborers, in four separate months in the 1890s. The high level of earnings and the high number of days worked for pumpmen, firemen, ashmen, and engineers and their assistants have been noted above. Notice how little their earnings vary from the relatively busy months of April 1890, February 1893, and March 1899 to the particularly dull month of December 1896. The "skilled men"—including blacksmiths sharpening mining tools, masons and carpenters building and maintaining structures to channel air throughout the distant reaches of the mine, and timbermen fashioning roof supports—did not work quite as much, but they did work quite steadily. As a result their earnings averaged more than $35 for each month surveyed. The average for teamsters was nearly as high, but they worked more days at a substantially lower rate.

Essentially, other company men worked, like the miners and their laborers, according to the demand for coal. They tended to earn close to or less than $35 per month but, in particular, their earnings dipped significantly in December 1896 when there was the least work at the mines, as measured by the amount of time operated by the breaker. Of course, quite a few of these workers tended to be young, especially in some of the larger categories, i.e.

TABLE 1.3
Average Days Worked by Company Men at Wanamie Colliery for Four Months in the 1890s

	Average Days (Per Month)	APRIL 1890		FEBRUARY 1893		DECEMBER 1896		MARCH 1899	
		No. of Workers	No. of Days	No. of Workers	No. of Days	No. of Workers	No. of Days	No. of Workers	No. of Days
Pumpmen	30.0	6	30.9	8	28.0	6	30.5	6	30.7
Firemen and Ashmen	28.1	10	25.1	10	26.5	8	30.3	9	30.7
Foremen and Bosses (in)	25.4	8	22.9	9	24.1	8	27.5	10	27.2
Foremen and Bosses (out)	24.9	7	24.3	8	22.5	8	26.6	8	26.1
Teamsters (out)	24.3	4	24.4	5	22.4	5	23.6	4	26.75
Engineers and Assistants	23.2	11	23.9	14	21.9	14	23.6	13	23.4
Skilled Men	20.7	14	19.4	18	22.8	21	18.1	15	22.5
Footmen, Planemen, and Headmen	18.0	5	18.6	4	24.15	10	11.4	10	17.9
Miscellaneous Laborers (in)	17.1	9	17.1	10	20.9	7	12.5	9	17.9
Miscellaneous Laborers (out)	16.6	26	17.15	33	18.7	39	11.9	32	18.5
Runners	16.2	8	17.9	13	20.1	9	10.7	9	16.2
Patchers, Oilers, Etc.	15.6	4	18.7	19	18.1	26	8.1	24	17.4
Drivers (in)	15.3	20	15.0	41	17.1	34	11.2	33	18.0
Topmen and Platform-men	14.4	15	16.9	19	16.7	21	8.7	14	15.3
Door Boys	14.1	16	15.7	12	16.4	3	8.2	2	16.05
Drivers (out)	13.4	4	14.4	4	16.2	5	6.9	6	16.2
Slate Pickers	11.2	106	13.6	102	14.2	103	6.25	107	10.6
Breaker	13.9	—	17.1	—	16.9	—	6.7 App.	—	15.0

TABLE 1.4
Earnings At Wanamie Colliery For Four Months in The 1890s

Position	Overall Avg. Earn. $	APRIL 1890 Col. A* $	Col. B*	Col. C* $	FEBRUARY 1893 Col. A* $	Col. B*	Col. C* $	DECEMBER 1896 Col. A* $	Col. B*	Col. C* $	MARCH 1899 Col. A* $	Col. B*	Col. C* $
Foremen and Bosses (in)	64.50	54.53	22.9	2.38	68.52	24.1	2.84	69.12	27.5	2.51	65.85	27.2	2.42
Pumpmen	54.96	56.30	30.9	1.82	51.82	28.0	1.85	55.62	30.5	1.82	56.11	30.7	1.83
Foremen and Bosses (out)	45.86	43.81	24.3	1.80	43.62	22.5	1.94	48.25	26.6	1.81	47.76	26.1	1.83
Firemen and Ashmen	43.26	36.96	25.1	1.47	40.31	26.5	1.52	47.63	30.3	1.57	48.12	30.7	1.57
Engineers and Assistants	41.96	41.51	23.9	1.74	39.71	21.9	1.81	43.25	23.6	1.83	43.38	23.4	1.86
Skilled Men	40.39	37.20	19.4	1.92	44.62	22.8	1.96	35.42	18.1	1.96	44.33	22.5	1.97
Teamsters (out)	36.36	36.21	24.4	1.49	33.60	22.4	1.50	35.50	23.6	1.50	40.12	26.75	1.50
Miners	36.33	36.09	17.3	2.09	42.09	19.2	2.19	24.72	12.1	2.04	42.43	20.0	2.12
Footmen, Planemen, and Headmen	32.09	33.25	18.6	1.79	44.60	24.15	1.85	19.51	11.4	1.71	31.01	17.9	1.73
Runners	29.56	32.62	17.9	1.82	35.94	20.1	1.79	19.22	10.7	1.80	30.48	16.2	1.88
Miscellaneous Laborers (in)	28.05	26.91	17.1	1.57	34.38	20.9	1.65	21.91	12.5	1.76	29.00	17.9	1.62
Drivers (in)	25.47	25.33	15.0	1.69	27.54	17.1	1.61	18.86	11.2	1.68	30.15	18.0	1.68
Miscellaneous Laborers (out)	24.63	26.15	17.15	1.52	26.25	18.7	1.41	18.08	11.9	1.52	28.06	18.5	1.51
Topmen and Platform-men	21.36	24.85	16.9	1.47	24.82	16.7	1.49	12.79	8.7	1.47	22.98	15.3	1.50
Miner's Laborers	20.74	19.24	10.8	1.78	22.53	12.7	1.78	14.61	8.3	1.76	26.59	15.5	1.71
Drivers (out)	15.92	18.35	14.4	1.28	19.17	16.2	1.18	7.98	6.9	1.15	18.20	16.2	1.13
Patchers, Oilers, Etc.	15.73	18.62	18.7	1.00	18.36	18.1	1.02	8.12	8.1	1.00	17.82	17.4	1.02
Door Boys	10.51	12.53	15.7	.80	11.78	16.4	.72	5.93	8.2	.72	11.79	16.05	.73
Slate Pickers	9.28	10.48	13.6	.77	12.20	14.2	.86	5.39	6.25	.86	9.07	10.6	.85

*Column A = Average Earnings

Column B = Average Days Worked

Column C = Average Earnings Per Day

drivers, runners, door boys, and the largest group of all, slate pickers and others who worked at the breaker, known collectively as "breaker boys." Commonly young mine workers would begin as slate pickers at eight or nine years of age or even earlier. Often they would move to jobs beneath the surface as door boys, tending major ventilation doors, and eventually as mule drivers and car runners, supplying cars in which the production of the miners and their laborers could be brought to the surface.

Any attempt to evaluate the standard of living that such a varied picture of earnings may have enabled workers and their families to achieve must begin with a figure that represents the income a family needed to live. Robert Hunter, a journalist and socialist from New York City at the turn of the century, commented in 1904 in his book *Poverty* that after estimating "in the most conservative way possible," approximately $460 a year was needed to defray the basic expenses of a family of five in the industrial communities of the New England states, New York, Pennsylvania, Indiana, Ohio, and Illinois.[31] Since the relative index of food prices in the North Atlantic region for 1890 equaled 88.2 percent of the index for 1904, Hunter's estimate can be multiplied by .882 to yield $405.72—his estimate deflated to reflect prices in 1890.[32] A family of five with children of ages seven, five, and two could conceivably survive on less, according to standards from various contemporary budget studies, a contemporary study of the anthracite region, and basic standards proposed by historian Daniel Walkowitz.[33] Such standards posit a survival-level budget of approximately $320 in 1890, a budget designed to meet no more than the standard set out by the pioneering British student of poverty, B. Seebohm Rowntree—"no allowance is made for any expenditure other than that required for the maintenance of merely physical efficiency."[34]

Of course, these budgets were for families, and throughout the late nineteenth and early twentieth centuries, large numbers of immigrants came to work in the anthracite mines as well as other industries without their families, at least at first. Their lives centered around living as cheaply as possible and saving as much money as possible, to send sums home to Europe either to support their families there or pay for family members to come to the United States. This facet of the experience of anthracite mine workers can be seen in the following excerpt from testimony taken by a committee of the U.S. House of Representatives in 1888. One of the members questioned Nichele Molinaro, a forty-nine-year-old Italian who had resided from 1882 to 1887 in Carbondale, Pennsylvania, near Scranton, where he had worked aboveground at a colliery. He had just returned from Italy where he had visited his wife and child.

Q. What have you been at work at?
A. In the Pennsylvania coal mines. . . .
Q. How much do you get there per day?

A. One dollar and twenty cents per day. . . .

Q. You know you will get a place [a job] right away?

A. I worked four years for the same man all the time.

Q. He is going to take you right back?

A. I suppose so. . . .

Q. Who paid for your ticket to come over?

A. It was my own money.

Q. Money you earned in Italy?

A. No, sir; in America.

Q. How much did you have when you left for Italy?

A. Whenever I used to have any money I used to send it home.

Q. You sent all your earnings home?

A. Yes, sir. . . .

Q. How much could you save a week while you were at work at Carbondale?

A. I could save nearly 100 francs a month—about $20.

Q. How much did it cost you a day to live at Carbondale?

A. Twenty cents. . . .

Q. How much did it cost you for lodging?

A. About $1 a month.

Q. And 20 cents a day for meals?

A. Yes, sir.

Q. Is that what the others spent?

A. Nearly the same.

Q. Did you live pretty well?

A. Yes, sir; very good.

Q. Then you saved about 90 cents a day?

A. 80 or 90 cents a day.[35]

Contemporary American observers took a very different view of such a mine worker's life. During the same hearings, H. H. Calclazer, a reporter for the *Philadelphia Record,* offered the following description of boarding arrangements he had witnessed in the coal fields:

A. I went up about a week ago . . . to Honey Brook, and this is merely an instance of the cases I have found there right along all through the coal regions and interviewed, through an interpreter, an Italian who could speak some English, and three or four men were standing around a shanty, such a place as an ordinary farmer would stow his tools during the winter, and a small farmer; not a large house, a very small house; there were no separate bunks in this house; but there was on either side, between the two extreme doors on either side of the house, rough planks upon which was scattered a little straw, and once in a while you would find a terribly filthy mattress filled with straw along both sides of the building, and in this building, these people told me, there lived in this little space forty of these Italians.

Q. What size building was it? . . .

A. . . . I should say it was 25 to 30 feet front; possibly 35 back, and not 15 feet high or deep in the gable.

Q. You say they lived there?

A. They lived there and cooked there and ate there and made it their home there. I have the exact dimensions of one other building there that I would like to quote. Here is one of the highest at Yorktown, and by actual measurement this house was 40 feet front, 12 feet deep, and 11 feet high. There are three rooms in each, and in some of these houses are domiciled from eighteen to twenty Hungarians.[36]

Such a description attests to the possibility of surviving at a level that may well have been at or below that imagined in the most stringent budget. More important, it demonstrates that some people in the anthracite region were living at very basic levels indeed. Certainly workers like Nichele Molinaro could not have lived otherwise if they were to save the sums they needed to make their journeys to the New World worthwhile. The most effective way to characterize the earnings of adult anthracite mine workers is that, like most industrial workers in this period, only a minority, and often a small minority, could be confident that they could support families with their income alone.[37] Families could survive on the $35 or so per month that most older workers who were employed steadily could receive, but generally they needed additional income to gain any sense of security, whether from taking in boarders or by sending children off to work. Male children, of course, had plenty of opportunity to work in and around the mines, and while females were legally prohibited from working there, an array of enterprises that needed their labor could be found throughout the anthracite region.[38]

WORKPLACE INJURIES AND PATERNALISM

Perhaps the most precipitous threat to security was also the most capricious. At least the vagaries of the market struck the majority of anthracite mine workers with a rough equality and allowed workers some opportunity to adapt. Accidents however had a far more immediate, unexpected, and devastating impact, suddenly destroying all of an individual's or family's painstakingly constructed strategies for security. The complex process of mining anthracite, bringing it to the surface, and preparing it for shipment was sufficiently fraught with danger to make the industry one of the world's most hazardous.

The state of Pennsylvania passed safety legislation first for Schuylkill County in 1869 and then for the entire anthracite industry in the following year. The latter code was prompted by the mining disaster at the DL & W's Avondale Colliery near Plymouth in Luzerne County on September 6, 1869, when ventilation problems caused an explosion in the mine shaft, resulting in the death of more than 100 mine workers. Much of that law, which according to one commentator was "the first significant mine safety law . . . in the United States," aimed at preventing another disaster like the one of Avondale. It mandated changes in ventilation procedures and a second exit for all mine workings, which might have enabled the workers at Avondale to escape. It also prohibited boys under the age of twelve from working underground. It outlined the responsibilities of supervisors concerning safety and set up a system of inspection by the state.[39] In addition, the law sought to discourage a broad range of risky activities by workers by making them crimes:

> Sec. 19. that any miner, workman, or other person, who shall knowingly injure any safety lamp, water gauge, barometer, air course, brattice or obstruct or throw open airways, or carry lighted pipes or matches into places that are worked by safety lamps, or handle or disturb any part of the machinery of the hoisting engine, or open a door and not have the same closed whereby danger is caused in the mine, or enter any place in the mine against caution, . . . or shall ride upon a loaded car or carriage in any shaft or slope, . . . or do any other act whereby the lives or the health of persons or the security of the mines or machinery is endangered; or any miner having charge of a working place in any coal mine or colliery who shall neglect or refuse to keep the roof properly propped and timbered to prevent the falling of coal, slate, or rock, every such person shall be deemed guilty of a misdemeanor.[40]

Such a law reflected the belief that a lack of attention to safety by mine workers was often the cause for accidents that befell them. This point of view, fervently maintained through the years by employers and mine inspectors, failed to take into account the nature of the work process.[41] Efforts to enhance safety were merely superimposed upon a system in which production, not safety, stood as the paramount goal. Not surprisingly, workers who faced the arduous task of providing for their families day after day chose all too frequently to ignore the potential for catastrophe that, through no design of their own, pervaded the jobs they performed.

The state continued to show its interest in the industry after 1870. In 1879 it provided for the construction of a "State Hospital for Injured Persons of the Anthracite Coal Region" in Schuylkill County, to care without charge for those hurt in work-related accidents. In 1881, Pennsylvania enacted legislation requiring all mines at which twenty or more workers were employed to provide some means to take injured mine workers to their homes or to hospitals.[42] In 1885, a revised, more extensive code was drafted by a committee of six mine operators, six miners, and six mine inspectors. This law strengthened the previously enacted standards on ventilation and mandated the responsibilities of a broad range of employees. The most detailed strictures were placed on foremen, who were required from that date to be certified by a district examining board. Furthermore, the law sought to regulate foremen's daily activities far more closely than previous legislation, requiring, for example, that they take certain specific steps where explosive gases were prevalent and that they visit "every working place in the mine at least once every alternate day." Miners were also given detailed instructions in how to care for their powder and blast safely. Similarly detailed instructions were applied to workers like firemen, who were required "to keep a constant watch" on their boilers, and younger workers, such as runners, who were told where to ride on a set of cars. The statute did strengthen the child labor provision by preventing any boy under twelve from working at a colliery in any capacity, thus addressing the common practice of having much younger boys work as slate pickers. The law also raised the age for starting work underground to fourteen. In addition, to provide for problems peculiar to individual collieries, the act ordered that "special rules" could be instituted, with the same force as the rest of the act, with the assent of the district inspector and the appropriate county court.[43] Finally, as mentioned above, in 1889 the state moved to certify miners.

As table 1.5 shows, while that legislation may have had a substantial impact in the first few years after its passage, after 1875 its effect was quite limited.[44] Fatal accident rates declined rapidly during the first years of state regulation. After 1874 there were no years in which the rate of fatal accidents per thousand employees exceeded four, as it had in 1870, 1871, 1873, and 1874. Similarly, after 1876, the number of tons mined per fatal accident approached and usually exceeded 100,000, a substantial improvement over the early and mid 1870s. However, progress in the 1880s and 1890s was inconsistent at best and by no means sufficient to cause a decline in the number of fatalities, which stood near or above four hundred throughout the 1890s and reached a peak of 502 in 1896. Nonfatal accident rates showed a somewhat steadier decline, but their number mounted alarmingly. Furthermore, since mine inspectors generally recorded only instances of "severe" injury, these statistics fail to provide a complete picture of the perils of anthracite mining. Peter Roberts noted that, in the 1890s, fully 148 and 147 of each 1,000 employees of the Delaware and Hudson Company and the Philadelphia and Reading Coal and Iron Company (P & R), respectively, who were enrolled in those companies' accident funds annually received benefits for injuries.[45] These rates exceed those derived from the data given in the mine inspectors' reports by a factor of twenty.

Frederick L. Hoffman, a statistician employed by the Prudential Insurance Company, noted that throughout the 1890s the anthracite industry suffered a higher rate of fatal accidents than bituminous coal mines in Pennsylvania, Ohio, Illinois, Great Britain, and New South Wales, Australia. For the decade, he found only seven occupations in the world more likely to be fatal than that of anthracite miner: Gloucester fisherman, railroad brake-

TABLE 1.5
Fatal And Nonfatal Accidents And Rates of Incidence In And Around
The Anthracite Coal Mines Of Pennsylvania, 1870–1899

Year	No. of Emp.	No. of Fatal Accidents	Fatal Accidents / 1000 Emp.	No. of Nonfatal Accidents	Nonfatal Accidents / 1000 Emp.	Number of Tons of Coal Mined	Tons of Coal Mined / Fatal Accidents	Tons of Coal Mined / Nonfatal Accidents
1870	35,600	211	5.93	N/A	N/A	12,653,575	59,970	N/A
1871	37,488	271	7.23	664	17.71	13,868,087	51,174	20,886
1872	44,745	229	5.12	611	13.66	13,899,976	60,699	22,750
1873	48,199	266	5.52	688	14.27	18,751,358	70,494	27,255
1874	53,402	262	4.91	558	10.45	17,794,857	65,629	31,890
1875	69,966	238	3.40	587	8.39	20,895,220	87,795	35,597
1876	70,474	228	3.24	458	6.50	19,611,071	86,013	42,819
1877	66,842	194	2.90	568	8.50	22,077,869	113,803	38,869
1878	63,964	189	2.95	503	7.86	18,661,577	98,739	37,101
1879	68,847	262	3.81	791	11.49	27,711,250	105,768	35,033
1880	73,373	202	2.75	670	9.13	24,843,476	122,988	37,080
1881	76,031	273	3.59	834	10.97	30,210,018	110,659	36,223
1882	83,242	293	3.52	815	9.79	30,867,301	105,349	37,874
1883	91,411	323	3.53	805	8.81	33,200,608	102,788	41,243
1884	101,078	332	3.28	848	8.39	32,561,390	98,076	38,398
1885	100,534	356	3.54	729	7.25	33,520,941	94,160	45,982
1886	103,034	279	2.71	807	7.83	34,064,543	122,095	42,211
1887	106,574	316	2.97	1048	9.83	37,137,251	117,523	35,436
1888	117,290	364	3.10	1032	8.80	41,638,426	114,391	40,347

1889	119,007	384	3.23	998	8.39	39,015,835	101,604	39,094
1890	109,166	378	3.46	1007	9.22	40,080,355	106,032	39,802
1891	123,345	427	3.46	1003	8.13	44,320,967	103,796	44,188
1892	129,797	396	3.05	1023	7.88	45,738,373	115,501	44,710
1893	138,002	445	3.22	1069	7.75	47,179,563	106,021	44,134
1894	139,655	439	3.14	921	6.59	45,506,179	103,659	49,410
1895	143,610	422	2.94	1075	7.49	51,207,000	121,344	47,634
1896	149,670	502	3.35	1165	7.78	48,074,330	95,766	41,266
1897	149,557	424	2.84	1106	7.40	46,947,354	110,725	42,448
1898	142,420	411	2.89	1134	7.96	47,145,174	114,708	41,574
1899	140,583	461	3.28	1030	7.33	54,034,224	117,211	47,649

man, railroad trainman (southern states), railroad flagman and switchman (southern states), bituminous miner in Washington state, bituminous miner in New Mexico, and diamond miner in South Africa. Several other positions in the anthracite industry—inside foreman, driver and runner, door boy and helper—were on Hoffman's list of the world's twenty-five most dangerous jobs.[46]

The staggering array of hazards that anthracite mine workers faced is further reflected in an incident that resulted in the death of ten men at the Kaska William colliery in Schuylkill County on May 9, 1889. As two of the topmen, Albert Fritz and his helper, John Decker, were leaving work at the end of the day, the outside foreman asked them to return to the shaft to place three more empty cars on the carriage so that they could be sent down the shaft for some development work to be done on the night shift. Fritz readied one car, moving it near to the entrance of the carriage and securing it with blocks, since he realized that ten men were ascending the shaft on the carriage. However, Decker, an eastern European who could not speak English, thought that Fritz signaled him to push the car to the carriage. He removed the blocks and sent the car into the shaft. The carriage and its occupants had only ascended halfway, and the massive mine car crashed into them, causing them to plummet more than 250 feet to their death.[47]

Workers, of course, struggled to build what defenses they could against the possibility of serious injury or death. As in so many other industrial communities, most subscribed to a benefit fund, generally connected with an ethnic or religious organization.[48] At many mines, workers subscribed to what was called the "keg fund," where proceeds from the sale of empty kegs of powder were collected along with dues payments and distributed to accident victims and their families.[49] Some anthracite mining companies were among the first in the nation to establish benefit funds. However, these efforts sometimes were met with suspicion on the part of workers, since they recognized the primary motivation behind them—to strengthen the workers' ties to the employer. For example, the P & R tried to set up its own plan in 1873, even though the Workingmen's Benevolent Association (WBA), a union that played a substantial role in the anthracite fields from 1868 to 1875, had such a plan. The company offered to contribute one day's worth of its earnings to start a benefit fund if the mine workers agreed to contribute their wages from a single day's work. However, the workers showed little interest.[50] The company required no contribution from its employees two years later, when it initiated a plan at the beginning of the "Long Strike," which resulted in the extinction of the WBA. Whenever a fatal accident occurred, the company would pay thirty dollars for funeral expenses and three dollars per week to the widow for one year, adding one dollar a week for each child.[51] After the union's defeat, the company endowed the fund with $20,000 and required workers who wanted to receive its benefits to contribute from five to thirty cents per month, depending on their job. This fund made payments for disability for up to six months as well as to the families of fatal accident victims, but while the workers provided most of the resources for the fund beside the endowment, the company appointed trustees to administer it.[52]

Companies who did not have such plans dealt with injuries to their employees on an ad hoc basis, albeit one that they had developed through years of experience. They had to decide whether or not to make any contribution to the victim or his family, and the injured party had to decide whether to take the company's offer or sue in a system in which it was most difficult to prove negligence on the part of the company. Company officials seemed to think they were being quite generous, but such generosity and sympathy as they might display was tempered if not submerged by their calculation of how cheaply the company could avoid being taken into court. To win a suit, workers or their heirs had to prove that a situation that produced an accident had exceeded the worker's assumption of risk and that neither the victim nor his fellow workers had contributed to the mishap.[53] In addition, the courts had held the foreman to be a "fellow servant" of the workers; thus, companies could not be held liable if a boss's negligence led to the injury or death of a worker. In 1891, the legislature mandated that an employer could indeed be sued by a worker injured through the foreman's negligence, but the state Supreme Court held that law unconstitutional. The Court maintained that the employer could not be held responsible for the negligence of foremen because through certification they had become "representatives of the State."[54] Nevertheless, despite the many protections the legal system afforded them, companies wanted to avoid going to court if they could, especially before juries who understandably tended to show sympathy for the plaintiff.

The process of careful calculation that underlay decisions to aid injured mine workers and their families is displayed in the correspondence of William R. Storrs, who from 1866 to 1894 ran the Coal Department of the DL & W, a leading producer and shipper of anthracite. In deciding how much or how little to offer an injured employee or his bereaved family, Storrs considered a variety of factors, from the work that the employee did to the amount of property he had accumulated and his importance to the company. For example, Thomas Watkins, inside foreman at the Cayuga colliery, died on October 14, 1889, of injuries suffered more than a month before. Storrs informed Samuel Sloan, president of the DL & W, that Watkins had worked for the company for over thirty years and had served eighteen at his last post. Although he had not worked in September, he had received his salary because the company expected him to recover. Storrs proposed that the DL & W pay his widow the $100 her husband would have earned for October. Watkins "was a good faithful man" who had left a "wife and three sons grown to manhood, with a little property saved from his earnings."[55] Sloan thought that the company could well afford to "do something more;"[56] and Storrs believed that half pay for four months, plus full pay for October, would suffice. He noted that "several [foremen] have been injured and two killed while I have been here—recognized in that way [by the aid given Watkins' widow] will encourage them."[57] Sloan thought that the company should even go beyond four months at half pay to six months.[58]

While the family of a foreman might place their trust in the company, those of other employees had learned that they must look out for themselves. On June 25, 1890, Storrs reported to Sloan that "a Mr. Dacy, many years a faithful laborer, fell down our Central Shaft, and was killed a few weeks ago." Storrs thought that this had occurred "through neglect of himself and man working with him;" however, "the Coroners Jury . . . censured the Company." Dacy "left wife and seven children," and lawyers were "trying to have the woman sue the Company." The widow had come to see Storrs but did not indicate what sum would be sufficient to keep her from suing. Storrs told Sloan: "I hope I can arrange for $250 or $300 and if so think it better than expense and chances of suit."[59]

For boys killed on the job, the company paid a smaller amount. On November 5, 1889, fourteen-year-old William Owens died after being run over by a mine car at the company's Hyde Park colliery. Storrs noted that William's father had been killed "by a fall of roof" six years previously. He gave the widowed mother twenty-five dollars and "agreed to pay her ten dollars a month for five months."[60] Negotiations concerning injured workers were far more complex. For example, on July 9, 1890, sixteen-year-old Anthony Lynch was caught between a coal car and the side of a mining chamber at the Bellevue colliery. The state mine inspector labeled him "slightly injured," but Storrs informed Sloan that the boy had been "seriously injured." Some three months after the accident, Lynch moved "about on crutches, with but little use of one leg." The boy's parents believed their son was "crippled for life," but Storrs told his boss that he thought the boy would "get better faster after settlement." Anthony's father had at first demanded $2,500, and Storrs had countered with $400. The father then dropped down to $1,500; but Storrs would only move to $500.[61] Two weeks later, after several negotiating sessions, the father said he could settle at $920 but, if the company rejected that, he would sue for $11,000. Storrs noted that "able, but bad lawyers" represented the man, and that the company might lose in court. Even an appeal thereafter could fail and, at that point, legal fees alone would cost the DL & W "two-thirds of the sum" demanded by the father.[62] Faced with this dilemma, President Sloan authorized the payment of $920.[63]

The important factor in these negotiations is not the relative generosity or cheapness of corporate executives like Storrs and Sloan. Far more noteworthy is the fact that their stance in negotiations was predicated upon business concerns. In addressing those concerns, they sought to preserve maximum freedom of action. As they did in managing the workplace, anthracite operators sought guidance only from their experience and their knowledge of market conditions. Storrs certainly did not see injured workers and their families as having any right to demand assistance from the company or the company having any obligation to help them. On two occasions he referred to the aid proffered by the DL & W as a "gratuity."[64] Negotiating with recalcitrant victims or their families to settle accident claims annoyed men like Storrs because they felt all too strongly the limitation, however slight, such dealings imposed on their freedom of action. Of course, far more galling was the intrusion of any outside party, like an attorney.

For managers like Storrs and Sloan, retaining their freedom of action in dealing with employees had a larger significance. Richard Sennett has viewed paternalism in the industrial context as a "false love," in which an authority figure claims paternal concern for his metaphorical children, but insists upon exercising that concern solely on his own terms. The false nature of the authority figure's professions of concern quickly comes to the surface whenever his authority is challenged. Although a genuine father figure would tolerate misbehavior from his children, encourage their desires for independence, and allow them the freedom to mature, the paternalistic authority figure will only care for his metaphorical children as long as they obey his rules and show no inclination to contest his control.[65] Sennett's analysis aptly describes the spirit with which the operators approached injured workers. Of course, they saw family members who threatened to go to court and their attorneys as little more than nettlesome annoyances. What they truly feared, and at the same time rejected as utterly illegitimate, was the challenge of labor organization.

2

The Failure of Labor Organization, 1875–1897

During the climactic anthracite coal strike of 1902, George F. Baer, president of the Philadelphia and Reading Coal and Iron Company (P & R), offered one of the best-known and most sweeping claims of paternal concern in the history of labor relations in America: "The rights and interests of the laboring man will be protected and cared for—not by the labor agitators, but by the Christian men to whom God in his infinite wisdom has given the control of the property interests of the country."[1] William R. Storrs said practically as much when, decrying the Pennsylvania legislature's efforts to pass legislation for workers, he stated that "the interests of the owner is the best guarantee for both [mine worker and owner]."[2]

Of course, Storrs's negotiations with accident victims and their families show the shallow and ultimately false nature of such a community of interest. Aside from a limited amount of help generally extracted from the company after the threat of a suit, workers were expected to take care of themselves. The nature and depth of management's concern for workers only truly manifested itself during a push for unionization. At such a time managers knew that workers could not be trusted and must be carefully shepherded by the company. Employers in the closing decades of the nineteenth century attacked labor unions as an onerous limitation upon economic freedom—that of workers who did not want to join and, of course, that of the employers. As Rowland Berthoff has made clear, the economic freedom that employers celebrated was, in labor relations, a "freedom to control," to exert unbridled power over their employees.[3]

Despite some occasional challenges from labor organizations, the men who ran the anthracite mines maintained that control relatively unchallenged for more than twenty years after the demise of the Workingmen's Benevolent Association (WBA) in 1875. That union wielded considerable power in the industry from 1868, presiding over several major strikes, tying wages to the price of coal, lobbying successfully for the passage of some of the safety legislation discussed in chapter 1, and participating in some of the earliest uses of formal arbitration in America. Nevertheless, it was swept from the anthracite region, particularly the Schuylkill field, where it had dominated the industry until the P & R began to purchase local lands in 1871. Under its president, Franklin B. Gowen, that firm proceeded to ensure that the industry in the Schuylkill field would have a single master.[4]

No union would be able to mount a challenge of similar significance for more than twenty years. Beginning in 1876, the Knights of Labor did establish a presence in the anthracite industry that would build slowly until its rapid demise after an unsuccessful walkout in 1887–88. The United Mine Workers of America (UMWA) had practically no representation in anthracite when it formed in 1890 from National Trade District 135 of the Knights of Labor and the National Progressive Union of the American Federation of Labor. It would not begin an organizing drive there until 1894. From that time, three years of laborious effort, filled with failure, would elapse before the UMWA would become a significant force in the industry. During those years, organization was sporadic, with short bursts of accomplishment followed by lengthy periods of decline. Although several organizers conducted successful campaigns in parts of the region, the organization they fostered had little staying power. The workers who responded to the organizers could not sustain a viable union, bedeviled as they were by withering underemployment and the meager earnings it brought. Constant disarray among the UMWA's leaders in anthracite only made matters worse, and the national organization lacked the strength to provide much support. Even without these obstacles, it was no easy task to build an industrial union of workers in widely differing jobs, with widely varying levels of skill, of an increasing diversity of ethnicity, and from three mining regions characterized by dissimilar local conditions and distinct histories. While the organizers' endeavors undoubtedly heightened the workers' awareness of the union, the UMWA's experience in anthracite from 1894 to 1897 demonstrated that organizing campaigns alone could not achieve unionization.

No effort to unionize the anthracite coal industry was likely to make progress without the spark of rank-and-file militancy at the workplace. Except for a flurry of such activity from 1885 through 1888 linked to the failed strike of 1887–88, relatively few job actions occurred at the local level. The operators' success in running the mines on a nonunion basis is further reflected in that almost no strikes from 1881 to 1894 had union involvement, except for less than one-third of those from 1885 to 1887. The level of rank-and-file militancy did not grow as the UMWA tried to organize from 1894 to 1897. That initial campaign showed that the union would not and could not generate militancy on its own.

"I CLAIM THEY HAVE NO BUSINESS BETWEEN US AND OUR MEN"

Anthracite mine workers joined in the "Great Uprising" of 1877, but their militancy, like that of railroad workers from St. Louis to Philadelphia, lacked coordination. Toward the end of July 1877, mine workers joined with their fellow employees on the railroads in walkouts against several major carriers in the Wyoming field. Like the railroad workers, the mine workers struck with apparent spontaneity and without encouragement from the Knights of Labor. As noted by Terence V. Powderly, a Scranton resident before he headed the Knights, the strike "began among those who had no KNOWL-EDGE OF THE KNIGHTS OF LABOR; they were not amenable to the laws of that order; knowing nothing of its existence, they could not take counsel from its members."[5] Mine workers held out for some three months before returning to work without any restoration of previous wage cuts. In a continuation of the pattern that had plagued the WBA in earlier walkouts, that strike never extended across the entire anthracite region. It spread to the Lehigh field but not into Schuylkill, in contrast to the "Long Strike" of 1875 in which the ill-fated WBA had succeeded in enlisting workers in Schuylkill and Lehigh but none from the Wyoming field.[6]

The strike may well have encouraged the growth of the Knights, since in 1877 nearly sixty local assemblies of the Knights were established among anthracite miners, and more than twenty other new assemblies were set up in the next year. However, the pace of organization then lagged, with only a handful of new assemblies formed in the early 1880s. Furthermore, many of those established in 1877 and 1878 did not survive until 1885 and 1886, when the Knights next achieved significant organizing success. They established nearly twenty assemblies in 1885 and forty-eight the following year. These assemblies generally had thirty to forty members and often many more, so in some years there must have been more than 2,000 active Knights in the anthracite coal industry.[7]

Still, neither the Knights nor the other union alive in anthracite in the 1880s, the Amalgamated Association of Miners and Laborers, took much militant action except for the strike year of 1887. According to the extensive listing of strikes compiled under the direction of U.S. Commissioner of Labor Carroll D. Wright, less than a quarter of all walkouts from 1881 through 1887 were called by a labor union, and only one prior to 1885 (see table 2.1).[8] Still, workers were able to win some gains through their own localized militancy. They achieved partial or complete success in almost 50 percent of the walkouts, compared to a success rate of nearly 57 percent nationwide in the period from 1881 through June 1894.[9] Just under half of the strikes were fought over workers' demands for an increase in wages or a refusal to submit to a reduction. However, in the rest of the walkouts, workers left their jobs to change some aspect of the complex and varied work rules under which they labored.

Not surprisingly, given the differentiation of work in the industry, all kinds of workers, young and old, walked out for a variety of reasons. For

TABLE 2.1
Strikes in the Anthracite Industry, 1881–1887

YEAR	TOTAL	ORDERED BY UNION	NUMBER OF STRIKES FOR INCREASE OR AGAINST REDUCTION	AT LEAST PARTIALLY SUCCESSFUL	ONE WEEK OR LONGER
1881	5	1	4	2	3
1882	9	0	5	3	4
1883	6	0	3	0	5
1884	3	0	1	2	3
1885	12	2	8	3	8
1886	6	0	6	3	3
1887	32	13	14	19	16
TOT	73	16	41	32	42

example, in August 1882, youthful drivers and runners at several mines in and around Wilkes-Barre left their jobs to protest the way in which their employers determined wages and hours. They complained that although miners and laborers were allowed to quit for the day as soon as they mined the standard number of cars, drivers and runners were expected to work a full day, regardless of the number of cars they brought to the miners and laborers. Management responded that these workers were paid for their time, rather than for the number of cars they handled, to prevent them from rushing cars through the mine. The strike ended in failure after eleven days. Excessive dockage—an issue that would be of special significance in the UMWA's turn-of-the-century strike wave and for many years thereafter—sparked five strikes in these years. In a related grievance over methods of payment, two walkouts occurred when miners insisted upon being paid for each ton of coal they mined, rather than each car. In two strikes, employees demanded semi-monthly payment of wages, and on two occasions workers walked out over being required to pay for the oil and cotton they used in their lamps. At Jeddo and Highland in the Lehigh field, workers at several mines struck in July 1884. They refused to sign contracts that would allow their employer to make deductions from their earnings to pay any bill presented against an employee by a local merchant. At those mines in the following year, miners struck to obtain payment for so-called dead work, which did not directly produce coal. The walkout in 1884 continued for some thirty-one days and ended in success, but the second one ended in failure after eighty days.[10]

The year 1885 saw more strikes in anthracite than any other year between 1881 and 1894 except 1887. While only two of that year's twelve disputes were recorded by the Bureau of Labor as having been ordered by a union, perhaps some of the walkouts provided an occasion for organizing. A noticeable increase in membership occurred in 1885 for both the Knights of Labor and the Amalgamated Association of Miners and Laborers, matching the nationwide trend.[11] Interest in organization was spurred by wage cuts of 10 percent across the Lehigh and Schuylkill fields, undertaken by some firms toward the end of 1884 and by others as late as the beginning of 1886.[12] The Amalgamated Association, the Knights, and a craft union to which some surface employees belonged—the Association of Eccentric Engineers—formed a joint committee to formulate a slate of demands. However, they received no response when they presented these demands to various companies in January 1886. In August the unions demanded that Lehigh operators restore the cut, but, once again, the companies did not respond.[13] Toward the end of that year, mine workers in the vicinity of Shamokin in the Schuylkill field won at least a partial rescission of that cut by threatening to walk out at several mines and actually striking at the Excelsior colliery, where they stayed out for more than a month.[14]

In 1887, a wave of some thirty-two strikes rippled through the industry, thirteen of which were called by unions. That year the unions' joint committee agreed upon wage proposals for both the Lehigh and Schuylkill fields and issued them to the companies. However, only a few small firms responded, stating that they had no choice but to follow the lead of their larger corporate brethren. Shortly thereafter, the committee decided to drop the operators in the Wyoming field to the north from its list of targets, since organization there had lagged.[15] That field had been dominated by corporate capital since the 1830s and had gone to great lengths to prevent the WBA from gaining a foothold at the end of the 1860s. By the 1880s it was the field in which more than half the mine workers produced more than half the coal,[16] so the failure to organize there put the unions in a weak position. Damaging unity further was the willingness of the largest anthracite producer, the P & R, to negotiate with the committee. Apparently that company could not afford a strike, since its corporate parent, the Reading Railroad, was in receivership. However, the P & R agreed to an increase of 8 percent to remain in force only until the first of the year, when the railroad would emerge from receivership. If the P & R's competitors in the Lehigh field had granted an increase by that time, the P & R would adjust its wage rates accordingly. If not, the P & R would return to its former scale. Most of the smaller operators in the Schuylkill field went along with the P & R's advance, so the strike was basically restricted to the Lehigh field at first.[17]

This was a recipe for disaster for the unions. Since the Lehigh field was the smallest of the three, a strike there would disrupt production the least. Perhaps more importantly, the strikers would see the other two fields producing as fully as possible while they tried to survive on whatever resources they had.[18] When the year ended with no agreement with the mine operators in Lehigh, the P & R cut its wages to the earlier level, and the workers in the Schuylkill field struck.[19] Still, with full work in the last few months the P & R had done very well, making 1887 one of the very few years in which the Reading's coal subsidiary turned a profit.[20] Most importantly, the workers in the Wyoming field showed no interest in striking. At the beginning of February, Knights of Labor there convened in Pittston and issued a mildly phrased demand calling for an increase of 15 percent. However, the Knights moved no further even though they received little or no response from most of the operators.[21] Meanwhile, in the Schuylkill field, the production of coal continued at a number of collieries, despite several violent episodes during the first week of February. As more mines opened for work, more and more workers abandoned the strike. The joint committee directed strikers in Schuylkill to return to work on February 20, after extracting weak promises from the P & R not to discriminate against strikers in reemployment and to discuss wages further after they had returned to work.[22]

The end of the strike in the Schuylkill field made continued resistance in the Lehigh field untenable, and by the close of the first week in March most mine workers there had returned to work. In Lehigh, the strike lasted for nearly six months, perhaps because of the particularly oppressive conditions that workers faced there. Lehigh was somewhat more remote than Wyoming and Schuylkill, especially in the area around Hazleton, which had the highest elevation of the entire anthracite region. Because of this relative isolation, the full-scale company town remained there for quite some time after it had begun to disappear in the other fields.[23] Company control of most of the commercial and institutional activity in these towns, from the company store to the company doctor and even to company collections for priests and ministers, had originated out of necessity in the wilderness. However, these towns had gradually evolved into industrial fiefdoms, many still controlled by men like Ariovistus Pardee. A Lehigh pioneer, Pardee helped open the region to exploitation by working with the railroads in the 1830s, and he started his own mining business in 1840. During the Lehigh strike, he turned seventy-seven.[24] He and his sons operated twelve collieries, which produced over 700,000 tons of coal, even in the strike-shortened year of 1887.[25] Pardee refused to have anything to do with the unions, and he led his fellow operators throughout the strike, both independents like him and large corporations like the Lehigh & Wilkes-Barre Coal Company.[26] Indeed, most operators, like businessmen across the nation, shared his attitude, and this antiunion ideology would set the tone for labor relations long after 1887. Pardee offered his views in detail in testimony before a committee of the U.S. House of Representatives investigating the strike.

Q. Will you state, then what objection you would have to conferring with your own men as Knights of Labor and as Amalgamated Association men?
A. I claim they have no business between us and our men.
Q. Do you claim that the men have no right to organize?
A. No; I do not care how many they organize, and they can belong to as many as they please.
Q. Then, if you have no objection to their organizing into labor organizations, what objection have you to conferring with them in that capacity?
A. Because I look upon the leaders of the organizations as meddlers. It is not the miners themselves, but I look upon the leaders of these associations as mischievous rascals, stirring up mischief all through the country. Did you ever know a time when there was so many causeless strikes as since the Knights of Labor have obtained the power they have now? . . .
Q. . . . If the men in fact did have cause to complain, would you object to confer with them?
A. No; not with our employés.
Q. Would you object to conferring with them, even if they came as representing some organized body?
A. I would not deal with them at all.
Q. Suppose the employés of these mines, in their various capacities, should organize; would you refuse to confer with them in that capacity?
A. I am not dealing with any organization or leaders of any organization. . . .
Q. Well, suppose the association known as the Miners' Amalgamated Association, composed exclusively of your miners, should send representatives to you in behalf of the men, would you treat with them?
A. If they would come as our employés I would treat with them, but as representing an association I would not. . . .
Q. Is there any sort of understanding between the operators of this country, any concert of action between them?
A. There has been a concert of action in this matter of the strike. . . . We are all of the same mind.[27]

With such attitudes, operators could be expected to remain vigilant against any hint of union activity. During the strike in Lehigh and Schuylkill, which had not involved his company, William R. Storrs declared that the "avowed object" of the Knights was "to control if not crush capital."[28] He attributed to them an attempt by miners in the winter of 1888–89 to persuade the Delaware, Lackawanna, and Western (DL & W) and other major firms in the Wyoming field to cut the price they paid for powder. After consulting extensively with other corporate leaders, Storrs formulated the plan of having foremen for the various companies poll the miners in their chambers. The miners had just two choices: a decrease in powder with a commensurate decrease in the rates they were paid or maintaining current rates for powder and for mining. Of course, they never got to choose what the various committees

TABLE 2.2
Strikes in the Anthracite Industry, 1/1/1888–6/30/1894

			NUMBER OF STRIKES		
			FOR INCREASE	*AT LEAST*	*ONE*
		ORDERED	*OR AGAINST*	*PARTIALLY*	*WEEK OR*
YEAR	*TOTAL*	*BY UNION*	*REDUCTION*	*SUCCESSFUL*	*LONGER*
1888	7	2	2	2	2
1889	5	0	1	1	3
1890	4	0	2	3	1
1891	6	0	0	4	3
1892	3	0	0	3	0
1893	6	0	3	4	3
1894	8	0	5	4	3
TOT	39	2	13	21	15

of workers who had visited Storrs that winter requested, a cut in the price of powder alone. Incredibly, Storrs managed to persuade himself that the vote for no change, by a margin of ten to one at the DL & W, showed the workers' unstinting support for the company.[29] But Storrs's confidence in the workers waned quickly, as fear of agitation over this issue continued to beset him.[30]

The decline of the Knights and of labor organization generally in the anthracite fields is reflected in the Bureau of Labor's comprehensive listing of strikes from 1888 to July 1894 (see table 2.2).[31] First, the level of militancy is rather consistent with that for the years 1881–86 (see table 2.1). Excluding the especially militant year of 1887, forty-one walkouts were recorded for the earlier six-year period, while in the six-and-a-half years covered in this table, thirty-nine strikes were recorded. Most notably, labor unions ordered only two and none after 1888. This sets labor militancy in the anthracite coal industry far apart from strike activity nationwide. In each year from 1881 to 1894, unions across the country ordered at least 63 percent of strikes recorded by the Bureau of Labor.[32]

One-third of the strikes listed in table 2.2 involved a wage cut or request for an increase, but the remaining two-thirds touched other workplace issues. Strikers included the youngest workers in the industry. In May 1888, some 100 slate pickers left their jobs for two days at a mine in Shamokin, but failed in their attempt to persuade their employer to reinstate a worker who had been discharged. During August of that year, twelve slate pickers at a mine in Kingston also struck for two days without success to curtail the imposition of overtime. At a strike in Minersville in February 1893, some ninety youthful workers—drivers, door boys, and slate pickers—demanded that their employer alter his method of timekeeping. Although they closed the mine for three days, they did not win their demand. Similarly, drivers and runners forced a mine in Parsons to close for three days in May 1894, but they did not obtain their demand for the discharge of a foreman.[33]

Older workers also struck over a wide variety of issues. For example, at a colliery in Shenandoah in January 1889, some fifty laborers left their jobs to persuade their employer to discharge a number of foreigners. That walkout lasted only two days and did not succeed. In a protracted dispute over the thorny issue of payment for tonnage workers, 110 miners and laborers in Plains Township closed one colliery from May 18 to June 14, 1894, in an effort to obtain an increase in the rate paid for filling certain coal cars. Although that walkout did not succeed, two other groups of miners and laborers, one in Scranton in February 1888 and one in Forty Fort in June 1893, won partial victories in strikes over the same issue.[34]

Workers achieved partial or complete success in some twenty-one walkouts, or more than half of the total, a figure that, in contrast to that for union involvement, almost reached the national average of 57 percent.[35] Still, based on the total number of walkouts, the anthracite mine workers do not appear to be an especially militant group. Thirty-nine strikes in six and a half years does not seem to be a large number, especially for an industry that employed more than 100,000 workers at any one time in and around more than 300 mines. Furthermore, only one or at most a handful of collieries were affected by each of these strikes.[36] Perhaps such localized walkouts, separated as they were from any unionization effort, merely served as the most readily available means by which unorganized workers might open negotiations over grievances. By stopping production, at least mine workers could rest assured that they would get their boss's attention.

THE EARLY STRUGGLES OF THE UMWA

The leaders of the recently founded UMWA were by no means impressed with the militancy of the anthracite mine workers. In June 1891, the *UMW Journal* commented that the anthracite workers' burdens were "of their own making," since they had not joined the union.[37] In March 1893, the *Journal* printed a letter taken from a newspaper in the anthracite region and gave it the headline: "Direct—From the Heart of Anthracite Serfdom—Account of the Astonishing Condition of Hard Coal Miners—Fraud, Oppression, Thievery in Various Forms."[38] Two months later, the *UMW Journal* reflected on a report that wages had been cut for certain classes of work at some collieries in the Schuylkill field: "We had thought that the men in the anthracite field were already down to their lowest existing notch, but it appears that their vampire-like masters think they can stand just a little more tapping."[39]

Regardless of the UMWA's harsh assessment of the anthracite mine workers, they proved themselves not totally averse to organization. John Rinn discovered this when he came into the Schuylkill field in July 1894 to solicit funds to support the members of his local in central Pennsylvania, who were engaged in the nationwide bituminous strike of 1894.[40] While Rinn found "collecting an up hill job," he also realized that "many miners cried out for organization." He applied to UMWA Secretary-Treasurer Patrick McBryde for an organizer's commission and went to work. Within one month, Rinn had organized thirteen locals, with considerable assistance from two other organizers, Philip H. Penna, the union's vice-president, and John Fahy, a member of the national executive board. These first UMWA locals in anthracite were located in north-central Schuylkill County and southeastern Northumberland County, between Mahanoy City and Shamokin.[41] As of October 13, 1894, forty-four locals had been formed, and Rinn and Fahy continued organizing and sought to expand the organization through the rest of the Schuylkill field.[42]

According to Rinn, many miners earned less than "one dollar per day after clearing expenses." Those expenses consisted not merely of the basic payments for supplies and for labor. First, many workers in the field traveled "from five to fifteen miles to their work in workman's trains, furnished by the coal company [P & R] at a charge of fourteen tickets for one dollar." That company also made deductions for its beneficial fund, and, according to Rinn, it made those deductions without reporting "how much was collected, . . . how much was paid out, . . . how much was left, [or] what was done with it." Also, Rinn had no love for the field's "all-the-time-sliding-down-sliding-scale," according to which underground workers' wages rose or fell 1 percent for every three cents the average price of a ton of coal in the field varied from the "basis" price. He pointed out that, at least since the demise of the WBA, which had originally proposed a sliding scale, no miner served on the committee that determined the average price of coal. Finally, the miners had little faith in the arbitrary allowance system, by which foremen could authorize additional payments to miners who confronted particularly difficult mining conditions. Rinn stated: "Many of the working breasts are very wet, and no matter how wet they may be the miner is paid nothing extra." Veins might dwindle in thickness to two feet in some places, which made it nearly impossible for the miner to earn a decent income. However, the miner received no extra payment.[43]

Representatives from the locals that comprised newly created District One of the UMWA convened on November 30, 1894, at Mahanoy City. There Rinn reported that, since the beginning of August, he and John Fahy had organized fifty-six locals. However, in recent weeks the pace of organizing had slowed. Only seven locals had been organized in November, because, according to Rinn, he and Fahy had been busy trying to revitalize several locals organized previously whose members had been "falling away." In addition, funds for organizing had been exhausted, and the district owed Rinn $177.30 for his efforts. This did not stop him from running for and winning the district's presidency. The officers elected with him demonstrated the union's interest in appealing to the various ethnic groups in the industry, with Charles Vitcufsky elected as vice-president, Patrick W. Doyle as secretary, and Emanuel Jenkyn as treasurer. Among other actions, the convention condemned the sliding scale and agreed on a constitution that set a minimum initiation fee of $.25.[44] At the UMWA's sixth national convention, in February 1895, the fledgling district had fifty votes, representing approximately 5,000 workers. Only two of the fifteen other districts in the UMWA had greater representation: the UMWA's heartland in Ohio and its western Pennsylvania district.[45]

A letter to the *UMW Journal* from a member of a local in Shamokin, one of the first organized in the district, painted a less positive picture. While the local had a substantial membership, it had "very little in the treasury." Workers had experienced a great deal of difficulty in paying their dues when the local was first organized in August 1894, when low coal prices caused 5 percent to be taken from underground workers' wages in accordance with the sliding scale. However, by January prices had fallen further, and, with wages 11 percent below the basis, even fewer workers paid their dues.[46]

The union's willingness to organize recent immigrants from eastern Europe and its success in doing so is reflected in a report by an organizer named James Dorsett. He described for the *UMW Journal* the promising beginnings of a "Lithuanian local," organized "last Sunday (forgive the day) at Mount Carmel." According to Dorsett, such successes served as a proper rebuke to "some of our most patriotic citizens" who claimed that foreigners would not join the union.[47]

John Rinn's report in May 1895 on the district's condition revealed that Secretary Doyle had resigned his post "for reasons best known to himself." However, in other respects, the district seemed strong. Rinn asked the members to consider taking action to persuade the coal companies to pay twice a month and to close their washeries until they could assure the mine workers at least four full days of work per week.[48] The washeries were highly mechanized facilities that reprocessed small sizes of coal that had been dumped on the waste piles in earlier years as unsalable. Workers referred to washery coal as coal "the company stole from the miner."[49]

The district's trials and tribulations mounted over the summer. Dorsett commented in July that most of the field's miners were "a disgrace to the name of men" since they did little else but find fault with the leaders of the union.[50] Three weeks later he reported that he and another member of his local had been discharged by their employer, the P & R, because of their activism.[51] Nevertheless, the editor of the *UMW Journal* counseled restraint for the anthracite mine workers, in spite of the difficult conditions they confronted. He believed that the coal companies, whose efforts to regulate the market had met with little success, hoped to provoke a strike during which the price of coal would skyrocket. The companies could then pocket sizable profits while blaming the workers and their union for the rise in prices. He advised the workers: "Let [the companies] goad and goad; but do not let them succeed in putting you in a false light before the public."[52]

Disarray persisted among the district's leaders. Secretary Thomas E. Maguire informed the members in September that Treasurer Jenkyn had resigned in order to "accept a position as inside foreman at Tremont." To make matters worse, although the district's executive board had appointed Eli Zimmerman to complete Jenkyn's term, Zimmerman had refused to serve. In addition, Maguire disagreed with certain changes in the district's constitution that President Rinn planned to propose at the next district convention. Instead of the existing procedure by which the secretary received $15 per month and the treasurer received 5 percent of the money he spent, Rinn favored paying a single secretary-treasurer $50 per month. But Maguire pointed out that in the three months since he had assumed both posts, his services had cost the district only $23 per month. In his view, these and other proposed changes tended "to create expense instead of to lessen it." He reminded the members that at that moment the district could not meet its indebtedness and advised them to make every effort they could "to help the district out of its present financial condition."[53]

At the district convention of September 20, after witnessing some bickering between Rinn and Maguire, the delegates decided against combining the offices of secretary and treasurer. The secretary's salary was set at $10 per month plus expenses, while the president's was increased by $10 per month, to $60, but without expenses, which had been permitted previously. The convention selected William E. Mellic of Shamokin as treasurer, and then passed unanimously a resolution of tribute to their "esteemed brother," former Treasurer Jenkyn. The resolution expressed thanks for the "able and prudent manner in which he had performed the duties of his office," and added:

> We, the members of the Mine Workers Union, regard the move he has made as a loss to us while we sincerely hope that it will prove a gain to him, and that his future will be as bright and prosperous as he can anticipate or desire.[54]

The district also passed a resolution to establish subdistricts throughout the territory covered by District One. Since district officials found themselves unable to organize in all areas of the Lehigh and Schuylkill fields because of a lack of funds, the work of organizing the subdistricts would "be left to the members of the various localities." Finally, the convention passed a resolution introduced by John Fahy calling for a wage increase. However, the resolution was so timid one could hardly characterize it as a "demand." It referred to both "the long period of industrial depression" that all had experienced and the "returning prosperity and advanced prices for necessities of life" that were anticipated. According to the resolution, during recent years the mine workers had suffered and proved "their desire for peace and harmony between themselves and their employers." The resolution then mentioned wage increases received by workers in other industries, some of which had been "voluntarily given by the employers." In particular, some bituminous operators had recently met with union representatives and agreed upon advances of 15 to 25 percent. Taking all of this into account, as well as prospects for a stronger demand for anthracite, mine workers "most respectfully" requested their employers to grant them an increase. The UMWA sent copies of the resolution to all the anthracite companies,[55] but if the district's leaders ever received a response, the *UMW Journal* made no mention of it.

A rise in coal prices beginning late in 1895 and continuing into 1896 caused wages to increase in the Lehigh and Schuylkill fields, where wages varied according to the price of coal.[56] However, since wages had plummeted as far as 17 percent below the basis in October 1895 in Schuylkill, an increase might well have been expected.[57] Still, improving wage rates did nothing to strengthen the union, as more disputes arose among its leaders. At the end of 1895, John Rinn was ousted from the district presidency amidst charges that his efforts had not justified the salary he received. One Patrick Carrol of Shenandoah replaced him, but, while Carrol was "a good man in labor circles, he was not a success as a leader among working-men." After a very brief tenure, he resigned under fire from Rinn's faction and was replaced, early in 1896, by John Fahy. Upon assuming the post, Fahy attempted to reinvigorate the district. He launched a series of rallies and reportedly made a special effort "to throw out his net for Lithuanians and Polanders" by engaging "speakers of those nationalities."[58] Although an editorial in the *UMW Journal* of March 26 referred to a recent district convention as the best since the birth of the district,[59] District One's representation at the seventh national convention, in April 1896, totaled only ten votes. This represented approximately 1,000 members in good standing, a drop of 80 percent from the previous year. Among the eight districts that voted, District One had fallen to fifth position.[60]

In later months, even though wages increased above basis rates, the district's condition grew steadily worse. Although Fahy continued to try to organize from time to time, by October he saw fit to chastise the field's mine workers for their apparent lack of interest. In addition, the editor of the *UMW*

FIGURE 2.1

John Fahy, President, UMWA District One, 1896–1899; President, UMWA District Nine, 1899–1912 (originally printed in *United Mine Workers Journal,* May 1902).

Journal, while praising Fahy's efforts, commented: "The entering wedge has already appeared in that region which is calculated, as soon as driven to the end, to split or take from the miners some of the advantages they yet retain."[61] From the fall of 1896, Fahy downplayed organizing and, at the UMWA's eighth national convention in January 1897, the district was entitled to only two votes, representing perhaps 200 members in good standing.[62]

Two basic causes can be cited for District One's failure to organize the anthracite region, or even the Schuylkill field, in 1895 and 1896. First, although the industry's economic condition was relatively weak when Rinn began his first organizing drive in the summer of 1894, it did not improve in 1895, and may even have worsened. The breakers worked half time or less for long periods, and wages slid further and further down the sliding scale. Early in 1895, Patrick W. Doyle, then secretary of the district, noted that collieries generally were in operation for only three days of seven hours each.[63] In July 1895, a correspondent of the *UMW Journal* reported that some laborers for the P & R were averaging less than $5 in earnings per week. At that point, most collieries were operating for only three nine-hour days per week.[64] By the time that coal prices began to advance early in 1896, to the extent that wages for April 1896 exceeded basis rates for the first month since February 1894, the district had been losing strength steadily for about a year.[65] Although the initial outburst of organizing had occurred during hard times, the persistence and worsening of such conditions made it most difficult for the UMWA to build on that first outpouring of support and expand or even sustain the organization.

The second cause for District One's failure lay deeply embedded in the work process and the informal, highly personal manner in which the mines were operated. Not only did the work force in anthracite consist of workers with many different levels of skill in many widely varying jobs, but access to the better jobs was often as dependent upon a man's relationship to his foreman as upon the skill he possessed. In one of his first communications to the *UMW Journal,* John Rinn reviled "the contract system." Under that system, he explained: "One man, perhaps a good friend of the bosses, can make $50 or $60 per month, while the man who performs the labor has to be content with $10 or $20 per month."[66] Approximately a year later, he disparaged the industry, which had "taken the boy from the schools, when only nine years of age and placed him in the breaker to pick slate at 30 cents to 50 cents per day." To make matters worse, boys often had to pay "the breaker bosses one or two dollars per month for being allowed to pick slate." According to Rinn, bribery and favoritism riddled the work process: "At some collieries you can get a breast for $5 and a better one for $10, but you will pay from $50 to $75 for a contract."[67]

Among the most exploited were recent immigrants from eastern Europe. A local newspaper reported that many bosses required them to pay from $20 to $40 to obtain employment. An unemployed Pole named Frank Lysenzski, who had been in the United States for several years, twice asked a foreman named Thomas Young for work. Young had refused him each time, but when Lysenzski returned to plead for a job once again, Young told him to speak with Frank Gray, a proprietor of a local grocery store. Gray informed Lysenzski that he could have work as a company laborer if he paid $25. When Lysenzski told him he could pay only $20, Gray told him that he could pay the remaining $5 on his first pay day and gave him a note to take to Young. However, Lysenzski brought the note to the company's superintendent, who promptly fired Young.[68]

Documentation of instances in which men were enticed to desert the union by operators' offers of promotions and contracts is scarce. However, two examples should prove instructive. First, as mentioned above, in 1895, Emanuel Jenkyn left his post as district treasurer to become a foreman. Interestingly, Jenkyn's departure was greeted not by accusations of betrayal, but by a resolution of praise and good wishes. Such a reaction may well demonstrate that many persons in the union sought similar preferment, or at least saw Jenkyn's action as justifiable. John Rinn saw corporate influence at work in the second example, the collapse of a local in Mahanoy City, one of the earliest locals established in anthracite. While he did not supply details in the following tortuous metaphor, Rinn's point is clear:

> A fight arose among [the local's] officers, and a mutiny among her crew, and to-day she lies on the seas of perdition and the black foam of grogg Sickness, supplied by the common enemy (corporate capital) besmears her decks, and the land lubbers who are responsible for her dissolution, of course they are contractors to-day aboard the great man of war (corporation).[69]

It is difficult to determine how common it was for operators to seek to lure ambitious men away from the union and thereby to sow seeds of dissension. Nevertheless, since operators had so many opportunities, embedded in the structure of work, to make such offers, they would surely have neglected one of their best weapons if they had not done so frequently. To mitigate the impact of such a strategy in the future, the UMWA would have to move more dramatically along a broader front to achieve the solidarity needed to build a full-fledged industrial union capable of withstanding such assaults. Only with the solidarity attained through dramatic collective action could the union overcome the numerous divisions in the work force and systematically attack the workers' grievances, many of which stemmed from the ad hoc, personal way in which mines were managed.

However, the UMWA did not come to such a realization as the result of its experience in Schuylkill. Fahy seemed prepared to abandon the work of organizing, for a short time at least, to turn to efforts where he had a better expectation of success. Although the district convention of October 15, 1896, passed a resolution calling on each local to pay ten cents per member "for the purpose of pushing the work of organizing," it devoted much more attention to efforts designed to influence Pennsylvania's legislature. To accomplish this, Fahy had written to candidates for the state assembly and senate in Schuylkill, Columbia, Northumberland, and Luzerne Counties and asked each to promise to support the following measures: "a semi-monthly pay law . . . a law abolishing company stores [and] . . . laws for the protection of health, life, and limb of coal workers."[70] Some six candidates for the senate agreed to Fahy's pledge, as did ten candidates for the assembly. Two other candidates did not sign the pledge, but each sent Fahy "an exceedingly strong letter," while only two candidates refused to extend any support.[71]

While he made no detailed report on the UMWA's effort to influence the elections themselves, Fahy seemed quite pleased at the district convention in December. He emphasized the special opportunity the union now had to win passage of favorable laws. He spoke of considerable interest among local businessmen in assisting the union's legislative effort, and he mentioned the possibility of establishing a "business men's auxiliary organization of the United Mine Workers of America." In its pursuit of cooperation with middle-class elements, the convention agreed to the following statement, which displayed its rationale for turning from organizing to political action:

> One of the chief fundamental principles of the United Mine Workers of America is that which looks to legislation for the best possible laws for the just protection of labor in its rights; believing as we do that to pursue a course of action along this line is in the end much more effective and of more lasting benefit to labor than strikes, boycotts, and such like methods, which seldom result in permanent good and usually tend to widen the breach between capital and labor, therefore we recognize the great importance of working people being properly represented in our national and state legislative halls.[72]

The union's legislative effort, which basically consisted of lobbying by Fahy, could claim several victories in 1897.[73] First, a legislative investigation into the conditions of the bituminous mine workers was expanded to include anthracite mine workers as well. Second, on June 15 the legislature enacted a statute prohibiting "any mine superintendent, mine foreman or assistant foreman" from receiving or soliciting any money "or other valuable consideration" from any employee or prospective employee to remain employed or to procure employment.[74]

The legislature also enacted legislation that showed the UMWA's ambivalence toward recent immigrants. Any employer of unnaturalized foreign-born males over twenty-one years of age was required to pay a tax of three cents for each day that such individuals were employed. Of course, the law permitted the employer to deduct the tax directly from the worker's wages.[75] Although Fahy had displayed considerable interest in organizing foreigners early in 1896, by lobbying for this legislation he fell into line with the UMWA's general policy of supporting attempts to restrict or discourage immigration.[76] He commented:

> What a world of good this law would do to the American citizens who try to earn their living in the coal mines, if the tax were one dollar per day. I have an idea it would also do the foreign-born . . . a power of good by keeping them out of the coal mines where all is cruel poverty and misery.[77]

The UMWA also won passage of a revised version of the miners' certificate law, first passed in 1889. That law had required all new miners to prove that they had worked at least two years as a miner's laborer. The revision tightened administrative procedures and qualifications for obtaining a certificate.[78] In its final legislative victory, the union persuaded the legislature to create a Bureau of Mines to enforce the state's mining laws and to scrutinize the conduct of its mine inspectors.[79] Direct lobbying by Fahy in Harrisburg apparently played an important part in enacting this legislation, which had not been passed in several previous attempts.[80]

Certainly, the union had reason to be proud of its legislative accomplishments. Nevertheless, one must wonder how much the UMWA thought it could accomplish by legislation alone. Without a new round of successes in organizing, these new laws would be unlikely to have much more impact upon the mine workers' condition than earlier enactments. Not only did the laws deal with a limited range of grievances, but these laws would be enforced only as mine workers demanded. But, in 1897 what remained of the UMWA in anthracite had all but abandoned its effort to build local unions capable of providing such support. Ironically, in his first year as president of the UMWA's anthracite district, John Fahy had moved from trying to bring the growing numbers of eastern and southern Europeans into the union to advocating legislation to discourage them from coming to the coal fields. Far more ironically, it would be the militancy of those immigrants, spurred in part by their opposition to the very tax for which Fahy lobbied, that would provide Fahy and the union an unprecedented opportunity to revive the UMWA in anthracite.

3

Militancy and Opportunity 1897–1899

The Lattimer Massacre of September 10, 1897, is one of a number of well-known episodes in American history in which law enforcement officials over-reacted pathologically to reasonably peaceful labor protest. The brute fact of the death of nineteen mine workers of recent immigrant stock at Lattimer makes that event memorable. However, its significance in the unionization of the anthracite coal industry stems from the month of rank-and-file militancy to which the Massacre was a response. That wave of militancy in the Lehigh field served as a turning point for the United Mine Workers of America (UMWA) in the anthracite region. In the strikes of August and September 1897, the rank and file displayed the capacity for militancy that would make unionization possible. The fledgling organization that arose encountered numerous difficulties and experienced little growth in 1898, a year in which the depression that beset the anthracite industry continued. But in 1899, demand for coal grew slowly and slack time began to decrease. Perhaps emboldened by the improving economic climate, more and more workers exhibited less and less patience toward a great many of the industry's work rules. Mine workers expressed their discontent in an ever-growing number of local strikes and, by walking off the job to protest particular regulations in the workplace, rebellious workers gave the UMWA the opportunities it needed. Where these walkouts began without the union's involvement, they generally allowed the union to establish itself. Where local UMWA leaders ordered these strikes, victory immeasurably strengthened the appeal of the union. Most importantly, by participating in such strikes workers gained the invaluable experience of joining together in a militant challenge to their bosses. By the beginning of the new century, these walkouts had not only added many names to the UMWA's membership rolls, they also had begun to build the solidarity necessary to mold a diverse population of mine workers into an industrial union.

THE ROAD TO AND FROM LATTIMER

The militancy of the summer of 1897 was not initiated by underground workers but by workers at stripping operations in the vicinity of Hazleton, where the most extensive strip mining of anthracite occurred. Workers in the strippings generally earned a lower daily wage than their subterranean counterparts, and the work process differed markedly from underground mining, with workers following behind a steam shovel to drill, blast, and load the newly exposed coal. Miners at strippings received a set sum per day, and the company paid their expenses. In addition, immigrants and their sons predominated in the strip-mining work force to a far greater extent than they did in the underground mines.[1] Finally, the area around Hazleton differed from much of the rest of the anthracite region in that company towns were far more common there and, for many operators, the revenues provided by the company store, company housing, and even payments deducted from each worker's pay to retain a company doctor contributed to profits.[2]

During his first year as superintendent of the Honey Brook division of the Lehigh and Wilkes-Barre Coal Company (L & W-B), Gomer Jones took steps to reduce costs. He eliminated a number of workers from the payroll, lowered wage rates for many others, and even raised the amount deducted from the workers' pay for each ton of coal they used. He encountered little overt resistance until, during the second week of August 1897, he ordered the consolidation of several mule stables at the company's strippings near Audenried into a single stable. The workers most affected by this change were the youthful mule drivers, many of whom would be compelled to travel further to get their mules in the morning and to return them at the end of the day. Several drivers met with Jones on Friday, August 13, to discuss the change, and some twenty-five to thirty-five drivers struck the next day. As the strikers milled around the colliery on Saturday, in the hope of dissuading others from going to work, an angry Gomer Jones confronted them.[3] William H. Storrs, son of William R. Storrs and assistant to his father at the Delaware, Lackawanna, and Western's (DL & W) Coal Department, gave the following description of the incident:

> The present strike came about through a consolidation of mine stables (in order that the services of one stable man might be dispensed with). Some of the boys [mule drivers] claimed that this change compelled them to walk four or five miles per day, and they asked to be paid for their time; this Mr. Jones refused.
>
> He had some words with these young men and, it is claimed, emphasized his remarks by swinging a club. This was followed by a personal attack on Mr. Jones, and had not other employees of the Company arrived just as they did, it would have been a serious matter for Jones.[4]

Of course, it is impossible to determine whether Jones used the club merely for emphasis or to attack the drivers, as the latter claimed. In any event, by Monday, August 16, most work had ceased at the L & W-B's nearby underground mines as well as its strippings, as some 2,000 workers walked out in sympathy with the drivers.[5] That evening, the mine workers met to formulate their demands. Not only did they call for wages to be returned to the figures that had prevailed before Jones lowered them, but they also demanded that all underground workers receive a 10 percent increase, and that the former price of coal to the workers be restored. Finally, the mine workers called for the removal of Gomer Jones because "he was partial to friends . . . [and] practiced economy at the expense of workers," whom he had "reduced to the verge of starvation wages."[6]

Having failed to reach an agreement with local company officials, the mine workers' committee, composed of representatives of each of the many nationalities in the work force, journeyed to New York on Wednesday, August 18, to confer with top officials of the L & W-B. On that day, John Fahy arrived to take advantage of the uprising to enroll the strikers in the UMWA. Although he apparently made no effort to take control of the strike, he did organize a number of local unions in several days. Meanwhile, on Friday, August 20, the mine workers' committee reached an agreement with company officials in which the company assuaged the drivers by promising to pay workers for all overtime. General Manager Elmer H. Lawall also agreed to investigate Jones's conduct and examine prevailing wage rates at nearby mining operations. If rates paid in the vicinity varied substantially from those paid by the L & W-B, the company promised to upgrade its own rates. In addition, Lawall announced that the workers could select their own doctors and would not be compelled to live in company houses. The men of the L & W-B returned to work on Monday, August 23.[7]

Unrest continued, perhaps prompted by the success of the L & W-B strikers. Once again young mine workers served as catalysts. On Wednesday, August 25, slate pickers, who claimed that they received lower wages than their counterparts at other collieries, walked off their jobs at A. S. Van Wickle's Coleraine breaker, located just to the east of Audenried. When bosses tried to bring immigrant workers in from the strippings to replace the boys and keep the breaker running, they instead surrounded the colliery office. There, Superintendent James E. Roderick persuaded them to return to work and select a committee later to meet with him the next day. However, after these talks proved fruitless, the workers decided to act. On the morning of Friday, August 27, a large group marched to Coleraine and induced those at work there to quit. The workers then marched several miles to Van Wickle's other major property, the Milnesville colliery, located to the north of Hazleton, and they succeeded in persuading the 1,000 workers there to leave their jobs. With the strike solidly established, a committee composed of representatives of the various nationalities employed by Van Wickle met with Roderick on the following day and secured a promise from him that if it could be demonstrated that other companies in the vicinity paid higher wages, he would adjust his company's wage scale accordingly.[8]

For the immigrants, the precipitating cause of the walkout seemed to be the three-cent-per-day wage tax on unnaturalized aliens, which John Fahy had supported so fervently. Saturday, August 21, apparently had been the first payday—at least for the workers at Coleraine—on which the tax had been deducted from wages. While the role played by the alien tax is not at all clear, several of the striking mine workers interviewed by newspaper reporters claimed that foreigners in Van Wickle's employ received lower wages for the same work than English-speaking employees.[9] Such blatant discrimination on the basis of nationality would seem to offer a company nothing more than an administrative nightmare. Thus, the workers' perception of wage discrimination can perhaps be explained by two factors—the wage tax and the wide variety of jobs in the industry, with many divided into several classes, each with a different wage rate. That foreigners may well have experienced considerable discrimination from foremen when they tried to move into better-paying jobs could only fortify perceptions of wage discrimination, which were compounded by the fact that workers who did not deal with the company store often received difficult work assignments or even faced dismissal.

On Wednesday, September 1, Superintendent Roderick announced increases for many of Van Wickle's stripping workers. This satisfied the strikers at Milnesville, the majority of whom worked at strippings, but not those at Coleraine, the majority of whom worked underground. While most of the men at Milnesville returned to work, most of those at Coleraine remained on strike. On the same day, at Audenried, General Manager Lawall and C. H. Warren, assistant to the president, met with the grievance committee of the L & W-B's workers. While Warren promised that the workers would receive fair treatment and expressed his hope that relations between the men and the bosses would improve, he made no mention of replacing Gomer Jones and made it clear that the company would not be pressured into firing him. After he presented detailed lists of wages at surrounding operations, Warren stated that, other than to raise the wages of stripping laborers who had been earning 90 cents per day to $1.00, no concessions were required since the company's rates were basically in line with those of its competitors. After the workers received the company's response, they resumed their walkout and sought, along with their counterparts from Coleraine, to extend the strike by undertaking marches throughout the Hazleton area.[10] Meanwhile, Thomas Duffy, secretary of the grievance committee of the L & W-B's workers, carried on negotiations with Lawall by telephone and telegraph. The marchers succeeded in idling many more mines, although some stayed idle only as long as marchers remained in the vicinity. Mine workers at many of these collieries then formulated their own sets of demands. And most of the men also heeded John Fahy's call to join the UMWA.[11]

As the strikers' ranks grew and marches became a daily occurrence, coal operators demanded that local authorities take action. On Tuesday, September 7, James L. Martin, sheriff of Luzerne County, issued a proclamation that declared: "A certain condition of turbulence and disorder exists in the neighborhood of the city of Hazleton." Also, Sheriff Martin deputized approximately 100 citizens to help maintain order.[12] Fahy implored workers to obey the law and to cease marching, but the strikers continued their tramps through the area.[13] By the end of the week, approximately 8,000 workers had joined the strike.[14] Meanwhile, Elmer Lawall of the L & W-B had decided to reopen negotiations with the committee of the company's employees.[15]

By Friday, September 10, the workers at Harwood colliery, owned by Calvin Pardee, had been on strike for several days, and John Fahy had organized a local union there.[16] On that day, in response to requests from workers at Lattimer, a large group of strikers from Harwood commenced a march to Lattimer with the intention of bringing that colliery of Pardee's into the strike. Marchers had tried to close Lattimer previously, but deputies had been able to repulse them.[17] The Harwood strikers confronted the sheriff and his men twice on Friday, the tenth, on their route around Hazleton. During the second confrontation, as the sheriff scuffled with several workers in an attempt to halt the march, the deputies fired directly into the crowd, killing nineteen and wounding perhaps fifty.[18]

The Massacre seemed first to encourage militancy and then, perhaps after some second thoughts by workers, discourage it. While approximately 2,000 more struck in the days immediately following the Massacre, and thousands of others threatened to do so, nearly all collieries had resumed operations by September 21, less than two weeks after the shootings. The swift ebb of militancy cannot be explained by the concessions which the companies offered, since some gave little or nothing and others offered relatively minor concessions.[19] The deployment of some 2,500 troops of the Pennsylvania National Guard on September 12 surely helps to explain it, although workers at several collieries did join the strike on the thirteenth and fourteenth.[20]

Perhaps the precipitous rise and fall of militancy in the Hazleton area in August and September 1897 can best be viewed as a consequence of the ebullient spontaneity that characterized the walkouts, marches, and even negotiations during the various strikes.[21] One aspect of that spontaneity was the fact that, although many of the demands presented at the different collieries were similar, no unified, region-wide set of demands was ever formulated. Consequently, the various companies could settle one strike after another by offering little to the workers, while complaining of their inability to pay employees any more than their competitors.[22]

The one man who might have provided overall leadership for the strike did not. While John Fahy took advantage of the numerous walkouts to enroll thousands of mine workers in the Lehigh field into the UMWA, he apparently made no attempt to take charge of the strike. In fact, Fahy received considerable credit from local newspapers for his moderation. When Calvin Pardee labeled him an agitator and added that "the men did not want to go out until they were stirred up by Mr. Fahy,"[23] Fahy responded tartly:

> In face of the fact that the miners were on strike and sent for me before I came among them, and that ever since my arrival in the Hazleton district, I have been complimented and congratulated by the press, clergy, and public in general because of the course which I have pursued . . . I deny in toto every charge made . . . in Mr. Pardee's interview.[24]

While the Lehigh strikes might have accomplished more if Fahy and the UMWA had tried to coordinate them, the union would have risked a crushing failure by doing so. By keeping his distance from the strikes, John Fahy was able to achieve the union's biggest success in anthracite since its earliest days in the Schuylkill field. From the end of August until the UMWA's national convention in January 1898, some sixty-four locals were organized or reorganized in District One, and the majority of those were located in the Hazleton area.[25] After the convention, the executive board of the UMWA, to which Fahy had been reelected after a year's hiatus, carried out the recent convention's resolution to establish the Lehigh field as a new district—District Seven.[26] Thomas Duffy, who had played an important role in the L & W-B's workers' committee, was elected president, and Benjamin James was elected secretary.[27] Just as significant for the union's future in anthracite was the UMWA's success in negotiating a contract in the bituminous coal industry's Central Competitive Field early in 1898. That epochal achievement heralded a far stronger national union that might be able to make substantial contributions to organizing efforts.[28]

The recent successes in Lehigh prompted further efforts in the southern portion of the Wyoming field, in the vicinity of Wilkes-Barre. After some initial organizing there, Fahy left the work in the hands of local men. By the end of March 1898, one Frank Gwisedoskey reported to the *UMW Journal* that the union had some 1,300 members in good standing in the area and some 9,000 total adherents. As had been the case in the Lehigh field during the previous summer, immigrants were showing the strongest interest in the union:

> The Polish, Litevish and Slavish elements are joining the union. The English-speaking people are very slow in coming in, especially the Americans. . . . They seem to have doubts about the organization being successful, they think it is a fraud to get their quarters.[29]

Gwisedoskey added that financing union activities had been difficult since the men had been working only two or three days per week and, consequently, many of them were unable to pay their dues regularly. In the next few weeks, he planned to organize some of the mine workers north of

Wilkes-Barre in West Pittston and Plymouth, where earlier attempts by Fahy had accomplished little. To facilitate organization, Gwisedoskey urged the UMWA to allow workers in and around Wilkes-Barre to form their own district.[30] However, Fahy, still president of District One, which at this point encompassed both the Wyoming and Schuylkill regions, opposed such a move. In March, Fahy wrote Michael Ratchford, president of the UMWA, approving Ratchford's denial of a district charter for the men of Wilkes-Barre. In Fahy's opinion:

> If the men themselves of the territory show they are able to and will push the work of organization among themselves to success, . . . they can have a district charter or even two of them if the charter be the only thing standing in the way . . . but up to date they have not properly shown that they will really do all this.[31]

As organizing efforts continued through 1898, it became clear that this year would bring no breakthrough in anthracite for the UMWA, and that the union would be fortunate merely to maintain its strength. Although veteran organizer Chris Evans reported favorably concerning several meetings he held in July in the vicinity of Wilkes-Barre,[32] his success was not sufficient to establish a solid foundation for organizing the entire area. A correspondent of the *UMW Journal,* who signed his letters as "Mine Worker," wrote toward the end of September that, even though some 4,000 workers had been enrolled in the Wilkes-Barre subdistrict of District One, not nearly that many were in good standing. He attributed the subdistrict's problems to the workers' meager earnings and the resulting lack of funds for organizing. Now that the mines were working somewhat more steadily, "Mine Worker" believed that if the national headquarters could send an organizer, organization would proceed sufficiently to justify the formation of a new district. He added: "Our local from a membership of several hundred dwindled down to two, but I am pleased to state that last week we had quite a meeting and soon expect to have it up to the old standard."[33]

In the late spring and early summer of 1898, the UMWA tried to organize two areas that had witnessed little union activity since the 1870s. One was the somewhat isolated southeastern portion of the Lehigh field, the Panther Creek Valley, bailiwick of the Lehigh Coal and Navigation Company. Chris Evans remarked after an organizing trip there that, even though two towns had solid locals, he had discovered that "the lost and strayed" were numerous and did not show much interest in "joining the gallant few" who were trying to establish the union throughout the valley.[34] Evans also tried his luck around Scranton, but had little success there. Although several successful mass meetings had been held, most mine workers in that area seemed afraid to get involved with the union.[35]

Even newly created District Seven faced a struggle to maintain its strength in the year following Lattimer. While Chris Evans reported considerable success in rallies throughout the Hazleton area in April and May 1898, he also detected a lack of effective organization in many parts of the district. Also, District Seven's financial condition was not particularly strong. At a convention in May, when Secretary Benjamin James reported that the lowest bid for printing the district's by-laws had been $65, the convention "decided to lay the matter over till times would improve."[36] According to James, many workers had as few as five days of work per month during the first half of 1898. However, he expected the district to "thrive" in the latter portion of the year, since steadier employment seemed likely. Nevertheless, James cautioned against militancy: "Let us not be hasty. Let us keep all strike agitations in the background until solidarity and anthracite coal miners are synonymous."[37]

To remind the union men of the accomplishments of the past year, the district sponsored a parade on September 10 along the route of the ill-fated march to Lattimer.[38] More than 2,300 men, representing thirty-seven locals, participated, and operators of collieries south of Hazleton, such as the L & W-B, made no effort to open their collieries for work on that day. However, to the north and east of the city, at the collieries owned by the Coxe and Pardee families, workers were told that "if they did not work [that day] they would have to seek employment elsewhere." Benjamin James reported that, despite the threats, some men from those collieries marched in the parade, but he added: "If the men paid no heed to the intimidations of these bosses who have no respect for themselves or any one else . . . [then] we would have had the largest parade that had ever been seen in Hazleton."[39]

As winter approached, most collieries in Lehigh worked five or six days per week, and James thought that the district's locals would "boom" as a result of the increase in employment.[40] However, the anticipated boom in organizing never occurred. In December, James reported that, while work had been "pretty steady," workers were "still drifting along in the same old way, seemingly content with their present condition." In describing that condition, James revealed the UMWA's basic thrust in its effort to organize mine workers, whether in the anthracite or bituminous fields. He pointed out that mine workers lacked "rules to govern them in their daily labor." For example, while foremen at some mines were giving "a fair price" for certain kinds of work that miners had to perform, at other mines the same work was "done without pay." He also charged that there was "no uniform wage for any class of work in and around the mines," and mentioned that at some collieries breaker boys received twenty cents more per day than elsewhere. Not surprisingly, at such collieries the boys persistently refused to join the union.[41] The UMWA's goal in anthracite, as in bituminous, was to negotiate an industrywide wage scale along with substantial regularization of work rules.[42] Yet these goals could never be accomplished without thorough organization. Clearly frustrated in his organizing efforts, James told the workers:

> Why stand around the street corners cursing your luck when you alone are to blame for it? In our present deplorable condition, we of the anthracite coal fields are a blot on civilization. Is there no lesson which can be imparted severe enough to teach you that you are powerless as individuals?[43]

Nearly four-and-a-half years after its initial foray into the anthracite industry, the UMWA still faced an arduous task of organizing. In March 1899, the *UMW Journal*'s frequent correspondent from Wilkes-Barre, "Mine Worker," wrote once again to present his diagnosis of and prescription for the organization's condition. Although he gave Benjamin James credit for recent efforts to rebuild the union in Wilkes-Barre, he maintained that much more had to be done there and throughout the anthracite fields. He thought it essential that organizers be dispatched to every field. He noted that in Schuylkill County, where John Fahy was "supposed to be president," there had once been ninety-four locals. However, he had learned that very few of these were still active. In his view, once organizing had proceeded sufficiently, several districts should be organized "under the Presidency of men of sand and sense." Such men "would lead the miners as they should go, and not truckle to them and let them go contrary to the constitution, common sense or business methods, and thus make egregious asses of themselves." He concisely summarized the history of the UMWA in anthracite—"As soon as one district is organized it is allowed to droop and die while another is being formed."[44]

BREAKING INTO THE WYOMING FIELD

Most ominous for the UMWA was the fact that, as of early 1899, the union had made little or no enduring progress among the workers of the Wyoming field, who constituted over 50 percent of the industry's work force. Workers there had not joined in the strike of 1887–88 and had played a relatively minor part in the strikes of the Workingmen's Benevolent Association in the late 1860s and early 1870s. However, their inability to organize on a regional scale prior to 1899 cannot be attributed solely to a lack of militancy. From the 1860s onward, the Wyoming mine workers had confronted large, financially healthy corporations that staunchly opposed labor organization and combated it skillfully. Nevertheless, during the latter half of the 1890s, a sufficient number and variety of job actions occurred to demonstrate a potential for militancy that would begin to be realized toward the end of 1899.

Some nine months before the Lattimer Massacre, a small group of workers at Archbald, near Scranton, rebelled with a spontaneity that strongly resembled the Lehigh strikes of the summer of 1897. As in those walkouts, the strikers were largely immigrants, and they provoked a response that, while less bloody than Lattimer, was similar in character. A group of some sixty Italian immigrants worked at the Forest Coal Company's mine "robbing pillars." This was the perilous final task before abandoning a mine, removing as many of the pillars of coal supporting the "roof" over the miners' heads as possible. One miner had supervised the immigrants until his discharge in November 1896, whereupon the company placed three miners in charge. Each of the miners received, as had their predecessor, six-and-a-half cents for each ton loaded by the laborers in his group, in addition to being paid for his own work. According to the *Wilkes-Barre Record,* ever since the change "the Italians showed a very angry disposition," and on Friday, December 4, they went out on strike. The strikers stated that they wanted to receive the six-and-a-half cents per ton themselves, since the contractors did little or nothing to entitle them to the money.[45] Although the company countered that the contractors were needed to insure the immigrants' safety, the latter responded that the contractors were quick to depart whenever danger threatened. On Saturday, December 5, an armed group of strikers blocked access to the mine by placing boulders at its entrance. The superintendent and outside foreman called in detectives from a local agency who, after withstanding a barrage of rocks, arrested the leaders, with the aid of the constable.[46] Meanwhile, the remainder of the strikers "entrenched themselves in their 'castle,' " a large wooden building in which about sixty of them resided with their families.[47] Several days later, most of the strikers were reported to have "taken to the woods," although some twenty-five did return to work.[48]

At the mines of the DL & W, militancy never lay far beneath the surface. In the aftermath of the Lattimer Massacre, officials of the company feared that protest might extend to their mines. On September 15, 1897, William H. Storrs informed President Samuel Sloan that some efforts had been made to organize their men. However, he added: "I cannot believe that our old men will go into such a union with the Huns & Poles & c." He mentioned that workers had met to consider striking at the mines of the Susquehanna Coal Company (SCC) in and around Nanticoke, at the southern edge of the Wyoming field, where the DL & W also had two mines. Storrs realized that the DL & W's mine workers might well be amenable to a strike, particularly since they had not had a great deal of work in recent weeks. He advised Sloan: "If we have [railroad] cars enough to work each of our mines every day, eight hours per day, during the continuance of this strike it will do more than anything else to keep them quiet." However, even if the demand for coal should increase considerably, Storrs advised against running the breakers more than eight hours per day. He feared that if the company did so, the newspapers would "call attention to 'full time at the mines,' " which workers might attribute to a shortage of coal on account of the strikes in the Hazleton area. In such an event, many of the DL & W's employees might conclude that "the time had arrived for a general turnout for higher wages for all anthracite workers."[49]

Although the turmoil in Lehigh subsided quickly, it apparently prompted some of the DL & W's workers to consider taking steps to better their condition. On October 15, Storrs reported to Sloan that the men at the Woodward colliery had appointed a committee that recently had met with company officials to request a cut in the price of powder. Although the committee from Woodward had been easily dissuaded from pursuing the matter, several days later some miners from the Pettebone colliery appointed a committee to request a reduction in powder along with other concessions. Storrs warned that "agitators" were "making a strong effort" to organize the men. Their demands were intended to call "attention to their organization, and if granted," would "do more than anything else to swell their ranks."[50] Storrs managed to deflect the committee's effort during what he described as "a long and pleasant interview" in which workers mentioned neither the price of powder nor the union.[51]

In the next two years young mine workers, principally mule drivers, initiated occasional episodes of militant protest at the DL & W's mines. Several of them struck at the Storrs colliery on a Saturday afternoon in the summer of 1898, claiming that they received no pay for the fifteen to thirty minutes they worked beyond the usual working time. Storrs informed Sloan that he had planned to close that colliery at some point to make repairs to the breaker, but he now had decided to halt operations the next day, to "give the boy[s] a chance to cool off."[52] Young men at the DL & W's Diamond colliery in Scranton walked off their jobs on Friday, June 2, 1899. That day had been scheduled as payday, but a number of older mine workers who served as volunteer firemen with the Tripp Park Hose Company requested that the bosses delay payday until Saturday. The Hose Company had planned its first annual picnic for that day, and the firemen reasoned that, having been paid on Saturday, the workers would spend more money at the picnic. The coal company agreed and decided to make that Saturday a holiday at the mine, but when the drivers received word of this on Friday, sixteen of them walked out of the mines and went to attend the circus. In response, the DL & W ordered all mine workers to report to work on Saturday and fired six of the drivers who had struck. These were older workers in their late teens whom the company accused of inciting the younger drivers to join them in the strike.[53]

Even without any effective union presence at their collieries, the managers of the DL & W feared the possibility of militant action. In a letter to Sloan on February 8, 1899, Storrs mentioned that, since the company had been operating four of its collieries considerably more than its other mines because of royalty arrangements, "some reckless fellow" might think that "if one or more of these breakers, shafts, or fanhouses were burnt or otherwise disabled," working time at the company's other mines would increase. He believed that "the Oxford breaker was set on fire last Spring in order that work might be resumed at the Archbald." While he admitted that his fears might be groundless, Storrs nevertheless thought that the company ought to consider insuring the four collieries.[54]

Although isolated incidents of militancy may well have occurred more frequently in 1898 and early 1899, the UMWA made little progress in the Wyoming field at that time. While there had been considerable union activity in the vicinity of Wilkes-Barre early in 1898, by February of the next year, when Benjamin James commenced an organizational drive, he reported that "not a single local union" was active[55] and that "very few" of the 25,000 mine workers there were organized.[56] When he first called a convention and advertised through the daily press that all the collieries, organized and unorganized, would be allowed to send delegates, he received very little response. However, a successful convention was held on March 26, which "about twenty-five delegates" attended, "all of them representing union men." Early in April, James noted that a local of some 400 "English-speaking people" had been organized in Carbondale and that in Nanticoke there was no hall in the town large enough to accommodate the members.[57]

One problem James faced in organizing workers was whether to organize workers on a colliery basis or by nationality, as some preferred but which the union tried to discourage. John Fahy had done this on a number of occasions in Lehigh in 1897. In discussing this issue in the *UMW Journal*, James stated that he had organized by nationality only at the request of the men involved. In Nanticoke, he had asked Polish mine workers if they desired to do so "as they (or a great many of them) do not understand the English language." However, "they were in favor of going with the English-speaking class and it was done."[58]

The UMWA's organization in the Schuylkill field had disintegrated so much by this time that District One was reorganized in a convention on May 23 in Scranton under the leadership of workers from the Wyoming field. Benjamin James, whom the convention thanked "for his earnest and indefatigable work," informed the assembled delegates that, in the three months since he had begun his current drive in the Wyoming field, thirty-two locals had been established. The district elected Thomas D. Nicholls and Frank D. Miller, both from Nanticoke, as president and vice-president, respectively, and C. W. Baxter of Providence, near Scranton, as secretary-treasurer.[59]

The reorganization of District One spurred John Fahy, who had not been reelected to the national executive board in 1899 and who lost the district presidency in the reorganization, to mount a counterattack from his headquarters in Shamokin. He initiated a campaign to persuade locals, especially those in the Schuylkill field, where he was still doing some organizing, not to send the per capita tax to the district and national officers but to one William Anderson, former treasurer of the district.[60] Complaining that national headquarters had long slighted both him and the Schuylkill mine workers, Fahy withheld these funds for several months in an attempt to pressure UMWA President John Mitchell, in his first year as president, to send organizers into the anthracite region, and into the Schuylkill field in particular.[61] However, in a stormy confrontation, Mitchell forced Fahy to relinquish control of the funds at a convention of the reorganized District One in August. In return, the men of the Schuylkill field were given permission to proceed to establish their own district.[62] In spite of its amicable resolution, this episode demonstrates the persistence of the interregional discord that had plagued labor organization in the anthracite region since the 1860s.

When he assumed the presidency of District One on May 23, 1899, Thomas D. Nicholls had not yet reached his twenty-ninth birthday. Born in Wilkes-Barre, he grew up in Nanticoke, began work as a breaker boy at age nine, and took a job inside the mines at age twelve. Little is known of his life from that time until he became district president, except that he showed ambition by taking correspondence courses in mine management and passed the examination for his state foreman's certificate in June 1897.[63] During a period of nearly a year and a half, from his election through the general anthracite strike of September and October 1900, Nicholls presided over a district in which militancy grew and spread dramatically. This militancy erupted in one local strike after another in which workers, organized or not, walked out over any of a wide variety of issues in strikes that affected from several hundred to several thousand workers. Taken as a whole, these strikes had three important effects. First, successful strikes sanctioned by union leaders served as an unmistakable lesson to the unorganized. Second, strikes by unorganized mine workers gave the union an opportunity not only to organize new locals at the striking collieries, but also to try to take control of such strikes and perhaps achieve new victories. Finally, the experience gained by workers and their leaders in these numerous strikes forged the solidarity essential to build a union capable of holding together throughout the industry-wide strikes of 1900 and 1902.

A particularly interesting dispute arose on June 28 at the Dorrance colliery in Wilkes-Barre, operated by the Lehigh Valley Coal Company (LV). Officials of the LV ordered miners at Dorrance, who worked in some of "the gassiest coal seams in the world,"[64] to cease using the traditional open-flame lamps which they clipped to their caps. Instead they were to use the Wolf safety lamp, reputedly the best safety lamp available. Frederick M. Chase, the company's assistant general superintendent, maintained that using the

FIGURE 3.1
Thomas D. Nicholls, President, UMWA District One, 1899–1909; Member of Congress, 1906–1910 (originally printed in *United Mine Workers Journal*, May 1902).

Wolf lamp would cause the miners little or no additional labor or expense. He stated that the company provided the lamps without charge, filled them with fuel, and cleaned them each evening. Concerning the issue of safety, he commented:

> To simply instruct men working in a gaseous mine to be careful in the use of the naked light is a very unwise policy. Even if all of the men are as careful as it is possible for them to be one of them may forget himself and leave open a door or walk into a body of gas and this act may cost a score of more of lives and the destruction of the colliery.[65]

However, the miners countered that the Wolf lamp not only gave off less light than the cap lamp, but it was also rather heavy and had to be held, hooked to the belt, or hung in a chamber, so that its light seldom could be made to shine directly where a miner was working. If the lamp's glass bonnet was broken, or the concentration of gas present rose above 6 percent, the flame was extinguished automatically.[66] Of course, the lamp had been designed intentionally with this feature, to prevent either an explosion or tampering by mine workers. However, the workers may have preferred the old-style safety lamps, whose flame required monitoring to determine the concentration of gas and could be drawn through the wire gauze surrounding it to light a fuse or even a pipe.[67] With the Wolf lamp in use, miners would be forbidden to light their own fuses and would be expected to wait for another employee, who would have the job of igniting charges, to come to the chamber. Such a system would inevitably cause delay.[68] Moreover, although the company's desire to prevent mine explosions was laudable, it was by no means altruistic. By using the Wolf lamp, the LV sought to prevent many thousands of dollars of losses which explosions could cause. The miners, however, were more concerned with avoiding a much more common source of accidents—falls of roof and coal that became more likely with the weaker light that safety lamps necessarily yielded.[69] Benjamin James of the UMWA succinctly summarized the miners' case against the lamp. In his view, the Wolf lamp might not only decrease safety by preventing miners from recognizing imminent roof falls, but it would also bring "a great reduction" in their wages, "because they could not mine as much coal with it as they could with the cap lamp."[70]

Apparently Dorrance had not been organized when the strike began, since Benjamin James formed a local of several hundred workers there on June 29.[71] In addition, the workers at Dorrance persuaded quite a few of their counterparts at other nearby LV properties to stay home as well.[72] Although the strikers had returned to work by July 10 and consented to use the Wolf lamp, this short strike had an impact beyond the issue over which it was fought.[73] It allowed the UMWA to organize the Dorrance colliery and probably also enabled the union to begin to organize the LV's other nearby mines as well.[74] Numerous small strikes throughout the area would have similar results.

In mid-July, shortly after Benjamin James organized the mine workers at the William A. colliery, located several miles south of Scranton, the men there struck over excessive dockage and "alleged favoritism to certain miners."[75] Several weeks later, the strikers returned to work after receiving a few concessions,[76] and Benjamin James could not resist the temptation to gloat. Previously, Congressman William L. Connell, who owned the colliery, had ordered James to leave his office, "claiming that if labor agitators would stay away there would be no trouble." Now, however, James was preparing to sign an agreement with the Congressman. James thought that Connell ought to realize that: "We control your men to-day, you know, so you must not be stubborn."[77]

At the beginning of August, just a few miles to the south of the William A. colliery, mine workers at the Babylon colliery, owned by Simpson and Watkins, struck over dockage. They returned to their jobs on August 14 after the company made some concessions,[78] but they did not remain at work for long. According to Benjamin James, once the workers had returned, a foreman named McCarthy "wanted the miners to load more on their cars, which would more than counterbalance the advances that had just been given them." When a number of miners refused to follow McCarthy's order and confronted him, the foreman and a Polish miner scuffled. Following that incident, two of "McCarthy's tools" reportedly held the Pole while McCarthy "again beat him." The workers immediately walked out and demanded McCarthy's dismissal.[79] Although there was no report of McCarthy's fate when the strike was settled in late September, the strikers did succeed in winning some increases in mining rates, as well as promises by the company to reduce dockage and not to compel men to deal with the company store.[80]

Yet another strike in the summer and fall of 1899 provided a glimpse of what the UMWA might be able to accomplish in the anthracite industry. The SCC, controlled by the Pennsylvania Railroad, employed approximately 4,000 workers at its several mines in Nanticoke and Glen Lyon. The first hint of trouble there came on the evening of July 25, when miners on the night shift complained that "the toppage required on the cars" was excessive and refused to go to work.[81] Like most companies in the Wyoming field, the SCC paid a certain sum per car of coal, and the company spared no effort to try to insure that the coal in the cars was as clean as possible and that the cars were as full as possible. In general, the procedures involved in penalizing, or "docking" miners for failing to load enough clean coal had never been calculated to breed trust for the operators among the miners. On the surface, far away from them, a docking boss decided whether or not a miner deserved credit for a full car as the contents of that car were dumped into the breaker. The cars came one after another, and for each one the docking boss had to decide not to dock, to dock one-quarter of a car, one-half, or even the entire car.[82]

While the docking boss's decisions regarding the topping, that is, the extent to which the coal had been heaped above the level of the top of the car, might seem less open to dispute than his rulings as to the proportion of dirt and other impurities in a car, consider the process. The company generally told the miner to load his cars so that each would have at least six inches of topping.[83] To accomplish this demanded no small amount of skill. As one miner described it, he would "take a row of chunks and put them along the top rail of the car and then fill with fine stuff or the best coal."[84] So, the six inches of topping consisted not merely of a mound in the middle of the car, but six inches around the edge of the car, with large pieces of coal holding the smaller pieces on the car.[85] However, since six inches of topping was required at the breaker, the miners and their laborers had to be sure to shovel several additional inches of coal on to the car. Some cars might have to travel more than a mile before they reached the surface, and throughout their journey they might be jostled over rough roads, collide with other cars, and ascend inclines. For any of these reasons, coal could fall out of even the best-constructed topping.[86]

If the docking boss saw less than the required topping, his task was to dock the car, even though the miner might well have topped the car sufficiently to withstand the general run of trips to the breaker. It is easy to imagine the chronic controversy that would result, especially where autocratic bosses held sway or when companies sought to widen their profit margins. To make matters worse, in this particular case, the SCC's underground bosses also insisted that miners top their cars generously. As a veteran miner related:

> The mine bosses, the fire bosses, were coming around the mines and telling us that we were not putting top enough on. I have been in my place and watched my laborer put ten inches on, and as high as a foot of topping on, and yet they said they only required six inches topping at the breaker. Things became unbearable.[87]

During the week of July 25, the SCC ordered miners to supply sixteen inches of topping in their chamber so that the company could be sure it received six inches at the breaker. After the men on the evening shift refused to comply, a committee of the company's miners met with Superintendent John H. Tonkin. When the committee informed him that it did not intend to follow the order, Tonkin ordered them to remove their tools from the colliery and not to return until they changed their minds. While it is not clear whether or not local and district leaders of the UMWA made the decision to contest the

FIGURE 3.2
Susquehanna Coal Company surveyors, 1889 (Courtesy of Jule Znaniecki).

company's crackdown on topping, Nanticoke was one of the best-organized towns in the Wyoming field. Little that occurred there, or in the SCC's mines, could have escaped the attention of union leaders, especially since Thomas Nicholls and Frank Miller, president and vice-president of the district, were employees of the company. In any event, the UMWA quickly took control of the strike and formulated a lengthy list of demands, which it presented to the company on July 31.[88]

These demands were designed to address a wide variety of problems. Miners not only sought to resolve the conflict over topping; they also demanded a schedule of payments to cover many of the specific conditions they had to face. No longer did they want to trust the company's largesse as displayed in the system of allowances. For example, they demanded that the company pay a specific sum, according to thickness, for the rock that they often had to blast to extract coal. Also, they called for a specific payment for each row of props they set, and additional payments for extra propping. Miners also wanted to receive an extra payment for building the road for coal cars from their chambers to the gangway, and they called on the company to send company men to repair the road in the chamber when that road required repair at a distance of fifty feet or more from the coal face. In addition, miners wanted the SCC either to have company men clear all cave-ins on roads in chambers or to pay the miners the daily wage of a company miner for doing so. Most importantly, the miners demanded that six inches of topping be required, not at the breaker, but in the chamber, and that dockage be limited to an average of 3 percent. Moreover, this was to be an intermediate step while the company arranged to "pay by weight, rather than by the car," in the near future. For the rest of the mine workers, the union demanded increases in wages ranging from 3.5 to 40 percent.[89]

The company's response demonstrates how sharply its thinking diverged from that of the mine workers. Regarding payments for blasting rock, General Manager Morris Williams held that the hardness of the rock should dictate payment and, in any event, the company had always compensated miners fairly for such work. Payment for basic propping was "included in the price paid for the car of coal," and the company would make "due allowance" for extra heavy propping. The company also refused to countenance any changes in payments for building or clearing roads in chambers. With regard to dockage, Williams stood on what he undoubtedly saw as an unassailable principle: "The dockage must always be governed absolutely on the merit of each car loaded." On the grievance that precipitated the strike, Williams stated that he found the demand for six inches of topping in the chamber "a strange one . . . after 25 years of compliance with an agreement to furnish six inches of topping at the breaker," which, he claimed, had "invariably been furnished.' Any experienced mine manager had no choice but to adapt the operation of his colliery to the constant changes in mining conditions. However, anthracite operators refused to consider any alterations in their venerable agreements, especially those made with groups of their employees uninfluenced by the meddling of a labor organization. In the company's view, the miners' demands for a different rule for topping and for payment by the car were "equivalent to a demand for an increase in wages," which, in its current state, the anthracite coal business would simply "not permit." Of course, the state of business similarly precluded raises for the SCC's company men.[90]

On August 24 and 25, at a special district convention in Wilkes-Barre, District One declared its full support for the strike. A committee was appointed whose members would station themselves at pay cars and offices around the district on paydays to solicit funds for the men of Nanticoke and Glen Lyon and their families. Also, in the following resolution, the convention sought to insure that the district concentrated its efforts on the current strike:

> We earnestly urge all union men to counsel their fellow working men in their respective places to stop all agitation of local grievances until our organization has been more fully perfected within our own territory and particularly that of the SCC.[91]

Nevertheless, this resolution did not prevent miners elsewhere in the district from taking militant action. At the Stevens Coal Company's colliery in West Pittston, miners had struck in July over excessive dockage. On September 5, strikers confronted a foreman, driver boss, and three other men on their way into the mine to repair pumps. As a crowd gathered, including several deputies, a fight ensued and shots were fired. About a dozen men were wounded in the melee, some quite seriously, and many were arrested.[92] The workers returned to their jobs at the beginning of October, after the company made a slight concession on mining rates.[93] In October, miners at the two collieries of Jermyn and Company south of Scranton, like so many of their counterparts, struck over dockage. The miners accused the company of docking one-quarter of their total production on a particular day. They also claimed that, when docking bosses failed to dock sufficiently to satisfy company officials, those officials added to the docking bosses' totals of docked cars after the tally sheets had been brought to the office. The miners returned to work after more than a month on strike when the company agreed to allow them to hire check–docking bosses to monitor the docking process.[94] Interestingly, this strike commenced only about a week after Benjamin James had been organizing in the vicinity.[95]

While District One's leaders concentrated their efforts and the district's resources on the strike at Nanticoke and Glen Lyon, others in the union continued to organize throughout the anthracite region. James kept busy in the

Scranton area and, to the south, the organization in the Schuylkill field returned to life as District Nine. On October 21, in Mount Carmel, some 106 delegates established the district and elected John Fahy as president. A glance at the names of the remaining officers reveals a conscious effort to maintain ethnic balance among the district's leaders: Vice-President Paul P. Pulaski, Secretary George Hartlein, and Treasurer Wilson G. Yoder. The district displayed a far less militant tone than District One, as evidenced by the following resolution passed at the inaugural convention: "We deprecate strikes, except as a last resort."[96]

As the Nanticoke strike continued, it exposed the distrust among the three anthracite fields which had for so many years sabotaged efforts to organize the industry. While the UMWA's national leaders apparently viewed the strike against the SCC as the unions' best opportunity for a major victory, and therefore focused their attention on it, leaders of the other anthracite districts displayed lukewarm support, or even hostility, toward the Nanticoke strike. In late September, Benjamin James accused John Fahy of "trying his best to defeat the miners on Strike, by advising men to withhold aid."[97] Early in December, as the Nanticoke strike neared its climax, Fahy informed Mitchell of the efforts made in his district to collect funds for the strikers. However, he added:

> I have often wished that this strike was over and that the men had won it, or that it had never started, because I believe that for quite a long while now it has in its effects been proving injurious to the progress and growth of the organization in other sections of the anthracite, by keeping men away from the organization through fear of strike etc.[98]

According to James, President Duffy of District Seven had his own reasons to fear militant action. In a letter to Mitchell in early October, James related that Duffy and one of his committee chairmen had recently been given "the best place in the colliery." In James's view this had caused many men to leave the union. He also mentioned that Duffy had been speaking at meetings throughout his district and had told the men that Mitchell intended to provoke a general anthracite strike in order to provide steadier employment to the bituminous mine workers and thus insure his reelection as UMWA president. With regard to the strike at Nanticoke, Duffy had reportedly told one group "that they had no use for the miners of . . . [the] upper end."[99]

Meanwhile, the mine workers of the SCC showed no sign of abandoning their strike. The company had agreed to some concessions—to stop harassing workers underground regarding topping and to make specific arrangements with miners regarding payment for blasting rock before such work was done, instead of the customary practice of haggling over such payments at the end of the month. However, the SCC would not consider further concessions, especially the higher wage schedule that the union had demanded for company men. So, on October 3, a mass meeting of strikers resolved not to return to work.[100] On October 9 and 10, a district convention at Carbondale agreed upon a levy of one dollar per member per month to aid the SCC strikers.[101] Benjamin James exulted on October 14 that "not a car of coal" had been hoisted since the beginning of the walkout.[102]

On October 19, the company posted lengthy notices, signed by Superintendent Tonkin, designed to lure the workers to return through a curious combination of carrot and stick. The notices detailed the SCC's concessions, which the company believed had not been reported properly. Tonkin also stated that the company had always paid competitive wages and was willing to investigate rates paid by companies in the surrounding area and to adjust its rates accordingly. However, the notice closed with a thinly veiled ultimatum. The SCC would resume work when and if a sufficient number of employees informed their bosses that they desired to return. Otherwise, the company would "abandon all hope of resuming operations until April 1, 1900."[103]

Having made its best effort to influence the strikers, the company tried to start one of its mines in Glen Lyon on October 26. To make its presence felt, the UMWA held a parade through the town at 6:00 A.M., before work commenced. At 6:30, a trolley came from Nanticoke to the mine, loaded with deputies and a few supervisory personnel. Pickets at the colliery let them enter, but no substantial influx of strikers followed them across the picket line. The supervisors sent several cars of coal that had been left in the mine to the breaker, and then they closed the mine once again. A company spokesman told the local press that, since the SCC had opened a colliery for work and had received so little response from the workers, it would keep its collieries closed until the men were "ready and willing to go to work."[104]

As the strike continued into November, some of the women in the community decided to take steps to stiffen resistance. Early on the morning of November 21, they went to several of the SCC's collieries to persuade workers who had not struck—supervisory personnel, engineers, and pumpmen—not to go to work.[105] According to Thomas Nicholls, the women, generally in groups of two, would merely take "scabs" by the arm and offer to escort them home. However, the *Wilkes-Barre Record* reported that some of the approximately 1,000 women at the collieries threatened or attacked those who insisted on going to work. Also, women were not the only ones involved in attempting to influence those who had not joined the strike. As a crowd approached an assistant foreman who had been deputized to protect the company's property, he fired his weapon and slightly wounded a fourteen-year-old boy, John Serowinski. By 8:30 A.M., a committee of strikers had persuaded most of the women to return home without further incident, and the women decided at a meeting that afternoon to cease their efforts.[106] The extent of community support that the Nanticoke strike enjoyed becomes all the more obvious in light of the success with which the boycott had been utilized against some strikebreakers. By the end of November, several of those who had been dissuaded by the women from going to work on the twenty-first came to Nicholls and asked him to "intercede for them in the union meeting," because no one would speak to them, and "they could not bear to be treated as dogs." The local unions agreed to allow anyone who had finally quit his job "to be recognized on the street as a man," but they would not admit any of them into the locals until "after the strike was won," in order to "avoid getting traitors in camp."[107]

The solidarity evinced by the strikers gave the SCC little choice but to reopen negotiations in the last week of November. Benjamin James, whom the company did not permit to participate in the negotiations because he was not one of its employees, hinted that the union might consider calling out workers at the collieries near Shamokin operated by other subsidiaries of the Pennsylvania Railroad.[108] In the negotiations, the union and the company apparently agreed to settle the question of topping along the lines of the company's earlier proposal to end underground supervision of topping.[109] Talks continued for several weeks, as the parties reached a series of compromises over various payments to miners and increases for some company men. A major obstacle to a settlement was the fate of the engineers and pumpmen who had walked out at the beginning of the strike. Although the company was willing to keep them in its employ, it refused to return them to their old jobs, since this would necessitate replacing the men whom the company had hired during the strike.[110] The UMWA committee insisted on reinstatement, but, on Saturday, December 12, the sixteen men involved got in contact with the committee and set up a meeting with Tonkin for Sunday. After speaking with him, they expressed satisfaction with the jobs he offered. On Monday, December 14, Tonkin and General Manager Williams signed a "Schedule of Prices and Wages" with the committee, prompting a "noisy demonstration of joy."[111]

The strikers obtained many of their demands, at least partially. Although the company would continue to pay miners by the car for coal rather than by weight, the miners won "the privilege to employ check–docking bosses at every breaker." Also, miners could rest assured that they would no longer have to argue with foremen over payments for blasting rock, but could count on receiving "$3.60 per lineal yard, one yard in thickness . . . in the Red Ash vein and $2.70 in all other veins."[112] In addition, miners won several concessions regarding props, chutes, and roads. The company men did not receive all the increases they had demanded, but many obtained raises. In particular, the mule drivers in some categories received increases approaching and even exceeding 10 percent.[113]

Most important of all, the rates to be paid for all of these various types of work had been agreed upon in face-to-face negotiations, and the agreement had been made public. The mine workers of the SCC had achieved the simple-sounding yet critical goal announced by Thomas Nicholls during the strike: "We are asking that a scale be adopted (as there is none at present), in order that all men might know what they are earning, and that all may be paid alike for the same work."[114] Thus, the SCC's workers had won firm ground from which they could resist reductions by the company or demand increases from it as market conditions or mining conditions changed. By striking for four-and-a-half months, they had brought a modicum of stability to their working lives.

During its first years in the anthracite industry, the UMWA did little to foster militancy among the mine workers. In the series of strikes that occurred in 1897 at the time of the Lattimer Massacre, the union won a foothold in the Lehigh field by playing little more than a passive role. However, workers achieved few concrete gains and organizing there stagnated in the aftermath of those walkouts, in which many more workers left their jobs than did so in the strike against the SCC. Still, that strike, which began over a particular issue of interest to a particular group of workers, developed into a labor dispute of far greater significance. Perhaps because workers at the SCC's mines were already largely organized, the miners' protest over topping expanded into a full-scale walkout to redress grievances harbored by various segments of the work force. During this lengthy strike, the workers demonstrated extraordinary solidarity, and, as a result, they won numerous concessions embodied in a formal agreement.

At the beginning of 1900, the UMWA had, for the first time, a realistic opportunity to organize the anthracite industry. With at least the framework of an organization in place in each field, the union could plot a strategy for organizing, rather than merely try to take advantage of local disputes as they occurred. With the assistance of the UMWA's national leaders, the districts could formulate a set of demands for the industry that would limit the interregional discord that had proved so damaging in the past. Meanwhile, in 1900, the anthracite mine workers would continue to protest against inequities in the work process and, as in 1899 and 1897, they would not hesitate to strike. However, the UMWA would discover that it could seldom control such walkouts as effectively as it had directed the strike against the SCC.

4

"Onward March": The Strike of 1900

In his report to the eleventh national convention of the United Mine Workers of America (UMWA) in January 1900, President John Mitchell characterized the growth of the union in the anthracite industry as "almost phenomenal." At the time of the convention, the three anthracite districts totaled nearly 9,000 members from more than eighty locals. Particularly breathtaking had been the rise of District One, which, less than a year after its reorganization, comprised more than 7,000 members and had quickly become the third largest of the UMWA's eighteen districts. Mitchell acknowledged that these gains had come only after considerable effort, but he expressed optimism for the future. He believed that the men of anthracite had begun to "realize the disadvantage and folly of isolation" and would soon "join with their fellow craftsmen in their onward march."[1]

For the UMWA in the anthracite industry, the immediate goal of that march was full-scale collective bargaining that would result in a contract that specified wages and working conditions throughout the industry. In pursuing that goal, the union aimed to duplicate its record of accomplishment in the bituminous industry, where, since 1898, the UMWA had negotiated agreements in joint conferences with the operators of the Central Competitive Field. Through the mechanism of the joint conference and a willingness to enforce its members' strict adherence to contracts, the UMWA saw itself as having brought labor peace to the bituminous industry.[2] It was eager to play a similar role in anthracite, but there the union confronted a group of operators who generally possessed greater financial strength than their counterparts in soft coal and exercised much more control over their market.[3] Perhaps as a consequence, anthracite operators had long exhibited an especially truculent attitude toward labor protest and organization.

The rank-and-file militancy that spurred the growth of the UMWA in the anthracite region only reinforced that hostility. Local strikes, so vital to the success of the union in 1899, especially in District One, did not abate in 1900. More and more strikes occurred over an ever-widening range of issues, and some walkouts developed into protracted disputes. Convinced that few genuine injustices beset their employees, the operators blamed the union for the burgeoning rebelliousness of the workers. Therefore, no matter how fervently union leaders promoted the joint conference and contract as the instruments that would bring harmony to the workplace, the operators shunned their entreaties. Ironically, however, the mine workers' militancy alarmed the leaders of the union as well, especially as they found that militancy more and more difficult to control. As the operators were learning, workers demanded immediate action on their grievances. Yet, in dealing with the union, mine workers showed little more patience than they did in dealing with their employers. Seldom did they wait for permission from district officials before they walked off the job. The leaders of the UMWA despaired over such persistent indiscipline as they sought to build an organization with which the operators might see fit to negotiate.

The rising tide of militancy, in District One in particular, coupled with the operators' utter rejection of the union's overtures, left the leaders of the UMWA little alternative to calling an industrywide strike in September 1900. This walkout was not equally popular in each of the three districts, but, after a shaky beginning, the union succeeded in closing down nearly all operations throughout the anthracite region. For the first time since 1871, the workers of the Wyoming, Lehigh, and Schuylkill fields had united in a strike, and this unity combined with John Mitchell's shrewd management of the walkout to achieve an important victory for the union. Mitchell's conservative tactics and businesslike demeanor so impressed powerful national political figures that they put pressure on the leading anthracite operators, which resulted in a settlement favorable to the mine workers. However, Mitchell's conservatism and his eagerness to compromise by no means assuaged the fears of the men who ran the mines, who had witnessed the revolutionary impact of successful collective action upon the rank and file. The compromise that concluded the strike of 1900 not only failed to resolve the most nettlesome grievances at the workplace, it also convinced the operators that they stood to lose their accustomed prerogatives of management if they failed to stand firm against further encroachment by the UMWA. Consequently, while the strike of 1900 strengthened the UMWA in anthracite, it also heightened the operators' determination to resist the union.

"WE HAVE ACTUALLY GOT TO FIGHT THEM"

Exhilarated by its success in the strike against the Susquehanna Coal Company (SCC), District One, in special convention on December 22, 1899, invited the district's operators to a joint conference to be held on January 9, 1900, in Scranton.[4] Of course, even the SCC in the recent strike had refused to recognize the union in any way, and other operators were no more eager to extend recognition. At the Delaware, Lackawanna, and Western (DL & W), opposition to labor organization remained steadfast, even though a new president and new head of the Coal Department had supplanted the regime of Samuel Sloan and William R. Storrs in 1899. President William H. Truesdale wrote Edwin E. Loomis on January 2, 1900, to acknowledge Loomis's recent letter, which had included a copy of the notice he received from District One. Truesdale concurred with Loomis's suggestion to ignore the notice and to hold a meeting of the operators to formulate a common strategy against the union.[5] No operators met with UMWA representatives either on January 9 or at the conference called subsequently by the union for January 18.[6]

Faced with this rebuff, District One requested that the national executive board move to initiate an industrywide strike.[7] At the meeting of the national board in February, the request received no support from those familiar with conditions in the other anthracite districts. John Fahy stated that the mine workers of District Nine had no interest in striking and that the district did not have "as many men organized as it should." Benjamin James doubted that workers at more than one-tenth of the collieries in District Seven would respond to a strike call. In any event, both he and Fahy agreed that, considering seasonal variations in anthracite production, the end of the summer would be a better time for a strike. James also noted that District One's President Nicholls had opposed a strike, but that the mine workers of his district, "intoxicated because of their success at Nanticoke," pressed for a walkout nonetheless. Since District One's request received no support from the other anthracite districts, the board rejected it. However, Mitchell stated that continued success in organizing could justify a "general movement for better conditions," which might necessitate a strike later in the year.[8]

The wave of local walkouts in the Wyoming field that began in the second half of 1899, of which the SCC strike was the most notable, continued to build in the early months of 1900. The most significant of these local strikes are listed in table 4.1.[9] Although full information could not be obtained on every one of these walkouts, the table reveals several basic trends. First, two occupational groups were the most likely to strike—miners and the youthful mule drivers, along with the runners who worked with them. Second, where miners were involved, dockage was the most prominent grievance. Third, miners were most adept at eliciting support from other workers, or at least at preventing any effort to run the mine involved. Fourth, longer walkouts became more common later in the year, with several persisting beyond the beginning of the industrywide walkout in September, which made it difficult to determine the result of two strikes. Finally, strikes occurred repeatedly at some mines. Not only do some companies appear more than once in the table, but the SCC and the Jermyn mines had also been on strike in 1899.

Table 4.1 also gives evidence of the beginning of a trend toward strikes linked to discrimination against union activists. For example, in the walkout against the Parrish Coal Company, a miner named Anthony Vishnefski was

TABLE 4.1
Local Strikes in Wyoming Field, January–August 1900

Month	Mine/Company	Workers/Grievance	Length	Other workers involved	Success
January	Cayuga/DL&W	Drivers/?	several days	no	no
February	Forest Mining Company	Drivers/?	several days	no	no
	Leggett's Creek/D&H	Drivers/?	several days	no	no
March	Warrior Run	Miners/Topping and dockage	several days	unclear	yes
	Forest Mining Company	Miners/weighing procedures and allowances	8 months	all at mine	yes
April	Mt. Pleasant	Miners in one vein/various increases	2 months	all at mine	partial
	Jermyn	Miners/dockage & discharge of activists	6 months	all at mine	unclear
	Temple Iron Company	Miners/dockage; Company men/increase	6 months	all at mine	unclear
May	Parrish Coal Company	Miners/discharge of activist	2 weeks	all at mine	partial
	SCC	Breaker boys	several days	all at mines	unclear
	SCC	Drivers and runners/discharge of activists	one day	no	unclear
June	D&H/4 mines	Drivers & Runners/wage rates	several days	all at mines	no
July	D&H/7 mines	Drivers and Runners/wage rates	several weeks	all at mines	no

fired supposedly because he had missed work for several days and thus his chamber had lagged behind surrounding ones, disrupting ventilation. However, the union maintained that Vishnefski's dismissal occurred because of his activism, and District President Nicholls stated that the company's superintendent had previously broken a local through such tactics. A committee of miners rejected the company's offer to give Vishnefski a chamber at its other mine, and on May 9 a group of Vishnefski's friends, strong union men who were mostly immigrants, began a strike. Some violence occurred the next day as strikers marched on the mine, but the walkout ended two weeks later when the local at the company's other mine voted against walking out in sympathy. Vishnefski accepted the chamber at that mine.[10]

Obviously, strikes could have a considerable disruptive impact, whether or not workers won their demands. In the strikes listed for June and July in table 4.1, youthful mine workers at several mines of the Delaware and Hudson (D & H) nearly precipitated a strike at all of the company's twenty-three mines. On June 6, runners and drivers left their jobs at the Marvine colliery, accusing the company of cutting their wages.[11] According to the *Scranton Times*, the company had downgraded a number of positions when boys were promoted. Consequently, a boy whose predecessor in a particular post might have received $1.38 per day found that he received only $1.25 for performing the same job.[12] Superintendent Charles C. Rose offered a very different explanation. He stated that the company had merely added "an internal price . . . between the two classes."[13] On June 8, drivers and runners at the Leggett's Creek, Dickson, and Von Storch mines joined the strike and idled those collieries. A total of 1,800 men and boys were out of work, and the older mine workers pledged support for the young strikers, while the drivers and runners of the four collieries organized their own UMWA local union. Nevertheless, work resumed soon thereafter when the boys accepted a promise by Rose to examine their grievances once they returned to work.[14]

In mid-July, drivers and runners walked out at the D & H's Grassy Island and Olyphant collieries. Two weeks later, after several attempts to persuade Rose to agree to a scale of wages, drivers and runners also left their jobs at the Eddy Creek, Dickson, Von Storch, Marvine, and Leggett's Creek collieries.[15] Rumors spread that the strike would be extended to all of the mines of the D & H, but Thomas Nicholls joined other community leaders, including two priests, to urge moderation. Local union officials met with Rose and other bosses, who promised to deal fairly with the boys once the strike ended. Operations resumed on August 3.[16]

Throughout the spring, UMWA leaders had expressed their uneasiness over the surging wave of strikes. At the end of March, Benjamin James advised the men of District One "to adhere more closely to the laws of the organization." He noted: "A number of strikes have occurred lately that were not approved of, or your troubles even brought to the attention of your District officers." James added that dealing with such strikes only distracted union officials from their ongoing duties, and he admonished District One's workers that the trend toward local strikes could only bring them "disgrace."[17] Charles J. Thain attributed the rash of strikes to the district's failure to sanction a district-wide strike in January after the operators ignored the union's summons to a joint conference. Still, he displayed considerable suspicion of the motives of those involved in local strikes. He believed that some of the strikes had been "fomented by tools of the coal companies" in order to weaken the organization. Other walkouts, he thought, had been "illegally declared" by men who had borne their grievances for years and expected redress as soon as they became organized. In his view, expanding the organization would bring the operators to terms, and he confidently believed that if the UMWA could demonstrate "sufficient strength," it would never have to strike, but would receive "reasonable concessions."[18]

At a meeting of District One's executive board, held while several D & H collieries were on strike in June, the district's leaders focused on the problem of local strikes. Shortly after that meeting, Benjamin James expressed his displeasure with the workers over their continuing recourse to such walkouts. He warned them bluntly that local strikes would "never remedy the evils" that anthracite mine workers were "forced to endure."[19] Thomas Nicholls conveyed the result of the board's deliberations to John Mitchell. Since so many of the district's workers were on strike, the board had considered ordering a walkout of workers at all the collieries of any company where workers at one or more of the company's collieries were on strike. However, this would necessitate a full-fledged strike against the D & H, as well as walkouts against several smaller firms. Nicholls had successfully argued against such an action, which he believed "might end very disastrously." Still, the district leaders faced growing pressure to move against the operators. Nicholls told Mitchell that a majority of the men in his district wanted to strike, and he added: "We have actually got to fight them and show them the folly of small strikes." Unfortunately for Nicholls and the other leaders, such attempts to calm the mine workers prompted the rank and file to begin to doubt the value of the union, since its leaders' main concern seemed to be to prevent strikes. Without supplying any evidence, Nicholls voiced the same suspicion that Thain had expressed two months previously: "The companies are trying to involve us in small strikes, and break our strength before we get ready to move together." Nicholls believed that the only salvation lay in "a decisive move at an early date." His executive board had authorized him to request that Mitchell call a joint convention of the anthracite districts. There the UMWA could request a conference with all of the operators and threaten to strike if they refused to negotiate.[20]

Although union leaders may have wished for less militancy from the workers of District One, they viewed the quiescence of workers to the south as a serious obstacle to the UMWA's success. District Seven's membership had declined from approximately 2000 members in 1898 to a mere 341 as of January 1900. At least District Nine had moved forward since its establishment in October 1899 to comprise nearly 1,500 members at the beginning of the year. However, in both of these districts, workers appeared hesitant to enroll in the union, and also showed little proclivity to confront their employers in local strikes. In reflecting on the modest successes he had realized in organizing in March and April in District Seven, Benjamin James commented: "The men in the Hazleton field can be brought into line, although the companies are placing many obstacles in the way." He also observed that the Lattimer Massacre still exerted "a deterring effect on the foreign-speaking people."[21]

Organizing in the Schuylkill field accelerated when John Fahy returned at the beginning of May from a sojourn that began when he went to the national convention in January.[22] Fahy and other organizers conducted meetings almost nightly throughout the district,[23] and, according to District Secretary George Hartlein, District Nine totaled approximately fifty-five locals by the end of the month.[24] This represented a substantial increase over the nineteen reported as of January. Nevertheless, despite this spurt in organization, the mine workers of District Nine, like those of District Seven, did not demonstrate the sort of militancy that had become increasingly common in District One. An incident related by Hartlein helps to show the difference between the districts. In June, a grievance committee from the local at the Short Mountain colliery in the Lykens Valley met with Superintendent Hood McKay to protest the discharge of a member of that committee. In collieries throughout the Wyoming field, workers walked out over far smaller provocations. However, no strike took place at Short Mountain, and this result could in no way be attributed to tactful behavior by McKay. The superintendent received the committee courteously at first, but when they told him why they had come, "the circus began." According to Hartlein: "He jumped, he danced, and he swore that he would at any time deal with his employees as individuals, as an organization, never." Furthermore, McKay made it quite clear "that no union should dictate to him what to do or what not to do." In Hartlein's opinion, only thoroughgoing organization could compel men like McKay to treat the UMWA with respect. Still, Hartlein prophesied that arrogance like McKay's would not survive for long in the anthracite region: "Wait, my gay duck, you will drop yet, and when you do the stench will be unbearable." Although he recognized the necessity for greater organizing efforts in the Lykens Valley, Hartlein stated that District Nine could not afford to send organizers there and requested that national headquarters do so.[25] Benjamin James, who seldom hesitated to comment on the problems of his colleagues, opined: "A district with over fifty locals, as I see by the *Journal* . . . should be able to keep at least some men in the field organizing."[26]

Rivalry between union leaders from the various districts increased with the growing level of UMWA activity in anthracite. In late June, Benjamin James, perhaps trying to impose some discipline from his post on the national executive board, excoriated District Seven President Thomas Duffy for the district's inactivity. James, who had been the first district secretary there, stated that he had heard "mutterings of discontent," and he warned Duffy that action must be taken to strengthen the organization. He expressed surprise that the district had not planned a mass meeting for July 4, and he commented that building the organization apparently had become "a secondary consideration." He added that "those who should" had failed to show a "proper interest" in the union, and that such laxity "must come to an end."[27]

Meanwhile, John Fahy tried to dissuade Mitchell from calling the convention of the three anthracite districts for which Nicholls had pleaded. He feared that such a gathering might not be well attended and urged Mitchell to countenance an industrywide strike only as a last resort. Instead, he suggested that the union's leaders hold a meeting to plan a new organizing campaign. Although Fahy believed that such an effort would surely require assistance from national headquarters, he wanted the campaign to be mounted as quietly as possible. He feared that operators might employ countermeasures, such as the blacklist, against a campaign promoted with the usual fanfare. Fahy's caution stemmed from his belief that the mine workers were "afflicted with a lack of confidence," and he paraphrased their supposed irresolution in the following passage:

> They wish that the organization was built up strong but that the work of organizing is going too slow and that the organization will not amount to anything among them, and that they do not care about the money they put into the organization and that they would gladly pay more if they thought the organization would grow strong because they believe that organization is a good thing . . . but what is the use of paying money into it if it won't grow etc.[28]

Fahy proceeded to express an attitude toward the rank and file that can only be labeled paternalistic: "In such matters coal workers talk and act like children." He believed that "if it were not for this . . . childishness among them," the UMWA would have "twice as many members." He further complained that during the past two months his district had received only forty-five dollars from the local unions; consequently he had not been able to do as much organizing as he would have liked. Fahy felt certain that if the district treasury had received half of the money that was "laying idle and doing no good in the locals," the rank and file would have been "gladly surprised" by what he could have accomplished.[29]

The hesitancy that Fahy detected among the mine workers of District Nine had little counterpart among the men of District One. At that district's quarterly convention on July 9 and 10, eight local unions presented a resolution demanding action. They had met in north Scranton three days before the convention and decried "the downward tendency" of the organization, which they attributed to the "waste of time and money in sending representatives to District conventions and accomplishing nothing." They called on the convention to discuss specific issues, such as the price of powder, semimonthly payment of wages, and the weighing of coal, and to appoint committees to formulate demands to be taken to the operators. The convention voted to include these matters among those to be discussed at a joint convention of the three anthracite districts, which it requested that national headquarters call for July 30.[30] In response to John Fahy's objection that July 30 was too early, the official convention call set August 13 as the opening date.[31]

Throughout 1900, prospects for a peaceful resolution of the differences between labor and capital grew increasingly remote as the operators remained steadfast in their determination not to deal with the UMWA. The response of one corporation, the DL & W, to the spread of unionization in 1900 may well have been typical. The DL & W moved to blunt the union's appeal by distributing to its employees thousands of antiunion circulars that cast aspersions on the motives of organizers.[32] In April, President Truesdale did not seem particularly concerned about the UMWA. He told Loomis: "I certainly hope that our men will use good judgment and good sense and not let a lot of outside fellows who have no real, substantial interest in their welfare induce them to give up their jobs." He foresaw little trouble for the company as long as the men held "steadily and firmly" to what he saw as "their present determination not to strike."[33] Nevertheless, Truesdale made sure that Loomis had arranged for someone to observe John Mitchell's activities while he was in Wilkes-Barre for the quarterly convention of District One in April.[34]

As the UMWA experienced more and more success, Truesdale and Loomis took bolder steps. Early in the year, Loomis had suggested to Truesdale one possible strategy against the union—persuading local merchants to use their influence to dissuade miners from joining. In August, Truesdale believed that the time had come to push such an effort "to the limit," in concert with "all the other operators," to prevent "the UMWA [from] carrying the day."[35] In addition, the company encouraged the formation of a company union named the Lackawanna Union. At its inaugural meeting at the end of July, when nominations for chairman were requested from the floor, someone suggested Benjamin James of the UMWA. However, those DL & W employees who had called the meeting declared James ineligible, since he did not work for the company. At that point, several hundred members of the UMWA, who apparently constituted a majority of those present, stalked out of the hall. The gentleman selected as chairman, one T. T. Morgan, a company man at the Bellevue colliery, told those who remained that, while labor surely deserved just remuneration, it ought to remain on friendly terms with capital.[36]

On August 10, the Lackawanna Union held its second meeting, and its leaders announced the result of a canvass reportedly made at the workplace to determine sentiment for and against the organization. In this "vote" it is likely that various supervisory personnel, or perhaps leaders of the Lackawanna Union, asked mine workers for their preference. The vote was conducted only at those of the company's collieries located near Scranton, and 2,643 workers expressed themselves in favor of the company union and 1,021 opposed it. This total of more than 3,600 votes equaled approximately one-half of the number of DL & W employees in the area.[37] If all workers were asked for their choice on a day when each of those collieries was in operation, then at least one-half of the workers refused to vote and another 15 percent voted against the company union.[38] Nevertheless, its leaders viewed the vote as an endorsement, and they proceeded to form the first local union and to frame a constitution.[39] Although the *Scranton Times* reported that the union had few members other than the officers, a committee from the Lackawanna Union did meet Loomis on September 6 to request an increase in wages of 10 percent. This meeting took place only several days before the UMWA issued its summons to all anthracite mine workers to strike on Monday, September 17.[40]

"THE GREATEST STRIKE IN THE HISTORY OF THE WORLD"

On August 15, at the conclusion of the convention of the three anthracite districts in Hazleton, the UMWA made its first formal move toward industrywide bargaining. The three district secretaries issued an invitation to all anthracite coal operators to meet with union representatives in a joint conference at Hazleton on August 27 to discuss a long list of grievances.[41] When the operators failed to do so, the three districts reconvened, and their scale committee converted the list of grievances into the following demands:

> We demand the abolition of the company store system, the reduction in the price of powder to $1.50 per keg, the abolition of the company dictating as to who shall be our doctors, abolition of the sliding scale now in practice in the Lehigh and Schuylkill regions, compliance with the semi-monthly pay law, and that all employees be paid in cash; abolition of the erroneous sys-

tem of having 3,360 lbs. to the ton, and that 2,240 lbs. constitute a ton; that an advance of 20 per cent be paid all classes of men now receiving less than $1.50 per day, that all classes of day labor now receiving $1.50 and not receiving $1.75 shall receive 15 per cent over present wages; that all day labor now receiving more than $1.75 shall be advanced 10 per cent; that no miner shall have at any time more than one breast, gang or other class of work, and shall only get his legal share of cars.

The committee also formulated a complex demand for an increase for miners, embodied in a framework of specific rates per ton for coal seams of different thicknesses in the various districts. Also demanded for District One was the right for miners to appoint a checkweighman.[42]

These demands provide a particularly detailed view of the dynamics of industrial unionism in the anthracite coal fields. Together, the various demands constitute a broad-based program for the entire spectrum of anthracite mine workers; yet, considered separately, each demand is best seen as an attempt to appeal to a regional or occupational group. Only three demands could ostensibly involve all of the mine workers at any single colliery—abolition of the company store, abolition of the company doctor, and semimonthly payment. However, many of the companies, particularly those in the Wyoming and Schuylkill fields, no longer had a company store or doctor, so that the appeal of these demands would be greatest in the Lehigh field, where they had been major grievances in the strikes of August and September 1897.[43] Nor would the demand for semimonthly payment have a uniform appeal throughout the anthracite region. While state law had mandated semimonthly payment since 1887, one amendment to the law enacted in 1891 to prevent companies from entering into agreements with workers to pay them other than twice a month was declared unconstitutional as an abridgment of freedom of contract.[44] Although some operators ignored the amendment and never paid more frequently than once a month, others not only tried semimonthly payment before the amendment was overturned, but they retained it thereafter. Those operators who did so included the largest anthracite producer, the Philadelphia and Reading (P & R), and one of the largest independents, Coxe Brothers and Company.[45]

The demands for increased wages for company men constituted a substantial inducement for that large group of workers in each of the anthracite fields to support the UMWA. Interestingly, the percentage increases demanded were not uniform for all company men, but were larger for those who earned a smaller daily wage. This demand combined a certain interest in leveling with an appeal to the largest number of workers. Perhaps the militancy of youthful mule drivers and slate pickers, most of whom earned less than $1.50 per day, lay behind the demand for a 20 percent increase for that group.[46]

The other demands addressed problems faced by the UMWA's most important constituency—the miners. Several of these demands were most relevant to the concerns of the miners of the Wyoming field, where local strikes had been fought over similar issues. The wage scale proposed for each field assumed that miners would no longer be paid by the car, as most were in Wyoming. Coal would be weighed if the UMWA's demands were adopted, and the miners would win the additional safeguard of having their own weighman rule along with the company's weighman on the conflict-ridden issue of dockage. In its recitation of grievances, the UMWA charged: "Dockage runs from 3 to 4 per cent to 12 and sometimes to 25 per cent, and no representation is allowed the miners in the matter." The union also broached the issue of topping, and stated that miners had been "compelled to place above the top of the car more coal than formerly, without increased compensation."[47] In addition, the union demanded the "abolition of the erroneous system of having 3,360 lbs. to the ton, and that 2,240 lbs. constitute a ton." This referred to the practice at some collieries, most of which were located in the northern portion of the Wyoming field, of paying not by the carload, but by the "mine ton," which had been "originally fixed at an amount above which it was found would produce 2,240 pounds of merchantable coal above pea or three-quarter inch size." The D & H, which paid by the "mine ton" at some of its collieries and by the car at others, insisted that it had decreased the number of pounds in the "mine ton" from time to time as the company had become able to sell more of the smaller sizes of coal. Furthermore, the D & H maintained that where its men were paid by the car, the company determined the rate for the carload by the number of mine tons that the car contained.[48] So the companies had a system, for which they claimed the respect owed to any venerable institution. However, the miners placed no faith in either the "mine ton" or payment by the car, and they would not be satisfied until the companies weighed their production in tons of 2,240 pounds, under the watchful eye of a checkweighman.

The miners of the Wyoming and Lehigh fields found just as much fault with the price that the companies charged them for powder. The price of powder had been set at $3.00 per keg late in the 1870s, and although the P & R had cut the price to $1.50 after the strike of 1888, the companies of the Lehigh and Wyoming fields had not lowered their price, except for a slight cut to $2.75 in 1893.[49] Meanwhile, the price of powder to the operator had plummeted below $1.00 per keg. While the UMWA viewed the high price of powder as one of the "greatest injustices" that anthracite miners faced,[50] the operators saw it as merely one factor in the overall picture of mining costs. The D & H claimed that the fall in the price it paid for powder had only partially compensated the company for the escalating cost of mining; nevertheless, the company had kept the same scale of wages in force since the early

1880s.[51] Yet, as long as the operators showed no willingness to discuss any of these matters with representatives of the UMWA, it seemed unlikely that they would be able to foster understanding among their employees for their point of view. Undoubtedly they preferred to persuade themselves that the miners had no genuine grievances. According to the D & H, the fact that the current scale of wages had remained in force "without disturbance" indicated that it was "not unfair to the miners."[52]

In spite of such protestations, most anthracite mine workers were no longer disposed to trust traditional procedures or the vagaries of the marketplace. In calling for the abolition of the sliding scale, the UMWA sought to eliminate a feature of labor relations originally obtained by the Workingmen's Benevolent Association in 1869, under which wages for workers in the Schuylkill and Lehigh fields varied according to the price of coal. However, since 1875 there had been no minimum below which wages could not fall, and mine workers lacked representation on the committee that monitored coal prices and thereby determined the level of wages.[53] The mine workers' disdain for the sliding scale is merely an example of the workers' tendency to limit more and more strictly the areas in which they considered their interests to coincide with those of the operators as fellow producers. Fewer and fewer mine workers trusted the operators to give them their due; no longer would they be content with the operators' judgment that their demands had "no warrant in present business conditions."[54]

In one demand in particular, the union showed the extent to which its basic principles diverged from those of the operators. By insisting that miners no longer be permitted to work "more than one breast, gang or other class of work" and demanding that each miner receive only "his legal share of cars," the UMWA hoped to equalize earnings and restrict favoritism.[55] The operators maintained, however, that any apparent inequities did not result from favoritism but from the differing levels of skill different miners displayed. Miners who received good places, an extra breast, or more cars were given them because, on the basis of their work in the past, the company could expect them to take full productive advantage of such perquisites. The D & H warned that the UMWA had a sinister objective behind such complaints— "to place all miners on an equality; the skillful and the unskilled are to be treated alike."[56]

Finally, implicit in the wage scales drafted for each field was the UMWA's desire to introduce some semblance of uniformity and fairness in miners' compensation. Although companies like the D & H insisted that their wage structures had internal consistency, the union wanted a wage scale for each anthracite field that had been hammered out in joint conference to insure that relatively equal work brought a relatively equal reward.[57] However, no such scale of wages could be constructed unless the companies conceded the

UMWA's overarching demand—the implicit recognition of the union that would accompany full-scale collective bargaining. Of course, this was the demand that the operators were least likely to grant. Throughout the final quarter of the nineteenth century, the operators' consistent denial of legitimacy to unions flowed from their paternalism. They fought the UMWA, not only because they viewed it as a competitor for control of their properties, but also because the union challenged the fundamental notions by which they justified their authority. Each success for the union provoked stronger denials of the UMWA's legitimacy from the operators, because each union victory served as a damning public refutation of the operators' efforts to maintain the fiction that they aimed to serve their employees' best interests as well as their own.

On August 29, the second Hazleton convention voted to request permission from the national executive board to initiate an industrywide strike on Monday, September 10. However, the board deferred the request so that John Mitchell could attempt to arrange a settlement through the mediation of Senator Marcus A. Hanna of Ohio, chairman of the Republican National Committee. As manager of President William McKinley's reelection campaign, Hanna perceived an anthracite strike during the campaign as a harshly discordant note amidst his carefully orchestrated drive to convince the nation's voters not to disturb the property that the McKinley administration had supposedly bought. In spite of his diligent efforts, Hanna failed to persuade representatives of the anthracite railroads to negotiate with Mitchell. On September 12, after a last-minute proposal of arbitration from Mitchell elicited no response from the companies, the board authorized a strike to begin on Monday, September 17.[58]

The operators seemed confident of victory. On September 7, in a letter to Loomis, William Truesdale noted the executive board's hesitancy to sanction the strike and observed that "the Treasury of the UMWA with a fund of $75,000 to support 100,000 or more anthracite miners during a protracted struggle should not prove very tempting bait to the miners to drop their work." He hoped that the mine workers would compare the condition of the DL & W's treasury to that of the UMWA and decide which of the two constituted a more reliable "means of support for themselves and their families."[59] As noted above, none of the operators responded to the union's call for arbitration, and the issuance of the strike call on September 12 did nothing to soften the operators' hard line. In what may have been a reference to Hanna, on September 13 Truesdale informed Loomis: "So far as I can see there is no disposition on the part of the representatives of the companies here in New York to enter into negotiations with any member of the UMWA or their political henchmen."[60] On September 17, only one-third of the 142,500 anthracite mine workers reported to their jobs, and almost all of these were in the Lehigh and Schuylkill fields.[61] Nonetheless, Truesdale assured Loomis on the twentieth that none of the operators was "likely to weaken in the least." He thought that the strike had made them "more determined than ever not to put their properties in the control of Mr. Mitchell and his United Mine Workers Assn."[62]

Because it took little time for the strike to become solidly established in the Wyoming field, UMWA leaders concentrated their efforts upon the Lehigh and Schuylkill fields. In the former, they sought to bring the 2,400 workers of G. B. Markle and Company, one of the largest independent operators, into the strike. Since 1885, workers there had been required to agree not to "be governed by any labor association" and to accept local arbitration of any disputes. This may well explain why, after the Lattimer Massacre, Markle's employees threatened to strike but failed to do so.[63] On September 14, two days after the UMWA had issued its strike call, a committee of workers presented its own set of demands to management. On September 19, both John Markle, son of the company's founder, and John Mitchell addressed a meeting of employees. Markle faced sharp questioning from the workers, but asked them in return: "Why should you let outsiders come in here and interfere with you?"[64] However, growing numbers of Markle's workers came to accept Mitchell's "interference," and most eventually decided to join the strike.[65]

The strike gathered momentum throughout the two southern fields during its first two weeks. On September 21, a confrontation between strikers and sheriff's deputies in Shenandoah in the Schuylkill field resulted in one death and several injuries; consequently Governor William A. Stone called out some 2,100 troops of the National Guard.[66] Nevertheless, by September 25, nearly one half of the P & R's collieries had been idled, and all had closed ten days later.[67] In the Lehigh field, strikers marched from colliery to colliery to persuade those still at work to leave their jobs.[68] By the end of the first week of October, the only substantial pocket of resistance to the UMWA that remained was at the far southeastern corner of the Lehigh field in the Panther Creek Valley, at the mines of the Lehigh Coal and Navigation Company (LC & N).

The LC & N was one of the first anthracite corporations, organized by Josiah White and Erskine Hazard in 1821.[69] Very few of its workers joined the UMWA despite several organizing efforts, and only a small number walked out in September. During a meeting of the company's board of managers in October, President Lewis A. Riley speculated as to why the workers had remained faithful to the LC & N. First, in his view, the company hired "a better class of workmen" than did other firms. However, he added that the "somewhat isolated" location of the LC & N's mines had limited the employees' contact with "the more turbulent element." Second, he stated that "the fair and just treatment" that had been shown to the workers "at all times" had helped to keep them loyal. Yet, he hastened to add that the company's firmness in the past had also helped to keep labor relations on a suitably even keel. Finally, Riley gave credit to superintendents and foremen for their "good judgment and kind disposition," but also told the board that the company planned to extend any concessions won by the strikers to its own workers.[70] Throughout these comments, Riley coupled each supposedly benevolent aspect of the LC & N's labor policy—that the men were better, the company fairer, and the bosses kinder—with more tangible factors such as the mines' isolation, the company's firmness, and its willingness to give its men whatever the strikers might receive. In reflecting upon labor relations, Riley, like so many other employers, combined expressions of paternal concern with more businesslike attitudes.

The strikers did their best to disrupt the LC & N's production. On the night of October 15, some 2,000 began to march into the Panther Creek Valley, under the leadership of the redoubtable "Mother" Mary Jones. Units of the Pennsylvania National Guard were sent to intercept the marchers. The marchers split into two groups and took separate routes. On the sixteenth, while the troops dispersed one column of strikers, the other succeeded in closing one of the LC & N's collieries and disrupting production at three others before the troops halted them as well.[71] Each of the collieries resumed regular production on the following day, and, early in November, after the strike had ended, the LC & N discovered that monthly production in October had reached a record level.[72] To reward the workers for their loyalty, the board of managers contributed $25,000 to the mine workers' beneficial fund.[73]

Undaunted by his earlier failure to arrange a settlement between Mitchell and the railroad presidents, Mark Hanna continued to warn the latter that the anthracite strike truly imperiled the reelection of McKinley. As a result of his persistence, beginning on September 29 the major coal companies posted notices at the mines offering an increase of 10 percent to all employees who would return to work. Those companies that sold powder to their miners at $2.75 per keg promised to reduce the price to $1.50, but they would consider that reduction as part of the wage increase.[74] Nevertheless, the strikers held their ranks throughout the anthracite region. When the P & R posted its notices on September 29, the company had not yet closed down all of its collieries. Management probably hoped that enough workers would return as a result of the notices so that the company could increase production. Instead, so few workers reported that all of the P & R's collieries were idle by October 5, as local union officials posted their own notices next to those of the company, telling the men not to return until ordered to do so by their local unions or by John Mitchell.[75]

On October 1, the *New York World* reported that, although Mitchell had not ordered locals to post notices in response to those posted by the P & R, he had "declared that the men would not be stampeded back to the mines."[76] At a mass meeting in Wilkes-Barre on October 2, Mitchell told a crowd of some 20,000:

> The greatest strike in the history of the world is drawing to a close. Already the great coal-carrying railroads have agreed to increase your wages 10 per cent, which is a great victory in itself. True, it is not enough; it does not satisfy us, but the time is not far distant when the anthracite coal miners will receive as much for their labor as any other class of workmen in the world. . . . This strike shall not be ended until a convention of anthracite miners shall so decide . . . I shall not decide the question of your going back to work. You must vote on that yourselves.[77]

Several days later, after most operators had posted notices offering the advance, Mitchell and the three district presidents from the anthracite region issued a call for a tri-district convention to begin at Scranton on October 12.[78] At that gathering, although some delegates clamored for the inclusion of other demands, such as recognition of the union and the sanctioning of checkweighmen, the delegates adopted the following report of the resolutions committee:

> That this convention accept an advance of 10 per cent, providing the operators will continue its payment until April 1st, 1901, and will abolish the sliding scale in the Lehigh and Schuylkill regions, the scale of wages in the last two named districts to remain stationary at 10 per cent above the present basis price, and that the companies will agree to adjust other grievances complained of with committees of their own employees.[79]

William Truesdale wrote to Loomis that he and most of the other railroad presidents were determined not to comply with the convention's terms. However, several of them feared that the P & R was "likely to break loose and make the concessions asked for."[80] On the seventeenth that company fulfilled expectations by announcing, along with the Lehigh Valley Coal Company, that it would post new notices in which the company would agree to abolish the sliding scale and to discuss any further grievances with its employees.[81] In response to a letter from Joseph S. Harris, president of the P & R, which advised him of that company's action, Truesdale stated that he did not oppose these additional concessions per se. However, he warned that the mine workers and the press would interpret the concessions "as a further victory of the UMW." This would only strengthen the union and make it more difficult for the operators to deal with their men "on an equitable basis."[82] Reflecting on the strike, Truesdale told Loomis that he saw the companies' original offer of

10 percent as "the chief mischief." He added: "This is where the fight should originally have been made and I certainly should have made it then if I had received support from any quarter . . . but I had none whatever.[83] Several days later, on October 24, most of the leading companies in the Wyoming field, including the DL & W, posted notices that specified the terms of the 10 percent advance for miners—an increase of 2.5 percent on mining rates along with a cut in the price of powder to $1.50 per keg.[84] However, on that day, Truesdale wrote Loomis that the operators would consider resuming the battle in earnest unless the UMWA called off the strike soon. He believed that if the mine workers did not return to work before the November election, "practically all" of the operators would agree to revoke their notices and offer "less favorable" terms to their men.[85]

However, on October 24, Mitchell, the presidents of the three anthracite districts, and members of the national executive board agreed to declare an end to the strike. During their meeting, Mitchell noted that if the strike were to continue the union would need to establish a system to provide relief for strikers. Many operators had basically accepted the union's terms, and he believed that those who had not done so would certainly fall into line once their competitors commenced operations.[86] Consequently, on the following day, the union leaders issued a proclamation in which the workers were directed to return to their jobs on Monday, October 29, at collieries where operators posted suitable notices. Recognizing that the settlement did not address a number of the mine workers' problems, the leaders emphasized that the operators had expressed willingness to meet with their employees to discuss grievances. Therefore, it fell to the workers to select committees when work resumed "to present grievances, in an orderly, businesslike manner, and ask that they be corrected." Also, since Pennsylvania law obliged operators to pay twice per month if their employees so demanded, the leaders urged the men not to hesitate to make such demands.[87] By Monday, almost all of the operators had posted notices that essentially accepted the union's terms, without, of course, making any reference to the union. Those few who did not post such notices by Monday, did so shortly thereafter, thus effectively ending the strike.[88] For many years to come, the day on which the workers returned to their jobs, October 29, would be celebrated throughout the anthracite region as "Mitchell Day."[89]

In the strike of 1900, the UMWA undoubtedly won a critical victory. However, an analysis of the settlement demonstrates just how arduous a struggle yet remained before the union could establish itself securely, much less provide security for its members. Although the union's leaders placed great emphasis on the operators' willingness to meet with committees of their employees, operators had traditionally done this in one manner or another. It remained to be seen whether or not the operators would bargain in good faith

with such committees over local issues, and whether the committees could combine the militancy and tactical sense necessary to obtain additional concessions. While the leaders of the UMWA frequently lauded the solidity of the settlement, even to the point of calling it a "contract," the way in which the operators communicated their acceptance of the settlement to the workers revealed the tenuous status of the union.[90] By posting notices, the operators maintained the fiction that they had not been pressured into granting concessions, but had merely decided on their own to institute changes that employees could accept or reject on an individual basis. Although John Mitchell retained considerable hope that the businesslike qualities of the UMWA would eventually be appreciated by the operators, the underlying reality was that they had refused to negotiate with Mitchell and his fellow union leaders. More importantly, while Mark Hanna would continue to try to persuade the operators that Mitchell was a most conservative labor leader with whom they would be well advised to deal, their superintendents and foremen, having received no order to the contrary, operated the mines in much the same way as they had before the UMWA came to the anthracite region. Throughout their lengthy experience, the owners, managers, and supervisors had seen unions come and go, and they thought they could afford to be patient.

5

Crisis of Authority

Throughout 1901, both management and the United Mine Workers of America (UMWA) struggled to assert their authority over the anthracite mine workers. Increasingly the mine workers rejected the authority of the coal operators, but they did not merely trade the authority of the company for that of the union. The UMWA sought greater control of the rank and file for more than obvious strategic reasons. The union hoped that it could impress upon management that it could in fact control the rank and file sufficiently to insure a new kind of labor peace through the process of joint conferences and contracts. However, that hope gradually ebbed, as it became clear that management, in true paternalist fashion, could not appreciate such authority as the union was able to wield. Showing little understanding of their workers, managers blamed rank-and-file militancy on the union and saw no possibility for labor peace as long as the UMWA remained in the anthracite fields.

As the union struggled to assert control over workers, it had to come to terms with the limits of that control. For many years, the UMWA would face the task of managing rank-and-file militancy. How far could it hope to extend its authority, which had only become credible with the rejection of much of management's? More important, how much control did the UMWA really want? The understandable preoccupation of the union with reining in the rank and file contained one transcendent peril—that the union might show itself as fundamentally opposed to the spirit of protest that lay at the very heart of the workers' struggle. As managers refused to even try to understand, rank-and-file militancy arose from the day-to-day violation of the workers' instinctive sense of fairness through the haphazard impact of the congeries of work rules under which they labored. Their resulting feelings of outrage constituted nothing less than the essential democratic impulse toward unionization.

PERSISTENT MILITANCY

When work resumed following the strike of 1900, the mine workers seemed determined to show their strength, confirmed by the strike's outcome. On November 2, near the end of the first week of work after the strike, William H. Truesdale of the Delaware, Lackawanna, and Western (DL & W) acknowledged receipt of a letter from Edwin E. Loomis that noted "the small annoyances and difficulties" that resulted from the independence shown by the company's mine workers, "particularly by the young men and boys." Expressing surprise that there had not been more trouble, Truesdale stated that he anticipated continuing problems in the enforcement of discipline and thought that the company would "have to submit to more or less annoyance." Truesdale also expressed regret that the workers were likely to demand semimonthly pay, but he offered no strategy to counter such a move.[1]

Several weeks later, Charles J. Thain reported that local committees had made considerable progress in obtaining semimonthly pay. The DL & W, the Lehigh and Wilkes-Barre Coal Company (L & W-B), and the Lehigh Valley Coal Company (LV) had already begun to pay every two weeks, and the Delaware and Hudson Company (D & H) had agreed to do so as of January 1, 1901.[2] Not only had the UMWA obtained this concession, demanded in the strike, but it also won permission from some operators for union men, paid by the miners, to monitor the judgment of the docking bosses.[3] Still, the workers' militancy did not abate as a consequence of these gains, and a variety of disputes arose throughout the anthracite region. Thain labeled "the topping question" as "the great stumbling block to peaceful relations between operator and miner."[4] Numerous brief strikes occurred over this issue at the mines of the L & W-B, and Thomas Nicholls found it necessary to meet with a committee of two delegates from each of the company's mines to discuss the problem. In the other districts, workers displayed a certain testiness as well. In the Lehigh field, mine workers for Coxe Brothers and Company quit early on election day, prompting the company to close several of its collieries for the remainder of the week. At the Colbert colliery in the Schuylkill field, several workers were fired for missing work to attend a funeral. The 300 employees there struck for a short while and returned when the company reinstated the workers.[5]

Another matter left unsettled by the strike revealed the friction between workers in the industry's two major job groupings—the miners and their laborers. Soon after work resumed, Benjamin James reported in the *UMW Journal* that some miners who paid their laborers directly had refused to give them the 10 percent advance mandated in the settlement of the strike. James stated that "the laborers contributed as much to the success of the strike as did the miner," and he reminded the miners: "We should not refuse to do unto our fellow men as we would have the operator do unto us." Obviously, many miners had not yet absorbed the ideals of industrial unionism. James went on to express his disdain for the system that prevailed throughout most of Districts One and Seven, in which the miner prepared the charges and blasted the coal for the laborer to load. He had heard that some operators planned to eliminate that system and have two men work each chamber as partners, and he believed that such a change could not come too soon.[6] In a report in mid-December on conditions in District One, Thain noted that some miners actually had cut the wages they paid their laborers. In his view, such men were "inoculated with selfish greed."[7] Meanwhile, at the Excelsior and Corbin collieries near Shamokin, several hundred laborers struck for several days over the miners' failure to pay them the advance.[8] In February 1901, Thain stated that some miners still refused to pay the 10 percent increase to their laborers.[9] To end the disunity that such disputes revealed, District One called in its January 1902 convention for those employers who paid the miner the earnings of both miner and laborer to deduct the laborer's wages from the miner's and pay them directly to the laborer.[10]

Toward the end of the year, mine workers struck one of the largest independent operators, the Kingston Coal Company of Edwardsville. In addition to check–docking bosses and semimonthly payment of wages, the UMWA grievance committee demanded the dismissal of outside foreman Thomas J. Morgan, who had demanded bribes from workers not only to get jobs but also to keep them. The miners further complained that new and repaired coal cars had been made somewhat larger than the 103 cubic-foot car which they maintained had been the company's standard since 1875. On December 16, the workers received the permission of District One's executive board to strike. In addition, the grievance committee threatened to call out the engineers, pumpmen, firemen, and fan runners within forty-eight hours, thereby presenting the company with the possibility of flooding in the mines and an increased likelihood of explosions. Two days later, the superintendents came to the UMWA's district headquarters and signed an agreement that ended the strike. They accepted semimonthly pay and check–docking bosses to be paid by collections from miners. Also they agreed to let an arbitration board that included District President Nicholls decide the fate of the foreman and the size of the coal cars. The arbitrators ruled in favor of the workers, although the company did not actually fire Morgan until the union issued an ultimatum.[11]

At the January 1901 convention of District One, President Nicholls noted that all anthracite mine workers had not emulated the orderly militancy of the employees of the Kingston Coal Company. Numerous local strikes had occurred "without proper authority." Nicholls argued that this could "bring the organization into disrepute" and destroy any possibility of a joint conference with the operators: "We must show our ability to control our members according to our laws and rules and that we can be depended upon to keep faithfully any agreement entered into."[12] Indeed, in discussing earlier a walkout in which workers demanded the discharge of a breaker boss, Nicholls had announced that the district would "not take any cognizance" of unauthorized strikes.[13] Charles J. Thain declared his support for Nicholls's policy, and re-

marked that wildcat strikers might lose their eagerness to strike if they would
"have to suffer the consequences of their precipitancy."[14]

Throughout the years of intense industrial conflict in the anthracite region from 1899 to 1902, the goal of the union remained constant—a contract
negotiated between the UMWA and the operators in joint conference. However, especially after the strike of 1900, the union's leaders assumed a conciliatory, almost supplicatory tone in their quest. Seldom did they even hint
at the possibility that the union could display so much strength that the operators would have no alternative to signing a contract. Instead, they hoped
that the operators would eventually notice the union's moderating effect upon
the workers' behavior and thus realize that a rapprochement could serve their
interests as well as those of the UMWA.

Episodes of militancy continued to occur in Districts Seven and Nine as
well as District One. Toward the end of December 1900, mine workers at the
Natalie colliery near Shamokin struck for several days so that fifteen blacksmiths and carpenters could receive the full increase won in the strike
settlement.[15] Meanwhile, employees of Leisenring and Company's Oak Hill
mine in Schuylkill County struck for several days over a variety of issues,
including the company's refusal to follow the district's tradition of giving a
full day's pay for the customary seven-hour day on Saturdays.[16] In early February 1901, some 250 employees at the Royal Oak Coal Company's colliery
in Shamokin left their jobs for several days and returned after the company
agreed to pay them twice each month.[17] In District Seven, 1,000 workers at
A. Pardee and Company's Cranberry mine struck for a short period because
the company scheduled its first semimonthly payday for January 19 rather
than January 15.[18] Several weeks later, strikers at Calvin Pardee and Company's Lattimer colliery abandoned their three-week long strike over the discharge of two drill runners.[19] Although the leaders of the two districts
apparently took no public stand on these walkouts, officials of District Nine
cracked down on a strike at the LV's Primrose mine in Mahanoy City, ordering the men to return to work after they investigated the strike and found
it unjustified.[20]

The UMWA's accomplishments across the anthracite fields, not only in
the strike of 1900 but also in the numerous militant episodes that occurred
during that year, persuaded thousands of mine workers to join the union. At
the end of 1900, the total membership of the three anthracite districts stood
at 53,161, nearly six times the 8,993 members in good standing at the end of
the previous year. District One, with 28,658 members, had become the second largest of all of the UMWA's twenty districts, and District Nine, with
19,773 enrolled, had become the fourth largest. Although District Seven, the
union's eleventh largest district, had only 4,730 members, it had grown more
than tenfold during 1900.[21]

However, with the approach of April 1, the date on which the operators' notices ending the previous year's strike expired, it remained unclear whether the UMWA's massive gains would overawe the operators or merely stiffen their resolve. William H. Truesdale had certainly developed no affection for the UMWA in the months following the strike. Writing in early February 1901 to Delos A. Chappell, president of a mining concern in Colorado, Truesdale congratulated Chappell on his "success in whipping out this organization" at his mines, but lamented that the anthracite operators had "it fastened on us in bad shape." Truesdale noted that the union had cost the operators a considerable sum of money and had caused them a great deal of trouble. He feared that the UMWA would soon present new demands, but he was unsure how forcefully his fellow railroad executives would resist them. He thought that they felt "very much less like making a fight now" than they had during the previous fall's strike.[22]

Nevertheless, Truesdale must have been heartened by the complete lack of favorable response that John Mitchell received to the telegrams he sent on February 15 inviting the presidents of the anthracite railroads to a joint conference with the UMWA in March. No operators attended the joint conference called by Mitchell for March 12 in Hazleton. Several days before the UMWA's delegates gathered there, many operators posted new notices that extended the terms then in effect for another year, to April 1, 1902. In response, the convention authorized Mitchell to try to arrange a conference with the operators before April 1. If that proved impossible, the union leaders were authorized to order an industrywide walkout.[23]

Mitchell did not like what he saw at the convention. In a letter to W. R. Fairley, a member of the national executive board, he characterized the 600 delegates in attendance as "about as wild a set of men" as he had ever seen: "The whole bunch wants to talk at the same time, and some of them have very decided opinions as to the proper method of running a labor organization." He was particularly distressed at the "disintegrating influences" which had arisen since the previous year's strike, and he told Fairley that charges were being made "against everybody, and by everybody." Mitchell planned to investigate the situation and punish those he believed to be promoting conflict.[24]

Mitchell sought to avoid a strike. In the hope of arranging a meeting with the operators, he enlisted the services of the National Civic Federation (NCF), established less than a year before to ameliorate various social ills, among them industrial strife. When the NCF's overtures proved fruitless, on March 19 Mitchell wrote William D. Ryan, a longtime friend and UMWA official from Illinois, and warned him not to be surprised if a strike occurred.[25] However, Mitchell then turned once again to Senator Mark Hanna and requested that Hanna persuade the railroad executives to hold discussions with Mitchell and the presidents of the anthracite districts.[26] At this point, Mitchell was supremely confident that he could control the union's decision regarding a strike, telling Ryan that the "miners will follow my advice without questioning whether it is right or wrong."[27] Mitchell met with both Hanna and George W. Perkins, a close associate of J. P. Morgan, who had gradually gained a controlling interest in most of the anthracite railroads during the 1890s. They arranged for Mitchell to meet with Eben B. Thomas, president of the Erie Railroad, which had recently acquired two large independent coal firms, the Pennsylvania Coal Company (PCC) and the Hillside Coal and Iron Company (HCI).[28]

Meeting with Mitchell on March 26, Thomas refused to make any concessions other than to agree to sanction discussions of grievances between the company's foremen and superintendents and committees of its workers. Mitchell saw this as "a very important concession."[29] However, it was never committed to writing and can best be viewed as a way in which Mitchell could avoid both a strike and the appearance of total capitulation. Although the second set of notices posted by the companies to settle the previous year's strike did not refer to the discussion of grievances with committees of their own employees, the UMWA's leaders had so interpreted the notices and urged the workers to form committees to present grievances. They had done so, and their militancy had secured a variety of concessions, most notably semimonthly pay.[30]

Mitchell further magnified the significance of his meeting with Thomas by convincing himself that it constituted an important step toward the eventual recognition of the union by the operators. After the meeting, he wrote UMWA Secretary-Treasurer William B. Wilson that he had "every reason to believe" that, if the union could maintain labor peace during the coming year, it would obtain full recognition.[31] Shortly thereafter, Hanna notified Mitchell that the Philadelphia and Reading (P & R) and the Pennsylvania Railroad had also consented to meet with committees to discuss grievances at their mines.[32]

The committee of the officers and executive board members of the anthracite districts, which had been empowered by the recent convention in Hazleton along with Mitchell to negotiate with the operators, unanimously approved the settlement Mitchell had arranged. They did so even though, according to Mitchell's secretary, many of them had come instructed by their districts to vote to strike unless full union recognition was achieved.[33] The union had not been recognized; nor had the committee, with the notable exception of Mitchell, spoken with any operators. Consequently, the committee tried to disguise its lack of success, informing the workers that "through the instrumentality and assistance of influential friends of organized labor, a conference was secured with representatives of the coal-carrying railroads."

Even though "the representatives of the operators listened attentively" to the union's arguments, they would not agree to a joint conference. Nevertheless, the operators were willing to meet with committees of men from their mines to adjust grievances. Furthermore, the committee assured the mine workers that if they would only abstain from local strikes in the coming months, "full and complete recognition would unquestionably be granted at future date."[34] Assessing the outcome of his talk with Thomas, Mitchell concluded that J. P. Morgan had induced Thomas to meet with him. Hanna told Mitchell that Morgan had begun to consider recognizing the union if it could maintain labor peace.[35] Mitchell viewed this as a small price to pay to achieve recognition.[36] However, Mitchell's craving for recognition and the security it would confer—a trait he shared with most other labor leaders—would increasingly place him at odds with mine workers who would continue to seek straightforward solutions to their everyday problems.[37] They had gradually learned that by walking out of the mines they could get quick attention to their grievances. That experience, combined with the vision of larger gains to be achieved through union solidarity, had led them to join the UMWA. By seeking to enforce labor peace in return for only the vaguest hints of recognition from corporate leaders, Mitchell would risk blunting the primary thrust behind the UMWA's progress in the anthracite industry.

During the remaining months of 1901, the leaders of the anthracite districts sought to strengthen the union by curtailing unauthorized strikes and by inducing all anthracite mine workers to join the UMWA. Nicholls of District One emphasized the first of these objectives in his report to the district convention in April. He noted that unsanctioned local strikes continued to occur sporadically. In his view, when grievances arose at the mines, too frequently mine workers left their jobs "without once thinking of the [UMWA's] law on the subject, or the propriety of taking such a step." Consequently, the operators maintained that the organization could not be controlled and certainly could not be depended upon to abide by an agreement. Still, Nicholls recognized that such walkouts stemmed from the numerous disputes that "out of necessity" occurred under the current system and could only be eliminated by the weighing of coal and the negotiation of a detailed scale of wages.[38]

Throughout the spring and into the summer of 1901, UMWA leaders repeatedly warned workers not to depend upon the union's support in unauthorized local walkouts. In the *UMW Journal,* Charles J. Thain described one such dispute, which occurred in mid-April at the LV's Midvale breaker near Wilkes-Barre. A foreman ordered a young man who was tending an engine in the breaker to leave his post to oil some other machinery. Since, as a general rule, he had been directed not to leave his post, he refused to comply. The boss then fired him as well as two others who refused to replace him. The company then decided to shut down the breaker, thereby idling some 1,100 men and boys in and around the surrounding mines. The grievance committee called on the district executive board after it failed to resolve the matter with company officials. However, the board sided with the company and maintained that all of the young men should have followed the boss's order and that the mine workers ought to return to work without insisting on reinstatement for the discharged youths. According to the board, those who refused to replace the young man who tended the engine should have done so, pending an investigation by the grievance committee. Thain stated that, "leaving out sentiment," that was the "logical and constitutional way to decide." He hoped that this episode would be related to "every local so that each mine worker would understand his duty in a similar situation." Furthermore, this case would clarify for the rank and file the determination of district officials to maintain "strict discipline and entire conformity with the constitution." By enforcing such discipline on its members, Thain believed that the UMWA could insist that the operators exact similarly high standards from their foremen.[39]

The leaders of District Nine took a similar stand. Militancy had increased considerably there, and organizer George Harris reported to Mitchell in May that workers often did not wait to consult district leaders before walking off their jobs.[40] In June, the district launched a campaign to establish grievance committees at every colliery. According to the *UMW Journal*, the purpose of establishing committees was to avoid "petty strikes" and to lessen friction.[41] On June 18, President John Fahy told the gathering that he and other district officials had dealt harshly with workers who struck without first forming committees to discuss the grievances with their bosses.[42]

The union's heightened effort to enforce labor peace is best reflected by its response to a strike by firemen in the summer of 1901. The UMWA had long maintained that firemen belonged in the UMWA along with the rest of the mine workers, but a craft union, the International Brotherhood of Stationary Firemen, also pursued them. On July 7, James A. Gerrity, secretary-treasurer of the Pennsylvania district of the Brotherhood, asked John Mitchell to support the firemen's demands for a cut in the work day from twelve to eight hours with no cut in pay. Gerrity feared that UMWA members might replace firemen if they struck, and he pointed out that, in and around Mt. Carmel in the Schuylkill field, mine workers refused to recognize the Brotherhood's working cards and had told its members that they would give them no support.[43] There is no evidence of a response from Mitchell, and on July 16 the firemen began their strike. However, very few firemen joined the strike in the Schuylkill and Lehigh fields, and even in the Wyoming field, where the firemen's union had its greatest strength in the anthracite region, the strike was far from complete. With some engineers and pumpmen joining the firemen, the walkout did close collieries in and around Scranton. Still, even in that area, firemen continued to work at several independently owned collieries that granted their demands and at the DL & W's mines, where quite a few firemen belonged to the UMWA. The executive board of District One soon declared its opposition to the strike and ordered all firemen, engineers, and pumpmen to stay on the job.[44] According to an editorial in the *UMW Journal*, the strike was a "flash in the pan" that demonstrated "the absolute necessity" that all workers in an around the mines belong to "one compact body instead of two or three separate organizations."[45]

At some mines, including those of the Susquehanna Coal Company (SCC) in Nanticoke, UMWA members replaced striking firemen. According to John Price, an official of one of the UMWA local unions there, those who had taken the places of the strikers were "Hungarians and Poles," many of whom had done so "out of revenge" against those firemen who had refused to walk out during the lengthy strike against the SCC in 1899. Price believed that UMWA members should continue to work, since the firemen's dispute did not affect them and the UMWA's executive board had not moved to support the firemen. He added that the firemen had not attempted to consult the UMWA locals before the strike began.[46] The union's opposition soon broke the strike, which the firemen's leaders called off after meeting with the executive boards of the anthracite districts on July 22. However, the UMWA did persuade most of the companies where firemen had walked out to reinstate them.[47] Several weeks later, John Mitchell discussed the firemen's strike in a speech in Plymouth, north of Wilkes-Barre. He expressed sympathy for them and reaffirmed the union's commitment to improve conditions for all workers in and around the mines. However, he emphasized that the firemen could never hope to obtain redress for their grievances without joining their fellow workers.[48]

According to an editorial in the *UMW Journal*, the most notable result of the union's opposition to the firemen's strike was the trust that the union gained among both the operators and the public:

> Every Mine Worker knows by bitter experience that the hardest thing with which his officials have had to contend is the distrust that the operators have of their ability to hold the members of the organization to the terms of a contract. While there is no reason, sound in morals or in logic, for this distrust, yet it is there and has to be met. The Mine Workers have as high sense of honor as any class of men, and are no more prone to break written or verbal contracts than the rest of mankind, yet, for some unknown reason, the great majority of operators profess to believe that they are, and anything which will tend to correct this false impression should receive the highest approbation of all Mine Workers. That strike was a critical moment in the affairs of the United Mine Workers.[49]

Eben Thomas's vague allusion to the possibility of full-scale negotiations if the mine workers behaved properly in 1901 was trumpeted once again as a species of contract, apparently all the more sacred because its terms had never been written. By moving against the firemen, the UMWA's leaders made certain that the operators would receive "the full benefit of the unwritten contract." Hence, the so-called contract held sway, even though it offered nothing concrete to the workers in return for the union's promise of labor peace, and in spite of the fact that the UMWA admitted the justice of the firemen's demands. In analyzing the union's tactics, the editorial noted:

> The advantages to be derived from this action are, first, it throws an irresistible public opinion on the side of the contentions of the Mine Worker. Second, it disarms hostile criticism and compels even the most sturdy opponent of labor organizations to admit that the Mine Workers are actuated by a high principle. Third, it strikes at the very foundation of the contention of operators that the organization can not compel obedience to its contracts.[50]

To build membership and enable the UMWA to exert more effective control over the work force, the union had initiated a policy of checking the working cards issued to all members in good standing. Delegates to the joint convention of the anthracite districts held in March resolved that once during each quarter a committee of each local union would check every employee for his card. Those without one would, at the very least, be encouraged to join the union or pay any arrearages in dues.[51] Many of District One's locals moved to institute the card system immediately and not surprisingly, operators balked at the inspection of cards on their property. As a result, district leaders sanctioned three brief strikes, two of which occurred at the mines of a major producer, the Temple Iron Company, which had experienced a lengthy walkout prior to the industrywide strike of 1900.[52] Further disagreement over the examination of working cards led to walkouts of several days at the DL & W's Woodward colliery,[53] located near Wilkes-Barre, and at one of the Scranton Coal Company's mines. At the latter, in May, a two-man committee inspecting working cards encountered a mine worker who said that he belonged to a different local, but declined to produce a card. When the committeemen directed him to leave the mine, he refused to go. The committeemen then led the rest of the workers out of the mine. The superintendent refused to let the committeemen return to work on the following day, and consequently the mine workers struck and the mines remained idle for about a week. The committeemen then tried to call out the workers at another of the company's mines nearby, but the superintendent kept those employees at work by threatening to close that mine for an indefinite period if the workers struck.[54]

In spite of the turmoil caused by the card inspections, Thomas Nicholls was determined not to abandon them. At a district convention in July, he pointed out that the inspections had induced "hundreds of new members" to enroll and had enriched the treasuries of the local unions. In his opinion, persisting in the examination of working cards was "of more importance than anything else."[55] During the summer, District Seven and District Nine moved to extend the inspection of working cards. The former resolved at its quarterly convention in July to systematize the examination of cards and to authorize the executive board to order strikes if necessary "to more fully unionize the employees throughout the District."[56] Resistance to card inspection by many operators was one of the chief issues discussed when the executive boards of the anthracite districts met on August 8, 9, and 10. In assessing responsibility for the numerous card-related disputes, the union officials blamed the bosses as well as those workers who still remained outside of the union. According to the UMWA, if the operators stopped interfering with the examination of cards and the recalcitrant workers joined the organization, prospects for labor peace would improve markedly. The executive boards insisted that the operators knew that cards could be examined "without interfering with the proper working of the collieries." Still, some superintendents opposed examination of cards on grounds that were "at best but technical." By doing so, they exacerbated labor relations instead of helping the UMWA to usher in an era of labor peace. To rectify the situation, local committees were directed to discuss the inspection of working cards with obstinate superintendents.[57]

While willing to sanction a walkout where it might seem necessary, the union's leaders feared unleashing the militancy of the rank and file. Although this militancy had proved essential to organizing as early as 1897, and had helped to build the solidarity which made the strike of 1900 successful, the union's leaders had always viewed with dismay spontaneous strikes that constituted a public denial of their authority. Throughout 1901 and into 1902 mine workers continued to walk off their jobs. Some actions resulted from local efforts to carry out district policy. However, such walkouts often proceeded beyond the control of district leaders. Just as important, many workers would continue to act on their own with no sanction from even their local leaders.

"ELIMINATE THE BOYS"

The extent and character of this persistent militancy can be seen most clearly in the actions of the young men, generally in their middle and late teens, who drove the mules and handled the coal cars that brought the miners' production to the surface. Outbursts of militancy from these workers had not been uncommon in the nonunion era. Once the union came, the drivers and runners seemed to display a special enthusiasm for the UMWA's goals and a remarkable eagerness to achieve them. Moreover, because of their strategic role in the production process, delivering cars to miners, drivers and runners could exert significant pressure on miners reluctant to join the union. In April 1901, at the beginning of the campaign in District One to inspect working cards, drivers and runners twice refused to deliver cars to nonunion miners at two of the Temple Iron Company's mines. In each instance, when the drivers and runners were discharged, all of the workers in the colliery walked out, for five days at one mine and a day and a half at the other.[58]

Drivers and runners also tried to enforce the union's general policy of seeking to equalize the distribution of mine cars. While miners were supposed to receive as many cars as they could load, in the distribution of cars mine managers generally gave a special priority to those miners doing development work, which opened new areas in a mine.[59] Although UMWA leaders had frequently deplored favoritism in car distribution and had demanded in the strike of 1900 that no miner should get more than his "legal share of cars," this demand received little attention at that time. After the strike, there is no evidence of directives from district leaders ordering local unions to equalize the distribution of cars. But many locals tried to do so, and while drivers and runners may not have formulated the policy, they risked their jobs to carry it out.

On several occasions during the fall of 1901 at the D & H's Jermyn colliery, drivers and runners refused to give miners performing development work all the cars that they wanted. In September, two miners working as partners were told that they should load no more cars than other miners. They met with Henry Collins of District One's executive board to explain their case, and he informed Thomas Nicholls that these men were doing necessary work that should be allowed to continue. Nicholls so informed the local, but in November, these miners were told once again that if they continued to load more cars than the chamber miners, they would be expelled from the union. When the miners met once again with Collins, he interceded on their behalf with Nicholls, but this time Nicholls told them they would have to settle the issue with the local. Consequently, when drivers once more limited the number of cars they gave them, the foreman discharged two drivers on December 12. On the next day he asked other boys to replace them; they refused and were also fired, thus idling a section of the mine. After a grievance committee met with the foreman, he agreed to reinstate the drivers if they would give the miners as many cars as they wanted. The drivers complied, but the local passed a resolution to expel from the union any miners who loaded more cars than their fellows. In its struggle to maintain discipline, the company turned to its last resort—a lockout. According to the foreman, Thomas R. Thomas, the D & H "wanted to control the men" and did not want "the Union to run the colliery."[60]

Drivers and runners struck for their own purposes too. In the fall of 1901, four drivers in a section of the HCI's Number Two colliery in Forest City, north of Scranton, demanded that the company add a driver to the crew to lighten their work. When their demand was refused, they walked out, and more than a week passed before the company could find other boys who would replace them.[61] In March 1902, most of the drivers at one of the HCI's collieries stopped work because they disagreed with the foreman's choice of a boy to be promoted to runner. When the foreman informed them that his word was law, the drivers and some other young workers walked out, idling much of the colliery for the remainder of the day. The foreman discharged the drivers but spared "three of the little door boys," who had also left their jobs.[62]

In one section of the D & H's Von Storch mine in August 1901, a group of drivers demanded reclassification of their work to a higher wage level. When the foreman refused, they walked off their jobs and idled that section. For the next month the foreman could find no boy who would agree to take the place of any of the strikers, and the company had to pay adult laborers to do so at a substantially higher wage.[63] Elsewhere in the same colliery one month later, the foreman fired a runner for alleged neglect of duty that resulted in an injury to a driver. All the employees in the mine then struck for one week in an unsuccessful effort to compel the company to reinstate the runner.[64]

Some small strikes occurred when foremen tried to discipline drivers who mistreated their mules. William Allen, superintendent for the Scranton Coal Company, told of a driver who, in May 1901, deliberately crashed a mine car into a mule standing in the middle of a roadway. The driver then brought the mule to Allen and "in a laughing manner said . . . 'That's a beauty now.' " Allen fired him, and subsequently, when Allen turned down a demand for his reinstatement, the drivers in that section of the colliery struck for one week, effectively idling that part of the mine.[65] David W. Evans, foreman at the Stevens Coal Company in West Pittston, made a special point one evening of expressing his displeasure to several drivers who galloped their mules into the barn at the end of the day. However, at the close of work the next day, he noticed that a group of drivers "waited altogether and started pell mell towards the barn, all in a body, with ten mules." On the following morning, Evans told them they would have to promise not to gallop their mules. The drivers refused, stating that they were in a hurry to finish work. They walked off the job, but after two days older mine workers persuaded them to return.[66]

Two other incidents demonstrate the extent to which the youthful drivers resented and resisted discipline. A driver boss at the Black Diamond Coal

Company in Carbondale noticed that a Polish driver named John had neglected several times to secure his cars at the edge of a grade. Fearing that a car might slide down the hill out of control and cause injury, the boss told John to secure his cars. John told him to go to hell and walked out of the mine. The entire work force struck on the next day; however they not only returned to work one day later, but the older mine workers also found a replacement for John.[67] A far more serious case of resistance occurred at the Clear Spring Coal Company located near West Pittston. Early one morning, a fire boss noticed that two ventilation doors, which were designed to close automatically, had been wired open. Such a disruption in ventilation might well have caused an explosion. A team of mules was found nearby, making the drivers the likely culprits. The foreman fired the boys who were responsible, and their fellow drivers walked out. However, an older UMWA member endorsed the firing and helped to persuade the strikers to return to work. Previously at that colliery, two other brief strikes had occurred when drivers were discharged for mistreating mules.[68]

Even the youngest mine workers resorted to militant action. In February 1901, the breaker boys at the Ontario mine of the Scranton Coal Company walked out for a day when, due to an unexpected thaw, the company canceled a sleigh ride it had planned for them.[69] One month later, the breaker boys at the LV's Maltby colliery struck for a day in an unsuccessful attempt to obtain a raise.[70] At the mines of the L & W-B, between the major strikes of 1900 and 1902, breaker boys struck on three separate occasions.[71]

In most of their numerous work stoppages, young mine workers consistently displayed a special kind of solidarity. Mine foreman David W. Evans attributed this to the influence of the UMWA. He admitted that boys occasionally complained about wages and conditions before the advent of the union. However, since the coming of the UMWA, not only had the number of incidents increased, but groups of boys would agree that if one was discharged all would strike. He held the UMWA responsible for the change: "The fruits go up certainly from the same teachings."[72] Other managers also realized that the drivers and other young mine workers had displayed remarkable militancy as organization spread throughout the anthracite region. When asked during the hearings of the Anthracite Coal Strike Commission, convened after the strike of 1902, which group of employees had presented the greatest discipline problem in recent years, Superintendent J. G. Hayes of the Peoples Coal Company of Scranton responded, "Boys."[73] Testifying before the same body, R. A. Phillips, then superintendent of the DL & W, stated that the union could improve itself if it would "eliminate the boys," whom he labeled "irresponsible."[74] His superior, William H. Truesdale, was horrified by the union's impact upon young workers. Discussing a prospective settlement of the strike of 1902, Truesdale demanded that the UMWA no longer be allowed to "poison" the minds of the nearly 20 percent of the union members that he claimed were between fourteen and twenty years of age.[75]

The leaders of the UMWA also sought more effective control over the young mine workers. After consultation with the presidents of the anthracite districts, John Mitchell announced a set of rules concerning mine workers under sixteen on August 13, 1902. The boys would be placed in auxiliary locals. Their initiation fee would be twenty-five cents, and they would be required to pay only one-half of regular dues.[76] Treasurers for adult locals would act as treasurers for the boys' locals, and the adult locals would elect a three-man committee to attend the boys' meetings and "exercise general supervision." The auxiliary locals would meet jointly with their seniors to elect delegates to district and national conventions, but each boy would have only one-half of a vote.[77]

"NO MAN CAN SERVE TWO MASTERS"

It is impossible to determine if Eben Thomas of the Erie Railroad was sincere in holding out to John Mitchell at the end of March the possibility of some sort of recognition if the union could end local strikes.[78] Whether or not he was, the burgeoning wave of job actions over the next few months confirmed for the operators their belief that the union had brought unrest to their mines, regardless of the union's considerable efforts to control it. Those efforts were quite strong verbally but much less so in practice, because district leaders must have come to realize the severe limitations they faced in trying to discipline the workers. It also became increasingly clear to union leaders that they would receive little credit from the operators for their efforts, vigorous though they may be, to foster labor peace. As job actions proliferated, the operators had less and less tolerance for them.

One mining executive in particular would come to play a leading role against the union. In April 1901, George F. Baer became president of the Philadelphia and Reading Coal and Iron Company and its parent, the Philadelphia and Reading Railroad. Toward the end of May, he wrote a number of his fellow executives to ask them to assist him in an effort to "get up and keep a record of all the strikes, disturbances and demands made through the labor organizations . . . from the first of April." This, of course, was the beginning of the period in which Thomas had told Mitchell the operators would be monitoring the UMWA's efforts to keep the peace. Baer had little interest in an evenhanded evaluation of such data, which he hoped "may be able to show how powerless the labor organizations have been to control the men, and how much annoyance and loss we are being subject to."[79]

The presidents of the anthracite districts gave voice to their doubts of the operators' sincerity in a letter to Mitchell in August. Nicholls, Duffy, and

Fahy had called a tri-district convention for August 27 in Hazleton and invited Mitchell to attend. They informed him that the actions of many of the operators had "caused a large number of people to doubt the sincerity of the employers in holding out the hope of a joint conference." Therefore, they asked Mitchell to ascertain the likelihood of such a conference. They noted that the lack of a written agreement promoted friction and that only a contract drawn up in a joint conference could insure peace.[80]

On August 17, in a speech to some 25,000 at Plymouth, John Mitchell castigated the D & H for its refusal to allow the examination of working cards. Still, he "strongly advised the men to keep their compact with the companies until April 1 at all hazards, and show them the true metal of which the union men were composed."[81] At the August 27 convention, officials from each district reported on the extent to which operators permitted the inspection of working cards. Most of the major operators in District One categorically forbade the examination of cards. Superintendent S. B. Thorne of the Temple Iron Company reportedly had threatened to discharge any foreman who permitted the inspection of cards. The SCC flatly refused to discuss the issue with a committee from the union. The Kingston Coal Company, with which Thomas Nicholls had settled several matters in a relatively peaceful fashion, had previously allowed the examination of working cards, but its superintendent informed a UMWA committee that the company would no longer do so. Only the Plymouth Coal Company, one of the smaller operators, accepted the inspection of cards. Reports from District Seven and District Nine were not as complete, but of the small number of operators surveyed, only one was reported as responding favorably. John Fahy stated that the P & R had agreed to permit card inspection, but it is difficult to believe that the company did this for long, if at all. Some months later, George Baer denied unequivocally that inspection of cards had been allowed.[82] Samuel D. Warriner, superintendent of the LV, which operated collieries in each district, went beyond prohibiting the inspection of cards. He also told a UMWA committee that all involved might "be dead before the joint conference."[83]

Confronting such sentiments, the UMWA's leaders began to lose patience with the operators. In a statement issued at the close of the convention, the union depicted itself as submitting stoically to a variety of indignities because it believed "that the contract entered into between employers and employees should be sacredly adhered to by both." Nevertheless, in spite of the UMWA's restraint, some bosses had shown a "persistent and well-defined antagonism . . . toward the United Mine Workers of America." Some companies had sought to destroy the union by discharging and suspending union activists, and several had altered wages for various jobs in violation of the notices posted in March. While the UMWA reaffirmed its desire to abide by the "present agreement," it insisted that the operators do the same. The union either did not believe or would not admit that the opposition it faced came from the top echelons of the anthracite railroads, stating that considerable friction had been caused by "underlings clothed with a little brief authority." Locals were urged to continue to examine working cards while a committee composed of Mitchell and the anthracite presidents would "proceed to the highest authority of the coal companies." They would attempt to obtain the operators' sanction for the inspection of cards, call attention "to the many violations of contract" by local supervisory personnel, and try to persuade the operators to schedule a joint conference before the notices expired on April 1, 1902. Finally, Mitchell and the district presidents were authorized by the convention to order strikes if necessary to secure the operators' compliance with the "contract."[84]

After the Hazleton convention in late August 1901, Mitchell redoubled his efforts to reach an understanding with the railroad executives who controlled most of the mines. Mark Hanna suggested that Mitchell meet again with Thomas, who had recently become chairman of the board of directors of the Erie. In a letter to Hanna on September 6, Mitchell seemed confident that Thomas would help to arrange a meeting with the railroad executives. Also, Mitchell stated that he was "quite sure" that Thomas and the other corporate officials did not know of the conduct of some of their superintendents and mine bosses, who Mitchell believed were "unquestionably going out of their way to antagonize" the union.[85] However, when Mitchell and the three presidents of the anthracite districts arrived in New York, they discovered that Thomas was in Europe. The Erie's president, Frederick D. Underwood, told them nothing could be done until Thomas returned, and he also stated that he did not believe that Thomas, in his statements of the previous March, had been speaking for any railroad but the Erie.[86]

What Mitchell and the presidents did not know was that even their brief meeting with Underwood showed a small break in the operators' facade. Baer and his fellow presidents were appalled that Underwood would hold such a meeting without consulting them and feared that Underwood might have committed them to attend, which they would not do. It is unclear whether Underwood planned to encourage Mitchell and the district presidents toward their goal of a joint conference when he first agreed to meet them. However, chastened by his fellow executives' horrified reaction, he gave no hint of a concession at the meeting. To reassure Baer and the others, he sent them a transcript.[87]

When Thomas returned in October, he refused to meet with Mitchell and would not even respond directly to letters Mitchell had left for him. Mitchell expressed his displeasure in a letter to Ralph M. Easley, head of the NCF, who had been acting as a go-between along with Hanna: "Personally, I have very little pride, but I do not intend to get down on my knees to Mr. Thomas or anyone else.'' Mitchell added ominously that, if the railroad executives were ''so sensitive'' that they could not receive a committee while their mines were in operation, they might have to receive one ''with their mines idle.'' He felt that his tireless work on behalf of harmony was not appreciated: ''If Mr. Thomas knew the efforts which I have made to keep down hostile action on the part of others he would not have refused to even reply to my letters.''[88] Easley assured him that Thomas had a very friendly attitude toward him; still, no meeting would occur until the end of March 1902, when the notices posted during the previous March had nearly expired.[89]

Throughout the autumn of 1901, militant action by the rank and file continued unabated, with and without union sanction. Workers at the Shamokin Coal Company's Natalie colliery walked out for a short period when the company refused to discharge a superintendent who sold the employees tickets for a raffle from which he stood to benefit. Edward McKay of the national executive board, members of District Nine's executive board, and even John Mitchell failed to dissuade the workers from striking.[90] To the north, at the Melville Coal Company's Lee colliery, located near Nanticoke, workers walked off their jobs in October over a variety of grievances, including the company's failure to pay wages promptly. Firemen, pumpmen, and other essential maintenance workers were included in the strike call, thus endangering the property; the executive board of District One did not sanction the strike. The company complained to the district and a member of the board advised the strikers to return to work and present their grievances to the company and the district officers. When the workers refused, Thomas Nicholls interceded. The president of the local at Lee admitted to Nicholls that he had little control over his men. Still, local and district officers continued to exercise their powers of persuasion and, ''after considerable effort . . . the men were induced to return.'' But on December 12, a group of drivers left their jobs for a brief period because the company failed to promote a door boy to fill an opening for a driver.[91]

Some local disputes became especially protracted. Workers at the Moffett colliery near Wilkes-Barre struck for more than two months when their employer reduced the rate paid per car to the miners. The district executive board endorsed the walkout and even allowed the local to call out maintenance workers. The strike ended in December after another company bought the colliery and reinstated the former rate.[92] A strike at the LV's Maltby colliery, also located near Wilkes-Barre, began during the summer of 1901 and continued through the industrywide walkout of 1902. Several firemen at Maltby left their jobs on July 16 in the short-lived firemen's strike, which the UMWA opposed, and management quickly replaced them. On the following day, several of the colliery's engineers walked out as well, refusing to run engines powered by "scab steam." The company replaced them also, and, on July 24, after the strike had ended, the company refused to reinstate the strikers. The other mine workers at Maltby continued to work until August 2, when they informed a foremen that they too could no longer work at a mine operated with "scab steam." Union leaders did not sanction the strike, and, even though the executive boards of the three anthracite districts ordered the men to abandon their strike shortly before the Hazleton convention, the strikers refused, and the colliery remained idle.[93] However, some of the men from Maltby obtained jobs at the mines of the Temple Iron Company, and when fifty of them were discharged in early November, Thomas Nicholls accused the operators of using a blacklist. The executive board of District One ordered a strike against Temple's collieries to begin on Monday, November 11, but the company capitulated and reinstated the Maltby mine workers.[94]

Upon learning of the possibility of a strike, Truesdale of the DL & W wrote his superintendent, E. E. Loomis, that he believed that the entire dispute could and should have been avoided. Truesdale noted that the superintendents of the leading operators in the Wyoming field had agreed previously to take "every possible precaution" to prevent the hiring of "men connected with any of the other companies who should at any time go out on a strike." In his view, "someone connected with the Temple Iron Company must have relaxed vigilance very much."[95] Several days later, in a letter to George Baer, president of the Temple Iron Company as well as the P & R, Truesdale returned to the question of neglect of duty. He pointed out that no problem would have occurred "if the same diligence had been used to prevent the employment of these men by the Temple Company as was afterwards followed to ferret out and locate these men that they might be discharged."[96]

These letters demonstrate much more than the operators' ability to compile a blacklist. More significantly, they reveal a serious defect in John Mitchell's strategy for obtaining a joint conference with the operators. Throughout the summer of 1901, he maintained that the men who ran the anthracite railroads did not realize what their superintendents and foremen were doing to antagonize the UMWA. Mitchell hoped that, by bringing these matters to the attention of the railroad executives, he could not only defuse various disputes but also lay the foundation for recognition of the union. However, the willingness to antagonize the UMWA came from the very top.

Truesdale vented his disgust with the UMWA and its fellow labor organizations in reflecting on the work of the annual convention of the American Federation of Labor (AFL) in December 1901 in Scranton. Truesdale took note of the "mass of resolutions" presented "pertaining to all possible subjects." He expressed his view that those attending the convention believed that they had a "special vocation in life to govern all the affairs of the universe." However, Truesdale found even more to worry him in the annual meeting of the NCF's Industrial Department, which took place in New York several days after the AFL convention adjourned. Senator Hanna had become chairman of the Industrial Department, and Samuel Gompers, president of the AFL, had become first vice-chairman.[97] Truesdale feared that politicians would exercise greater influence than employers in labor disputes to come before the NCF, thus "the real merits of any matter" would be ignored. Of course, the uneasy truce between the anthracite operators and the UMWA had been a leading item on the NCF's agenda for several months, and Truesdale had "no doubt" that Hanna had committed the operators, "to a certain extent anyhow, to the recognition of Mr. Mitchell's organization." Truesdale believed that the operators had to become "fully armed" to combat any such move and to explain why they would not negotiate with Mitchell.[98]

The basic attitudes that informed the operators' approach toward labor relations were delineated by George Baer in an address entitled "Work is Worship," which he presented as president of the board of trustees of Franklin and Marshall College in Lancaster, Pennsylvania, on January 16, 1902. Reminding his audience that "man was not made to be a loafer," he enunciated several "fundamental truths," among them: "All men, as laborers, are not equal," and "the owner of property has a right to control its lawful use." In elaborating upon his final truth—"the most society can do is to give every man an equal chance of developing and using his powers, and to secure him in his reward according to his work"—Baer explained his objections to labor unions. Although he asserted that laborers had the right to organize and could use "all lawful means" to improve their lot, including leaving their jobs "singly or in a body," he argued for strict limits on the means unions could employ to achieve their objectives.

> To-day there is no greater absolute despotism and tyranny on the earth than the power which forbids a man to work because of some other man's quarrels. The nod of a despot, causing the arrest of any man in his kingdom, represents no more arbitrary power than the edict which issues in the name of labor, whereby a workman, without a grievance, must stand with folded arms and see his family suffer for bread, because he is in terror of the ostracism, if not the personal violence, which follows an attempt to be a free man.
>
> We must have the courage and the Christian heroism to denounce all oppression of labor, whether by capital or by labor itself, and to frown upon the demagogues, politicians and agitators who try to terrorize us into silence on this subject.[99]

In expanding upon the theme of "oppression of labor by labor itself," Baer made no specific mention of any particular dispute. However, there can be little doubt that the recent activities of the UMWA in the anthracite region had helped to shape his views concerning one union strategy that he found particularly oppressive.

In some trades, employers are not permitted to employ workmen without labor organization cards. Union men will not work with non-union men. Was ever greater tyranny practised by one set of men over their fellow men? Work will not be worship in the country until it is universally conceded that no man shall be deprived of his right to work, by law, by force, by threats, by social ostracism, by boycott, or by insult; . . . no man shall be denied the right to work as many hours as he pleases, and at any price he pleases, and no man shall be boycotted because he employs non-union labor. Labor may organize, but it may not tyrannize.[100]

Viewed in such a light, any contract between an employer and an organization of employees would infringe upon the rights of the individual so long as a single worker desired the right to work more hours for less pay. Consequently, Baer disparaged annual meetings between employers and employees to negotiate terms of employment. He accused labor unions of seeking "to make an impassable gulf" between labor and capital and maintained that the "modern theory of labor organizations" was based, not on harmonizing relations between workers and employer, but on dividing them into "two great hostile camps." In describing the harm that would result from negotiating with labor organizations, Baer caricatured the system of joint conferences the UMWA sought in the anthracite fields.

Peace is only to be a temporary thing, brought about by formulating a truce between the two contending armies, which shall terminate at the end of the year. In the meantime, the leaders of the hostile camps are to be fully occupied during the whole of the year in adjusting the thousand and one various misunderstandings as to the true meaning of the terms of the truce. The business is to be carried on by dividing authority, each hostile camp having representatives to determine when and how the work shall be done. This is violating the old rule that "No man can serve two masters."[101]

Unwilling to share authority with the workers, Baer would brook no interference from outside parties either. In rejecting the feasibility of mediation in labor disputes, Baer referred specifically to the NCF. In his view, that organization was "based on the delusive and impracticable idea" that relations between capital and labor could be adjusted amicably by a board not selected by the parties themselves.[102] He expanded on this point in discussing the NCF in an earlier letter to Eben B. Thomas. Baer granted that groups like the NCF, with their high-minded ideals and goals, might serve a useful purpose if they restricted themselves to being "mere teachers and promulgators of sound doctrine." However, they could do little good by trying "to put their theoretical teaching in practical form.'' The world's problems would have been solved long ago if ''wisdom and justice and fair-dealing would necessarily flow from conferences between the leaders of divergent interests.'' But, he continued, ''this is a world of conflict. It is, perhaps, cruel to say that the conflict always has and, perhaps, always will result in the 'survival of the fittest,' . . . it is the law of the universe.''[103]

In the struggle over authority in the workplace, George F. Baer could see no room for compromise. He did not shrink from conflict, and even seemed to welcome it. By the beginning of 1902, he and his fellow operators were willing to accept conflict to reestablish their authority. Union leaders were considerably more divided on the issue. In 1902 they would continue to hope that the operators would recognize the union's legitimacy in some form. They had not yet realized what Baer had long understood. The struggle for unionization in the anthracite coal fields was much less a question of legitimacy than one of power.

6

The Strike of 1902

The anthracite coal strike of 1902 stands as one of the titanic industrial struggles in American history. One hundred fifty thousand mine workers and their families confronted some of the nation's oldest and most powerful railroad corporations for five-and-a-half months. Other significant interests were also affected, principally millions of consumers of hard coal. The anthracite industry produced what most Americans in the northeastern United States at the turn of the century considered a necessity. Traditionally production was strongest in the summer so consumers could accumulate stockpiles for the fall. As the strike continued from the spring through the summer, the needs of those consumers seemed to represent perfectly the dawning concern for "the public interest" which would exemplify the Progressive Era. Concern for that consumer, along with an eagerness to play a larger role in the nation's economic life, induced President Theodore Roosevelt to intervene in the walkout. His politically inspired need to serve the public interest and deal justly with the parties to the strike resulted in, for the first time in American history, even-handed federal intervention between labor and capital.

No intervention would have occurred if the material interests involved had not been so great. However, the conflict between the operators and the union was not primarily over money. The strike of 1902 was so long and so bitter because of the threat posed by the mine workers under the leadership of the United Mine Workers of America (UMWA) to the operators' control of the work force and their business. Under public pressure, President Roosevelt decided that the consumers' interest demanded an end to the strike regardless of the principles involved. As would become increasingly common throughout the twentieth century, the principles at stake in the strike would be submerged in calculations of material gain and loss for each of the affected parties.

"HOW CAN WE FACE OUR LOCALS?"

As 1902 began, the UMWA could challenge Baer and the other railroad executives from a position of unprecedented strength. The three anthracite districts totaled some 78,437 members, or more than half of all anthracite mine workers. The proportion of union members was even higher, since allowance must be made for the many workers under sixteen who, according to the union's rules, were not recorded as full members.[1] Anthracite membership had increased nearly 50 percent over the previous year. District One had become the largest of all twenty UMWA districts, with 45,005 members, while District Nine remained the fourth largest, with 23,376. District Seven had more than doubled in size to become the union's seventh largest district, with a total of 10,056 members.[2]

Those in charge of the anthracite districts proceeded to take a number of steps designed to manage their organizations more effectively. At District One's semiannual convention in January, President Nicholls reported severe losses in membership for a number of locals in which the members worked at several different collieries in a locality rather than a single one. Most of those locals had been organized by ethnicity. The district addressed the issue by designating a particular local for the workers at each mine.[3] Also, the convention empowered the district executive board to suspend for a maximum of three months any local that allowed its members to strike without authorization from the board.[4]

At District Seven's semiannual convention in January, the delegates decided that the district's business could be conducted more efficiently if district conventions were called only once a year.[5] Furthermore, in discussing initiation fees, Districts Seven and Nine showed that adding to the union's ranks was not their primary concern. The former kept its fee at five dollars, the highest figure for the three anthracite districts, and at its convention, District Nine considered increasing its fee to that amount.[6] In addition, President John Fahy of District Nine suggested that the district make a special effort to drop mine workers who were no longer in good standing from the membership rolls.[7]

In his report on the situation in anthracite to the UMWA's national convention in Indianapolis in January 1902, John Mitchell noted that, while the inspection of working cards had been responsible for increases in the union's membership, "strange to relate, the companies—evidently acting in concert," had grown more and more unyielding in their refusal to permit the inspection of cards on their property. In Mitchell's view, the companies' resistance had "practically destroyed the usefulness of the working card," and he advised the delegates to substitute buttons, which members in good standing would receive each quarter. Theoretically, buttons would be much easier for each local union's committee to check, thus eliminating one of the operator's major complaints about the inspection of cards—that the process of inspection greatly disrupted work.[8] Nevertheless, although their acceptance of the buttons may be viewed as a step designed to calm tensions, the delegates also directly confronted the possibility of a strike by offering "all possible assistance" to the anthracite mine workers if no joint conference occurred and an industrywide walkout resulted.[9]

The mine workers' propensity toward spontaneous militancy, particularly that of the younger workers, had by no means subsided, as several brief strikes that occurred at opposite ends of the anthracite region in the latter half of February demonstrate. Near Shamokin in the Schuylkill field, workers struck at the Hickory Ridge colliery, complaining that the clerk there had overcharged them for mining supplies. Nearby, at the Colbert colliery, breaker boys walked out for one day in an unsuccessful attempt to induce the company to replace their boss.[10] In the Wyoming field, workers in the Delaware, Lackawanna, and Western's (DL & W) collieries from time to time had expressed their dislike for a system initiated at or near the beginning of the year in which underground workers were required to check in and out of the mine. The company claimed that it had instituted this procedure to enable bosses to know who was underground in the event of an accident. However, the system also allowed the company to keep track of the actual amount of time spent underground by miners, who generally were free to leave their chambers and quit work when they pleased. At the Hampton colliery, located west of Scranton, drivers struck against the check-in system. With the entire colliery idle as a result, Thomas Nicholls, after considerable effort, succeeded in persuading the drivers to return several days later.[11]

As an industrywide strike appeared more and more likely, the operators realized that a walkout in 1902 would become a public relations contest and mobilized for it. For example, the DL & W proceeded to take full advantage of the data generated by its check-in system to record the amount of time that its miners spent underground, so that it could claim later that very few miners worked ten hours per day.[12] On January 17, 1902, the railroad presidents met to discuss the outlook for a strike and to consider whether or not they needed to order any changes in labor policies. Their goal, in the words of William H. Truesdale, was to make sure "agitators" could not find "a weak place in existing arrangements . . . which would be difficult to defend before the public."[13]

Truesdale expected that the UMWA would press the operators to accept arbitration by the National Civic Federation (NCF). He believed that the railroad presidents would never consent, but still they would have "to be prepared . . . to show by the most conclusive reasons and facts available" that they could negotiate wages only as they had traditionally done. The anthracite railroad presidents ordered their superintendents to prepare material on wages and working conditions that could "form the basis of a reply to any communication . . . from the Civic Federation or anyone else." In doing so, the superintendents were expected to address the following concerns:

> That the eight-hour day is impracticable and unreasonable and as such cannot be considered; that the payment for mining coal by the ton instead of by the car as generally prevails, would prove very much more cumbersome and burdensome, both to the operators and miners, than the per car basis. Also

that a uniform rate of pay for doing certain dead work or development work about the mines is entirely impracticable owing to the different conditions in the different mines.[14]

Moreover, by displaying the many different rates of payment for mining, which varied from company to company, mine to mine, and even vein to vein, the superintendents could try to demonstrate "the impossibility" of formulating a scale of wages in a joint conference. To supply further ammunition, Truesdale suggested that Loomis gather information concerning disputes between the company and its employees in the preceding year. Also, the DL & W's president requested an estimate of the percentage of boys and young men—"impulsive and without the judgment and experience of men of maturer years"—in the UMWA. Truesdale believed that youths were "practically . . . controlling [the union] and its policy."[15]

Truesdale and his fellow railroad presidents also wanted the superintendents to deal with the potentially embarrassing issue of the hours worked by firemen. They should recommend "changes that for one thing would not make a prima facie case against" the companies, "such as under any circumstances working . . . men twenty-four hours except in case of accident."[16] Truesdale's prodding induced Superintendent Loomis to inaugurate a new schedule for the DL & W's firemen several weeks later. They had traditionally alternated between the night shift and the day shift, and had exchanged shifts by working twenty-four hours every other Sunday. This allowed them a holiday on the alternate Sunday, but required that they work an average of seven shifts per week. However, to eliminate the twenty-four-hour stint, the company wanted the firemen who previously would have worked from 6 A.M. Sunday to 6 A.M. Monday to work from 6 A.M. to 4 P.M. on Sunday. Their counterparts, who had been on the night shift, instead of taking the whole day off and returning to work at 6 A.M. to begin work on the day shift, would work half of the night shift, from 4 P.M. to approximately 11 P.M. The firemen who had left work at 4 P.M. would then work from about 11 P.M. to 6 A.M., whereupon they would be replaced, and the workers would have exchanged shifts.[17]

The DL & W sought to make the new schedule palatable to the firemen by giving them a full shift's pay for each additional half shift. Consequently, the firemen would be paid for two more shifts every four weeks, thus increasing their pay by approximately 7 percent.[18] While firemen at most of the DL & W's collieries acquiesced in the plan, those at the Pettebone colliery near Wilkes-Barre rejected it, largely because they wanted to continue to stay at home on alternate Sundays. When they told their bosses that they preferred the old schedule, they were informed that if they wished to be exempted from the new schedule, they would have to file a written request. The firemen refused, perhaps because they feared that such a request might be interpreted as an endorsement of their old schedule, thus undermining the UMWA's effort to win an eight-hour day. When the bosses insisted that the twenty-four-hour shift must be eliminated, the firemen either walked off their jobs or were discharged on February 22, according to company and union reports respectively. Within several days, the firemen at the company's Woodward and Avondale collieries nearby also walked out, and the 2,500 other workers at all three collieries joined them.[19] The executive board of District One announced its support for the strike and, according to the *UMW Journal*, other companies who had similar plans to eliminate the twenty-four-hour stint did not implement them for fear of walkouts at their mines. The *Journal* noted further that the union's staunch support for the firemen would enable the UMWA to organize them more completely.[20]

On February 13, John Mitchell and the presidents of the anthracite districts notified Eben B. Thomas of the Erie that, since "the verbal contract" between Thomas, "representing the coal operators, and the committee representing the anthracite mine workers" would expire shortly, they wanted to arrange a joint conference with the operators for March 12.[21] In his reply, Thomas denied that, in his meeting with Mitchell in March 1901, he had represented any coal interests other than those controlled by the Erie. In any event, he believed that the UMWA did not deserve recognition, since labor relations had become considerably more contentious during the past year. He added that numerous work stoppages had caused a sizable decline in productivity, and that there had been "an apparent disposition on the part of the younger element to keep the whole territory in a condition of unrest." Moreover, Thomas could not envision negotiating a truly comprehensive agreement with the UMWA under any circumstances. He believed that it would be impossible "to bring about a condition approaching uniformity" throughout the anthracite industry; thus "any agreement would necessarily have to be of the broadest and most indefinite character on account of the varying conditions." Of course, this was precisely the opposite of the specific, detailed agreement that the UMWA desired. Even so, Thomas could foresee nothing but "endless strife, ill feeling, and petty strikes" arising from "the interpretation of . . . a general agreement." He suggested that negotiations would pose "an entirely different question" if the UMWA were composed entirely of English-speaking adults." However, in an industry in which the work force included "over twenty different nationalities" and one in which "approximately 20 percent" of the workers were "boys and youths under twenty-one," Thomas did not believe that the union could exercise sufficient control over its members to be a party to any useful agreement.[22]

Mitchell and the presidents of the anthracite districts issued a call for delegates to convene in Shamokin in the Schuylkill field on March 18. Several days before the delegates gathered, the operators posted notices extending existing wage arrangements for another year.[23] Consequently, the delegates were in a truculent mood when the convention opened, and they agreed to resolutions that sanctioned strikes at all mines of the DL & W in support of the strikers at Pettebone, Woodward, and Avondale. They also sanctioned a walkout against the Delaware and Hudson (D & H), if that company refused to rescind a new work rule that miners there found particularly obnoxious.[24] On the question of a possible industrywide walkout, Thomas Nicholls introduced a militant resolution that called for the convention to send its demands to each company. If the companies did not implement them by April 1, a strike would commence. Even if negotiations were pending, work would be suspended to await the outcome. President Mitchell would have authority to negotiate for a joint conference or to consider any proposal presented by the operators. However, he would have to submit any prospective settlement to a convention for ratification. Finally, the mine workers would accept arbitration if the operators did so.[25]

John Fahy offered a more moderate resolution. It referred to the mine workers' ''keen disappointment'' over the operators' refusal to meet with the union in joint conference and blamed the operators for ''shattering'' the workers' hopes for a ''harmonious relationship'' with their employers. Still, regardless of this disappointment, the union would continue to follow its ''well-defined policy of absolute fairness and self-sacrifice,'' which had earned for the UMWA ''the approbation and respect of the great American public.'' According to this resolution, Mitchell, the officers of the anthracite districts, and the members of the national executive board would continue to try to arrange a joint conference and employ the ''kind offices of the Civic Federation, and of all good and public-spirited citizens to this end.'' If the union officials failed in their quest for a joint conference and could not negotiate a settlement in any other way, they were authorized to decide upon a strike or other course of action without calling a convention.[26]

Mitchell charted a middle course between the two resolutions. Noting that the UMWA had reached ''the supreme crisis'' in anthracite, he criticized Nicholls's resolution for limiting his and the union's options. He told the delegates that if he was to lead them in a strike, he did not want someone else to ''name the terms, name the field, name the day and name the hour of the fight.'' Almost chiding the delegates, he reminded them that he had ''directed enough fights'' so that he knew ''a little more about them than everybody else.'' Still, Mitchell objected to Fahy's resolution because it so closely resembled the course the union pursued in March 1901. Mitchell assured the delegates that the union would not have accepted that settlement ''had it not been for the promises held out and the hope given'' that the operators agree to a joint conference in 1902.[27]

Mitchell warned the delegates: ''If you do strike you will strike a long time; . . . you will have to win.'' He asked them to consider whether this was the best time to strike, and he offered the truly radical alternative of a nationwide walkout of mine workers, both bituminous and anthracite, at an unspecified time in the future: "If you can go on and strengthen your organization until that day comes when the miners of the entire country will join hands and strike, from ocean to ocean for the complete emancipation of the coal miners; then, in my judgment is the proper time to strike." Finally, Mitchell referred to the dissension he had witnessed during the convention and reminded the delegates that unity was essential for success: "When the crisis comes you must not feel as you have been in this convention; talking of District One and District Seven and . . . District Nine; when that time comes there will be no district lines to divide you; you will have to be as you were a year and a half ago, fighting as one man."[28]

Mitchell recommended a final appeal for mediation by the Industrial Department of the NCF.[29] The convention adopted a resolution that provided for such an appeal and the selection of a committee to represent the union. If the NCF's mediation failed, the executive boards of the anthracite districts were authorized to order a strike on a date that seemed to them most conducive to success. However, to prevent the operators from amassing stockpiles of coal, if no strike had been declared by April 1, work at the mines would be restricted to only three days per week.[30]

After Mitchell contacted Mark Hanna, chairman of the Industrial Department, on March 24, a committee of the NCF then invited the operators to send representatives to meet with the mine workers' committee. Under pressure from J. P. Morgan's associate, George W. Perkins, Baer of the Philadelphia and Reading (P & R), Thomas of the Erie, Truesdale of the DL & W, and Robert M. Olyphant, president of the D & H, agreed to attend. At the meeting, the railroad executives demanded that all efforts to restrict production must cease. They maintained that while they had no intention of discriminating against members of the UMWA, union members must no longer refuse to work with nonunion men. Finally, they insisted that the UMWA abandon its primary goal—to negotiate a comprehensive agreement on an industrywide basis.

> By reason of the different conditions, varying not only with the districts but with the miners themselves, thus rendering absolutely impossible anything approaching uniform conditions, each mine must arrange either individually or through its committees with the superintendents or managers any questions affecting wages or grievances.[31]

The representatives of the UMWA countered these demands with their own, formulated at the Shamokin convention. For workers paid by the hour, day, or week, the UMWA sought a "minimum day wage scale" and an eight-hour day with no change in salary. Although the latter demand surely appealed to all company men, the engineers, pumpmen, firemen, and ashmen who worked twelve-hour days would obviously welcome it most. For contract miners, the UMWA called for an increase of 23 percent in the rates paid for mining where geological conditions made the weighing of coal impossible. Elsewhere, the union demanded that the miners' production be weighed in tons of 2,240 pounds, for which miners would receive a minimum of sixty cents per ton. Price differentials among the various veins would be retained. Finally, the UMWA called for union recognition and full-scale collective bargaining with the operators.[32]

Both parties agreed to confer once again in thirty days, during which the UMWA would neither order an industrywide strike nor restrict production to three days per week. In return, the operators promised to make no attempt to stockpile coal. On April 26, the NCF committee met again with the UMWA committee and the railroad executives. When that conference produced no progress, negotiations continued between two subcommittees—Baer, Thomas, and Truesdale for the operators and Mitchell, Nicholls, Duffy, and Fahy for the workers. Throughout two days of discussions, the UMWA leaders insisted upon some sort of concession, while the executives refused to budge and merely stated that they would welcome meetings of this kind periodically to discuss grievances.[33] At one point Mitchell and the anthracite presidents modified and simplified their demands, asking for (1) an advance of 10 percent, (2) a nine-hour day, and (3) the weighing of coal. The operators rejected the offer. During the negotiations, Mitchell and the district presidents stood firm, not only against the railroad executives, but also against George Perkins, who naively believed that the mere occurrence of a meeting should suffice to prevent a strike.[34] After the negotiations broke off, the NCF committee, with Mitchell's concurrence, asked the executives if they would agree to an increase of 5 percent. Once that offer had been rejected, Perkins suggested that Mitchell consider a settlement that would extend beyond the one-year period customary for UMWA agreements. Mitchell refused. On May 3, he summoned the executive boards of the anthracite districts to meet in Scranton on May 7 to decide whether or not to strike.[35]

Significantly, the members of the executive boards could not agree on a course of action. This not only shows division within the union hierarchy but, just as important, the existence of a democratic climate in which union leaders felt free to differ. Thirteen expressed opposition to a strike, eleven were in favor, and four were undecided. Several of those who advocated a walkout stated that they did so only because they could see no alternative, while others who opposed a strike stated that they personally favored striking but believed the workers to be opposed. After a proposal for arbitration wired to the railroad executives received no positive response, the executive board members called for a tri-district convention. They directed the union's members to suspend work on Monday, May 12, pending the decision of the convention.[36]

Production ceased throughout the anthracite fields as local unions selected delegates who met in Hazleton on May 14.[37] Mitchell and several other top leaders argued against a strike. George Hartlein, secretary of District Nine, maintained that those who favored a walkout seemed to want "to strike for the sake of striking" and had formulated no strategy for victory. In his view, the UMWA had taken greater strides forward than any other organization in a similar length of time and would risk little if it decided not to strike. He reminded the delegates: "You are not asked one-cent reduction, you are not asked to retrograde one step."[38] John Dempsey, secretary of District One, thought that the operators wanted to force a strike, and he wondered why the delegates should risk destroying the organization. He urged the convention to consider soberly the prospects for a successful strike.

> Let us realize, gentlemen, that if we call a strike now it will not be a short one. I hope you all realize that the operators are not going to humiliate themselves again by granting you an increase after a short period of idleness. If we strike now we strike until there is not a pound of coal in the United States they can get to burn; you will strike as long as they can stand it; and I dare say they can stand it better than any miner can stand it.[39]

In his remarks, John Mitchell emphasized that he wanted no delegates to violate their instructions. Nevertheless, he did not hesitate to express his views, which closely resembled those of Hartlein and Dempsey. He reviewed the history of the UMWA in the anthracite region, recounting the early rebuffs it had received from the operators, his meeting with E. B. Thomas in March 1901, and the recent negotiations. He asserted that the UMWA had grown steadily in the operators' esteem and that, in the latest talks, the operators had virtually agreed to recognize the union. He admitted that they had not done so openly, yet they had agreed to meet with worker committees to discuss any and all grievances. Mitchell noted that the operators no longer cared whether those committees were composed of men from their own mines or leading union officials. He warned the delegates that a strike would endanger all of these gains, that it would be "either a grand and mighty triumph" or would return the union to the precarious status it held before the strike of 1900. Although he had heard many say that their present condition was worse than before the strike, he begged to differ. He asked them to consider carefully whether or not they felt "a greater degree of security" than they had before that strike.[40]

A delegate named Llewellyn from District One believed that the time for moderation had long since passed. He told the convention:

> I believe our noble leader and all our officers have been as conservative as any labor leaders the world has ever seen. I claim that through their action

we have actually gone down on our knees to the operators. Shall we go on our knees again? No, we shall not lick their feet.[41]

Some leading district officials also favored a strike. Thomas Nicholls told the delegates that, while he could not assure them that the union would win a strike, he did believe that victory was possible.[42] Andrew E. Matti, vice-president of District Seven, displayed greater enthusiasm. He disagreed with those who believed that the UMWA lacked the resources needed for victory. He reminded the delegates that they had "fought before without ammunition." In his view, the gains the union had made since 1900 increased the likelihood of success.

If we do fight I want to fight standing up and not lying on my back. We have a better show for winning now than we did in 1900. I know I am better prepared to fight now than I was at that time. Then I knew nothing about the union, now I know at least a little bit about it.[43]

An unnamed delegate from District One stated that, in contrast to those who opposed a walkout, he believed that the UMWA would risk its survival if it failed to strike. He admonished his fellow delegates that "if they did not put up a fight," the "smashing up" of the Union could conceivably follow.[44] A delegate from District Nine named Clauser advocated a walkout and also hinted that the UMWA could lose credibility among the rank and file if it refused to strike. He asked the convention:

How can we face our locals if we decide to go on with the old prices until April 1st [1903]? When the last strike was called [there] was not a Union man in our place. Now they are in the Union. In the meeting that selected me as the delegate to this convention the members went wild. They were solidly in favor of striking for better conditions.[45]

John De Silva, a member of District Nine's executive board, examined the issue from a somewhat different perspective. He told the delegates that he was "perplexed," since both those opposed to a strike and those in favor of one maintained that the union's survival was in jeopardy if the convention failed to abide by their wishes. De Silva stated that the opposing parties' prophecies of doom troubled him more than the dilemma of whether or not to strike. He then related his experience as a soldier for the Union at Fredericksburg, where he was among the last group in that battle to attack Confederate positions. He and his fellows were forced to retreat, but they returned to fight many times thereafter. The lesson was quite clear:

When this organization can make up its mind that it will face the enemy, and if it gets whipped retreat, reorganize, and come up again, then we will have gained a victory greater than we have gained before. To be successful all that labor organizations need is to be able to stand defeat and come up and fight another day.[46]

In anthracite, the UMWA had not yet achieved the "victory" that De Silva envisioned, and its survival hung in the balance. As John Dempsey warned the delegates, a strike in 1902 would be far more difficult to win than the strike of 1900. By May 1902, the mine operators had marshaled their considerable resources and were fully prepared to do battle. No one realized this more than John Mitchell, who pointed out to the delegates that by striking they would jeopardize all that they had worked so hard to accomplish. By refusing to strike in the face of corporate intransigence, the UMWA could, for the time being, insure its survival and preserve its accomplishments. However, by ordering such a course of action, the delegates risked losing the respect of the rank and file, especially those who, because of their participation in local walkouts, had come to anticipate an industrywide strike just as eagerly as their bosses. Thus the delegates faced a truly harrowing choice— to risk the survival of the UMWA or to spurn the militant spirit which had brought the union to life.

By a vote of 461 1/3 to 349 2/3, or approximately 57 to 43 percent, the convention decided to make permanent the temporary suspension declared by the executive boards.[47] The closeness of the vote, the fact that it went against the advice of John Mitchell, and the openness of the discussion that preceded it all show the democratic character of the UMWA in the anthracite districts. In just a few years, the democratic yearnings of the mine workers had grown from occasional spontaneous protest to a variety of tactically sophisticated job actions. But those democratic yearnings found expression at another level through the instrumentality of the UMWA. Merely by serving as a haven for the disgruntled, the UMWA provided substantial support for protest, despite its leaders' earnest inveighing against unauthorized strikes. But mine workers not only took shelter in the union, many participated in it and could, on occasion, move it to express their will.

"I NEVER WAS SO DETERMINED IN MY LIFE"

The operators clearly expected the strike to be a long one. After negotiations with the UMWA committee had broken off, Baer wrote Thomas and Truesdale, addressing them as "Co-Partners in Patience."

> We are all satisfied that it is impracticable to increase the cost of mining coal. The question then is: Shall we stand squarely on a business proposition, and take whatever comes, or shall we commit voluntary suicide?
>
> I never was so determined in my life. I can afford to stand a strike, and the losses that will result therefrom; but I cannot afford, with my eyes open, voluntarily to bankrupt my Company by inviting losses that any man

charged with the responsibility of management would say were unnecessary and unwise.

What we need for the moment is courage. We all believe that the conclusions we have reached are the only conclusions that can be reached. It is not only the judgment of the Presidents, but there is not an officer in our employ that does not heartily concur in the soundness of the conclusions we have reached.

I write this earnestly, because I believe if we stand solid and firm, we will win.[48]

Nor was there much likelihood, as the strike got underway, of intervention from higher corporate powers, in particular, J. P. Morgan. The man who kept him posted, George Perkins, had little sympathy for the UMWA. Informing Morgan, who was in Venice at the time, that the strike had begun, Perkins referred to Mitchell as a "bituminous man" who "went into the anthracite field unbidden and attempted an organization which, as a matter of fact, he never has been able to perfect." These sentiments indicate how closely Perkins had been listening to the anthracite executives. Still, Perkins promised to keep Morgan informed, adding that if he and his associates saw "any indications of serious complications," they would "not hesitate to ask you to step in and suggest some way of compromise."[49]

Having declared the strike, the leaders of the UMWA moved vigorously to take the initiative. One week after the convention, the presidents and secretaries of the anthracite districts, along with John Mitchell, met to decide whether or not to order out on strike those workers whose labor was deemed essential to prevent the collieries from flooding. They agreed to permit these workers, who had been exempted from the original strike order, to remain at their jobs only if their employers granted them an eight-hour day at no change in pay, as demanded at the convention in Shamokin in March. While at least one of the smaller operators complied with the UMWA's demand, the large companies refused.[50] However, because of the bitterness that lingered from the union's effort to break the firemen's strike of July 1901, as well as the UMWA's failure to organize the firemen, pumpmen, and engineers effectively, many remained at work.[51] Still, by calling out these men, as the UMWA had not done during the strike of 1900, the union made it clear that it would not hesitate to take the militant steps a battle for survival might require.

As a lengthy strike became a more and more likely prospect, a variety of business and labor groups, as well as a number of newspapers, called on President Roosevelt to mediate the dispute. On June 8 Roosevelt directed Carroll D. Wright, Commissioner of Labor, to conduct an investigation. Wright interviewed leading executives of the various railroads as well as John Mitchell, and he also collected a number of documents submitted by both parties.

Wright completed his report within two weeks, but it was not made public until September.[52] Overall, Wright believed that he had never before encountered a strike that "presented so many varying conditions, conflicting views, and irritating complaints."[53]

In discussing the particular issues involved in the walkout, such as hours of work, the weighing of coal, the profitability of the companies, and the alleged indiscipline of the workers, Wright generally avoided expressing an opinion regarding the merits of either party's position. However, he did display considerable sensitivity concerning the suspicion that miners harbored toward many of the arcane arrangements by which their employers determined their earnings. After discussing grievances concerning topping and dockage, which lay behind the UMWA's demand that the miners' production be weighed, Wright noted that "all these things irritate." He added that, whether or not the miners' grievances could be proved, the perception of unfairness had a substantial impact upon the men.[54] Wright blamed poor management for engendering the mistrust that characterized the relationship between the contending parties.

> It is represented to me by reputable parties who have no interest in the mining business one way or the other that the chief difficulty lies in lack of organization. This is shown by the existence of many practices in the management of coal mines which appear to be unwise, unfair, and calculated to work hardship. There are many prosperous miners in the coal region, and of course there is also, as in every industry, great destitution. The whole problem is an extremely complex one, and involves many practices that have been built up through long years. The mine owners too often have regarded the average miner as unreasonable, and likely to be unruly when occasion offered. The miner has come to regard the average owner as greedy and ready to do anything which will take advantage of him.[55]

Wright offered suggestions for a settlement. He recommended first, that the UMWA cease interfering with nonunion workers, and second, that the anthracite workers form an organization separate from the UMWA.[56] Operators commonly had attributed much of their suspicion of the UMWA to the union's contractual relations with numerous bituminous operators, who were competing more and more extensively with their counterparts in anthracite.[57] Third, Wright agreed with the union that miners should be paid by the ton wherever possible, and he also suggested that the employers grant a nine-hour day for six months "as an experiment," to be continued thereafter unless productivity was "materially reduced." Finally, Wright also called for the establishment of a "joint committee on conciliation," to consist of representatives of the operators and the proposed organization of anthracite mine workers. The first duty of such a board would be to investigate, with the help of experts, "all conditions relative to mining anthracite coal." However, the purpose of such an investigation would not be to mandate a settlement, but to provide "verifiable information" that could serve as a basis for collective bargaining.[58]

While the operators shunned all efforts toward a settlement, John Mitchell drew attention to both the UMWA's willingness and the operators' refusal to accept arbitration. As he had in 1900, Mitchell cultivated the good will of the public by skillfully depicting the UMWA as a conservative, respectable labor organization whose demands were moderate and just.[59] However, in the midst of this effort, he was obliged to call a convention to consider whether or not all bituminous mine workers should strike in sympathy with their brethren in anthracite. UMWA districts in Michigan and West Virginia had begun their own strikes and joined with the three anthracite districts to petition for a special national convention, which opened in Indianapolis on July 17.[60]

Mitchell believed a sympathetic strike to be a disastrous step that would sully the union's public image and lose the support of Mark Hanna and the NCF. Furthermore, such a strike would openly repudiate one of the UMWA's primary justifications for collective bargaining—that it would bring stability to labor relations.[61] Mitchell opened the proceedings in Indianapolis by presenting a plan in which nonstriking UMWA members would remain on the job and contribute at least one dollar a week for the men of the anthracite districts, who to that point had received no assistance from the national union. In his speech to the delegates, Mitchell emphasized the impact the convention's actions would have on public opinion.

> If this convention . . . legislates judiciously, I feel confident that public sentiment will be so concentrated against the arrogant and unreasonable attitude of the anthracite coal operators that they will be forced to yield and to make a settlement . . . which will insure living wages and fair conditions of employment, that will render future strikes, with their attendant sufferings and losses, unnecessary.[62]

There was exceedingly little support expressed for a sympathetic strike at the convention, although it is unclear whether this should be attributed to Mitchell's leadership or to a genuine lack of enthusiasm for such a strike. John De Silva of District Nine stated that if the convention had been held several weeks earlier, most of the anthracite delegates would have come instructed to support a sympathetic strike. However, most delegates had been "authorized to carry out the recommendations of President John Mitchell" instead.[63] None of the bituminous delegates spoke in favor of a sympathetic strike, while only one anthracite delegate did so.[64] Other delegates from the anthracite districts claimed that they were unsure of the overall stance of their delegation and requested time to confer.[65] After they did so, John Dempsey of District One announced that the anthracite districts supported Mitchell's plan for relief.[66] Thomas Nicholls added that, while some newspapers had stated that he favored a nationwide walkout, he only wanted financial help.[67] Several bituminous delegates argued for an amendment to allow the other striking districts to share in the money to be raised by Mitchell's plan. However, Mitchell noted that the union had provided considerable aid to those districts and would continue to do so. The delegates voted down the amendment and adopted his plan.[68]

The relief plan was a most extensive one, demonstrating the substantial support that a national union like the UMWA could mobilize, even for a massive strike affecting hundreds of thousands. The plan was crafted to show the anthracite workers that they were not the only ones willing to make sacrifices. To get as much money as soon as possible, the national treasury committed $50,000 to the strikers and requested all districts, subdistricts and local unions to donate from whatever surplus they might have. Workers were assessed either 10 percent of their gross earnings or one dollar per week. To demonstrate the support of union officials to the public as well as the strikers, UMWA officers and organizers were assessed 25 percent of their salary. In addition, plans for a nationwide fundraising campaign were formulated. The first relief funds were issued on July 23.[69]

The strike showed no signs of weakening. During its first two months, coal was produced only at the washeries, highly mechanized operations that salvaged small sizes of coal from the massive refuse banks that had accumulated over many years.[70] Efforts in August and September to reopen mines met with little success, as very few workers returned to their jobs and those who did encountered intense and occasionally violent opposition from other members of the community.[71] While many recent immigrants from eastern and southern Europe left the region to find work elsewhere, those who remained displayed a particularly spirited solidarity. In Shenandoah on July 30, a mob composed primarily of Polish and Lithuanian immigrants attacked a deputy sheriff while he escorted three machinists returning from their work at the P & R's Shenandoah colliery. In the ensuing fracas, the deputy's brother was beaten to death when he tried to come to his brother's aid. Several other officers incurred injuries when they attempted to restore order, and the crowd dispersed only when the sheriff of Schuylkill County arrived with reinforcements. Shortly thereafter, Governor William Stone dispatched 1,500 soldiers of the Pennsylvania National Guard to Shenandoah. One month later, state troops were also sent to the Panther Creek Valley, where workers generally supported this strike, in contrast to their stance in 1900. Overall, the presence of the National Guard had little impact on the walkout.[72]

During the remainder of the summer, Mitchell received several proposals from individuals connected either with the NCF or with J. P. Morgan. According to these plans, the mine workers would return to their jobs while Morgan arranged for an investigation of the industry, the conclusions of which he would persuade the operators to accept. Throughout these negotiations, Mitchell insisted that the mine workers receive some form of concession, either recognition of the union or at least a promise from the operators that they would accept the results of an investigation. In any event, these discussions were consistently overshadowed by the operators' staunch opposition to arbitration and their dogged resistance to pressure, whether from the press, politicians, or even Morgan's associates.[73]

In a letter he wrote early in September, Truesdale of the DL & W showed that, nearly four months into the walkout, the operators' stance had not changed.

> The vital question in this strike, from the operators' standpoint, is whether they shall resume the control and operation of their properties which they, as owners are entitled to and which they in a manner lost, as a result of the strike in the fall of 1900—or whether the leaders of the United Mine Workers organization shall further extend their control over these great and valuable coal properties. The question of whether the miners and mine employees of the anthracite companies should get more pay, less hours' work, have their coal paid by weight instead of by car, etc. etc., were mere make-weights with the leaders to aid them in securing what they were really after. . . . The leaders in inducing the miners to strike, merely made use of them for their own selfish, individual ends. It is my firm belief that the operators will never yield . . . but will continue to the end on its present lines, no matter what time it may take or what it will cost.[74]

As the summer drew to a close, the operators' intransigence, coupled with the union's readiness to accept arbitration, generated considerable public support for the UMWA.[75] Nevertheless, the public's dislike for the operators' arrogance would have mattered little if the strike had not posed the threat of a severe coal shortage throughout the northeastern part of the nation for the upcoming winter. As Robert H. Wiebe has pointed out, there was little distress as late as mid-September, since many easterners had turned to bituminous coal to replace the anthracite they preferred.[76] However, toward the end of that month, bituminous prices jumped unexpectedly as railroads that ran from the bituminous fields to the Atlantic seaboard, pressed to supply freight cars for agricultural products, limited the number of cars available to carry bituminous while demand for it moved toward a peak.[77] Until that point, the high price of anthracite had not frightened most consumers, who apparently were willing to make the adjustments necessary to use the smokier fuel.[78] However, when the price of bituminous soared as well, the public did not hesitate to communicate its dismay to elected officials.[79]

Meanwhile, the operators redoubled their efforts to induce mine workers to abandon the strike, but to no avail. Circulars appeared in various languages with the obvious purpose of fomenting ethnic discord. One implored its readers:

> Who is going to take care of you? Who gives your friends and relatives good chambers? Are they your countrymen? No, all Irish. Do John Mitchell, Fahy, Duffy, and Nicholls work for you? No, for themselves and their own class, the Irish. They use you and your countrymen to win their battle. . . . Name the man (among your countrymen) who ever had a fat place in the "Union." Did you ever hear of such a man? No, that is not for you. A pocket full of money is better than strike benefit which is half stolen before you see it. The men who own the mines and pay you are better friends to you than those who lied to you and are still lying. Send a good friend to them and he will get a good place for you. Save your money. Don't pay dues to a union.[80]

Some companies preferred more discreet methods. On September 25, Thomas Nicholls issued a statement to the members of District One, warning them of the activities of one Michael Grimes, who had worked as a foreman for several companies. Nicholls accused Grimes of offering the sum of $4,300 to the officers of an unspecified local if they could persuade their members to adopt a resolution calling for an immediate return to work. According to Nicholls, Grimes assured the officers that they "would be taken care of" if exposed. He promised them "any position under the company that they were able to fill," but told them not to ask for the jobs until three months after the end of the strike.[81]

As public clamor over coal supplies grew, President Roosevelt became increasingly sensitive to the impact that fear of a coal famine might have upon Republican fortunes if it still gripped the voters during the midterm elections in November. On October 1 he invited John Mitchell and several representatives of the major operators to meet with him on October 3. In that conference, Roosevelt acknowledged that he had no legal justification for intervening, but nevertheless he requested that mining resume as soon as possible to prevent further distress to the public.[82] Mitchell then seized the initiative. He not only offered to meet with the coal company presidents; he also expressed the union's willingness to accept arbitration under the President's aegis, and he suggested that Roosevelt appoint a commission.[83] However, the operators' representatives showed no interest in Mitchell's proposals. George F. Baer of the P & R stated that if state authorities would only perform their duty and restore order, thousands of mine workers would flock back to their jobs.[84] Nevertheless, Baer did make one conciliatory offer. If the workers "at any particular colliery" could not settle "any alleged grievances" with their employer, these grievances could then "be referred to the Judges of the Court of Common Pleas of the district in which the colliery is situated for final determination."[85]

Representatives of the Erie, D & H, DL & W, and independent operators also offered little in the way of concessions.[86] William H. Truesdale took the UMWA to task for its baneful influence on youthful mine workers.

> One-sixth of the membership of this illegal organization is composed of young men and boys between the ages of fourteen and twenty. . . . These young men and boys during the past two years have had their young, immature minds poisoned with the most dangerous, anarchistic, distorted, wicked views and errors concerning the rights of citizenship and property that any one can possibly conceive of; all through the teachings of the United Mine Workers' Association.[87]

In sharp contrast, Mitchell carefully avoided adding to the acrimony that so pervaded the conference. Nonetheless, when the President asked him if he would agree to Baer's offer of piecemeal arbitration through local judges, Mitchell said he would not. When Roosevelt asked the operators' representatives if they could accept Mitchell's proposal for either collective bargaining or arbitration, they refused as well. The conference had apparently accomplished nothing.[88]

Still, the operators' unyielding posture did generate considerable public disfavor and increased pressure upon them to compromise. Several days after the conference, Roosevelt asked Mitchell if he would order the workers to return while the President formed a commission to investigate their grievances and worked to persuade the operators to accept the commission's findings. Mitchell rejected the offer. He wrote Roosevelt that the mine workers had "no reason" to believe that the operators would abide by the recommendations of any such commission. The operators made a slight move toward compromise. On October 8, Roosevelt received word that they would accept arbitration of disputed issues before a court higher than the Court of Common Pleas, which the President could select. This rather obscure proposal acknowledged that the President had a role to play in mediating the strike and showed some flexibility regarding arbitration.[89]

Meanwhile, the operators received requests to consider arbitration from elements of the business community not connected with the NCF, such as the National Association of Manufacturers and railroad magnate Edward H. Harriman. As Roosevelt contemplated the appointment of a commission to investigate the industry and the strike in greater depth than Carroll Wright had done in June, Elihu Root, Secretary of War, suggested a possible compromise to J. P. Morgan. On October 9, Root wrote Morgan and asked him to consider whether or not the operators might accept arbitration if the contending parties in the proceedings were the employers and their employees, rather than the employers and the UMWA. This would allow the operators to avoid extending any semblance of official recognition to the UMWA. Morgan invited Root to meet with him two days later, and at that time they agreed to a plan which Morgan then referred to the operators for approval. However, the operators insisted that the panel to be appointed by the President consist of individuals with particular qualifications.[90] The operators' proposal, released to the public on October 13, called for five commissioners: a military engineer, a judge of the federal court for the eastern district of Pennsylvania, a mining engineer not connected with the coal business, a veteran of the anthracite industry in both its "physical and commercial features," and a "man of prominence, eminent as a sociologist."[91]

When the President relayed this offer to Mitchell, the UMWA's president expressed misgivings about the proposed makeup of the commission. Roosevelt gained Mitchell's approval by promising to expand the panel by adding a representative of organized labor and a prominent Catholic clergyman. When the operators balked at the appointment of a representative from labor, Roosevelt named such a man as the "sociologist" without consulting the operators. They had little choice but to accept these changes, and on October 16 the executive boards of the three anthracite districts met with Mitchell and called for a convention to meet in Wilkes-Barre on October 20. They recommended that the delegates accept the jurisdiction of the commission and return to work. Although several delegates expressed fear that the operators might not allow all strikers, in particular the pumpmen, engineers, and firemen, to return to their jobs, the convention gave the commission its unanimous endorsement and ordered an end to the strike.[92]

After more than five months of idleness, the mine workers had won the right to submit their grievances to a reasonably impartial tribunal. John Mitchell undoubtedly deserves much of the credit he has received from historians for skillfully conducting the strike. As a result of his careful cultivation of public opinion, groups who surely harbored suspicions toward labor organizations in general—business and political leaders as well as large segments of the public—could nevertheless sympathize with and support the UMWA in this strike.[93] Just as significant, Mitchell and the UMWA retained the strikers' trust. The union collected more than two million dollars in aid and apparently received few complaints over its distribution efforts. Mitchell took special care to make sure that recent immigrant groups were treated fairly in the process. While even that massive sum provided only a limited amount of help for needy strikers, it gave them tangible evidence of sympathy and support from their own union and other workers across the nation and even overseas.[94]

Yet, the skillful management of the strike by Mitchell and his lieutenants would still have accomplished nothing if the vast majority of the mine workers had not believed in the cause sufficiently to maintain the strike faithfully in their own communities. They not only stayed away from work, but many also engaged in acts of intimidation toward those who continued to work. Still, they did so with enough subtlety and selectivity to maintain the strike's effectiveness without sacrificing the UMWA's respectability.[95] Their solidarity was not primarily the result of skillful leadership, but of their identification of the union's cause with their own interests. At least a sizable minority of the anthracite mine workers had done so before 1902, which was only the culmination of several years of local agitation and organizing directed toward bringing about a new regime in the workplace. The numerous hardships and irritations endured by mine workers had prompted them not only to join the union, but also to undertake local strikes at mines across the anthracite region. Their recollection of their grievances and of the collective action they had already taken provided a powerful incentive for mine workers to remain loyal during the strike of 1902. The workers' struggle for a fairer workplace and the operators' insistence on their own standards had long constituted the essence of the anthracite industry's conflict-ridden industrial relations climate. The numerous issues spawned by these very different concepts of fairness would be described and disputed in exhaustive detail before the Anthracite Coal Strike Commission.

7

The Anthracite Coal Strike Commission

The three-and-a-half months of hearings held by the Anthracite Coal Strike Commission depict the work regime in great detail. Testimony before the Commission displayed the variety of work rules that operators had formulated in an ad hoc response to such diverse concerns as local geological conditions, consumer demand, and the difficulty of monitoring workers' activities underground. With the rise of the United Mine Workers of America (UMWA), more and more mine workers had come to believe that some work rules constituted little more than a thinly veiled attempt to cheat them, while they viewed other rules and procedures as simply inhumane. Overall, most employees viewed the regime under which they labored with suspicion and distrust, inasmuch as they believed that the rules that governed their labor consistently worked to their disadvantage. In contrast, operators defended the work regime doggedly, ostensibly because they saw their work rules as fair, but, more importantly, because they were determined not to surrender the authority they had traditionally wielded.

In their testimony, mine workers and their bosses presented a great many examples of the day-to-day struggle over authority in the workplace. Because of the relative freedom from close supervision that mine workers enjoyed, that struggle was fought over a wide variety of issues, such as hours of work, the extent of dockage and its accuracy, variations in the rates paid for certain work and in the size of coal cars, and of course, the demeanor shown by bosses while exercising authority. Workers viewed these issues in the context of their own experience of how various rules had been applied in particular instances. Not surprisingly, they displayed considerable sensitivity toward abuses that had occurred. In contrast, bosses paid little attention to individual cases and focused instead upon their primary concern—the continued profitability of mining operations. They sought to place work rules and procedures within the context of the pressures that operators faced from their competitors and the consumer. They tried to justify their authority by appealing to such broader concerns and thus, in essence, dismissed the experience of the individual worker as irrelevant.

If workers had acquiesced in such an approach to their work, they would have abandoned their right to exercise some semblance of control over a fundamental part of their lives. Through protest, workers asserted the validity of their experience and challenged their bosses' attempt to subsume that experience within the supposedly larger realities of supply and demand. Determined to achieve greater security in the workplace, anthracite mine workers, with the indispensable assistance of the UMWA, had arrived at a consensus in opposition to the prevailing distribution of authority.

The hearings, which began on October 27, revolved around the demands of the "union mine workers," presented by John Mitchell, who appeared as the "Representative of the Anthracite Mine Workers," not as president of the UMWA.[1] In these demands, which closely resembled those approved at the convention of the anthracite districts in March in Shamokin, the union called for the weighing of coal wherever feasible and a minimum rate of sixty cents per ton for tons of 2,240 pounds, with differentials between mines to be retained. Also, contract miners would receive an increase of 20 percent in their rates. For those paid a set wage by the day, hour, or week, hours were to be reduced by 20 percent with no reduction in pay. Finally, the union called for an agreement between the UMWA and the operators encompassing not only "conditions of employment" but also "satisfactory methods for the adjustment of grievances."[2]

"MINERS, AS A CLASS . . . ARE SUSPICIOUS"

Testimony from labor and from management regarding the demand for the weighing of coal displayed fully the dynamics of the workplace in anthracite and the nature of the work regime. Where miners were paid by the car, walkouts had often occurred over dockage that miners thought unfair and over disputes about the actual volume of the coal cars they were expected to fill. However, the UMWA demanded the weighing of coal "wherever practicable," because in many mines in the Lehigh and Schuylkill fields, coal veins were inclined substantially from the horizontal, and consequently refuse and coal could not be effectively separated in the chambers. Miners who worked such veins were paid a certain sum for each yard they advanced their chambers.[3] The union also called specifically for coal to be weighed in tons of 2,240 pounds. Some 30 percent of the coal in the Wyoming field was weighed, but miners in those cases were paid by the "mine ton" or "miner's ton," which in 1902 generally stood at more than 3,000 pounds, so that the companies could compensate themselves for the refuse yielded in the mining and preparation of anthracite.[4]

Miners were paid by the car for nearly three-quarters of the coal mined in the Wyoming field, where over half of the anthracite was produced. In the Lehigh and Schuylkill fields, approximately one-quarter of the coal was paid for by the car.[5] This standard of payment had engendered considerable

FIGURE 7.1
At the bottom of the shaft, circa 1900
(Courtesy of Hugh Moore Historical Park and Museums)

mistrust among the miners. At the Shamokin convention, the scale committee had charged that mine cars throughout the anthracite fields, "as though made of live oak," had grown in capacity, and that many miners had been loading more and more coal for the same price per car.[6] While such an accusation was by no means easy to prove, the miners' suspicions were surely heightened by the many different sizes of cars that operators used. To facilitate production, operators generally used the largest cars that the layout of the mine and height of seams of coal would permit.[7] At some mines, cars of particular sizes might be segregated for use only in certain portions of the workings, while in other mines cars of various sizes might circulate indiscriminately. Moreover, cars often needed repairs or would have to be replaced, further complicating a situation in which an ostensibly invariable standard of measurement, the car, could vary considerably.

James Gallagher, a sixty-year-old miner who had worked for G. B. Markle and Company in the Lehigh field from the time that he arrived in the United States from Ireland in 1871, believed that many of that firm's cars had indeed grown. He explained to the Commission that the company's blacksmith, who repaired many cars, had often told the miners that the iron lining fitted to mine cars originally would no longer fit after the cars had been in use for sometime. Gradually, cars became from two to four inches wider. The company did not add to the rate per car for such subtle increases in volume, although Gallagher did admit that the company had paid more when it introduced a new car that was larger. Frank Ray, another miner for Markle, described one particular way in which the renovation of cars could add to their volume. Cars that had once been lined with wooden boards were relined with sheet iron, which was thinner and thereby increased the inside volume of the cars.[8]

Miners reported similar difficulties at the Delaware, Lackawanna, and Western's (DL & W) operations, where the company generally used mine cars of more than one size at each mine and paid the miners a single rate based in theory on an average of the various sizes. A committee at one of the company's collieries had examined the cars there and noted that iron-bottomed cars held eighty-six cubic feet of coal while wood-bottomed ones held only eighty-three cubic feet. Under pressure from the committee, the company agreed to increase its rate for all cars at that mine by one cent to $.99. David T. Davis, who worked at another DL & W colliery, testified that the superintendent there had informed him that the mine had seven different sizes of mine cars, ranging in volume from just over sixty-six cubic feet to seventy-and-one-half cubic feet. There the company paid $1.01 for each car of coal, or slightly more than at the aforementioned colliery.[9] Whether or not this discrepancy, as well as many others like it, was actually justified by differences in mining conditions, one can readily understand why such situations might cause some miners to grumble.

R. A. Phillips, general superintendent for the DL & W, tried to explain to the Commission his company's policy regarding mine cars.[10] He insisted that the DL & W had no more than two sizes of cars at any single colliery. Concerning the dispute over the iron-bottomed and wood-bottomed cars, he noted that there was no particular pattern in their distribution to the miners, that a miner could get an iron-bottomed car one day but not the next. He had explained to the committee of miners that it would be impossible to differentiate between the wood-bottomed and iron-bottomed cars as they were being unloaded, and thus the company could not give a larger price to miners for loading the bigger car. Consequently, Phillips had suggested that the disparity in volume between the sizes be prorated among all of the cars. He maintained that the iron bottom was not installed in order to enlarge the car, but merely to facilitate emptying the cars at the breaker.[11]

The Commission compiled a list of car sizes from several of the leading operators. For a majority of the collieries listed, only one size of car was reported. Nonetheless, the list did reveal a number of situations that seemingly could justify the miners' lack of faith in payment by the car. For example, the Philadelphia and Reading's (P & R) Maple Hill colliery had only one size of car. However, twelve different rates were paid for this car, from $.75 to $1.25, supposedly according to the difficulty of mining conditions. Where a colliery used cars of several sizes, matters grew increasingly complex. At the P & R's Phoenix colliery, four different sizes were in use, ranging from seventy-four to ninety-four cubic feet in volume. Miners might receive any of five rates on each car, from $.70 to $1.05. Similarly, the Temple Iron Company's Mount Lookout colliery had four different sizes of cars and two rates for each, so for each ton of coal he mined, a miner might receive any of eight different rates.[12]

Merely calculating a rate per ton where payment was made by car was a complex task, since anthracite varies considerably in specific gravity, and the space occupied by various grades and sizes ranges from thirty-six and one-half to forty-three cubic feet per ton.[13] Significantly, however, witnesses for the operators took little note of this complicating factor, and their testimony showed that companies determined rates through an ad hoc process, rather than through any set of precise calculations. When developing a new vein, bosses would take into account rates for nearby veins, bargain with the miners over a likely rate, and later refine that bargain on the basis of the miners' earnings in that vein.[14] While this process may have seemed eminently fair to the operators, miners who received those rates per car long after they had been set could hardly be blamed for viewing them as arbitrary. Of course, discontent over particular rates was exacerbated by the different sizes of cars in use at many collieries as well as the uneven nature of repairs to cars. Indeed, it would have been difficult to persuade a miner who had been receiving quite a few of a colliery's bigger cars that the different sizes had been averaged fairly to yield the company's rate. One would encounter similar difficulty trying to convince a miner who had to load a car with a newly lined iron bottom or one enlarged by its sagging sides that the company took care to insure that it received no extra coal from the miner.[15]

Like payment by car, payment by the miner's ton was a most complex matter, and this complexity provided numerous opportunities for conflict between miner and operator. The scale committee at the Shamokin convention called for coal to be weighed "at the legal number of pounds per ton" so that companies would "not have the liberty . . . to increase the number of pounds per ton."[16] Still, at least in principle, the miner's ton did not merely constitute a blatant attempt to extract more coal from the miner. It was set at a figure calculated to include sufficient material to yield for the operator on the average 2,240 pounds of coal in the so-called prepared sizes, such as chestnut, egg, and larger sizes of coal on which operators generally could earn a profit.[17] The miner's ton, in effect at many collieries north of Scranton, had been instituted in the 1870s. Two employees of the Delaware and Hudson (D & H), P. H. McCormick and Thomas Malone, informed the Commission that, prior to 1877, at many of its mines, the company had paid according to each actual ton of material that miners sent to the surface. However, in that year, the company notified the miners that it would henceforward require a ton of coal in the profitable prepared sizes for each "ton" credited to the miner, and it began to pay miners for each miner's ton of approximately 3,000 pounds.[18] For several years before and after 1877, to insure that the company received as little of the unprofitable smaller sizes as possible, the D & H ordered its miners and laborers to sort through their coal before loading it, by using a rake with prongs three inches apart. Whatever pieces of coal could not be caught in the prongs of the rake were not to be loaded into the car.[19]

To convey to the miners the company's commitment to the principle of the miner's ton, or possibly to persuade them of its legitimacy, the D & H, as well as other operators, would periodically compare the total number of miner's tons for which the miners received credit to the number of tons of prepared sizes that the company shipped to market. The companies apparently did nothing in case of a shortfall, but if the marketed tons exceeded the miner's tons, each miner would receive a prorated portion of the surplus.[20] However, the operators did not hesitate to increase the miner's ton, particularly during the early years. Alexander Bryden, a superintendent for the Pennsylvania Coal Company (PCC), told the Commission that in 1870 the company wanted to substitute payment by the car for payment by the ton. When the miners objected, the company established a miner's ton of approximately 2,800 pounds. When that amount proved insufficient to yield a ton of prepared sizes, the company increased it in several steps until it exceeded 3,000 pounds. Yet, according to Bryden, the company paid for many more miner's tons than it received in tons of prepared coal.[21]

As of 1902, the three leading companies who paid many of their miners by the miner's ton were the D & H, the PCC, and the Hillside Coal and Iron Company (HCI). The D & H paid miners in its collieries south of Providence, near Scranton, by the car, and those to the north according to a miner's ton ranging from 3,080 to 3,192 pounds at different collieries.[22] Yet Charles C. Rose, the company's superintendent, informed the Commission that each miner's ton there yielded approximately 80 percent of 2,240 pounds of profitable sizes on the average. Rose stated that only by including smaller sizes, such as buckwheat and pea, which were sold at a loss, and birds-eye and rice, which were used for fuel around the mines, did the miner's ton yield more than 2,240 pounds of coal.[23] All of the collieries of the PCC and the HCI, both controlled by the Erie Railroad, paid according to the miner's ton. W. A. May, general manager of both firms, pointed out that miners at each colliery, at least at some point, had agreed to the miner's ton. The terms of those agreements differed to some extent from one mine to another. At each of the PCC's collieries, the miner's ton equaled 3,024 pounds, but for the HCI's mines, it ranged from 3,000 to 3,248 pounds.[24] May stated that at two of his mines the company refunded any excess of tons of profitable sizes over the number of miner's tons to the miners on a pro rata basis. Interestingly, however, at the other collieries the amount of material actually yielded by the miner's ton did not enter into the bargain. According to May, the miners at the HCI's Forest City colliery, for example, had agreed in 1892 to a rate of $.74 for each 3,248 pounds they mined, after docking for impurities and regardless of the amount of prepared sizes yielded.[25]

The discussion before the Commission of the miner's ton revolved around the question of who should bear the burden or reap the benefit of changes in the workplace and in the industry. The operators emphasized that they currently gave miners credit for any size of coal they loaded, whereas in the 1870s they had only accepted the profitable prepared sizes.[26] The miners pointed out that advances in preparation and marketing had allowed the companies in recent years to reclaim and sell the smallest sizes, so those sizes did generate some revenue.[27] In addition, more and more miners had to mine veins that contained a larger proportion of impurities than those they had once mined.[28] Should these miners have to load more material so the company could receive its ton of prepared sizes from the miner's ton? As companies realized that the market for the largest sizes of anthracite, lump and grate, was declining, they crushed those sizes to produce more of popular sizes, such as stove and chestnut. In the process, however, the breaker also produced more of the unprofitable smaller sizes.[29] Should the miners have to sacrifice to compensate for the resulting decrease in profitable sizes per miner's ton? Even if, as the operators maintained, the miner's ton worked more to the miner's advantage than it had when instituted in the 1870s, the replacement at that time of the legal ton as a standard for payment by the miner's ton could only be viewed as yet another way to make miners mine more coal for no more money. Still, amidst all of the controversy over the miner's ton, one point is quite clear—miners had no more faith in that method of payment than in payment by the car.

Regardless of whether miners were paid by the car or the miner's ton, each car of coal they sent to the surface was examined by the docking boss, who could take a portion of a car or even an entire car from a miner if he thought it was not loaded properly or contained too much slate or dirt. One mine car after another would be moved in rapid succession to the edge of a chute at the top of the breaker, where its contents would be tipped into the chute, which was inclined at an angle of about twenty degrees.[30] The docking boss would stand near the chute, amidst billowing dust, and try to determine the amount of refuse in each car. In no way could the process be labeled objective. W. A. May told the Commission that the amount of dockage depended "entirely upon the judgment of the docking boss."[31] Although the miners at some collieries employed a check–docking boss to monitor the docking boss's judgment, most companies had successfully resisted this innovation.[32] To complicate matters further, standards for docking varied at different collieries, even ones operated by the same firm. Samuel D. Warriner, general superintendent of the Lehigh Valley Coal Company (LV), explained his company's practice to the Commission.

> In our operations, although the theory of the bargain is that the coal shall be clean, yet certain elements are allowed in certain veins. In one place we allow 300 pounds to the car and in other places we may allow up to 800 or 900 pounds, and for impurities below that . . . no dockage is made.[33]

Docking surely generated considerable discontent at one of G. B. Markle's collieries. Peter G. Gallagher, who worked there as a miner for five years before he was appointed as an organizer for the UMWA, explained the problem to the Commission. He testified that he had learned from his father and other veteran miners that, in arriving at the rate it paid for cars of coal, the company had assumed that eight of each forty-eight cubic feet of material sent to the surface would be refuse, with the remaining forty cubic feet equaling a ton. Docking persisted there, nevertheless. Gallagher made his point in response to questions from mine workers' counsel Daniel J. McCarthy.

Q. [McCarthy] From your experience in the mines of G. B. Markle and Company does the average car contain more dirt and refuse than eight feet to the ton?

A. [Gallagher] During my experience, and during my work with G. B. Markle and Company, in the average work which I worked at, there was nothing there other than bone, what they call bone coal, with about an inch to an inch and a half of slate on that. The vein average from eight to fourteen feet and when it struck a roll or a fall it runs up to forty feet thick.

Q. So it would be impossible to put in the cars eight feet of dirt and refuse to a ton?

A. It would be impossible if a man loaded it as he blasted it. A man could put that much slate in the car provided he would throw back what he would get and reserve it for one car; but taking the vein as a whole he could not put that much refuse and slate in a car. . . .

Q. Now, if you know, was not this arrangement that you have heard from the old miners made to allow eight feet to eliminate the question of docking entirely?

A. That was my understanding of it.[34]

Figures for dockage varied considerably for different operators. The Peoples Coal Company in Scranton docked its miners an average of 1.9 percent in the months prior to the strike of 1902.[35] Representatives of the Lehigh and Wilkes-Barre Coal Company (L & W-B) and William Connell and Company informed the Commission that dockage in 1901 at their collieries averaged 2.9 and 2.7 percent respectively.[36] W. A. May reported that dockage at the PCC equaled an average figure of 1.05 percent, while the HCI's figure was 3.5 percent.[37] Dockage differed from shaft to shaft, as well as from company to company, according to Anthony Sherman, who served as checkweighman at Clifford colliery, operated by the HCI. Coal from two shafts came to that breaker for processing, and Sherman kept track of how much each shaft's mines had been docked. During the three months preceding the strike of 1902, dockage averaged 9.2 percent at one shaft and 4.5 percent at the other. Furthermore, Sherman testified that dockage could vary by several percentage points form one month to another at the same shaft.[38]

Throughout the anthracite fields, operators maintained a more rigorous check on the cleanliness of the coal sent out of the mines through what the miners called "the courthouse." From time to time, before a car of coal was dumped into the breaker, it would be diverted so it could be carefully examined to determine the amount of refuse that it contained. The courthouse not only allowed the operator to monitor the accuracy of the docking process but also to prove to some miners that they were actually sending a sizable proportion of waste to the surface.[39] Nevertheless, miners displayed little faith in the courthouse. William Mates, a veteran miner for the L & W-B, told the

Commission that the courthouse had "neither judge nor jury nor justice." Mates pointed out that the employees who examined the cars weighed only the slate and other refuse they found in the car and not the coal. If the waste exceeded 400 pounds, the miner would be docked at least one-quarter of a car. This process did not fill Mates with confidence in his employers. "They don't dock you by weight, they dock you what they please."[40]

At some collieries a boss might call a miner out of the mine to separate the coal from the waste for one of his cars, apparently as some form of punishment for sending out dirty coal. John Farari, an immigrant miner for Coxe Brothers and Company who also served as vice-president of his UMWA local, recounted for the Commission his experience on a cold day in 1896.[41]

> I loaded the car and that coal is sent to the breaker, and in the breaker they won't take it, and [they] send it back to the slate bench. . . . Then they called me out of the mine, and I took my shovel and pick, me and my buddy (that was my brother) and we go to the slate bench . . . and take the coal off the car and pick in it, and put the big lumps of coal on the scale and dump on the other side and let it down on the bench. And after doing that, we take that coal again, the big lumps of coal and put them in the car and send it to the breaker and they dock me a quarter anyhow.[42]

Farari added that the miners there were no longer willing to leave the mines at management's call to sort through their cars.[43] However, assertive miners could take advantage of the courthouse to correct docking they thought to be unjust. Paul Dunleavy, a veteran miner for G. B. Markle and Company and treasurer of a UMWA local, told the Commission how he once responded to several days of heavy dockage. He complained to the foreman and demanded that any of his cars which were docked be sent over to the courthouse. Shortly thereafter, when he was docked again, he went to the courthouse to examine the coal and refuse that the workers there had unloaded and sorted.

> There was an eight-quart bucket full of what they call slate, and the man that did the examining or cleaning of the coal was there, and I said; "Do you call this slate?" He says: "Yes." I got hold of the biggest of those pieces and broke it on a stone, and there was probably one-eighth of an inch of a shell of rock, and the rest of it was clean coal. I said: "Do you call that slate?" He says: "It looked like slate to me. It goes for slate." The breaker boss was passing at the time, and I said to him: "Do you call this slate?" . . . He says: "No, Paul, I do not." I says: "I want to show you much slate is in this coal." So the breaker boss stopped there with us, me and the other man, and examined it, and picked it out, and over one-half of what I had was thrown to one side for coal with the breaker boss watching us. I can take a solemn oath that I could carry what rock was left for slate, to my home, a distance of a quarter of a mile.[44]

Since differentiating between coal and slate apparently was no simple task, the miners' lack of confidence in the docking process should come as no surprise. Yet, for many miners this lack of confidence had developed into a profound distrust, based upon a suspicion that the amount docked by the company had little or no relationship to the amount of refuse actually in a car. The testimony of Edward Ridgway, docking boss at the Temple Iron Company's Mount Lookout colliery until he was fired for his refusal to replace pumpmen and firemen during the 1902 strike, provided evidence of that suspicion. According to Ridgway, when he was hired as docking boss in 1893, his foreman ordered him to dock a certain percentage over the course of each month, regardless of the contents of the mine cars.[45] W. H. Dettrey, a veteran miner at Coxe Brothers and Company's Derringer colliery, where he served as president of the UMWA local, told the Commission of a similar episode which occurred early in 1900.

> I had trouble with the docking, like many more of the men. I went to the outside foreman, who is the overseer of the dock boss, and made a complaint to him time and time again . . . and he replied in this way. "We cannot help it. We have a certain percentage marked up in the breaker, and we have got to make that at the end of the week. I says "Do you mean to tell me you have got to make it out of the men?" He said: "We have got to make it."[46]

Representatives for the companies denied that they docked according to any standard other than the amount of refuse in the car.[47] Furthermore, some superintendents told of having seen miners deliberately loading refuse into their cars after breaking it into pieces so the docking boss would be unable to detect it. Alexander Bryden of the PCC stated that he had witnessed miners pulverizing slate and rock with a sledgehammer so that it would not be noticed as the car was dumped into the breaker.[48] W. G. Thomas of the Black Diamond Coal Company in Carbondale also told the Commission of his company's difficulties.

> We have a streak of impurity in the coal that will go anywhere from six inches to eighteen inches in thickness. If that is taken out and left in the mines without being broken up we can get along very nicely. But we go in the mines and find men breaking it up. Now those are the things we have to contend with when we pay by weight.[49]

Evidently, the operators and their managers had no more trust of the miners than the miners had of them. Consider the following exchange between W. A. May and Clarence Darrow, one of the mine workers' counsel, during Darrow's cross-examination concerning docking:

> Q. [Darrow] Is not that your experience, that men are more or less suspicious of your docking boss, and is not that one of the reasons why they

asked for a check–docking boss? In other words, would they ask for a check–docking boss if they thought your docking was always fair?

A. [May] I think that can fairly be answered yes, because the miners, as a class, I think are suspicious.[50]

Of course, May did not mention that docking essentially was institutionalized suspicion of the miner, and that the very nature of the process bred suspicion. The miner and his laborer had to mine and load coal without much light, so that often it would be no easy task to distinguish coal from refuse, both of which could be intermingled in a vein.[51] Consequently, even if he trusted the docking boss's judgment, the miner could justifiably claim that the refuse in his car resulted from the conditions he faced rather than from his own neglect. Furthermore, decisions on docking were made hundreds of feet above the miner, who had no opportunity to participate, unless he chose to confront the company at the courthouse, as did Paul Dunleavy. Still, as in Dunleavy's case, even at the courthouse the miner and the men examining the coal could differ over the quality of the material in the car. By defending the docking process and attributing the miners' objections to their suspicious natures, managers like May merely showed their insensitivity to their workers' concerns. Discontent and conflict would necessarily result wherever so integral a part of the work process engendered so many occasions for suspicion.

"I MAY STAY IN JUST AS LONG FOR ONE CAR AS FOR SIX"

The demands presented to the Commission on behalf of miners not only included the weighing of coal but also increases of 20 percent in contract rates. The data compiled by the Commission's staff on the earnings of miners offer few clear conclusions other than to demonstrate the extent to which miners' earnings varied. Tables 7.1[52] and 7.2[53] show the average annual and daily net earnings at each colliery of the LV and L & W-B for miners who worked throughout 1901. For both companies, more than $200 separated the mine with the lowest average annual earnings from the one with the highest. At the LV's Spring Brook colliery and the L & W-B's Stanton colliery, those miners who worked throughout the year averaged only $465.37 and $451.07, respectively. However, at the LV's Hazleton shaft miners averaged $667.27, and at the L & W-B's South Wilkes-Barre colliery, miners averaged $686.08. Tables 7.3[54] and 7.4[55] give a more detailed picture of miners' net earnings for each company. Interestingly, the earnings profiles for the companies are quite similar, with over 80 percent of each firm's miners falling between $400 and $800. For the LV, 19.1 percent earned from $400 to $500, 31.9 percent earned from $500 to $600, 22.1 percent earned from $600 to $700, and 10.1 percent earned from $700 to $800. For the L & W-B, 17.7 percent earned from $400 to $500, 31.2 percent earned from $500 to $600, 21.9 percent earned from $600 to $700, and 11.3 percent earned from $700 to $800. In each of these segments, the miners worked, on an average, more than 80 percent of the days on which the breaker started.

Many miners were not employed as steadily as the miners in tables 7.1 through 7.4. Earnings for such miners could well have fallen below $400 per year and thus approached the minimum budget standard for a family of five formulated in chapter 1. The figure for such a budget of approximately $320, when inflated approximately 4 percent to account for the increase in prices from 1890 to 1901,[56] becomes $332.80. Table 7.5 displays the net earnings for 1901 of all miners employed by the DL & W, regardless of their tenure.[57] A total of 31.9 percent did not work an average of 80 percent of the days on which the breaker started, and all of these workers earned less than $300. The 16.1 percent of the miners who earned under $200 worked 19 percent of the days the breaker started, an average of only fifty days altogether.

Still, the DL & W had a more stable work force than either the HCI or the P & R. At the former, from April 1, 1901, through March 31, 1902, as shown in table 7.6, 67.1 percent of the miners worked less than 80 percent of the days on which the breaker started, on the average.[58] Some three-fifths of these, or 51.4 percent of the total, earned less than $400 and worked less than 70 percent of the days that the breaker started. Table 7.7 shows the miners of the P & R to be an even more transient group.[59] From November 1, 1900 through October 31, 1901, some 72.6 percent of them worked, on an average, less than 80 percent of the days that the breaker started. Nearly 90 percent of these, or 65 percent of the total, earned less than $400. Some 48.9 percent of the P & R's miners worked an average of 11 percent of the days that the breaker started, that is, only twenty-eight days.

Clarence Darrow told the Commission that he had been informed that a colliery where earnings were low tended to have more "floaters" than did more remunerative mines.[60] Data presented by the P & R for the Indian Ridge colliery, which Darrow labeled as one where the miners' earnings were quite low, show the extent to which such floaters could dominate a colliery's work force. There only fifty-two of the 496 miners, or 10.5 percent, worked an average of at least 80 percent of the 252 days on which the breaker commenced operations. This group comprised the 3 percent of that colliery's miners who earned over $600 and the 7.5 percent who earned between $400 and $600. The remainder of the miners, 89.5 percent, earned under $400 at the colliery and worked less than 80 percent of the days on which the breaker started. Most significantly, some 78.2 percent of the miners at Indian Ridge earned under $200, and these men worked an average of only twenty-five days, or less than 10 percent of the days on which the breaker started.[61]

So, at least at some of the collieries, most miners tended not to spend much time at a particular colliery. The Commission's hearings tell us little

TABLE 7.1

Average Net Earnings of Contract Miners Who Worked Throughout 1901,
for Each of the Collieries of the Lehigh Valley Coal Company

Collieries	Miners	Days breaker started	Average days on which miners worked	Percent of breaker starts worked by miners	Average annual earnings	Average daily earnings	Percent of total miners reported
Hazleton Shaft	41	288	256	88.9	$667.27	$2.61	4.5
Hazleton No. 1	85	284	257	90.5	656.41	2.55	9.2
Packer No. 3	49	268	231	86.2	644.32	2.80	5.3
Exeter	77	276	252	91.3	595.74	2.36	8.3
Primrose	10	253	212	83.8	594.75	2.81	1.1
William A.	126	280	254	90.7	587.18	2.31	13.7
Dorrance	74	273	243	89.0	576.26	2.38	8.0
Packer No. 2	12	282	231	81.9	566.21	2.45	1.3
Packer No. 5	27	247	211	85.4	565.17	2.68	2.9
Heidelberg No. 2	33	264	245	92.8	563.99	2.30	3.6
Seneca	87	290	239	82.4	546.87	2.29	9.4
Franklin	52	222	193	86.9	536.10	2.78	5.6
Heidelberg No. 1	30	266	236	88.7	527.86	2.24	3.3
Henry	46	268	239	89.2	522.38	2.19	5.0
Centralia	53	236	211	89.4	522.34	2.48	5.7
Prospect	63	268	229	85.4	501.43	2.19	6.8
Spring Brook	58	230	194	84.3	465.37	2.40	6.3
Totals and Averages	923	264	236	89.4	568.17	2.41	100.0

TABLE 7.2
Average Net Earnings of Contract Miners Who Worked Throughout 1901, for Each of the Collieries of the Lehigh and Wilkes-Barre Coal Company

Collieries	Miners	Days breaker started	Average days on which miners worked	Percent of breaker starts worked by miners	Average annual earnings	Average daily earnings	Percent of total miners reported
South Wilkes-Barre	121	276	250	90.6	$686.08	$2.74	11.1
Lance	111	277	258	93.1	667.09	2.59	10.2
Maxwell	80	271	242	89.3	627.33	2.57	7.4
Reynolds	64	272	254	93.4	609.21	2.40	5.9
Nottingham	222	275	255	92.7	593.93	2.33	20.4
Audenried	78	268	237	88.4	577.58	2.43	7.2
Wanamie	81	263	234	89.0	574.33	2.46	7.4
Hollenbeck No. 2	116	244	234	95.9	564.27	2.41	10.7
Honey Brook	43	268	232	86.5	561.58	2.42	3.9
Sugar Notch	69	239	209	87.4	509.51	2.44	6.3
Stanton	103	190	185	97.4	451.07	2.44	9.5
Totals and Averages	1,088	258	238	92.2	589.05	2.47	100.0

TABLE 7.3

Average Net Earnings of Contract Miners Who Worked
for the Lehigh Valley Coal Company Throughout 1901

Classified annual earnings	Miners	Average days on which miners worked	Percent of breaker starts worked by miners	Percent of total miners reported	Average daily earnings
$1,000 or over	10	254	97	1.1	N/A
$900 or under $1,000	10	252	96	1.1	$3.77
$800 or under $900	33	258	98	3.6	3.29
$700 or under $800	93	250	95	10.1	3.00
$600 or under $700	204	249	95	22.1	2.61
$500 or under $600	295	238	91	31.9	2.31
$400 or under $500	176	221	84	19.1	2.04
$300 or under $400	76	206	78	8.2	1.70
$200 or under $300	16	185	70	1.7	1.35
Under $200	10	159	60	1.1	N/A
Totals and Averages	923	236	89	100.0	2.41

about that group, but it is unlikely that many of these men went from mine to mine in an optimistic, confident search for better opportunities and higher earnings. Tables 7.3 through 7.7 show that the smaller a portion of the year a miner worked at a colliery, the more likely he was to earn a lower amount per day. Probably only an extraordinary miner could count on garnering consistently high earnings while moving from place to place. Most of the so-called floaters could well have been marginal miners with less skill and experience than their more settled counterparts. According to Jacob P. Jones, paymaster for the P & R, the "Poles and Hungarians" in particular moved from colliery to colliery very frequently.[62] Such relatively recent immigrants, who tended to have little or no experience in mining,[63] may often have moved from mine to mine in response to short-term demand for increased production. While the total annual earnings of such transient miners must have generally exceeded the lowest figures recorded in the tables, it is difficult to believe that most of them could attain the level of earnings of those miners who remained at one colliery.

The Commission not only sought to determine the amount of money that miners earned; it also considered the extent to which miners exerted themselves in earning that money. At most companies, miners could quit work when they chose, and witnesses for the companies emphasized that very few miners worked a full ten-hour day or even the entire time that the breaker

TABLE 7.4
Average Net Earnings of Contract Miners Who Worked for
the Lehigh and Wilkes-Barre Coal Company Throughout 1901

Classified annual earnings	Miners	Average days on which miners worked	Percent of breaker starts worked by miners	Percent of total miners reported	Average daily earnings
$1,000 or over	9	273	106	0.8	N/A
$900 or under $1,000	28	263	102	2.6	$3.60
$800 or under $900	58	255	99	5.3	3.33
$700 or under $800	123	255	99	11.3	2.94
$600 or under $700	238	248	96	21.9	2.62
$500 or under $600	340	241	93	31.2	2.28
$400 or under $500	193	224	87	17.7	2.01
$300 or under $400	80	195	76	7.4	1.80
$200 or under $300	15	169	65	1.4	1.48
Under $200	4	169	65	.4	N/A
Totals and Averages	1,088	238	92	100.0	2.47

operated, generally seven to eight hours.[64] Charles C. Rose of the D & H told the Commission that, although he believed that a miner should remain at his job for at least eight hours a day, very few did so.[65] Alexander Bryden of the PCC stated that most of that company's miners were in the mines from six to seven hours a day, and that the average amount of time was closer to six hours than seven.[66]

R. A. Phillips of the DL & W informed the Commission that his company's miners generally entered the mines at 6:30 or 7 A.M. and would leave as early as 9 A.M. and as late as 3 P.M. He stated that the company had experienced considerable difficulty in trying to enforce a rule instituted several years previously that required all miners to stay in their chambers until at least noon. Phillips added that the miners, "particularly those in the good places," tended to leave work as soon as they could, often by 9 or 10 A.M. He complained that many were so anxious to go home that they neglected to keep their chambers in a safe condition. He added that quite frequently they failed to blast a sufficient amount of coal to enable their laborers to load the expected number of cars. Phillips also told the Commission of the DL & W's "peg system," in which the underground workers were checked in and out of the mines by means of a peg-board. Since this procedure had been instituted, the company had recorded the amount of time that miners spent in the mine, and according to Phillips they were there "about 60 percent of the breaker

TABLE 7.5
Average Net Earnings of Contract Miners Who Worked for the Delaware,
Lackawanna, and Western Railroad Company During 1901

Classified annual earnings	Miners	Average days on which miners worked	Percent of breaker starts worked by miners	Percent of total miners reported	Average daily earnings
$1,000 or over	56	251	96	1.6	N/A
$900 or under $1,000	44	257	98	1.3	$3.70
$800 or under $900	104	259	99	3.0	3.28
$700 or under $800	303	266	102	8.8	2.82
$600 or under $700	639	260	99	18.6	2.50
$500 or under $600	761	245	93	22.2	2.24
$400 or under $500	433	213	81	12.6	2.11
$300 or under $400	313	170	65	9.1	2.06
$200 or under $300	231	122	47	6.7	2.05
Under $200	554	50	19	16.1	N/A
Totals and Averages	3,438	200	76	100.0	2.36

time." As he explained, "If the breaker was working ten hours it would be six hours; if it worked eight hours it would be 4.8 hours, five hours it would be three hours and so on."[67]

William Allen, inside superintendent for several properties operated by the Scranton Coal Company, was not impressed by the working habits of either the laborers or miners he supervised. Concerning the former, he told the Commission that they did not work continuously, and that he had often seen laborers resting rather than separating refuse from the coal. He said that often they did nothing if they did not have a car to load. With regard to miners, he stated that, on the average, they spent six hours a day in the mines.[68] When asked if most miners worked "the entire time" while in the mine, he responded:

No, . . . that is when we speak of work as continuous work, they do not. They may sometimes sit down and talk with their laborers, or sit down and talk with their fellow miners, for half an hour. . . . Anyone familiar with the workings of mines will know that the miners and men will often congregate together and talk for ten or fifteen or twenty minutes or half an hour. They sit down there and have their lunch at nine or ten o'clock.[69]

Not surprisingly, the miners offered the Commission a very different view. Peter G. Gallagher testified that he worked an average of eight hours a day for G. B. Markle. While he admitted that on some days he worked fewer

TABLE 7.6

Average Net Earnings of Contract Miners Who Worked for the Hillside Coal
and Iron Company During the Year Ending March 31, 1902

Classified annual earnings	Miners	Average days on which miners worked	Percent of breaker starts worked by miners	Percent of total miners reported	Average daily earnings
$1,000 or over	24	210	83	2.4	N/A
$900 or under $1,000	8	225	89	.8	$4.22
$800 or under $900	20	215	85	2.0	3.95
$700 or under $800	36	216	85	3.5	3.47
$600 or under $700	109	226	89	10.8	2.87
$500 or under $600	136	215	85	13.4	2.56
$400 or under $500	159	191	75	15.7	2.36
$300 or under $400	117	161	64	11.6	2.17
$200 or under $300	95	106	42	9.4	2.36
Under $200	307	41	16	30.4	N/A
Totals and Averages	1,011	143	57	100.0	2.57

hours, he also stated that often he worked for as long as fourteen hours. He added that at times before the strike of 1900, he would be "staggering on the gangway, from working in bad air," and still his boss would threaten to discharge him if he left the mine before 6 or 7 P.M.[70] W. H. Dettrey told of the efforts of Coxe Brothers and Company to regulate their miners' time strictly. That firm required contract miners to report at 7 A.M. and remain on the job until 5 P.M. If a miner failed to do so, he could be suspended for at least one or two days.[71] While management maintained that this rule had been in effect for many years, Dettrey stated that the company had made some effort to enforce it only since the strike of 1900. He added that some bosses insisted that miners stay even if they did not receive mine cars.

> Men after entering the mines at seven in the morning have laid there until two o'clock without receiving a mine car. They laid there up to two o'clock on account of wreckage in that part of the mine. And if they attempted to go home before that time, they would be suspended that day or probably two or more in addition to that. If they laid there from dinner time until ten minutes to five, and then started to go home, and they met the mule driver three-quarters of a mile further, with a trip of cars going to their place, if they failed to go back that carried with it a suspension of three days.[72]

However, most miners could leave their chambers when they chose, and this was a major component of the relative independence they enjoyed when compared to most industrial workers.[73] Yet, the length of time that miners

TABLE 7.7
Average Net Earnings of Contract Miners Who Worked at Nine Selected
Collieries of the Philadelphia and Reading Coal and Iron Company
During the Year Ending October 31, 1901

Classified annual earnings	Miners	Average days on which miners worked	Percent of breaker starts worked by miners	Percent of total miners reported	Average daily earnings
$1,000 or over	24	266	102	1.3	N/A
$900 or under $1,000	32	254	97	1.7	$3.74
$800 or under $900	46	250	96	2.5	3.40
$700 or under $800	86	245	94	4.7	3.06
$600 or under $700	130	231	88	7.0	2.81
$500 or under $600	188	215	82	10.2	2.56
$400 or under $500	140	181	69	7.6	2.49
$300 or under $400	136	143	55	7.4	2.45
$200 or under $300	160	103	39	8.7	2.42
Under $200	901	28	11	48.9	N/A
Totals and Averages	1,843	111	42	100.0	2.75

worked depended less upon their desire for leisure than upon concrete elements in the work process. In the Wyoming field, where most veins were relatively flat, miners generally worked with laborers. A miner would leave his chamber once he had blasted what he believed to be a sufficient amount of coal to keep his laborer busy for the remainder of the day. Since the laborer would seldom work longer than a full ten-hour day, this arrangement allowed the miner to leave after working seven or eight hours, or even less.[74] Edward Roderick, mine inspector for the first anthracite district, which comprised collieries north and east of Scranton, told the Commission that he doubted that the miners in his district spent an average of five hours underground. He had seen miners leaving work as early as 8 A.M.[75] However, Henry McMillan, a superintendent for the PCC, testified that miners who loaded their own coal generally worked at least nine hours per day.[76]

In the Lehigh and Schuylkill fields, many veins pitched severely. In such veins, no laborer was needed to load coal, since the coal, once it was blasted, would run out of the chamber by gravity and would be loaded into cars at the gangway by other employees. Yet, since work in pitching veins required considerable experience and skill, two miners worked such veins together as partners or "butties." Because they could work simultaneously, they tended to work a longer day than miners in veins that did not pitch. William Stein, inspector for the sixth anthracite district, which comprised collieries in northern Schuylkill County, told the Commission that miners there left the mines between 2 P.M. and 6:30 P.M.[77]

Miners attributed their tendency to leave their chambers early to the inability of the companies to supply them with a sufficient number of mine cars. In the relatively flat veins where coal was loaded in the chambers, miners and laborers could accomplish little unless they received cars in which their product could be hauled away. Peter Ingoldsby, a longtime miner for the D & H, told the Commission that, although miners at the Grassy Island colliery were expected to mine six cars per day, they would seldom obtain more than three cars. He maintained that he was willing to work as late as 6 P.M. if he received enough cars, but he had often left work before noon after receiving just one or two cars, or sometimes none at all.[78] John F. Murray, a veteran miner for the LV, stated that he generally worked for eight or nine hours a day, and that he would seldom receive as many cars as he could load. As he explained:

> I may stay in just as long for one car as I would for six. That is the way in the mines. A man may go in in the morning and stay there until two or three o'clock and not get one car. There may be accidents along this road, or a break somewhere, and he will not get a thing for his day.[79]

William Atwell, a miner at the Hillside shaft of the HCI, testified that his foreman had told the miners that the company needed more cars there. Although they had heard for some time that the company had ordered them, none had arrived yet.[80] W. A. May, superintendent for the HCI, admitted that the company did not have a sufficient number of cars at that colliery.[81] Charles C. Rose, superintendent for the D & H, acknowledged that miners often complained about a shortage of cars and he admitted that his company had experienced problems in supplying its miners with cars. He told the Commission that the company had "so many difficulties to contend with in a mine" that it could not insure that miners would always receive as many cars as they wanted.[82]

"HE IS NOT SUPPOSED TO SLEEP"

The demands formulated by the UMWA on behalf of the miners called for wage increases and a change in the way in which wages were determined. In contrast, for those workers paid by the day, week, or month—the company men—the UMWA's demand made no mention of wages. Instead, the union called for a reduction in hours of 20 percent, a figure equal to the wage increase sought for contract miners.[83] Although this demand contemplated the substitution of the eight-hour day for the ten-hour day, few workers in anthracite worked ten hours a day on any consistent basis. The amount of time worked by most company men depended upon the length of time that the breaker operated. While most company men worked somewhat longer hours than the breaker, quite frequently the breaker was not in operation for eight hours, much less ten. Data compiled for the Commission from nine of the largest anthracite operators shows that in 1901 the breakers averaged more than eight hours of operation per day at only two firms. For four of the nine companies, breakers operated for less than eight hours on more than half of the days of operation.[84]

Although many of their employees already worked closer to eight hours each day rather than ten, the operators nevertheless resisted the eight-hour day. Samuel D. Warriner of the LV told the Commission that the eight-hour day would result in "decreased output not only per day, but also a decreased annual output, annual maximum output." He pointed out that, while the LV generally had sufficient demand during 1901 to justify operating its collieries for ten hours on most days, the breakers actually operated on the average approximately eight hours per day. The production of coal depended upon the coordination of a number of processes, some of which involved the operation of complex machinery. Hence, according to Warriner, there were "bound to be" problems each day. As he explained:

> If eight hours . . . were to be the maximum, the infinite number of delays in a colliery would result in their [the employees] being unable to work eight hours, and [the work day] would be reduced to six or seven hours per day on an average.[85]

Nevertheless, some of the most important workers in the anthracite industry consistently worked a ten-hour day and longer—the firemen, pumpmen, and engineers, whose positions had to be manned around the clock. Workers in these jobs either worked twelve-hour shifts or alternated between ten hours on the day shift, which for some tasks was extremely taxing, and a fourteen-hour night shift. Usually they would work eight shifts one week and six shifts the next, switching back and forth every two weeks from night to day and from day to night. Every other Sunday each of them would work a full twenty-four hours, not merely to exchange shifts, but also to enable his counterpart on the other shift to have a day off from work.[86] Counsel for the mine workers focused on these employees as the most poignant examples of exploited company men, while the attorneys for the operators refused to apologize for the regime under which these men worked.

William E. Markwick, a veteran of more than twenty years with the DL & W, was one of the hoisting engineers who joined the strike, and his testimony before the Commission shows why he did so. He portrayed his work as arduous and nerve-racking, especially so since he often had to work more than the usual fourteen shifts every two weeks, including twenty-four hour shifts on alternate Sundays. He stated that at times when the engineer on the other shift at his engine did not come to work, he had to work three, four, or even five consecutive shifts. During the hours that the breaker operated, he would have to hoist from ninety to one-hundred cars of coal per hour, in addition to letting mine workers down into the mine in the morning and bringing them up in the afternoon. Markwick told the Commission that operating the engine required considerable strength, and that most men would need to use both hands to pull the levers that controlled the carriage that brought men and materials to and from the surface.[87] Most important, this work necessitated that the engineer concentrate continually on the signals he received from inside the mine and on the feel of the load.

> The foot [of the shaft] bell would be on one side and the head [of the shaft] bell would be on the other, and you would have to go by the different sounds of those bells. . . . Now, your constant attention was there from morning to night, and you had to watch your weight as you started your load. You had one bell for a car of coal, and you had one bell if they sent a carriage up empty, and as soon as they would start, you would have to notice your load, whether the carriage was full or empty. And the next would be a load of men. In that way, our attention was there continuously. One second's inattention was liable to cause thousands of dollars worth of damage, if not sacrifice of life, because the engines would hoist a car from the bottom to the top in sixteen to eighteen seconds.[88]

Markwick's job was made all the more taxing because he had to stand while performing it. Also, he worked near steam pipes, which, while undoubtedly providing welcome warmth in winter, made his work area unbearably hot in summer. During cross-examination, when an attorney for the DL & W asked why he joined the strike, he not only said that he believed eight hours to be a sufficient length of time for an engineer to work each day; he also mentioned that the company had kept him on the far more strenuous day shift for eleven consecutive months. Apparently Markwick, who had been charged with destroying company property during the strike, had special reason to be militant.[89]

Jackson Aulsbach, a fireman for Coxe Brothers and Company, described his work to the Commission. He had to keep the fires burning properly, keep the boilers clean, and also clean the flues, of which there were approximately 140 in each boiler. In his work, he not only had to shovel a great deal of coal, he also had to break up the coal pile during the winter when it became covered with ice.[90] John E. Doyle, a fireman for some thirteen years, testified that he had to shovel more than fifteen tons of coal during a shift. He and another fireman had to tend fifteen boilers.[91] One coal operator, John C. Haddock, who was trying to sell his small company, informed the Commission that efforts to economize in feeding boilers had made the firemen's job more arduous. Where companies used a cheaper grade of coal to fire their boilers, more coal might have to be shoveled, and hence he believed that hours for firemen should be reduced.[92]

However, witnesses for the operators presented a very different picture of the amount of effort demanded from engineers and firemen. Thomas J. Williams, a district superintendent for the DL & W, stated that on the night shift an engineer had very little to do. He only had to check his machinery from time to time, lower the pumpman to his pumps and hoist him to the surface, and also lower various other workers down into the mine early in the morning before the day shift began. According to Williams, on the night shift an engineer could possibly sleep for five to six hours.[93] Not surprisingly, Clarence Darrow subjected Williams to a probing cross-examination.

> Q. [Darrow] Did you mean to tell the Commission that during the twelve hours in which an engineer is on duty that he can sleep a portion of the time?
> A. [Williams] He is not supposed to sleep. . . .
> Q. No. What would you do with a man if you were to stumble along and happen to find him asleep?
> A. Well, the first time I may notify him to keep awake.
> Q. Yes. You do not furnish folding beds, or any such arrangement as that . . . ?
> A. No.
> Q. Or even cots?
> A. No, sir.
> Q. Nor any bedding of any kind?
> A. No bedding of any kind.[94]

Still, attorneys for the DL & W pressed the point by calling Michael McHugh, a one-time engineer who later had become a fireman for the company, to testify. McHugh declared that engineers commonly slept four to six hours on the night shift, and he added that he had seen William Markwick asleep on the job. He also stated that, where two firemen worked together during the night shift, one could rest while the other attended to their work. Nevertheless, in cross-examination, Darrow forced McHugh to admit that firemen and engineers were supposed to stay awake, and that where an engineer or firemen had to monitor the engines that propelled ventilation fans, a disaster could occur if those engines malfunctioned during an unofficial rest period.[95]

Witnesses for the leading operators saw the engineers, firemen, and pumpmen as having the easiest and most secure jobs at the collieries. An outside foreman for the Temple Iron Company, who had once worked as an engineer, testified that his work on the night shift was so easy that one night he was able to sleep for ten hours.[96] McHugh of the DL & W told the Commission that he could not recall a fireman being discharged during the previous five or six years.[97] John Veith, mining superintendent for the P & R since 1878, stated that pumpmen had a particularly easy job, since they only had to oil their pumps periodically and make sure that they were operating properly. He added that many mine workers sought jobs as firemen because they hoped to become engineers and that many firemen did so. Furthermore, he pointed out that such jobs were "steady work, every day in the year."[98] John McGuire, a division superintendent for the same company, told the Commission that he knew of pumpmen who quit because they found their work "too lazy a job."[99]

The operators and the mine workers utilized fundamentally different standards to determine how intensely and for how long a period employers could rightfully expect their employees to labor. The mine workers seemed to evaluate their work according to their own commonsense standards, which consisted of such matters as the labor involved, the money earned, and the stress encountered. In evaluating particular jobs, the men who worked in them tended to apply their standards in absolute terms, deciding whether or not their hours were too long or their work was too hard on the basis of their experience. With regard to the eight-hour day, the self-evident symmetry of eight hours for work, eight hours for sleep, and eight hours for recreation had long appealed to workers.[100] Engineers and firemen who testified for the mine workers tried to convey their feeling that twelve hours at their labors were simply too many. In contrast, witnesses for the operators examined these jobs in relative terms—they seemed to demand less physical labor and they were in greater demand than other positions in and around the mines.

Similarly, miners viewed dockage, the miner's ton, and payment by the car as unfair in and of themselves, or, at the very least, open to considerable abuse. Meanwhile, the operators saw these traditional features of the work regime as merely convenient, time-tested methods useful in determining appropriate wages. They were far less concerned with the impact of these methods upon the individual miner than with the overall level of wages, which they believed must ultimately depend upon the profitability of mining. To the operators, all of the workers' concerns—justice at the workplace, steady employment, safety, and higher wages—were subject to profitability and its determinants, supply and demand.

Undoubtedly, mine workers wanted to earn more money. However, they were not market-conscious economic men who simply sought to reap as much as they could from their labor. In their testimony before the Anthracite Coal Strike Commission, they focused upon the injustices they encountered day after day in the workplace. As a result of their experience on the job, they had come to share standards of fairness that were continually violated by the work rules and procedures under which they labored. Those standards were not openly declared, but they were implicit in the UMWA's demands and in the workers' testimony. Throughout that testimony, the mine workers sought to persuade the Commission to recognize those standards and implement far-reaching reforms in the workplace.

THE COMMISSION DECIDES

After almost five months of deliberations, the Coal Strike Commission issued its award on March 21, 1903, to govern labor relations in the anthracite industry for three years until its expiration on March 31, 1906. In many respects the award was quite favorable to the mine workers. For the company men, the Commission showed that it had carefully considered the particular problems of a number of the various occupational groups. Some of them actually received more than the original demand for a 20 percent reduction in hours of labor with no cut in pay. The Commission singled out engineers who hoisted water, for example, to receive the same daily wage for an eight-hour day that they had received for their customary twelve hours. Firemen, who generally worked a twelve-hour shift as well, also obtained an eight-hour day at the same daily wage. Engineers other than those who hoisted water, as well as pumpmen, did not win any reduction in the hours they worked each day, but they did receive a 5 percent wage increase and a holiday every Sunday. All other company men obtained a reduction in the work day from ten hours to nine at their former rate of pay per day, which amounted to a 10 percent decrease in hours and an increase of 11 1/9 percent in the hourly rate.[101]

Similarly, contract miners received an increase of 10 percent on their rates, or one-half of what the union requested from the Commission.[102] In its report, the Commission estimated annual earnings for miners employed throughout the year at approximately $560 and noted that the average daily earnings of miners did "not compare unfavorably with that in other industries requiring substantially equal skill and training."[103] However, in justifying the increase, the Commission acknowledged the great variation in days worked from mine to mine and from year to year, the variation in mining conditions from one chamber to another, the increased cost of living since 1900 (9.8 percent), and finally, "the hazardous nature of the employment."[104]

The anthracite mine workers received little else from the Commission, which consistently refused to challenge the basic work practices of the industry. The miners did not win their demand for payment by weight for tons of 2,240 pounds wherever possible. But the Commission confirmed their right to remedies they had previously sought with some success—the check-weighman and the check–docking boss.[105] In its report, the Commission displayed its conservative bent by asserting that in altering "conditions of life and work which have been the outcome of years of experience and which affect large numbers of persons,'' great care must be taken "to avoid embarrassing the situation in the endeavor to amend it."[106] By commenting that "any measure of work performed, as a basis for payment, must in a certain sense be arbitrary,'' the Commission showed little understanding of the depth of the miners' suspicion of payment by the miner's ton and by the car. Instead, it chose to dwell on the hardships mine operators who paid by the car might face if they were ordered to pay by weight. To install scales, they would have to reconstruct their breakers, or perhaps place the scales at the foot of each shaft.[107] However, the Commission failed to consider that the cost of such changes might prove relatively small when balanced against the increased trust that could result.

The Commission gave little consideration to the other portion of the UMWA's demand for payment by weight—that 60 cents per ton be established as a minimum rate, with prevailing differentials among the mines to be maintained. According to the Commission:

> This demand could not have been made in full understanding of its practical effect, for coal is now mined at a cost varying from 19 to 59 cents a ton, the miner's earnings being up to the average level. Sixty cents per ton of 2,240 pounds as a minimum, and the maintenance of differentials now existing in the various mines on that basis, would result in many instances in an increase of 300 per cent over present cost, and would throw into confusion the whole matter of compensation and the business of mining.[108]

In its desire to avoid disrupting "the business of mining," the Commission may well have missed an opportunity to dispel some of the confusion that had always characterized "the whole matter of compensation." The various methods of payment and the staggering array of wage rates in the anthracite industry had long generated confusion and distrust, which led to a great many disputes. While the standard of sixty cents per ton may not have been carefully calculated, it did demonstrate the miners' desire for some sort of standard. By failing to mandate any standard whatsoever, the Commission showed considerably more sympathy for the concerns of the operators than for those of the workers.[109]

Many representatives of operators had accused the union of restricting production by limiting the number of cars miners could load. Witnesses and counsel for the UMWA responded that such action had been taken at those mines that were plagued by a shortage of cars. The union had limited some miners, especially those performing development work, which companies wanted to proceed as rapidly as possible. But it had done so only to make sure that the other miners received their fair share of cars.[110] In its award, the Commission sought to address this controversy in a most modest way by directing the operators to distribute cars "as uniformly and as equitably as possible," while enjoining the mine workers not to restrict anyone's production.[111] The Commission also moved to end the common practice of miner's laborers receiving their pay in saloons. Since many companies did not deduct the laborer's pay from the miner's, the workers had gone to their local saloons on payday to obtain change as well as refreshment. While the Commission did not see this as a particularly grievous problem, it nevertheless ordered that all companies arrange to make the deductions and pay the laborers.[112] Here the Commission could insist on equity without disturbing production unduly. Interestingly however, the Commission made no mention of extending the 10 percent increase to the miner's laborers, perhaps inadvertently, perhaps seeing them as employees of the miners rather than the companies. Assuming that the Commission had meant for the laborers to have the increase, the Board of Conciliation that the Commission established to rule on anthracite disputes moved quickly once it had been organized to insure that the laborers received the increase.[113]

Perhaps to encourage mine workers to believe that their interests coincided with those of the operators, the Commission exhumed the sliding scale, which had been abandoned in the Lehigh and Schuylkill fields as a result of the strike of 1900. Recognizing that the primary drawback of the old scale was that it set no floor beneath which wage rates would not continue to slide along with coal prices, even if they fell precipitously, the Commission formulated a scale that could only operate to the workers' advantage. Yet the scale was not intended to add substantially to workers' wages, but to enable workers to share in profits if the price of coal should become "abnormally high." When the average price paid for white ash coal at New York harbor rose above $4.50 per ton, mine workers' earnings would be advanced 1 percent for every increase of five cents. To carry out this part of its award, the Commission ordered each operator to file a statement of all rates paid for each occupation as of April 1, 1902, with the United States Commissioner of Labor. Of course, such data would not be used in any industrywide study directed toward the eventual standardization of rates. Rather, the Commission merely wanted to insure that its new sliding scale operated properly.[114]

The Commission did not mandate a collective bargaining contract between the operators and the union and would only order an end to discrimination "on account of membership or nonmembership in any labor organization."[115] Although it recognized the vital role played by the UMWA during the strike and endorsed labor organization and collective bargaining in principle, the Commission noted that the UMWA per se had no official standing before it. The agreement between J. P. Morgan and Elihu Root that had led to the establishment of the Commission had hinged on this point. What the Commission did give the UMWA was representation on the Board of

Conciliation that it established. That Board, the Commission's most significant innovation, would have three members representing mine workers and three representing operators. The Board would rule on disputes that workers and management at any mine or mines could not settle themselves, and no strike or lockout would occur while the Board considered a dispute. If the Board could not reach a decision, the matter would be referred to an umpire to be appointed by one of the federal judges of the third circuit, in practice George Gray, chairman of the Coal Strike Commission. Still, in establishing the Conciliation Board, the Commission scrupulously avoided any direct reference to the union or its anthracite districts, stating that each of the workers' representatives could be appointed by "an organization" in each of three districts which represented a majority of the mine workers.[116]

In establishing the Conciliation Board, the Anthracite Coal Strike Commission showed that it realized that it had not resolved most matters of dispute in the anthracite industry. It further realized that, in the controversies that would necessarily arise, the mine workers and, in fact if not in name, the UMWA must have a voice. It is not surprising that the Commission avoided thoroughgoing reform on the industry. Given the diverse backgrounds of the Commission's members and the complexity of the industry, the Commission's concern for the status quo is not difficult to understand. However, no group would ever again have the opportunity or the authority to enact the fundamental changes that might have alleviated the endemic conflict that had come to characterize the industry. Operators would view the Commission's failure to order changes as an endorsement of the workplace regime in anthracite. Workers would continue to challenge the inequities of that regime, but the Board of Conciliation would show little sympathy for that challenge. The leaders of the UMWA, both frustrated and strengthened by the quasi recognition the union received from the Commission, found they had little choice but to build upon what the union had won from the Commission, and try to ignore what it had not been able to win.

8

Twilight Bargaining: 1903–1906

When the award of the Anthracite Coal Strike Commission was made public on March 21, 1903, the press generally viewed the settlement as a victory for the mine workers and their union.[1] John Mitchell pronounced the award "on the whole, a decided victory for the miners," and Clarence Darrow called it "in every respect . . . a substantial victory for the men."[2] However, representatives of the coal companies found much to their liking in the award and the report that accompanied it. While George F. Baer of the Philadelphia and Reading (P & R) remained silent, an attorney who had represented another firm before the Commission, Francis I. Gowen, stated that he saw the Commission's decision as mainly a victory for the operators.[3] Privately, William H. Truesdale of the Delaware, Lackawanna, and Western (DL & W) went much further in a letter to his company's attorney, Everett Warren. He called the decision "a great and sweeping victory," which he believed would be "of lasting benefit" to the operators. The Commission's refusal to mandate recognition of the United Mine Workers of America (UMWA) pleased him especially. He saw the wage increase and reduction in hours as "no more than we all expected."[4]

Although each side could appreciate various aspects of the award, the actual implementation of the award appeared consistently to favor the operators. When constituted in June 1903, the Board of Conciliation included the three presidents of the UMWA's anthracite districts and three leading anthracite executives. In the Board, UMWA leaders saw a form of the recognition they had so fervently desired. Furthermore, they hoped to use the Board to pursue a variety of reforms that the workers had not obtained from the Commission. However, the umpire to whom most difficult cases were referred in the Board's first year, Carroll D. Wright, saw the Board's role as limited merely to interpreting the award, not mediating labor relations more broadly. His rulings enabled the operators to take advantage of the award to perpetuate the work regime.

At the same time, UMWA leaders faced the task of maintaining the union's strength without the crisis atmosphere of impending conflict or the check-off of union dues, which had long stabilized membership in the Central Competitive Field. In anthracite, they faced a workforce characterized by considerable turnover and increasingly populated by immigrants from eastern and southern Europe. In contrast to most unions, the UMWA had consistently succeeded in organizing such workers, both in the anthracite and bituminous fields.[5] However, in the wake of the triumphal strike of 1902, few of its leaders could have fully understood the very different, devilishly prosaic task before them. Belonging to the union in anthracite demanded from workers an especially strong level of commitment to trade unionism—voluntary dues payment. Signs of union weakness, the intensity of workers' struggle to make ends meet, and a human tendency toward apathy made it difficult for many of the intensely pragmatic mine workers to justify that commitment.[6] As memories of 1902 faded, more and more drifted away from the union. Confronting this response after a practically unbroken series of victories from the bituminous strike of 1897 through the anthracite and bituminous settlements of 1903, Mitchell and district leaders paternalistically excoriated those who would not maintain their membership as unappreciative of the union and unwilling to act in their own best interest.

Outside of anthracite, John Mitchell and the UMWA faced a variety of arguably more significant problems—a downturn in the bituminous industry, the disruption of the joint conference system in the Central Competitive Field, the failure of a series of strikes in areas that proved far harder to organize than anthracite, and a burgeoning national drive for the open shop. To complicate matters, in an era that was only beginning to come to grips with bureaucracy, both unionists and coal operators across the nation insisted on Mitchell's personal intercession in most matters of importance. Demands upon his time and energy were so overwhelming that they could only reinforce his tendency toward conservatism. He retained great stature among anthracite mine workers and brought tens of thousands back into the union in an organizing drive in 1905. However, in the long run, his stature may have led him to believe he could pay less attention to their interests. He clearly had no stomach for highly risky simultaneous strikes in 1906 in both the anthracite and bituminous fields.

Although many workers found the limitations of the award of the Coal Strike Commission annoying and disliked the decisions of the Board, the anthracite districts in 1906 accepted a three-year renewal of the status quo in a precedent-setting document signed by both operators' and workers' representatives, albeit without formal recognition of the union. Furthermore, the failure of the UMWA to extract any substantial gains from the operators through industrywide bargaining in 1906 concealed its considerable accomplishments since 1903 on the local level. Disputes over the many workplace issues left unresolved by the award presented numerous opportunities for the union to represent workers, just as similar disputes had offered the union the occasion to organize workers before 1902. As the Board of Conciliation proved itself ineffective in managing day-to-day labor relations, workers and managers too sought to avoid it for all but the most contentious controversies. To get striking workers back on the job as soon as possible, operators would at least talk with committees of union men and often with union leaders themselves, whether or not most of their employees belonged to the organization. In both local and industrywide bargaining, the UMWA stood in a kind of twilight status. It was by no means fully recognized as the voice of the workers, but managers increasingly acknowledged it as a force with whom they could deal.

THE LIMITATIONS OF CONCILIATION

Immediate reaction in the anthracite region to the award of the Coal Strike Commission was largely but not entirely positive. On the editorial page and in banner headlines, local newspapers proclaimed a great victory for workers. Union veteran John DeSilva of Mahanoy City labeled it "the greatest [victory] ever for organized labor."[7] Some dissatisfaction was noted with the compromise nature of the settlement, but the papers reported that it subsided quickly. William Dettrey, the recently elected president of District Seven, thought that the award would eliminate strikes and added that "the more the award . . . is studied, the better we like it." Some immigrant company men were reported to be disappointed by what they received—the nine-hour day at their previous daily rate. They had less interest in reduced hours than higher cash earnings.[8] The most significant discontent came from the Commission's failure to mandate payment by weight, an issue that had generated so many local strikes and would continue to do so. Thomas D. Nicholls of District One openly stated that he was "very disappointed." However, a mass meeting of mine workers in Wilkes-Barre on March 23 was reported to have shown satisfaction with the award once they were assured, in what proved to be a false hope, that the question of payment by weight could be brought before the Board of Conciliation.[9]

While noting that the award did not require that the operators negotiate a contract, the editor of the *UMW Journal* expressed confidence that, as a result of the award, "contractual relations . . . must naturally follow in a short time." Meanwhile, the workers should treat the award as if it were a contract.

> The *Journal* would urge with all its power that the mine workers honorably abide by the award in both spirit and letter. To carry out its decrees faithfully and keep inviolate its admonitions. To use tact, judgement, and fair play in all of their relations and do nothing by word or act which will discredit their noble officials or the work of their attorneys or the commission. Let the petty mine bosses and superintendents have a complete monopoly on faithless acts and breaches of contract. They have had it in the past and if there should be any such evil work the world will know where to place it.[10]

The union leaders' sanguine view of the award hinged on their confidence that the Conciliation Board would interpret the award and resolve disputes in a satisfactory manner. The men who ran the UMWA had long deplored unauthorized local strikes as violations of union discipline. With the advent of the Conciliation Board, they hoped to dissuade discontented workers from striking by assuring them that they would receive a fair hearing.

In the weeks following the announcement of the award, before the Board organized, numerous disputes arose concerning the award's implementation.[11] The most notable of these began on Saturday, April 18, in the Schuylkill field, when thousands of workers, obeying the instructions of their district leaders, refused to work a nine-hour day. Traditionally, companies in that region had required a maximum of only eight hours on Saturday but, armed with the Commission's award, they tried to institute nine hours as a day's work on Saturday, as well as during the rest of the week. The mine workers could not imagine that the Commission had intended to increase their hours in any way. In response, on Monday, April 20, several operators, in particular the P & R, closed down a number of their collieries, idling some 30,000 mine workers. The lockout ended several days later after John Mitchell and the presidents of the anthracite districts ordered the men to allow the Conciliation Board to settle the matter.[12]

Mitchell wanted to protect the public image of the UMWA and give the conciliation process a chance to work, but his patience and that of his men would be tested further by the operators. Initially their representatives to the Board refused to meet with the district presidents, who had been chosen to represent the workers on the Board at a joint meeting of the UMWA district executive boards in April.[13] The operators demanded that the mine workers select their representatives on a district-by-district basis.[14] Rumors of a possible strike spread as the union leaders called a tri-district convention, which opened on June 15. There, however, the delegates from each district, in joint and separate votes, elected the district presidents to serve on the Conciliation Board. They also agreed to submit their grievances to the Board.[15]

Once the Board organized, the district presidents displayed their disdain for local strikes, which continued to occur sporadically over a variety of issues.[16] When the Board met to formulate procedures, the district leaders agreed with the operators' representatives to refuse to consider any grievance as long as workers were on strike. They also agreed that the "organization representing the majority of the mine workers" would assume the responsibility of persuading striking workers to return to their jobs. Furthermore, in what would provide some formal sanction for a union role in local disputes, the Board decided that all grievances would first be presented to the mine foreman and then to the superintendent before being referred for Board action.[17]

Carroll D. Wright did not hand down his decision for a deadlocked Board of Conciliation on the dispute over hours of work on Saturday in the Schuylkill field until January 2, 1904. He refused to sustain the mine workers' grievance, basing his decision on an exceedingly literal interpretation of the award of the Coal Strike Commission. While this sort of approach would become the norm as labor arbitration developed in the twentieth century,[18] anthracite mine workers viewed it and similar rulings by Wright as ill-conceived. By focusing on the text of the Commission's award, Wright ruled that the Commission had *not* established a nine-hour day.[19] He ignored the accompanying narrative, which had included the statement "that a reduction of the hours of labor from ten to nine would be fair to both employee and employer."[20] While he noted that the nine-hour day had become standard since the award had been announced, Wright ruled that the award only required employers to pay company men as much for nine hours of work as they had previously paid for ten. Wright emphasized, however, that the mine workers and operators were free to come to their own agreement concerning hours. Despite the decision, both parties retained the nine-hour day.[21]

The P & R's decision to try to get more hours from its workers on Saturdays may have reflected the flintiness of George F. Baer, but at least one railroad president, William H. Truesdale of the DL & W, began to display a somewhat different attitude. While he had consistently been a staunch foe of the union, in the months after the award was issued he was careful not to offer the mine workers any offense and counseled his fellow executives along the same lines. Shortly after the award had been announced, he took issue with Baer's contention, also shared by several other operators, that the Commission intended its 10 percent increase for miners to apply to net rather than gross wages. He saw Baer's interpretation of the award as erroneous, and predicted danger in implementing that interpretation.

> I believe if this is done the miners will immediately appeal to Mitchell and his district presidents, and the latter will take it up and make a great fuss and blow about it, using it as an argument why those of the miners who are in arrears in their dues to the UMWA should pay up their delinquent dues and stick by their organization, as by so doing can they only hope and expect to get justice from the operators.[22]

The Board interpreted the award similarly when the controversy came before it.[23] While Truesdale's flexibility certainly preceded any shown by Baer, it raised the possibility that other corporate executives might eventually adopt such an approach.

Such flexibility did not come easily or often. Even when the mine workers received a favorable ruling from Wright, they might encounter resistance. The Commission had given miners the right to appoint checkweighmen and

FIGURE 8.1
Truesdale breaker, Delaware, Lackawanna, and Western Railroad (Courtesy of
Hugh Moore Historical Park and Museums—DL & W Collection).

check–docking bosses at any mine where a majority wanted them. Further,
the Commission had allowed the checkers' salaries to be paid with deductions
made by the companies from the miners' wages. A dispute arose with several
companies in the Wyoming field over whether or not the union could insist on
deductions from all miners at a colliery, including those who had not requested a checkweighman or check–docking boss. Company representatives
noted that the Board had ruled on July 9, 1903, that miners who wanted
checkweighmen and check–docking bosses should sign a legal release to allow deductions. Representatives of the mine workers pointed to a later decision by Wright on a somewhat different issue, in which he assumed that all
miners would face deductions where a majority called for a checkweighman
or check–docking boss. Several companies refused to make full deductions
as a result of that decision of April 8, 1904, and a clarification Wright issued
at the request of Thomas Nicholls did not change their minds.[24] At the annual convention of District One, which took place during the controversy,
Nicholls referred to other forms of employer harassment over this matter:

Company officials . . . placed every obstacle in [the miners'] way by making objections to the list of names [of those who wanted a checkweighman]. . . . Some lists were refused because they were written with lead pencil. Others, because miners who could not write had not placed their mark on the list.[25]

The convention authorized the district executive board to order strikes where companies remained intransigent. But Nicholls did not do so, and all members of the Conciliation Board agreed to call upon Judge George Gray to resolve the impasse. Several companies were persuaded to cease their resistance before he rendered his decision on September 24, 1904, in favor of deducting the checkers' wages from all miners without any legal release wherever a majority had requested.[26]

Still other sources of discord demanded resolution. Approximately one-fifth of the grievances filed in the Board's first three years concerned workers who had not been rehired in the aftermath of the strike but believed they were entitled to reemployment. The majority of these cases resulted in apparently acceptable arrangements for rehiring.[27] Nevertheless, in most cases on broader issues, Wright's strict adherence to the letter of the award caused growing disenchantment among mine workers. Wright upheld, in principle, the employer's right to discharge workers for any reason whatsoever, except for membership in the UMWA (such discrimination had been expressly prohibited by the Coal Strike Commission).[28] Furthermore, he generally saw little evidence of such discrimination, and instead called in several cases for employers to rehire workers simply because the Commission's award had called for the rehiring of strikers.[29] Union officials expressed their discontent, with the *UMW Journal* predicting that this ruling would "cause ceaseless and increasing friction."[30] When miners complained to the Board that operators, by altering work rules, had compelled them to do more work but had not increased mining rates, Wright held that the Board could do nothing as long as operators paid miners at a rate 10 percent higher than that paid before the strike of 1902.[31] Similarly, Wright refused to sustain a grievance presented by runners at the Delaware and Hudson's (D & H) mines in and around Plymouth, who complained that, although the company classified almost all runners as third-class runners, third-class and first-class runners generally performed the same work. Although Wright noted that matching classifications to the work done "must be considered a matter of justice," still the company had not violated the award by failing to do so. He declared that "the Anthracite Coal Strike Commission did not undertake to deal with the character of the work performed," but had left that to be settled between employees and employer.[32]

Still, if the Board proved unwilling to reform the industry, neither did it show any interest in serving as a disciplinary agency when workers struck, as some employers wanted. The five grievances brought by employers against striking workers in the Board's first three years received neither rapid nor favorable action. In three cases involving such issues as strikes over the scheduling of payday, holidays ordered by a union local for its picnic, and general absenteeism, two were withdrawn and one was reported more than a year later to have been "amicably adjusted."[33] Two other grievances filed by operators against their employees similarly accomplished nothing for the companies. The Silver Brook Coal Company asked the Board to order its employees to pay damages to the company for strikes at the end of 1903 and in May 1904, but withdrew the grievance.[34] In a particularly interesting dispute that shows the depth of distrust over methods of payment, in August 1904 the Pennsylvania Coal Company (PCC) brought its miners at Barnum colliery before the Board because they walked out for more than two weeks over the accuracy of the scales. That firm generally paid its miners by weight, but by the "miner's ton," which included a certain amount beyond the ton that was assumed to constitute waste. At Barnum, as the result of an "exhaustive test . . . [supervisors believed] that the scales were overweighing the coal in the miners' cars." The scales were adjusted and the checkweighman was notified on August 1, but two days later the miners walked out. According to the company, the miners were allowed to choose an expert, who verified the scales' accuracy. But the miners still insisted on additional tests before returning to work, which the company thought they had promised to do pending the first test. The final outcome of this dispute is not referred to by the Board, since the case was reported withdrawn some months later.[35]

In its first three years, some 150 cases were brought before the Board, but 115 of these, or more than 75 percent, were presented in the last nine months of 1903.[36] Matters had become sufficiently stabilized that John Mitchell could report to the UMWA national convention in January 1904 that "since the close of the anthracite strike the relations of miners and operators have grown steadily more cordial. With very few exceptions the award of the Commission has been rightly observed and a new era of cooperative peace and contentment has reigned."[37]

Mitchell's view was overly sanguine. Workplace disputes continued to arise after 1903, but the role of the Board changed. Both the union and the operators came to realize that the Board was incapable of resolving day-to-day problems efficiently. After it had dealt with the original flurry of grievances, especially those that concerned rehiring of strikers, the Board became largely an ultimate arbiter in particularly difficult cases. Otherwise, operators either met openly with union leaders or with committees of their own employees who were most likely local leaders advised by district officials. For example, a firm like the Kingston Coal Company, which had come to an agreement with the UMWA as early as December 1900 (see chapter 5), solved problems with its workers outside of the Conciliation Board. In May

1904 a joint committee of three company officials and three mine workers, including Benjamin McEnaney, long active in the union and later elected president of District One, reached an agreement on disputed docking procedures.[38] In another instance of cooperation with the union, in August 1905, the Lehigh Coal and Navigation Company (LC & N) wrote to subdistrict one of District Seven to ask that the members approve an increase in contributions to the firm's benevolent fund.[39]

Relations between the UMWA and Coxe Brothers and Company, a leading independent producer in the Lehigh field, had never been cordial. In November 1905, the editor of the *UMW Journal* rejoiced over the dismissal of longtime superintendent Edgar Kudlich, calling him "the greatest source of irritation and ill feeling and the greatest obstacle to industrial peace in the anthracite region."[40] This company was brought before the Board in its first three years more often than any other except the far-larger P & R.[41] Still, Kudlich held at least one meeting with District Seven President and Board of Conciliation member William Dettrey, and he responded in detail to the demands of union locals.[42] While these negotiations seem to have done little to improve labor relations, nevertheless they did occur.[43]

Yet another form of such local "twilight" bargaining can be seen at the PCC and the Hillside Coal and Iron Company, jointly controlled by the Erie Railroad. In May 1905 this firm was labeled by the UMWA, along with Coxe Brothers, as one of the chief corporate troublemakers in the anthracite region. According to the *UMW Journal,* the Erie had "pursued a course totally unworthy of a great corporation and seem[ed] destitute of the faith which holds mankind together."[44] Interestingly, this indictment came in the midst of a dispute that was preceded by union efforts at "the reorganization of the Erie employés."[45] That walkout at two of the company's mines in Dunmore over docking procedures and the appointment of a check–docking boss was settled to the satisfaction of the local union and the district executive board.[46] Three months later, a committee of mine workers from the company's various collieries was selected—at a meeting that included District President Nicholls and other UMWA officials—to meet with General Manager W. A. May. Their grievances included docking, distribution of cars, and the lack of a receipt they could take home with their pay. May carefully indicated that he was responding to the "requests of your committee representing employees of the Pennsylvania Coal Company and the Hillside Coal and Iron Company," and the committee received few tangible concessions other than a promise to provide receipts.[47] Moreover, grievances over these issues would continue to fester in coming years at these mines. Still, the union had played an important role in negotiations.

Such mixed results could have given the union's leaders little confidence, especially since the membership of the anthracite districts showed a slow but steady decline. Even before the Coal Strike Commission announced its award, John Mitchell had expressed concern that the mine workers had been slow to pay their union dues in the aftermath of the strike.[48] However, his apprehension at that time may have been mitigated by the report he received in April 1903 from Adam Ryscavage, vice-president of District One, that members there were paying arrearages in dues and new members were coming into the union.[49] Nonetheless, by the fall UMWA leaders realized that maintaining the organization in anthracite would require considerable effort. A series of meetings on October 30 for Mitchell Day opened an organizing campaign. In an address to a banquet in Scranton, John Mitchell made clear his displeasure in a chastizing, paternalistic tone that anthracite miners would hear over and over again.

> My attention has been called to the fact that some men who struck for five-and-a-half months have taken the position that it is unnecessary to belong to the union, to pay their dues, to pay their assessments, to attend meetings because the award lasts for three years. I respect, I honor, I revere every man who struck for five-and-a-half months, especially do I honor and revere the wives and children of these men. But let me say, and I wish that what I say could be heard throughout the length and breadth of the anthracite field, that I have more respect for the man who worked during the anthracite strike than I have for the man who refused to belong to the union now.[50]

District officials similarly excoriated the backsliders. At a meeting in Pittston in February 1904, John Fallon, national executive board member for District One, deplored the need to "hold smokers to smoke out the poor union men."[51] In July 1904, President Thomas Nicholls took official note of his district's declining membership at its annual convention. He reported that "a large number of members have failed to pay up arrearages, and attend our meetings, since the strike of 1902 ended." While district officers had "endeavored by all means in their power to awaken those delinquents," he observed that it would require "constant agitation to keep a portion of our members alive to the necessity of strengthening and perfecting our organization."[52]

In an address to a mass meeting in Forrestville, the national executive board member from District Nine, Miles Dougherty, ridiculed "the young fellows who wear the high collars and who sip soda water through a straw with their best girls, but who forgot to pay their dues."[53] In January 1905, a workers' newspaper in District Seven named the *Toilers' Defense* referred to non–dues paying "ingrates . . . [who] preferred spending fifty cents with a scab in a side-room bar." Noting that the district had less than a majority of its mine workers in good standing, the *Defense* addressed the slackers: "But you say you are just as good a striker as the good union man. You are a brazen liar. The best striker is the man who prepares for a strike in time of peace. . . . This the dues dodger don't do."[54]

The number of members reported in the anthracite districts for 1903 and 1904 never reached the level attained at the end of 1901—78,437. Some 56,334 were recorded for December 1903. Despite organizing efforts, December 1904 showed a considerable decline to 41,893. Membership figures ranged during 1904 from 50,119 for February to 37,706 for July.[55] Still, official union figures may have been pessimistic regarding actual membership. At the 1904 convention of District One, Secretary-Treasurer John Dempsey reported that membership for many locals had declined in approximately the same proportion as the increase in the per capita tax to be sent to the district, from three to five cents, so that the amounts sent by these locals had remained practically the same.[56]

Nonetheless, no one tried to deny that a decline in membership had occurred in the anthracite districts. Was it the result of a conscious decision by workers to abandon the union because of its failure to win recognition and other concessions from the Coal Strike Commission? Was it because of intense disappointment over the work of the Board of Conciliation?[57] Certainly there was substantial discontent over a number of Board decisions; still, it seems unlikely that such disappointment would cause mine workers who followed such issues closely to abandon so quickly the organization they had supported with such vigor during the strike of 1902. Those who might have wanted a more militant approach could have tried to express that militancy through opposition to union leaders as well as action at the workplace, but there is relatively little evidence of either, especially in 1904 and 1905. Since 1899, anthracite mine workers had defied UMWA leaders in local strikes and even in their decision to strike in 1902 against the wishes of John Mitchell. Surely there is no evidence of a sudden antidemocratic transformation of the union. Retaining 50 to 60 percent of its membership may not have been an impressive accomplishment in the wake of 1902, but it did reflect a good deal of staying power.

Two structural factors help to explain the decline in membership—an increase in the UMWA's initiation fee and, of course, the lack of the checkoff in the anthracite districts. To encourage uniformity, the national convention in January 1903 raised the initiation fee to $10 for all except boys, who would pay $2.50.[58] However, in July at the annual convention of District One, where the fee had been $3, a resolution was offered calling on the District to request a dispensation, since many workers would "not affiliate owing to the high initiation fee." The convention did not adopt this resolution, and instead adopted one calling for any local that initiated anyone for less than the mandated fee to be fined $50.[59] Nevertheless, this concern persisted. In a resolution presented to the 1904 national convention, a local from Shamokin in District Nine linked the initiation fee to the lack of the check-off.

> WHEREAS, The findings of the Anthracite Strike Commission are such that we cannot properly control a large percentage of the men employed in and around the anthracite mines, and WHEREAS, We have now many who are delinquents, and it is our desire that every inducement be offered to those people to again become members in good standing, therefore be it Resolved . . . that the initiation fee be fixed for a limited time, at least within this jurisdiction, so that no excuse can be offered for a continuation of their present action.[60]

With the substantial turnover common in the anthracite industry at the turn of the century (see chapter 1), a high initiation fee might be especially damaging. Ten dollars was by no means an inconsequential sum—a full week's pay or more, even for many adult workers. National headquarters realized this in 1904 and granted dispensations to each of the anthracite districts in February and March and extended them throughout the remainder of the year. Initiation fees were reduced to $3, less for workers at especially low wages.[61] From membership figures, the impact of the dispensations was clearly modest, although the reduced fees may well have kept membership from sliding further.

The anthracite districts needed more than dispensations from national headquarters. However, the high level of attention the UMWA and Mitchell in particular had paid to anthracite from 1900 through 1902 could only be expected to diminish thereafter. Whatever their membership, the anthracite districts had minority status in the UMWA. That was reflected most clearly by the failure of Thomas Nicholls of District One to unseat incumbent UMWA Vice-President Tom L. Lewis in 1903, losing by a margin of 69 to 31 percent.[62] While Mitchell seemed to have some sympathy for Nicholls's candidacy against his longtime rival Lewis, there is no evidence that he made any public endorsement of it.[63] No one from the anthracite districts would attain national office until 1925.

"YOU CANNOT DO WITHOUT THE UNION"

The practically unbroken series of triumphs for the UMWA—from the successful bituminous strike of 1897 and the Central Competitive Field contract of 1898 to the anthracite strike and award and an increase of more than 10 percent in the Central Competitive Field in 1903[64]—came to a halt in 1904. The UMWA's difficulties were part of an antiunion trend nationwide, which noted reformer Jane Addams reflected on in August 1904: "In spite of the fact that sympathy for trades-unions never rose so high in America as during the long anthracite-coal strike, the past two years offered undoubted evidence of a reaction against the cause of organized labor."[65]

The death of Ohio Senator Mark Hanna on February 15, 1904, symbolized the changing climate for the UMWA.[66] Despite or perhaps because of the negative public image he had acquired in the 1890s, Hanna had worked to become the embodiment of the progressively inclined, public-spirited businessman, especially where labor was involved. His personal relationship with Mitchell was close, and Mitchell called for mine workers to take an afternoon off to honor the memory of the Senator.[67] But while Hanna's demise took from the UMWA an influential friend, its main significance lay elsewhere. The death of Hanna reflected the declining importance of an organization with which both Hanna and Mitchell had worked closely from its founding several years before, the National Civic Federation (NCF). One of its major emphases was to promote harmony between capital and labor through trade agreements. The UMWA's contract in the Central Competitive Field was the outstanding example. However, by 1903 the NCF was coming under a strong attack from employers who abhorred not only the prospect of trade agreements but the very notion of unionism. In 1902, David M. Parry and several like-minded businessmen had taken over the National Association of Manufacturers (NAM) and quickly transformed it into the vehicle for their open-shop crusade.[68] Hanna, who had become president of the NCF, contributed in no small way to its influence. But the influence of the NCF stemmed from the perception that the trade agreements it called for appeared to represent, for a short while at least, the wave of the future. Six years of labor peace achieved through the series of agreements in the Central Competitive Field justified this sort of thinking, as did the settlement of the 1902 anthracite strike, which Hanna and the NCF had tried to mediate before it began. But the aggressive tactics of Parry and his confederates gave an official voice to virulent antiunionism (which had hardly diminished in management circles) and, perhaps more importantly, made it a "respectable" alternative to the NCF's approach.[69]

In the Central Competitive Field, an economic downturn inspired coal operators to try to retrieve some of the wage concessions they had made in the previous year. With negotiations deadlocked early in February, Ralph M. Easley of the NCF reminded Mitchell that a strike would not merely be the concern of the mine workers and the operators.

> I cannot help but feel that a failure to effect a settlement will be a great blow at the joint trade agreement movement. We have held up the bituminous system of contracts as the ideal one. Our enemies the "Parryites" are praying for a rupture. They say the joint trade agreement is only good when it gives the union what it asks for. The recent reports on joint trade agreements in

England show that in the mining industry there have been reductions as well as increases, depending entirely on commercial conditions.[70]

The operators insisted that their final offer was a cut of 5.55 percent. In March the union held a referendum in which mine workers could choose between a strike and the reduction, to last for two years until April 1, 1906, the day following the expiration of the award of the Anthracite Coal Strike Commission. Mitchell, Vice-President Lewis, and Secretary-Treasurer William B. Wilson exerted their influence against a walkout. They pointed to the gains made in the Central Competitive Field since 1897—wage increases, the eight-hour day, and the check-off—and went on to mention the possibility that the organization's "weak links," like West Virginia and western Pennsylvania, might not join a strike. Significantly they used Easley's argument, noting that "two years of peace" would "demonstrate that a Trade Union can, when the occasion arises, gracefully accept a reduction as well as strenuously insist upon an advance."[71] In a statement to a special convention held on March 5 and 7, several days before the vote, Wilson noted that to accept a reduction "would do more to suppress Parryism with all its attendant evils than any other move."[72] In the referendum, the bituminous mine workers accepted the cut for the next two years by a margin of 60 to 40 percent.[73]

At the convention called prior to the vote, Wilson analyzed the interdependence between anthracite and bituminous in explaining why the bituminous mine workers had received such a favorable settlement in 1903:

> Who is there among you that believes that if the anthracite strike had not occurred in 1902 we would have been able to secure any advance in 1903? The strike of the anthracite coal fields resulted in producing a scarcity of domestic coal in the West, a scarcity of domestic and steam coal in the East, and created an abnormal market for bituminous coal.[74]

Higher prices resulting from the anthracite strike had enabled bituminous miners to insist on a big increase in 1903. Also, the fact that they were at work during the strike allowed them to provide massive amounts of aid to their anthracite brothers. As a union committee had noted at the 1903 convention, "should either field inaugurate a strike, they must, of a necessity, depend largely upon the support of the other for a successful termination."[75]

By contrast, UMWA leaders referred to a very different sort of interdependence in a letter to union members that Mitchell, Lewis, and Wilson coauthored on the eve of the referendum. They stated that acceptance of the wage cut would "cause our contracts to expire at the same time as the Anthracite Award and place us then in a position to act with greater unity, if we so desired, than we could at any other time."[76] This raised, however modestly, the prospect of a strike of both anthracite and bituminous mine workers, idling the entire coal industry. Such a move could conceivably give the UMWA bargaining power of breathtaking scope.

At the annual convention of the UMWA in January 1905, Mitchell faced a number of difficult problems, most notably a failed strike in Colorado. Mitchell's refusal to continue to provide support for the strikers after eight months had incensed some in the union, most conspicuously "Mother" Mary Jones, as well as prominent socialists like Eugene V. Debs, who had been highly critical of the award of the Coal Strike Commission. Difficult strikes—all of which eventually would fail—had begun the previous year in Alabama, Tennessee, central Pennsylvania, and West Virginia.[77] Still, while it may not have been the major problem he had to confront, Mitchell noted the decline in membership in the anthracite fields and chastised the mine workers there:

> It is a source of keen regret and disappointment that I am compelled to report a loss of membership in the anthracite region and an apparent lack of interest on the part of the mine workers in that field. What reasons there can be for this seeming indifference I am unable to conceive. It certainly can not be attributed to any failure on the part of the organization to protect and safeguard the welfare and material advancement of the men employed there.[78]

John Mitchell knew that he would have little chance of negotiating a contract with the coal operators when the Commission's award expired in 1906 if the union's ranks in the anthracite fields were depleted. Shortly after the convention, he began to plan a personal organizing campaign in the anthracite districts for that summer with a full commitment of resources from the national union. Beginning in June, his tour revealed the depth of the union's difficulties. His papers contain data on the status of about seventy local unions located in the vicinity of the sites for his many speeches. Few towns were as bad as Olyphant in District One, where only 268 of some 2,374 workers at four collieries, or 11 percent, belonged to the locals there. However, seldom did more than one-third of the workers belong at any of the mines.[79] In addressing the faithful, lapsed, and fallen, Mitchell focused on several themes. He praised those who had stuck with the union, but addressed most of his remarks to those who had not, expressing amazement over their disloyalty.

> I can understand the logic of men who leave the union if it suffers defeats, I can understand the process of reasoning which leads many men to abandon their organization, when their organization engages in strikes and suffers defeats, but I cannot understand the logic, I cannot understand the process of reasoning which impels men to leave the union and become non-unionists in times of victory. The United Mine Workers of America, during the five years that it has been strong in this field, has suffered not one single defeat. Every strike in which we have been engaged has been, if not a complete, at least a partial victory.[80]

He reviewed the history of the UMWA in anthracite, noting the perils workers faced before the arrival of the union and admitting the limited nature of the victory of 1902. In referring to the end of that strike, Mitchell chose not to mention the UMWA's eagerness to accept arbitration: "Circumstances entirely beyond our control compelled us to defer to the wishes—not only to the wishes but to the imperative demands—of the public as expressed through the President of the United States. We were compelled to quit fighting." He further noted that "we did not get all we wanted; we did not get all we demanded; we did not get as much as we hoped for."[81] Nevertheless, the limitations of that settlement in no way justified staying out of the union, and Mitchell chided those who had:

> Gentlemen, this is your fight. It is the fight of your wives and children. The United Mine Workers of America would live and prosper even if every man in the anthracite fields were to leave it. The union can do without you; you cannot do without the union. You confer no favor upon the union when you pay dues to it; it is you who are favored by being permitted to pay to the union. Some men think that when the officers of the union come along to appeal to them to pay their just dues, they want the money for their own salaries. Does any man here think the salary you pay keeps me in this work? If he does, he is mistaken. . . .
>
> My friends, the struggle is hard, the contest is unequal enough even when every workman is a member of the union. It is too bad that, instead of concentrating our efforts against those that would oppress you, we must spend nearly the whole year appealing to the non-union men to come into line and fight with us. It is discouraging at times, but if you won't fight for yourselves, then we shall have to fight for you; if you will not defend your own wives and your babies, then we shall defend them for you.
>
> My friends, I am not afraid of Mr. Baer; Mr. Baer is not afraid of me. Do you know who I am afraid of: I am afraid of the men who don't belong to the union. If all men belonged to the union, Mr. Baer would be more afraid of me.[82]

Mitchell spoke to four or five meetings a week across the anthracite fields, including one of perhaps 150,000 in Wilkes-Barre in August where he introduced President Theodore Roosevelt at a joint meeting arranged with the Catholic Total Abstinence Society.[83] If anthracite mine workers found the tone of his speeches condescending, they showed no evidence of it. The *Pottsville Chronicle* offered the following account of one mass meeting:

> That the anthracite miner regards John Mitchell with something akin to reverence was demonstrated Saturday evening in the Schuylkill Valley, when the leader of the United Mine Workers of America made an address at New Philadelphia. Along the entire route from Pottsville to the place of meeting, which was made in carriages, were congregated knots of mine workers and

their families who most enthusiastically cheered Mitchell as he passed, and made rushes toward the carriage he occupied in order that they might say they touched the vehicle in which the miners' leader was seated.[84]

By the end of August, Mitchell was ebullient. He informed his longtime associate William D. Ryan, Secretary-Treasurer of District Twelve, that he was being "received more as a conquering hero than as an ordinary 'labor skate.' " On a more pragmatic note, Mitchell added that he felt "free to confess that the absence of the check-off is a serious hindrance to the complete organization of this field."[85] In September, Mitchell informed Ralph Easley that "within the next two months . . . we shall have practically a solid organization here."[86] In the first six months of 1905, totals for the three anthracite districts ranged from a low of 29,682 in January 1905 to a high of 53,215 in March. For the latter half of the year, totals ranged from 36,397 for July, when Mitchell had only been in the region for several weeks, to 80,488 for November. Membership levels continued to exceed the former peak of 78,437 attained on the eve of 1902 in February and March 1906 with totals of 83,550 and 80,388 respectively.[87] With a massive effort fueled by an extension of dispensations for initiation fees, John Mitchell and the UMWA had reorganized the anthracite districts.[88]

Mitchell's aim, as it had been since 1900, was to gain an audience with the presidents of the coal railroads that could lead to a trade agreement. At the beginning of his organizing campaign in June, he had met privately with William L. Connell, an independent operator on the Conciliation Board, to discuss the upcoming expiration of the award.[89] Toward the end of the summer, his success in persuading most anthracite mine workers to join or rejoin the union made him confident that he could achieve a settlement with the railroad presidents. On September 4 he wrote to a friend that he hoped "to have the contract signed . . . before the expiration of the agreement in the bituminous field."[90] Encouraging Mitchell toward his goal of a conference with the railroad presidents was Easley of the NCF. On September 8, he informed Mitchell that in a recent conversation, Frederick D. Underwood, president of the Erie Railroad, noted that his company had made agreements with several railroad brotherhoods and that there was "no reason" why it shouldn't make a contract with the UMWA, since the union had a good track record of keeping its agreements. However, to pave the way for a full-scale meeting with the operators, Easley advised Mitchell to prevent his "boys from putting out threats or 'ultimatums' " that would make the union look bad before the public.[91] Mitchell agreed and even moved to correct any misimpression that may have been conveyed in recent reports in the press concerning his organizing drive.[92]

Movement toward some sort of formal meeting between operators and the UMWA accelerated as a special convention of the anthracite districts approached in December. Easley had not been able to obtain any agreement from the other railroad presidents to negotiate with union leaders. Still, Easley reported to Mitchell that the Erie's president wanted him to know that "there was absolutely no bitterness in the minds of any of the operators."[93] However, Mitchell probably obtained a somewhat different impression from an article in the *North American Review* by the President of the D & H, David Willcox. Offering a highly favorable assessment of the award of the Coal Strike Commission, Willcox maintained that the employers had "no desire to disturb such results . . . and are willing to continue the present arrangements indefinitely." More ominously for Mitchell, he added:

> . . . everything suggested as the subject of a general contract has been secured by the award. Therefore, no contract with the union is necessary for the protection of the employees. . . . The illogical and illegal scheme of having all the labor employed in a great industry controlled by one organization and compelling all the employers to enter into contracts with the organization, rather than with their own employees, is rapidly passing away, and agreements of employment are fast reverting to their natural form of arrangements between the parties concerned.[94]

Shortly before the delegates of the anthracite districts convened in Shamokin on December 14 to formulate their strategy, Charles P. Neill, head of the U.S. Bureau of Labor, met with the most influential of the railroad presidents, George F. Baer. Neill reported to Mitchell that "on some points" Baer was "very fixed and determined," and would "not consider the proposal of a contract." However, Neill did believe that Baer might accept a formal meeting between a committee representing the operators and one from the UMWA. While Baer did not agree to such a meeting at that time, Neill believed that "there was an entire absence of bitterness in his attitude." He suggested a strategy to facilitate a meeting:

> If the Convention makes definite demands, the operators may say that since they are not willing to grant any of the demands they can not see any necessity for conference, but if the Convention would make its demands in executive session, and allow no official statement of what they were, but instead appoint a committee to confer with the operators, they could not then take this stand.[95]

At the Shamokin convention, Mitchell succeeded in persuading the anthracite delegates to adopt such a strategy, but he acknowledged opposition to it. He knew that many expected adoption of "certain specific demands, among them . . . the eight hour work-day, the weighing of coal, uniform wages for the same classes of labor, increased wages for outside men." However, he believed that with a set of demands "the prospect of securing a conference with the railroad presidents would be much less . . . it would be giving to the operators our plans in advance of knowing theirs.'' He reassured delegates that the members of the committee selected to meet the operators—the district presidents and members of district executive boards—''know your grievances, know your hopes, they know the things you want.'' Introducing his customary note of caution, he added that he was ''not too sure'' that the committee would be able to obtain what the mine workers wanted, and that the attitude of the operators did not offer ''much encouragement.'' He emphasized the importance of such demands as recognition of the union and the eight-hour day if ''permanent industrial peace'' were ever to be established, but did not suggest militant action as the means to achieve them.

> Now, my fellow workmen, I am as anxious as man can be to see a relationship established between the anthracite miners and their employers that will make strikes and lock-outs for all time unnecessary. I am not here to denounce them; I am anxious for their friendship for you; I am anxious to have them agree to such conditions of employment as will prove advantageous and fair to you without being unfair to them.[96]

This strategy provoked no open dissent, but on the third and final day of the convention the delegates convened in executive session, amidst reports that some delegates disagreed with the decision not to formulate a set of demands in public. With apparent sincerity, Mitchell urged dissenters to speak out:

> Gentlemen, we might as well understand one another here, because if there is any criticism or disapproval it is better to express it in the convention than to express it outside. . . . And I want to say this to the delegates—and I hope they will believe me when I say this—that I shall regard it in no sense as an offense for delegates to disagree with me. I don't want any delegate to vote for a proposition simply because I advocate it.[97]

The convention then agreed to give ''the preference of the floor'' to dissatisfied delegates, although this led one delegate to complain, ''If we give the floor to the growlers the rest of us may have to sit here all day.''[98] This statement moved Mitchell to call again for open discussion while subtly raising the spectre of disloyalty.

> The delegates may be reluctant to speak because they may feel that the overwhelming sentiment of the convention is in favor of the action taken yesterday. They may fear they will not be given a respectful hearing. If the delegates have any regard for my wishes they will give as respectful hearing to the dissenting delegates as they have given to me. It is not wrong for a delegate to disagree, and radically disagree, . . . However, I am satisfied the dissatisfaction has not been expressed by our delegates. It is as I feared, there are men in Shamokin who are not delegates who are trying to create dissention among our people. I have known for many months that our entire

organization was honeycombed with men employed and sent here for the purpose of creating dissention.[99]

Several delegates proceeded to mention some local matters that had been referred to the negotiating committee,[100] but one issue did arouse considerable discussion: the Conciliation Board. Delegate George Evans stated that his local was "positively disgusted" with it and added that many of those who had deserted the UMWA had done so because they "at first placed too much faith in the conciliation board."[101] Several of the delegates focused on the lengthy delays that had plagued the Board's proceedings. Evans stated: "When they delay these things for a year or a year and a half . . . [the men] think they are getting buncoed." He also advocated allowing locals to strike if the board failed to act quickly on their grievances.[102] One delegate complained that even when the Board decided in favor of the workers, operators could be quite laggard in implementing its rulings.[103] A delegate named Hahn eloquently talked of the troubles he faced in bringing a case before the Board:

> The case came before the board and I was the main witness. Out of twelve men working in the place I could only get one poor miner to stand by me, and two other men working in another part of the mine also came with me. The others all had some excuse to get out of it. While the matter was brought before the public, and the foreman and superintendent were also held up to the gaze of the public, I was brought to the attention of the operators. Where is there any protection for me in such a case? I think the man who seeks to uphold principles and wages should be given some protection. If you can only get one man out of a hundred who dares stand up before the bosses to demand union wages and principles he should be protected. Give a man a good place and good wages and he does not give a snap of his fingers for other men. That has been proved in the past. Men in our region who have become active in the locals have fallen down and ceased working for our interests. Why? Because they were given better places than their fellow workmen. Today they give me starvation wages because I stood up for union principles.[104]

Mitchell acknowledged the criticism of the Board and noted that he had heard it from "hundreds of men." He stated that he believed that the operators' representatives on the Board often desired "to prolong these cases so as to wear them out." Perhaps to dampen discontent, he quite inaccurately stated that the miners had "won a vast majority of the cases referred to the board" and "practically every case referred to an umpire."[105] Nevertheless, he did make an interesting point regarding the Board's larger impact.

> Gentlemen, the greatest advantage that comes to us from the Board of Conciliation is not the cases we win, nor does it come to us from the cases re-

ferred to the board. The great benefit that has come to the miners by the creation of the Board of Conciliation has been the cases not referred to it. *The existence of the board has deterred unfair foremen and superintendents from imposing on our men,* because they knew that their actions were subject to review and that the review of their actions meant that the public would have information as to what they were doing. So I say it has been the fear on the part of the foremen that their actions would be reviewed by a board and by the public that has given us the greatest benefit and is my strongest reason for wanting the board continued in existence. [emphasis added][106]

Thomas Nicholls, who served on the Board with the other two district presidents, made it clear that he realized its deficiencies. He stated that men had "brought grievances before the board and . . . died before the grievances were settled."[107] But President John Fahy of District Nine attributed the Board's shortcomings to the union's weakness:

Before we had the Union you never had a Board of Conciliation; the nearest thing to it was what might be called a board of damnation—take it or get out. The only way we can have a Board of Conciliation that will be effective is to be big enough to make the other fellow agree to the decisions. You cannot expect conciliation as long as men remain outside the Union. . . . Just as soon as the award of the Anthracite Coal Strike Commission went into effect just that soon some men jumped the switch, got out of the Union, and did not pay a cent until a short time ago. If you want conciliation, stick to the Union.[108]

Evidence of that apathy had been brought out in a number of ways in the convention. A delegate named Penman, who once belonged to the Workingmen's Benevolent Association, stated:

Gentlemen, all we want to do as a working class is to put our shoulders to the wheel, stick to our Union, pay our dues and all will be well with us. I belong to Local 105, and for some time we had a great deal of trouble in organizing. We used to have meetings at which there was hardly a quorum. When the district officers came to visit us we were ashamed. Thank God, however, we have passed that stage and are now in better condition.[109]

Further evidence of the union's weakness arose when a delegate named Sweeny from District Nine noted that boys, whose initiation fee was much smaller, had been selling their working buttons, which indicated that they had paid their dues, to older workers. This led to discussion of, but apparently no coordinated action toward, allowing workers who earned less than seven dollars a week to be initiated at the boys' rate and not pay full dues, as at least District Nine had done for a time.[110] In discussing where buttons ought to be worn, one delegate noted that some members were "afraid to wear their buttons." He asked his fellow delegates: "If we are afraid of recognition at home, how are we to get recognition from the operators?"[111]

"IT HAS BEEN PEACEFUL"

John Mitchell's elaborate maneuvering toward some sort of recognition came to fruition when the operators agreed to meet as a committee with the UMWA representatives. Mitchell observed that "it . . . would be very difficult for them to refuse a meeting of some kind," especially considering his "very conciliatory letter" of December 20, 1905. He did not even use his official letterhead, so that the operators "would not be confronted upon opening the communications, with the objectionable title of the organization."[112] Nevertheless, he did mention in the letter that he wanted to meet before January 12, 1906, since that was the date on which the UMWA would hold its annual convention and that "many, if not all, of the members" would attend.[113] Baer responded that he would be willing to meet along with the other railroad and coal company presidents, but that due to the press of business, he would prefer to meet after January 16.[114]

The union committee did not hold its first meeting with the operators until February 15, just six weeks before the expiration of the Strike Commission's award. This meeting followed the disappointing opening session of the joint conference of the UMWA and bituminous operators. In those negotiations, the union had demanded an increase of more than 12 percent and the extension of bargaining to cover the Southwest field, while the operators called for a renewal of the 1904 agreement and refused to extend the agreement to the Southwest field. When the UMWA annual convention reconvened after those unsuccessful negotiations, W. D. Ryan, Mitchell's close friend, set a militant tone by offering a resolution calling for rejection of a renewal of the 1904 agreement along with a promise to accept "no contract . . . in any district until we all get a settlement or go down in defeat together." The resolution passed with only three dissenting votes, but one was cast by Pat Dolan of Pittsburgh, president of District Five. Dolan's vote led to his condemnation by fellow western Pennsylvania delegates.[115] Subsequently mine workers from throughout the district petitioned for his removal, which the International Executive Board endorsed. However, Dolan stubbornly refused for several months to surrender his office, so Mitchell not only faced the possibility of a strike in bituminous for the first time since 1897 but an internal battle in one of the largest districts in the Central Competitive Field.[116]

On February 15, some twenty-five anthracite coal executives met with a mine workers' delegation of thirty-four, headed by Mitchell and composed of the district officers and board members and the national board members from the districts. In his opening statement, Mitchell sounded a cordial note, expressing "the gratification of the miners upon this the first meeting . . . strictly between ourselves." He referred to the Coal Strike Commission as composed of men, "many of whom were not familiar with either the operation of mines or . . . with the methods of working them." While he believed that all could agree that the three years during which the award had been in effect had "been more satisfactory than any other period," he still thought that they could reach an agreement that would "remove some of the matters which we believe to be inimical to our interests and not advantageous to yours," thus guaranteeing "industrial peace." He then proceeded, undoubtedly by design, to present the mine workers' demands in a vague and undemanding way. First, he called for an eight-hour day, which he noted had been "accorded to mine workers in nearly every other part of our own country and, indeed, in . . . most of the countries of Europe." He next requested that wage rates be made uniform for workers performing the same job. Along the same line he called for "a fixed and definite scale of wages . . . for dead work," that is, work by miners not immediately directed toward mining coal. Mitchell also made a general request for higher wages, noting that workers "should share the increase of profits" in prosperous times "and . . . in times of depression they should share the burden." He revived the demand for payment for coal by weight. Finally, while he noted that the Board of Conciliation had "done very much to maintain peaceful relations," he called for reorganizing it so that grievances could no longer "drag along months and months without a decision."[117]

The response of the coal executives was courteous but reserved. Baer of the P & R did not think that "a general discussion of the statement . . . so clearly made" by Mitchell could lead to much progress. He suggested that the mine workers designate a subcommittee to "formulate just what they desire and their reasons for it," to which a subcommittee of the operators could respond. Mitchell stated that "the miners would not be able to present a detailed scale as to their demands very soon," and thus expressed his hope that those present could "canvass general propositions . . . to know where we are at . . . [to] avoid a possible disagreement." However, none of the executives showed any interest in such an exploratory discussion.[118]

The UMWA negotiators agreed to appoint a subcommittee, but in discussing plans for proceeding, Eben Thomas, who had become president of the Lehigh Valley Railroad (LV) after his long association with the Erie, asked a question that had long been at the center of the operators' rejection of negotiations with the union—how many men on the committee were "actually employed in the collieries." When Mitchell noted that only four were so employed and the others were "actually employed by the miners," the only negative reaction was Baer's, apparently in jest: "They are not workers like we are.'' This session adjourned cordially with an agreement for two sub-committees of seven to proceed to negotiate.[119]

This brief meeting revealed the prospect of a new model of labor relations in the anthracite industry. In 1906 the mining companies were willing to carry on industrywide negotiations with the UMWA. This constituted de facto recognition, assuming some sort of agreement would result. There had been several meetings in March and April 1902 between operators and Mitchell and district officials at which substantive issues were discussed, but those meetings had been forced upon the operators by the NCF.[120] Interestingly, Mitchell's vagueness in the UMWA's opening presentations may well have been a tactic to necessitate further talks and thus publicize the operators' apparent recognition of the union as the bargaining agent for their employees.

Twelve days after the negotiating session of February 15, Mitchell sent Baer a draft of a detailed one-year contract. The document provided for the eight-hour day and a detailed wage scale for nearly 150 different tasks both inside and outside the mines. Contract miners were slated to receive not only an increase of 10 percent, but also standardization of cars for each vein at a colliery, standard rates for dead work, the weighing of coal ''wherever . . . practicable,'' an equal distribution of cars, and a detailed procedure for the appointment and payment of checkweighmen and check–docking bosses. To resolve grievances more effectively, the employees at each mine would select a ''mine committee.'' Companies would be required to respond to all grievances within a week. The Conciliation Board would be retained, but if a decision was in favor of the employee, employers would be required to pay those who had filed the grievance ''six cents on each dollar held by them'' for the period of the grievance. Also, while strikes would be prohibited when a grievance was under consideration, should an operator refuse to comply with a Board decision, the employees reserved the right to strike. In addition, discharged employees could present their firing as a legitimate grievance, as they had been unable to do under the rulings of Carroll D. Wright except for reasons of union discrimination. Finally, the UMWA called for check-off of union dues.[121]

Baer's response may have surprised Mitchell. In his letter of February 28, he acknowledged receipt of the ''propositions'' but noted that no explanation accompanied them.[122] Mitchell's response on March 1 betrayed his fear that the face-to-face negotiations he had pursued so assiduously might be at an end. He stated that he had understood that the proposal would be the subject of discussion at their next meeting, and that he hoped Baer would ''agree . . . that a personal discussion would lead to more satisfactory results.'' Still, Mitchell proceeded to give a brief explanation of the basic points of the proposal.[123] The operators' response on March 9, however, made it clear that they were in no mood to make concessions. Referring to the text of the award of the Anthracite Coal Strike Commission, they claimed that the Commission had been called to settle "all questions at issue between the respective companies and their own employees" and had also, in the Conciliation Board, established a "satisfactory method for the adjustment of grievances which from time to time may arise." In their opinion the Commission had arrived at its award after "probably the most conscientious and exhaustive examination ever given to any similar matter," and the award had "not been the subject of serious criticism." They believed that "the only question properly open" was whether there were "any new facts" that raised "new questions." They believed that "no such new facts" had been "brought to public attention," and added "with great respect that nothing of the sort" was contained in the UMWA's proposals. Still, they proceeded to examine each point of the proposed contract and, after referring time and time again to the Commission's award, concluded that no change was warranted. Finally, the operators offered a very simple counterproposal—continuation of the award for three years.[124]

However disappointing the operators' response must have been for Mitchell, he did not have much time to reflect upon it. Not only did the award expire in three weeks, but the bituminous miners were having little success in coming to an agreement to replace their contract. The UMWA gathered in a special convention on March 15, adjourned while discussions with the bituminous operators continued, and then agreed, after the collapse of those talks just prior to the contract deadline, to allow the bituminous districts to bargain separately. This move greatly moderated the impact of a bituminous walkout on April 1, since the various districts made no commitment to return together or to insist on the inclusion of nonunion fields like West Virginia in any new contract. Vice-President Lewis openly opposed this strategy, which not only jettisoned the solidarity called for in the Ryan Resolution but more importantly signaled the abandonment of the joint conference system for the Central Competitive Field. The convention accepted Mitchell's decision for this new departure, but some 200 delegates of the approximately 1,100 assembled were reported in opposition.[125] Even with this victory, Mitchell faced the task of monitoring negotiations and strikes in the various districts. Shouldering such burdens, he could not focus on matters in the anthracite region to the extent they deserved, *especially if any sort of effective strike were to be conducted.*

On March 16, Mitchell wrote Baer, telling him that his committee was "keenly disappointed to learn that our demands were rejected *in toto*," and questioned the operators' stance by noting that the Strike Commission had been "in doubt as to the permanency of its findings." In a somewhat supplicatory tone, he stated that the union had hoped "that our adherence to the letter and spirit of the award, and the absence of local or general strikes during the past three years, would have appealed more strongly to your confidence and that we might reasonably expect serious consideration of our claims.'' Again showing his fear that face-to-face negotiations might not resume, he stated that his committee believed that neither party could ''afford to break off negotiations in this abrupt manner.'' Mitchell further warned that the mine workers could not ''with any degree of contentment and satisfaction, continue to work under present conditions'' and added that he hoped that the committees would meet again to ''strive earnestly and conscientiously to reconcile our differences.''[126]

Maintaining the operators' calculatedly civil approach to the union, Baer responded on March 20 that his committee had always assumed that all involved would meet again. He even chided Mitchell for not responding to the operators' ''counter-proposition . . . to continue the existing conditions,'' which had ''been so highly beneficial to the miners and to the community.'' He noted that Mitchell had informed E. B. Thomas by telephone that the UMWA committee could not meet before March 26. Baer added that the operators were ''prepared to meet . . . at any time you may name.''[127] Mitchell, of course, was trying to manage matters at the bituminous convention, where negotiations with the operators broke off on March 29 and the convention decided to allow district-by-district bargaining on March 30.[128] Only on March 29 did Mitchell write Baer to ask for a meeting,[129] and on the following day Mitchell and the general committee directed all anthracite workers except essential maintenance personnel to suspend work on Monday, April 2, pending the outcome of negotiations.[130]

The two anthracite subcommittees met in New York on April 3, with the newspapers reporting a full-scale walkout across the anthracite fields and a strike of similar proportions not only in the Central Competitive Field but also in the Southwest field. A total of one-half million mine workers were on strike across the nation, although prospects for a quick settlement were good in a number of bituminous districts.[131] In his opening statement, Mitchell told the operators that ''a very large number'' of their men employed received wages ''too low . . . to maintain them properly,'' lower than that received by ''men of like capacity in every other mining district in America.'' He believed that the companies' increased earnings showed that they could afford higher wages. In closing, he invited the operators to ''endeavor jointly to build a scale which will be fair to you and fair to us.''[132]

Baer replied, ''Is that the only proposition you have to make?'' Mitchell stated that was all he was ''authorized to make.''[133] Perhaps to keep the meeting going, the mine workers' representatives then took the initiative, bringing up such issues as labor costs and the profitability of the railroads and their anthracite coal operations. The operators expressed a willingness to show relevant figures, but did not give any sign of budging from their position that they could not grant a pay increase.[134] While these topics occasioned considerable discussion, Mitchell received no response when he sought to correct a "very great misapprehension" on the part of the operators—that the UMWA demanded a closed shop. Mitchell pointed out that the union only wanted the companies to make deductions for the union from those employees who were willing to request officially that those deductions be made.[135] When Thomas Nicholls later brought up the matter of "the agreement with our organization," Baer responded: "That we need not discuss." Still, E. B. Thomas, who was chairing the meeting, stated that "Mr. Nicholls is entitled to be heard."[136]

Nicholls expressed his belief that the only way for an agreement to be "carried out properly" was for it to be made between the operators and the UMWA. Baer responded: "On the contrary three years have obtained . . . without any agreement with your organization and they have been the most peaceful and the most satisfactory that have ever obtained."[137] Nicholls's response revealed not only the conservatism of the union leaders but their fundamental optimism, displayed consistently since 1900 despite considerable evidence to the contrary, that they could show the railroad presidents that the union actually could benefit the companies. After stating that he and his colleagues had not found the past three years "satisfactory," he added:

> It has been peaceful, and we have done our best to make it peaceful. We have at times suffered loss because we hoped that if we could show you that we were reasonable people, not hot-headed and unreasonable, that then, knowing that, you would be willing to agree with us.[138]

Mitchell proceeded to argue for a wage increase, referring to increased earnings for the companies, higher wages for bituminous miners, and a Department of Labor study showing an increased cost of living. None of this persuaded the operators, who noted that mine workers had received noncumulative increases from the sliding scale averaging approximately 4 percent per year since April 1903.[139] President William Dettrey of District Seven pleaded for equalization of wages for the same work: "I cannot for the life of me understand why one man in the Lehigh Valley region doing the same kind of work should receive $1.17 or $1.29 or $1.35, when in the other two regions that position pays from $1.43 to $1.55 or $1.60." That only prompted E. B. Thomas to ask: "Has it ever occurred to you that the other regions might be paying too much?"[140] Baer then posed the "socialistic problem" of whether "all men should be paid alike in the same occupation." Mitchell stated that the UMWA only looked to establish a minimum. To him and his union, it was a "false philosophy," for "all men to receive the same wages," but "all men performing the same kind of work [should] receive a certain uniform minimum wage."[141]

The most acrimonious moment of the meeting occurred shortly before adjournment when Baer read a telegram from Wilkes-Barre stating that company hands at one colliery had been assaulted the day before and Thomas referred to a telephone message he had received about another disturbance. When Nicholls said he was "sorry to hear anything of the kind," Baer's response displayed the pique he may have been trying to suppress:

Yes, you are always sorry. You are sitting here and my men are being injured. We are trying to have peace. . . . It is not very nice gentlemen, for you people in the midst of these negotiations to have called out your men and then when we are sitting here to have telegrams like this coming to us. I believe, of course, you will do what you can to stop it and I hope you will, but it is not very soothing to one's nerves.[142]

Although the committees met four more times, the meeting of April 3 was the only one in which substantive, detailed discussion took place. Each proposal made by correspondence was made public, giving the parties little room for maneuver.[143] They reconvened on April 5, and in that meeting the UMWA committee offered to accept arbitration from the Board of Conciliation, with Judge George Gray, chairman of the Strike Commission, to serve as umpire. In the very brief discussion that followed, Willcox of the D & H asked whether "all of the propositions . . . contained in the draft of contract" would be submitted to arbitration, and Mitchell stated that they would.[144] When the committees reconvened on April 10, Baer presented the operators' rejection of the union's arbitration proposal. He noted that the union contemplated arbitration by a body with which they had expressed "dissatisfaction" and had even contemplated abolishing. Further, the operators were dismayed that one of the issues to be arbitrated would be an agreement with the UMWA, which had not been within the Strike Commission's purview. However, they returned to their primary argument—that they could not "assent to re-open the fundamental questions decided" by that body, which had "formulated principles and rules of right" that "received the hearty assent of all good citizens of the land."[145]

As an alternative to renewing the award however, the mining companies offered their own proposal for limited arbitration. They suggested convening such members of the Coal Strike Commission as could serve "to decide whether any changes in the conditions of the Anthracite Industry" had occurred. Although the operators had expressed their view that no increase in wages was merited, they did express willingness to arbitrate "wages or rates of payment . . . either by way of increase or reduction," as well as the "adjustment of complaints through the Conciliation Board or otherwise." They favored submitting those issues to the Strike Commission rather than the Conciliation Board because the former would be "composed of disinterested parties." While the union committee had wanted any award to last for two years to 1908, the operators suggested that any change in the Commission's award should last until 1909, to "avoid introducing into purely business questions the political considerations of a presidential campaign." Baer added that the operators would be willing to pay all the expenses of the Commission, if paying half would be an "inconvenience" to the mine workers. After conferring with his committee, Mitchell stated that, on first hearing, the offer did "not appeal to us favorably" and asked if the operators would "present arguments for the reduction of wages." Baer responded affirmatively, and the committees adjourned for two days.[146]

Not surprisingly, the UMWA committee rejected the operators' counterproposal. Still, "to remove . . . even the suspicion of obduracy," the UMWA altered its original contract proposal to exclude reference to an agreement with the UMWA, substituting the term "anthracite mine workers" instead. This revised contract could then be considered in a full-scale arbitration before members of the Coal Strike Commission. After a brief recess, Baer responded that the operators could not accept that and would submit a formal reply in writing.[147] In that response, the operators noted that, in originally appointing the Strike Commission, President Roosevelt had instructed it "to endeavor to establish the relations between the employers and the wage earners in the anthracite region on a just and *permanent* basis."[148] Once again they stated that the mine workers' arguments had not persuaded them that significant change had taken place. In closing they stated that the responsibility for the suspension rested with the mine workers, since "there was no good reason for ordering the men to stop work pending our negotiations, which had been delayed by you."[149]

On April 24, Mitchell met in Wilkes-Barre with his negotiating committee. He told the press that the suspension had injured no one, and that most mine workers would have worked partial weeks at best had it not occurred. While a few small incidents of intimidation or property destruction had been reported, there seemed to be practically no effort by the operators to mine coal with nonunion workers.[150] In writing on April 26, the committee labeled the operators' proposal of limited arbitration as one to "arbitrate to ascertain whether or not there is anything to arbitrate, and then restrict within narrow limits the scope of the investigation." They then offered "two separate and distinct propositions," first to increase wages for workers receiving less than a dollar a day by 15 percent, those earning between $1.00 and $1.25 by 12.5 percent, 10 percent for those earning between $1.25 and $1.50, and 7.5 percent for those earning from $1.50 to $1.75. All other workers, including contract miners, would receive an increase of 5 percent. The other would be to add "an advance equal to ten cents per ton upon the total production of anthracite coal" to the wages of all workers, apportioned "in such manner as may be mutually determined between our respective committees."[151] On that same day the committee issued a call for a convention of anthracite delegates to begin on Thursday, May 3, to consider whether or not to make the suspension a full-fledged strike.[152] The operators rejected the union's latest proposals in a letter dated April 27. In keeping with the putative concern for the consumer they were careful to claim throughout the negotiations, they stated that both proposals would have too great an impact on the price of coal. The first would increase costs far more than ten cents per ton and the second would do so as well if the operators were to have any chance of recouping their increased costs, in particular those connected with the sliding scale.[153]

With no further negotiations on the horizon, locals began to elect delegates to the convention. Reportedly some locals instructed them to vote for a strike unless the operators offered concessions, while others instructed delegates to support whatever course Mitchell favored. The most violent incident of the suspension occurred on April 30, when approximately twenty members of the state constabulary rode into Mt. Carmel in the Schuylkill field in response to complaints of attacks on workers at the nearby Sayre colliery of the LV. Fearing that arrests would be made, a crowd of what was estimated at between several hundred and two thousand, mostly foreigners, threw rocks at the troopers, who fired into the crowd, wounding perhaps seventeen. This incident added to strike sentiment. Initial reports concerning the convention indicated strong support for a strike, and the members of the joint committee were reported as "outspoken" in favoring one. However, at the first session of the convention, no second was offered for a delegate's motion that the suspension be turned into a strike. After that, the convention went into executive session. According to press reports, on the next day the convention agreed to refer matters to the negotiating committee.[154]

National Secretary-Treasurer William B. Wilson closed the afternoon session with an address to the delegates. While he expressed no preference for or against a strike, he did introduce a note of caution. He stated that what had "struck" him "most forcibly" among the arguments he had heard was that going back to work without concessions would constitute "defeat and the destruction of the organization." To this he responded: "Gentlemen, when a body of men fully realizes the importance of being organized, when they realize the advantages that come to them through the association with each other, no condition of affairs that may be forced upon them by circumstances can ever mean their defeat or destruction." He then brought up a matter that had long been the subject of contention at anthracite gatherings—the cost of membership.

> I know that in the Anthracite region there has been a great deal of kicking and a great deal of criticism because members of the organization believed the dues were too high.

The men in the Anthracite field had received their training—as many of us had—under the old Knights of Labor system, where the dues of the organization was six cents a quarter. Having received our training under an organization that required us to pay but six cents a quarter to the general fund and six cents to the district . . . naturally we thought it burdensome when the taxes became twenty-five cents a month. We felt it was a burden, and some of us objected, but, my friends, no great army was ever put in the field and no great industrial warfare was ever waged for any period of time unless the sinews of war were provided for from some source. . . . Cheap organizations can only produce cheap results.[155]

The press still maintained that the majority of delegates wanted to strike, but mentioned that the "radicals" had already made their strongest push.[156] That afternoon Mitchell and the committee met, and the members showed little sympathy for a strike, in contrast to the division of opinion they had expressed prior to the 1902 walkout (see chapter 6). The vice-president of District Nine, Paul Pulaski, spoke first, maintaining "that the forign [*sic*] speaking mine workers ar not in favor of a strike under any circumstances at the present time." Each of the district presidents then stated he preferred to accept a renewal of the award rather than strike, as did the members of the National Executive Board from the anthracite districts. One of them, Miles Dougherty of District Nine, noted that men would demand relief in case a full-fledged strike was declared. Secretary-Treasurer John T. Dempsey of District One and John P. Gallagher, his counterpart in District Seven, pointed out that workers had already been demanding relief. Board member Thomas J. Richards of District Nine and the vice-presidents of Districts One and Seven respectively, Adam Ryscavage and Andrew Matti, stated that immigrant workers did not want to strike. No one spoke in favor of a strike, and only the slightest doubts were uttered by other speakers. Edward Harris, board member from District Nine, stated that he had "changed his mind since coming into the meeting" and was opposed to a strike. According to James Clark of District Nine, the men were divided, but he was personally opposed to striking. Ralph Simmons, board member from District Seven, noted that although the members of his local favored a strike, he was opposed. Several other members of the committee voiced concerns about relief if a strike occurred. Speaking last, William Carne of District One said he opposed a strike, but pointed out that some men feared that "injury will be done to organization if men go back without consesson [*sic*]."[157] It would be hard to imagine that Mitchell had not guided the group's deliberations. Still, in 1902 he had not been able to lead most district officials or a majority of delegates away from a strike.[158]

Mitchell informed the convention of the committee's recommendation and denied that acceptance of the operators' terms would constitute retreat.

He stated that the operators' proposal to recall members of the Strike Commission to arbitrate wages "very likely would . . . secure an advance in wages for the lowest paid men; but . . . might reduce the wages of the higher paid men to give it to the lower paid men." In his view, any leveling process "must [level] up, not down." He also brought up the prospect of an unsuccessful strike, not mentioning that the suspension had been maintained with little difficulty up to that point.

> If I were sure that you could stand long enough to win, that you would stand firm enough to succeed, I would advise you to strike. . . . But from information reaching me from every part of the region I am fearful that our own people are not inclined to strike; and while I believe they would respond to the instruction of this convention and their organization, nevertheless on the part of many it would be a strike with which they would not be in sympathy.[159]

After the committee's recommendation was translated into several languages, the convention adopted it without a dissenting vote and adjourned to await the return of the committee, which journeyed to New York to meet with the operators.[160] Mitchell tried to persuade the operators to accept a term of only two years for the agreement, however they insisted on three years to ensure that it would not expire during a presidential year. Mitchell importuned the operators to "go that far to meet us," but they would not be moved.[161] Mitchell and his committee accepted the three-year term and signed the agreement. It did not refer to the UMWA; and Mitchell, the district leaders, and the operators signed without any reference to their official positions. The union representatives merely signed on the right side of the agreement, and the operators' representatives signed on the left. From that point, the meeting became quite cordial. In a concession of some significance, the operators agreed verbally to allow dues to be collected and notices of union meetings to be posted on their property.[162]

The committee returned to Scranton and the convention endorsed the final agreement. In trying to explain why better terms were not achieved, Dettrey and Fahy pointed to the overall lack of support for the union.[163] Mitchell closed the convention by admitting disappointment over the lack of any advance, but he emphasized the importance of the operators' having signed an agreement with the union's officers, if not with the UMWA itself. Finally he reflected dramatically on his organizing tour of the previous summer.

> I want to make this announcement for the first time: Had that tour not been made there would have been a reduction in wages. My information is that the railroad presidents had decided to increase the hours of labor from nine to ten: to require that the engineers work 7 days in the week instead of 6; to require the firemen to work 12 hours instead of 8, so that if this information is correct you have won a victory.[164]

Mitchell did not give the source for this information, and the following day the operators issued denials that they had had any such intention.[165] Whether or not the operators planned to make reductions, they were prepared for a lengthy strike, having accumulated millions of tons of coal in stock.[166] In 1902 they had been perfectly willing to reject arbitration after five months even with winter approaching and their coal stocks utterly depleted. In any event, newspapers that had stressed the anthracite delegates' eagerness to strike reversed themselves, emphasizing that most mine workers, especially English-speaking ones, were satisfied with the convention's decision. Some foreign workers were reported angry and likely to leave the union, but it was not clear whether they were more annoyed by the fact that no strike had been called or that they had lost several paychecks during the suspension for no apparent benefit.[167]

Whether or not Mitchell's pessimistic assessment of a strike's outcome was accurate, he had another reason to try to settle matters quickly in anthracite. While some workers in the Central Competitive Field had gone back to work in April, most remained on strike into June, and some 12,000 were still out at the end of July.[168] In reporting the decision not to strike in the anthracite fields, the *UMW Journal* stated that "the resumption in the anthracite will be the means of furnishing a source of revenue to help aid the financially weak districts in the bituminous fields."[169] However, Thomas Nicholls noted that many men in District One abandoned the union over its assessment of fifty cents per member per week in June and July 1906 to support the bituminous workers. Nicholls recalled local meetings where men walked out declaring they would not pay.[170] At the very least, the assessment made it far less likely that the men who returned to the union on the eve of the suspension would maintain their membership. While the amount of money was surely a factor, the men of anthracite could not have liked paying so some bituminous mine workers might obtain an increase that their leaders had told them they could not get. In the aftermath of the suspension, membership in the anthracite region declined rapidly, from 80,000 in March to stabilize at approximately 30,000 for the last few months of 1906.[171]

Some anthracite mine workers may have left the union because they felt betrayed over the UMWA's failure to strike. But it is difficult to imagine that a full-scale nationwide walkout in April 1906 for militant demands could have succeeded. The UMWA faced a diverse group of coal operators and would have had no relief available from mine workers still on the job. The climate of public opinion toward labor unions was less sympathetic than in 1902 when, of course, only the anthracite workers had struck. A massive unified strike across the entire coal industry would, at the very least, have quickly led to pressure from the federal government for compromise. Surely, the precedent of the Coal Strike Commission would not be lost on the same president who had appointed it in 1902. Still, the strategy John Mitchell pursued in 1906, first offering the prospect of a militant nationwide strike only to abandon it piecemeal must have demoralized many anthracite mine workers. Others, looking more pragmatically at the union, saw little reason to maintain their membership for the next three years with an agreement in place.

The twilight status of the UMWA in anthracite must have made it especially difficult for workers to appreciate their union. Their leaders had bargained with coal operators, but they won practically no tangible gains. In the signed agreement that resulted, the union was not even mentioned by name. At some mines, the union might have a vigorous presence; at others it might have none at all. Union leaders, ever mindful of the progress that they and the union had made in anthracite, could not understand why workers might avoid paying dues. Perhaps trying to forget their lack of success in 1906, they refused to take any blame. Instead, as membership fell, they came to view the workers more and more critically, and showed less and less interest in trying to keep them in the union.

9

Demoralization and Rebirth, 1906–1916

The decline of the anthracite districts that began after the 1906 agreement proceeded steadily for nearly six years. In 1908, John Mitchell's successor as president of the United Mine Workers of America (UMWA), former Vice-President Tom L. Lewis, labeled "the attitude of the membership" in the anthracite region as "border[ing] on complete demoralization."[1] In 1909, the union failed again to win any significant concessions in agreeing to another three-year renewal of the award of the Anthracite Coal Strike Commission. By that point, a most onerous cycle had emerged for the UMWA in anthracite. Declining membership gave the union less influence with the operators, a lack of progress in industrywide bargaining emphasized the union's weakness to the rank and file, and membership figures continued to plummet, reemphasizing the union's weakness. In the closing months of 1911, total membership reached its lowest levels since before the 1900 strike, giving little expectation of success in negotiations for another agreement in 1912.

These difficult years for the union display both the strength and weakness of its hold on anthracite mine workers. The union's strength is reflected in its ability to survive and even extend its influence in some ways despite declining membership. However, the union's weakness can be seen in the strategy it employed—taking little more than what the operators would allow it to have. The lack of the check-off reflected the union's weakness, making it dependent on workers to pay dues. Yet that dependence forced the anthracite districts to retain a democratic character that, when combined with the pragmatic independence of the rank and file, kept alive the possibility of a resurgence.

An indispensable element in the success of the UMWA had been its willingness to organize immigrants from eastern and southern Europe. However, in the aftermath of the strike of 1902, union leaders failed to make a consistent commitment of the massive resources needed to keep most of those workers in the union and to enroll the ever-growing numbers of their newly arrived brethren. By 1910, more than 53 percent of anthracite mine workers had been born in eastern and southern Europe, up from approximately half that figure ten years before.[2] In areas where those immigrants predominated

205

FIGURE 9.1
Polish mine workers, Nanticoke, Pennsylvania, Circa 1910. Seated on the right
is Joe Chrzan, standing on the right is Martin Znaniecki (Courtesy of
Jule Znaniecki).

in the mines, the UMWA was at its weakest, and obviously, the union could not improve its weakened condition without them.

A combination of events in 1912 allowed the union to enroll many of those workers, bringing a majority of anthracite mine workers into the union for the first time since John Mitchell's reorganizing drive of 1905. Increased demand for coal and a willingness to risk a strike enabled the UMWA to win its first significant gains from the operators in direct negotiations. By shrewdly following up contract gains with a massive organizing effort, the anthracite districts were able to rebuild. But the infusion of new blood brought the ferment of democracy. Periodic election battles and local militancy to build membership caused considerable turmoil, but as negotiations approached for yet another contract in 1916, the anthracite districts retained greater strength than they had previously between contracts. With demand for anthracite forcing underemployment to a historic low, the UMWA won significant gains once again in 1916. Still, these gains, like the award of the Anthracite Coal Strike Commission in 1903, did little to reform the workplace, and the operators remained adamant against giving union men the security of the closed shop. Despite the union's successes, there remained plenty to complain about for anthracite mine workers, who had learned not only that the union could win important benefits for them, but that they could influence the union.

"PASSIVE SUPPORT"

Discontent arose quickly in the wake of the 1906 settlement. In July 1906, at District One's annual convention, a resolution that called for eliminating salary for members of the district's executive board was tabled by a close vote of sixty-three to forty-five. Board members were accused of "fast sapping the life of the organization, putting it under an enormous daily expense and rendering no service in return."[3] Declining membership surely affected the district's treasury. By December, the executive board decided that the district's financial condition was so weak that it had to suspend paying salary to board members other than officers.[4] However, these problems apparently had no effect on the personal popularity of District President Thomas Nicholls. In November 1906 he won election to Congress as a Democrat, receiving more than 60 percent of the vote to defeat an incumbent.[5] This victory made Nicholls one of two UMWA leaders elected to Congress as part of the American Federation of Labor's effort to encourage trade unionists to run for political office.[6] Still, its significance for District One is less clear. It shows that Nicholls did not look upon the task of strengthening his embattled district as one worthy of his full attention.

At the 1907 UMWA convention, John Mitchell noted that membership in the anthracite districts had declined to approximately the same level as when he began his organizing drive in June 1905. He could not explain the "indifference and negligence" of the anthracite mine workers, but promised to increase organizing there so the workers could be "saved from themselves."[7] Mitchell planned a trip to the anthracite fields in May to organize, but that was prevented by illness.[8] That summer, Mitchell proposed that several presidents "of the well-organized districts" conduct speaking tours in the anthracite region and West Virginia.[9] However, when he broached this plan at a meeting of the executive boards of the anthracite districts, it received such a negative reaction that he abandoned it.[10] Instead, the boards initiated their own drive. National headquarters fortified the campaign with a dispensation reducing initiation or reinstatement fees to only two dollars and a loan of $5,000 to enable District One to pay salary to all its executive board members so they could organize.[11] This effort had a limited impact at best. At the end of 1907, total membership for the UMWA in the anthracite industry stood at only 23,000, and at its next year's convention, District One was forced to eliminate four executive board positions.[12]

In addressing his final UMWA convention as president in January 1908, having announced his retirement several months before, John Mitchell compared the men of anthracite in a most unflattering way with their counterparts in other areas where the union was weak.

> In the bituminous districts named . . . the miners refrain from joining the organization because of the relentless hostility of the operators and the heartless prosecution to which they subject anyone who has the temerity to assert his right to join the union of his craft. . . . Whereas in the anthracite districts there is little or no discrimination against our members. The men are free to join or not to join the union without interference from the mine owners, and the actions of thousands of them in leaving it or in refusing to become members of it is due entirely to apathy and indifference, supplemented by a fallacious belief that it is necessary to establish a strong organization only on the eve of the expiration of their contract with the operators.[13]

Despite declining membership, the UMWA maintained an important presence in local disputes. An uncommonly lengthy walkout at the Jermyn Coal Company in District One lasted from February to August 1906. Union officials played a role in negotiations, and the district provided relief to the strikers.[14] In some cases union officials prevented strikes, as at Kehley Run colliery in November 1908. Terrence Ginley and James Clark, board members from District Nine, met with the superintendent in a dispute over payment for timber and props, and the members were sufficiently satisfied with the result that they decided against striking.[15]

Use of the Conciliation Board continued to decline, with only twenty-three grievances filed during the three years that followed the 1906 agreement. In July 1907, the new president of District Seven, John F. McElhenny, noted the decline in grievances submitted, but stated "it is because we feel that the coal companies are not inclined to abide by any decisions, and the men would rather use endeavors along other lines than bring them to the . . . board." Declining membership also helps explain the decrease in cases, since the union was generally responsible for bringing grievances before the Board. Not surprisingly, union officials were sometimes reluctant to deal with the grievances of the growing number of nonunion men.[16]

One Board decision shows how both the Board and the 1906 agreement could, on occasion, work for the union. In the fall of 1907, several UMWA organizers were ordered off the property of various companies in the Wyoming field. The UMWA appealed to the Board, noting the operators' verbal promise, at the end of negotiations in 1906, to allow collection of union dues and posting of notices of union meetings on their property. Only one of the companies responded to the grievance. The Delaware, Lackawanna, and Western (DL & W) stated that it only told the organizer to leave because he was too close to the pay window, and it included a statement by a committee of the local union at that colliery stating that it had "never been interfered with nor asked to discontinue the collection of dues." Upholding the union, the Conciliation Board formalized the operators' verbal commitment, noting that in making collections and posting notices "there should be no interference . . . [with] the expeditious payment of the employees . . . [or] with men at work."[17] Unfortunately for the union, workers did not hesitate to refuse to pay their dues, even when collected at the mines. District Nine President Fahy told his members in the fall of 1908 that such collections had produced good results, but needed to be "put . . . thoroughly into effect." He realized, however, that "collecting dues at the collieries is inconvenient, and at times . . . unpleasant . . . especially for the men who do the collecting."[18]

Prospects for the next contract were not good. As a result of the nationwide economic downturn that began in the fall of 1907, underemployment in 1908 and 1909 was more severe than it had been for several years.[19] When the new UMWA president, T. L. Lewis, began another organizing drive in the summer of 1908, he avoided militant rhetoric. More significantly, he spent much less time in the region than had Mitchell three years before, and his campaign had only a modest impact.[20] In spite of dispensations extended through the year, membership only climbed from 23,000 at the end of 1907 to 30,000 by the end of 1908.[21]

When the three anthracite districts gathered in October 1908 to plan strategy for the upcoming negotiations, they drafted ambitious demands similar to those of 1906, 1902, and 1900. These included recognition of the union, the eight-hour day, payment by weight for miners, and "a definite and more uniform'' wage scale for company men, to include increases of 10 percent for those earning under $1.50 per day and 5 percent for those earning from $1.50 to $2.00.[22] But anthracite leaders were looking for new and perhaps easier worlds to conquer. President Fahy of District Nine, who had lost a race for the Republican nomination to Congress some months before,[23] ran for national secretary-treasurer with support from President Lewis. However, George Hartlein, secretary-treasurer of the same district, showed his longtime dislike for Fahy by running as well. The secretary-treasurer of District One, John T. Dempsey, was a candidate for vice-president on a slate opposed to Lewis. None of the anthracite men won national office and, to add to the disarray in the anthracite districts, President Nicholls of District One left that office on account of ill health before negotiations commenced.[24]

When the union committee first met the operators on March 11, 1909, just three weeks before the expiration of the agreement, the operators showed no more interest in making concessions than they had in 1906 and offered only to maintain the Commission's award for three more years.[25] In joint convention in March, the three districts decided to keep working after April 1 if no agreement could be reached.[26] The union committee conferred with the operators several times in April, and eventually accepted their terms with a few minor additions to the 1906 agreement. Most notably, rates for new work could not be less than those paid under the Commission's award for similar work, and the understanding on dues collection and the posting of notices was formalized as part of the contract.[27] While the operators remained insistent in refusing any sort of recognition to the union, an interesting change occurred in the way in which the agreement was signed. The signatures were grouped under two headings: ''On behalf of the Anthracite Operators'' and ''On behalf of the Representatives of the Anthracite Mine Workers.'' No such headings had appeared in the 1906 agreement.[28]

Two national organizers noted the positive impact the settlement had on how ''the general public, and especially . . . the business element'' viewed the union. The press and businessmen in Wilkes-Barre reportedly wanted all mine workers to join the UMWA.[29] The problem, of course, was to convince the men to do so. Over the years, organizers had found it hard to understand that more and more workers needed convincing. They may have found the task of continual organizing daunting, especially with the limited resources available. More important, in keeping with the disparaging remarks national and district leaders had directed toward the anthracite mine workers, the organizers may have viewed the task as demeaning, given the stature and accomplishments of the union as they saw it. Peter Kelly, a longtime local leader from Jermyn in the Wyoming field, critically analyzed the approach of many organizers in a Mitchell Day address in 1909:

Many of our mine workers are puzzled, confused and amused at the attitude of some of the organizers who are ever telling the mine worker of the enormous money gain the organization has achieved for him, and this in the face of the fact that the mine worker has no money at all, and in numerous instances he is heavily in debt.

It is not right for an organizer to say that he would prefer to shake the hand of a "scab" or of a "strikebreaker" than that of a man who fails to pay his dues in the union. It is not right for him to say that the man who receives the sliding scale and [is] not a member of the organization is a thief.[30]

In May and June 1910, the predominantly immigrant workers of the Pennsylvania Coal Company (PCC) reminded union organizers of their potential for militancy and the yawning gap between them and the UMWA. The PCC, most of whose mines were located between Wilkes-Barre and Scranton in and around Pittston, had by no means eliminated its labor problems as a result of the August 1905 arrangement it reached with its employees, counseled by union leaders. A familiar grievance—excessive dockage—had played a role in brief walkouts in November 1907 and September 1908.[31] In June 1909, union officials held a mass meeting in Pittston to consider the issue.[32] This was an especially contentious matter in the mines of the PCC, where most miners were paid by the miner's ton. No concrete action resulted from the meeting. The union had become especially weak in the PCC's collieries, where an increasingly large proportion of workers were Italians. District One President Benjamin McEnaney referred to these mines as "practically speaking unorganized."[33] Some workers there had shown sympathy for the Industrial Workers of the World (IWW), or "Wobblies." A Wobbly local had been in place in Old Forge as early as April 1907, and one of the IWW's ablest organizers, Joseph Ettor, spent several months organizing in and around Scranton in late 1908 and the first few months of 1909.[34]

Still, Ettor had long since departed when a brief strike occurred at the #9 colliery in Pittston on May 3, 1910, over dockage and the use of new coal cars. In a meeting with the superintendent, the UMWA local union committee assured him that nonunion men had started the strike. They had been enrolled in the union and the implication was that they would not strike again.[35] Two weeks later another walkout occurred at the PCC's #1 colliery at the IWW's stronghold in Old Forge. Workers at the #9 colliery went out again too, stating that the company had declined to take action on most of their grievances. Two days later, another colliery struck over the same issues— excessive dockage and the miner's ton. Several other mines were out by May 24, at which point some 12,000 employees were on strike.[36]

Interestingly, the IWW claimed no credit for the strike and received none in local newspaper accounts. The UMWA certainly didn't want any. When

FIGURE 9.2
Old Forge breaker, Pennsylvania Coal Company (Courtesy of Hugh Moore Historical Park and Museums—Pennsylvania Coal Company Collection).

the company claimed that the union had induced the workers to strike, President McEnaney called the charge "not only incorrect, but deliberately false."[37] The union used the opportunity the strike provided to sign up workers and even played a role in the selection of committees of strikers to meet with management. Still, its influence with the strikers was quite limited. The Conciliation Board, with the full backing of the union, called on the strikers to return to work and discuss grievances with PCC officials. If that failed to yield results, the Board promised, it would act on the grievances within five days. Union leaders presented that offer to the strikers, but they rejected it.[38]

The PCC held some preliminary discussions with a committee representing workers, but it refused to deal substantively with grievances until the men returned to work. As the strike spread to the PCC's mines at Dunmore, north of Scranton, the union's executive board ordered the members of the twelve locals at the affected mines to meet to fix a date to return to work. Even after the PCC's general manager, W. A. May, gave union leaders a written guarantee that the company would deal with the grievances within forty-eight hours after the men returned, the workers still held out.[39] The strike did not end until the area's Italian consul, Chevalier Fortunato Tiscar, took on the role of mediator. On Monday, June 6, May refused to meet a committee of thirty workers from the company's collieries as Tiscar asked him to do, insisting that they first return to work. However, May did agree to meet with Tiscar himself and, after that meeting, May spoke with a committee of six mine workers, two local priests, two "influential Italians" from Pittston, and Tiscar. The strikers' committee also met with the district executive board and, on the following day, May met with Tiscar and McEnaney and gave them another written guarantee that the PCC would address the grievances. This satisfied the strikers, who agreed to return on June 8 and June 9.[40]

The difficulty over ending the strike shows not only the depth of the workers' distrust of the company but also their lack of faith in the union, which certainly harbored its own suspicions of the immigrant mine workers. The *UMW Journal* blamed the walkout on "agitation by the IWW's" and once again adopted a chiding, paternalistic tone: "By and by the anthracite miners will learn that there is only room for one organization, that their place is in it, and they should remain in it if they do not expect to see encroachments made on their rights."[41]

General Manager May and his lieutenants met with district officials and a committee of strikers from each colliery on June 30 and July 1. Each point on their lengthy list of grievances involved the kind of work rules that had consistently bred disputes throughout the history of the industry. The PCC would not agree to abolish docking as workers demanded, but it did agree to add "pea" coal, a small size increasingly used by consumers, to the sizes that would make up the ton of profitable coal that the miner's ton was supposed to contain. The company also offered to comply with the demand to stop cars on the scales to weight them, if workers at each colliery still desired. But first it intended to make tests it believed would prove the accuracy of the old procedure. To address further the worker's concerns on dockage, the company also promised to compare the amount of salable coal it sent out with the miner's tons it received and pay the miners for any discrepancy. The PCC agreed to the demand that it abolish the practice of hiring workers from its other collieries only if they had a "recommendation card" from their former boss. Additional concessions included payment of a stated hourly rate to miners and laborers who were taken out of their chambers to do work for the company.[42]

As a result of the strike, almost 5,000 workers joined the UMWA at the PCC's mines.[43] Reportedly the PCC also stopped discouraging the employment of checkweighmen and check–docking bosses.[44] Workers at all the company's mines accepted the agreement except those at Old Forge. The company implemented it there anyway, and some of the mine workers struck on August 18. Whether or not these were Wobblies is unclear but, after several days marked by violence between strikers and state troopers, UMWA organizer Martin Memolo convinced the strikers to return to work.[45]

The increase of membership in District One from the PCC strikes did not last long. Few new members could have been eager to pay an assessment enacted at a special international convention called in August concerning strikes in various bituminous fields.[46] On top of the assessment, most UMWA organizers in the anthracite region were to be laid off as part of a retrenchment effort to address the union's precarious financial condition.[47] By year's end, membership in the anthracite districts stood at just over 21,000, with some forty-three local unions abandoned during the year and only one new local organized. In both January and April 1911, membership dropped below 10,000, and in the latter month there were fewer paid-up members than there had been in December 1899.[48]

Still, in the winter of 1911, a curious spark of life arose from the practically moribund anthracite districts. The 1911 international convention, after considerable controversy, passed a resolution requiring any UMWA member to withdraw from the union if he became a mine boss or member of the National Civic Federation (NCF). This was an attempt on the part of President Lewis, who had been defeated for reelection, to embarrass his old rival John Mitchell. After leaving the union's presidency, Mitchell had become chairman of the Trade Agreement Department of the NCF. Although the vast majority of delegates from Districts One, Seven, and Nine supported the resolution, it generated considerable protest from local unions in anthracite. A number of workers condemned it in letters to the *UMW Journal,* and at least nine anthracite locals passed resolutions calling for a referendum vote on the question.[49]

Still, the Mitchell dispute had no discernible impact on union membership, and the persistent weakness of the anthracite districts was of critical importance as the union began to prepare to negotiate another agreement with the operators. When the districts convened in October 1911, they put together a militant set of demands that closely resembled those of 1906 and 1909. These included the eight-hour day, "a more convenient and uniform system of adjusting local grievances," an advance of 20 percent, payment by weight where possible in tons of 2,240 pounds, and union recognition with the check-off. Added to the demands was a promise to strike if necessary, in stark contrast to the reluctance to do so in 1909.[50]

The UMWA had some reason for confidence as it approached negotiations in 1912. The union experienced some organizing success in the early months of 1912, bringing the membership of the districts back to 29,225 in March 1912.[51] In addition, the union had come to the realization that its stature in anthracite was not fully reflected by its membership figures. As UMWA Vice-President Frank J. Hayes put it in January 1912, "our strength in this particular field is not measured altogether by our membership, but somewhat by the great public forces in sympathy with our cause and the passive support, at least, of practically all the mine workers in the region."[52] Just as important was a strong demand for anthracite, which gave workers unaccustomed economic leverage. In 1910, a trend of increasing demand had caused underemployment to decline so much that the mines averaged 229 days worked, the highest number since 1883. That trend accelerated in 1911, with days worked reaching an all-time high of 246.[53] Any lengthy strike in 1912 would exact a substantial toll from operators' profits. Furthermore, 1912 was a presidential year, and the operators would surely want to avoid the all-too-likely possibility of meddling by politicians if a walkout continued into the campaign season.

"SORRY WE CAN'T KILL THE FATTED CALF IN HIS HONOR"

The anthracite mine workers' strong bargaining position enabled the UMWA for the first time to get past the operators' insistence, once again presented by George F. Baer, on a renewal of the old agreement. Negotiations broke off on March 15, and on March 29 the union declared a suspension of work for all except essential maintenance personnel. When negotiations resumed on April 10, Baer suggested that the Anthracite Coal Strike Commission be reconvened to determine what may have changed in the industry. But he soon dropped that familiar ploy, and when the union gave up its insistence on the check-off, the parties came to an agreement. That agreement contained the first substantive gains for the workers since 1902, but they were relatively modest. The UMWA obtained neither recognition nor the eight-hour day nor payment by weight, but it did receive a wage increase of 10 percent. However, that concession was not quite as generous as it appeared, since the agreement also abolished the sliding scale, which had allowed for increases that averaged slightly more than 4 percent since 1903. Contract miners and laborers were guaranteed the rates of company miners and laborers when doing company work and miners were also promised an equitable division of mine cars, as the Coal Strike Commission had recommended nine years earlier. Most importantly, to expedite the handling of grievances, a committee of no more than three workers would be established at each mine to consider grievances with company officials and refer them to the Board of Conciliation as necessary. Company officials and these committees would meet to list all rates of pay as of April 1, 1902, to clarify the basis for the increase. In the agreement, the operators moved a bit closer to a formal expression of recognition for the UMWA by allowing the international president and district presidents to sign it "on behalf of the Anthracite Mine Workers' Organization."[54]

Some mine workers and their leaders thought that union negotiators could have done better. When the subcommittee of district presidents and international union statistician William Green, serving in place of President John P. White (who had become ill), presented the agreement to the executive boards of the anthracite districts, they refused to endorse it. They instructed the subcommittee to return to the bargaining table to get additional concessions. When that failed, many locals instructed delegates to the convention called for mid-May to reject the agreement.[55]

Thus President White, having recovered from his illness, faced a difficult task of persuading the delegates to accept the agreement at their convention. White seemed both defensive and combative, challenging the delegates: "Show me how you can wring more from the anthracite operators." He recognized that "no contract [would] meet the expectations" of the men of the anthracite region unless it included union recognition and the check-off, but he emphasized how difficult these concessions were to obtain: "My friends, listen to what I say, not for what it may mean to me, but for what it may mean to you! When you wring the closed shop from George Baer and his associates you will fight, and you will fight as you did before," referring to the strike of 1902. Still, he noted that recognition had not been won then, when a great many more were in the union. Ominously he asked the delegates, "What is your condition today?"[56]

As so many other UMWA leaders had over the years, White chided the anthracite mine workers, at least those who opposed the agreement. He found it ludicrous that the workers of a region where so few belonged to the union were prepared to insist on the check-off: "Men who would not join the union for fifty cents are demanding that an industrial conflict be waged to make them come into the union and have somebody else check their dues off! Who ever heard of such a philosophy!" He reminded the workers of the "large and losing strikes" he had inherited from the previous administration, in which workers had fought in vain for the right to organize. According to White: "If they had the opportunity you men have in the anthracite field they would be members of the United Mine Workers' organization."[57]

As they had in past conventions, the anthracite delegates proved amenable to their leader's arguments. They accepted the agreement by a comfortable margin of five to one, 323 to 64.[58] But this agreement led to the rebirth of the union. The concessions won were sufficiently tangible to get the attention of workers. Most notably, the provision that established a committee at each colliery greatly facilitated the handling of grievances and energized the union at the local level.[59] With a dispensation in force lowering the initiation and reinstatement fee from ten dollars to two, membership rose above 46,000 in July. That month, President White took advantage of the union's enhanced status by beginning an organizing tour *after* the agreement had been signed. In more than a month in the region, he spoke to some fifty-eight mass meetings. By September the anthracite districts had exceeded their previous peak membership of some 83,000 in February 1906, in the aftermath of John Mitchell's campaign in the summer of 1905. By November, more than 100,000 men were in good standing, and in April 1913, membership peaked at more than 129,000.[60] The business manager of the *UMW Journal* called the anthracite unionist a "prodigal son" and jestingly lamented, "Sorry that we can't kill the fatted calf in his honor. Blame the meat trust."[61]

As thousands joined and returned to the union in the summer of 1912, the districts instituted "button day," on which union committees checked workers to make sure they had the current union button issued for paying dues. This method of encouraging membership, which had not been employed on any general basis since 1901, led quite logically to the "button strike," in which union men refused to work with nonunion men. As Table 9.1 shows, such walkouts were especially common in 1913, as many locals were seeking to consolidate the gains they had made in the previous year. Of course, the operators staunchly opposed button strikes, and in some cases locked workers out for a week or so to punish them. In August 1913, the UMWA petitioned

TABLE 9.1
"Petty" Strikes, 1913–1916

YEAR	WORKERS ON STRIKE	TOTAL DAYS LOST
1913	64,086	481,678
1914	26,115	179,743
1915	30,325	214,691
1916	79,481	955,067

the Conciliation Board to consider instituting the check-off, maintaining that it would obviate "annoying button strikes." The companies denied the request.[62]

In District Seven, union leaders used militant action to make the smallest district the strongest one. Thomas Kennedy had taken over as president of the district in 1910 at the age of twenty-three.[63] He came from Lansford in the Panther Creek Valley, which had been a union stronghold ever since 1902.[64] That strength may well be reflected by a series of button strikes that took place there in August and September 1911, when the union was far weaker than a year later.[65] The district quickly gained a reputation as the best-organized district.[66] In September 1912, some 5,000 men walked out at the mines of the company that dominated the Panther Creek Valley—the Lehigh Coal and Navigation Company—over the refusal of two brothers named Miller to join the union. Kennedy ordered the strikers to return to work after company officials informed him that the Millers had left town. A little over a week later, President White summoned Kennedy and three other district officials to West Virginia to express his displeasure with such walkouts. The officers then issued a circular to their members stating that White deplored the "numerous petty strikes" that had occurred in recent months and that the workers should avoid such strikes in the future.[67]

District Nine's campaign that summer to have committees check mine workers for buttons on a quarterly basis also had a positive impact. A successful button strike was reported at the Buck Run mine, and a local union in Williamstown claimed it had achieved " a closed shop."[69] The recording secretary of a Shamokin local deplored the strong measures some wanted to use against nonunion men: "Some will say we will get a baseball bat and use it to force them into the union. . . . Shame that we should have to hear United Mine Workers utter such propositions."[70] The district participated fully in the massive growth of membership, in some months exceeding the totals of the larger District One.[71] Many of those new members apparently wanted a change at the top of District Nine. In December 1912, John Fahy, the district's only president since its establishment in October 1899, was turned out of office. James Matthews defeated him by a margin of almost two to one.[72]

In District One, militancy arose from the rank and file as mine workers not only took advantage of the agreement of 1912 to form mine committees but sought to develop that workplace instrument into a new, potent force in the industry and the union. Mine committees at the various collieries of several of the large corporations that dominated District One realized that the committees for each company needed to work together on an ongoing basis. So workers brought the committees together to form a "general grievance committee" for various companies. The general committees could conceivably have worked with district leaders as well as against them, but an adversary relationship emerged quickly in the first year after the 1912 agreement.[73] Over the next decade, the general grievance committees would provide the basis for a vigorous insurgent movement and function at times as practically a rival labor organization.

The general grievance committee of the DL & W called a strike for February 1, 1913, at eight of that company's mines over the failure of engineers to join the union. The general committee had met with the company's superintendent and accused him of encouraging the engineers to stay out of the union. He denied that charge and warned that a strike would violate the agreement between the operators and the UMWA. Workers for the DL & W struck for one day in defiance of the union, but were persuaded to return by President John T. Dempsey.[74] This was by no means the only strike over union membership in District One. Thomas Holton, who would unsuccessfully challenge an incumbent for a district board post in 1913 and 1915, reported to the *UMW Journal* in March 1913 that "numerous petty strikes" had occurred in the district over that issue. While he noted that these walkouts violated the agreement, he believed that they demonstrated "the gallant effort [being] made to perfect the organization."[75]

Dempsey had served as secretary of the district from 1900 and became president without opposition in August 1911.[76] Nor was he opposed when he won reelection in July 1912, as the union's revival commenced.[77] By the following winter, a number of general grievance committees had been organized and they had begun to move against Dempsey. They called themselves the "Progressive Party" and tried to enlist locals to support their slate for district office against Dempsey and his allies. In his report to the district's 1913 convention in July, Dempsey criticized their efforts:

> During the past seven or eight months . . . emissaries of this party have been encountered everywhere; money was raised; political literature printed and circulated in the halls of the local unions and elsewhere; visiting committees organized, who went from local to local condemning officers, contracts and most everything else, the result being that wherever an officer went in the pursuit of his duties, he was confronted with some of these committeemen, no matter what he said or done in the interest of the union, he was condemned and ridiculed.[78]

Dempsey won reelection with more than 60 percent of the vote, as did his secretary-treasurer, John Mack.[79] Enoch Williams, secretary of the DL & W's general grievance committee, gave Dempsey credit for being a "better general than any man we got," but alluded to voting improprieties on Dempsey's behalf.[80] Defeated presidential candidate Thomas W. Davis accused the victors of practicing "the rottenest politics ever playing in the state of Pennsylvania," and responded to the charges of some delegates that he was sympathetic to the IWW.

I don't believe in the I.W.W. nor their tactics; I believe, men, that when you make a contract, live up to it; I don't believe in breaking a contract after we made it; I don't believe in breaking machinery and the direct action people do. I believe in being a trade unionist every day in the year, election day included, and when you people use your both arms against the people that are grinding us down, that's the day we will be respected.[81]

Dempsey had also condemned "numerous petty strikes for trivial causes" that had occurred in previous months, noting that they had occasioned "much resentment and bitterness on the part of the operators" and could not "result in any permanent good for our organization or its membership."[82] It is not clear how much Dempsey opposed militant action per se, but he did oppose it when it occurred under the aegis of the general grievance committees. In June 1914, another dispute arose between the DL & W's general committee and management. The company had instituted a mine "patrol" system designed, in the words of the superintendent, "solely for the purpose of giving the face of the working place closer supervision, so as to eliminate or greatly reduce the number of . . . accidents."[83] The general committee of the DL & W believed that the company's motive in enhancing supervision went well beyond safety concerns. Heightening the controversy was the company's refusal, after initially explaining the patrol system to a subcommittee of the general committee, to negotiate further. The general committee threatened to strike on August 1, and even ordered locals to hold strike votes.[84] It showed no interest in consulting district leaders, and Dempsey attended only one meeting of the general grievance committee prior to another meeting on July 30 of the general committee and some "150 prominent union men," where he advised against a strike.[85] A walkout was averted when the general committee agreed to submit a report on the patrol system to district officials who would, "for the first time in local mining history," discuss the dispute directly with DL & W officials.[86] In its statement, the general committee maintained that the strike threat had served its purpose, noting that "the failure of the district officers to have grievances quickly adjusted has created a feeling of dissatisfaction in the minds of all classes of employees."[87]

In accordance with time-honored democratic practice, Dempsey moved to co-opt some of his opponents. When John Fallon, veteran member of the international executive board, died in October 1913, Dempsey replaced him with Thomas Davis, his opponent for the presidency.[88] An opposition slate lost by a somewhat larger margin in 1915, and there was notably less discussion of election fraud.[89] David Fowler, president of the DL & W general committee, won election to the district executive board in 1915 after narrowly losing two years before. At the district convention in 1915, he stated that the district administration had given the general committees "permission to meet.''[90] Still, the general grievance committees would remain as an alternative source of power in the district, and some of their leaders, Enoch Williams in particular, retained their skepticism toward Dempsey and his administration. In the next few years, the general grievance committees of District One would serve as a democratic symbol of insurgency originating in the workplace. The intractable workplace problems of District One would make it relatively easy for the insurgents to find new recruits.

''ANY DELEGATE FOUND HISSING . . .''

Ever since most anthracite mine workers returned to the union, they had begun to acquire a new image at UMWA headquarters. In contrast to previous years, most of them not only paid assessments, but even gave additional contributions to support strikes like that of eastern Ohio miners in 1914–15.[91] Early in 1915, the editor of the *UMW Journal* marveled at the transformation:

> There was a time when the organized miners in the bituminous fields, remembering the ready aid they afforded the anthracite miners in the strikes of 1900 and 1902, and the indifference displayed by these same miners for a period of many years, were inclined to charge the men of the anthracite regions with the black sin of ingratitude.
>
> The loyalty to the organization shown by the men of the hard coal regions . . . especially in the last year, has completely lifted such stigma from them.[92]

President White understood the need for ongoing organizing in the anthracite fields, even though membership did not decline as precipitously between agreements as it had in previous years. In the closing months of 1913, the three districts generally totaled more than 90,000 members.[93] Perhaps District One showed the largest decline thereafter, dipping below 30,000 in several months in 1914.[94] To strengthen the union for negotiations in 1916, President White spent more than a month and a half in the anthracite fields during the summer of 1915, addressing some sixty-eight meetings. His goal was to raise the rate of membership above the 70 percent overall claimed by the union.[95]

Despite White's campaign, membership in District One was far less than that, generally staying below 30,000 for the last half of 1915.[96] Delegates to the biennial district convention that summer discussed a variety of obstacles to strengthening the organization. President Dempsey brought up an important issue in the management of union locals—lax bonding procedures for local officials, treasurers in particular. One local at a mine in Old Forge that had enrolled all 1,200 employees there fell apart after some $1,400 was lost, and the workers shifted their allegiance to the IWW. Dempsey added that the Old Forge case was in no way unique.[97] Consistent and effective examination of union buttons had also been difficult to achieve. Some members gave buttons to friends or family members. A number of locals abandoned the use of buttons and checked dues records or receipts instead. A delegate named O'Neill described the most effective, but ultimately most burdensome method of maintaining membership:

> [W]e have a better system altogether and no expense attached. We have a very active committee, a committee from the Local with the spirit of unionism in their make-up. We don't have to coax anyone in our colliery to join the Union, we know everyone in the colliery and know him to be a member, and if he ain't we make him one.[98]

While District One continued to show weakness in 1916, District Seven maintained its strong organization. District Nine also did well, often pushing its membership above 30,000, thus exceeding the substantially larger District One during some months.[99] A continuing willingness to resort to button strikes in the anthracite districts certainly played a role in organizing success. As can be seen from Table 9.1, local walkouts increased markedly in 1915 and much more in 1916, in what may have been a show of force for the benefit of the operators.

Most of the demands of anthracite mine workers for the contract to be negotiated in 1916 were familiar: a 20 percent wage increase, an eight-hour day, union recognition, a speedier grievance procedure, payment by weight, and prohibition of contract miners having more than one working place. In an attempt to extend formal bargaining down to the district level to deal with a variety of thorny problems, the union called for "arrangement of detailed wage scales and the settlement of internal questions . . . [by] representatives of the operators and miners of each district." A new demand called for "a readjustment of the machine mining scale" to address one of the few technological innovations affecting the actual mining of anthracite. From this point, machine mining and machine loading would move very slowly into some of the relatively flat veins of District One.[100] With negotiations looming in both anthracite and bituminous, the UMWA played down militant action. In October 1915, the editor of the *UMW Journal* announced that the union saw no need to suspend operations if contracts were not completed by the deadline: "There was a time . . . when any difference of opinion between employers and employees could only be adjusted by a display of solidarity on the part of the latter; but, in the organized fields, at least, that time has passed."[101] The union may have adopted this approach because of increased slack time in both bituminous and anthracite in 1915. The latter averaged some 230 days of work, a large figure historically, but smaller than any year since 1910.[102]

The IWW offered its own response to the approaching expiration of the 1912 agreement by conducting a membership campaign in the summer of 1915. On February 1, 1916, a UMWA button strike at a mine of the Lehigh Valley Coal Company at Duryea near Pittston, apparently with some support from the company, resulted in several Wobblies being compelled to join the UMWA. This spurred the IWW to hold a convention at Old Forge on February 6 in which ten locals were represented by forty-six delegates. That one-day gathering adopted twenty demands, some of which resembled those of the UMWA, such as the eight-hour day and restricting each miner to only one chamber. Others showed a more intense commitment to leveling the work force, or at least improving conditions for the lowest-paid workers through such measures as the abolition of piecework and specific daily minimum wage rates for all workers. The Wobblies' major effort coming out of the convention was a month-long strike at the Greenwood mine of the Delaware and Hudson, which ended in defeat in mid-March.[103] Overall, the IWW exerted itself fitfully. The only public notice that it received from UMWA leaders came early in April when President White and President Matthews of District Nine warned workers against joining Wobbly-inspired work stoppages in violation of the no-suspension policy.[104]

As in 1906 and 1912, the simultaneous expiration of bituminous and anthracite agreements complicated negotiations. They did not really get underway in anthracite until the end of March, but the union's no-suspension policy allowed them to be conducted at a leisurely pace. However, that pace rankled restive mine workers, and the UMWA negotiators urged the operators to move more quickly to offer counterproposals. When those proposals were less than satisfying, as was the operators' refusal to budge on union recognition and the check-off, the UMWA committee broke off negotiations toward the end of April. They called a tri-district convention for May 2 that would have the power to call an industrywide walkout. However, the union soon returned to the bargaining table and the parties reached agreement at the end of a marathon fourteen-hour session on Sunday morning, April 30. The operators made substantial concessions—such as the eight-hour day, an agreement on machine mining, and a wage increase of 7 percent for miners and 3 percent for company men, who would benefit most from the shorter day. These terms reportedly had been enhanced somewhat from the proposals the operators had made before the union broke off negotiations. But to obtain them, the union negotiators abandoned recognition and the check-off.[105]

In contrast to the previous agreement, this one received the endorsement of the executive boards of the anthracite districts.[106] Nevertheless, many delegates expressed their displeasure with it at the convention. The reading of the agreement occasioned enough vocal discontent to prompt President White to intone from the chair that "any delegate found hissing—expression of speech that belongs to geese—will not be tolerated."[107] Delegate George Evans of District One bemoaned the failure to obtain the perennial demand for payment by weight, which he thought was still "one of the most vital questions confronting the Anthracite Coal men today." Another District One delegate named Quinn told the convention that his company had successfully insisted on removing him as a check–docking boss because he had represented the miners too vigorously.[108]

Most criticism centered on the inability of the negotiators to win the closed shop. In large part this reflected the understandable weariness local leaders had long expressed with the task of trying to keep workers in the union. One delegate complained that locals at the PCC's mines had deteriorated badly and the IWW had made substantial gains: "If we can't have the check-off system up there how are we going to hold them, or the closed shop? We can't hold them today, and if we can't get the closed shop we won't hold them hereafter."[109] A delegate from District Nine explained that, by 1915, his local had lost more than half of the 400 members it had in 1913. Recently membership had increased substantially, but "they are coming in just merely because of the closed shop; and we told them that we would get it this time, and they are afraid of that and they are coming in fast, and if they don't get the closed shop now they won't have 50 men in Pine Grove local."[110]

Other delegates saw the closed shop as a way to end discrimination against union activists. According to a delegate named Yodzio, "The Grievance Committees are discriminated against; the agreement is abused that has expired, and there is nothing in this agreement, I can see, is going to prevent the bosses and superintendents from abusing you."[111] Delegate Grogan from District One wondered why the operators resisted a closed-shop agreement. He referred to the petty strikes that operators had complained about across the anthracite fields and the agitation of the IWW in his district. In one dispute, the IWW had organized laborers who threatened to strike, and the company asked for the support of the UMWA local. The delegate mused, "They expect the United Mine Workers to stand by them, but still they won't give the United Mine Workers recognition."[112]

White responded by criticizing those who opposed the agreement for putting "all your eggs to the basket of recognition." He emphasized, along with District Seven President Kennedy, that the public would not have much sympathy with any strike called solely to obtain the check-off. For White, such a strike was an "unsavory proposition to go before the public on. . . . [T]he natural question is asked of us if we love this Union so well and it has accomplished so much for us, why are we not loyal enough to it to pay our own dues?" He focused on the somewhat stronger recognition the union had achieved and the benefits he thought would flow from that. The district presidents had signed the agreement as presidents of Districts One, Seven, and Nine of "the Anthracite Mine Workers Organization," rather than just as individuals on the organization's behalf in 1912. More significant for the officers, the "Organization" had been named in the contract as the "party of the first part" and the operators as the "party of the second part." They maintained that this contract language would allow them to pursue the closed shop further. They also thought it would provide an opportunity to eliminate a problem about which the union had complained since 1900, but which had proliferated in recent years, namely, contractors managing work in numerous chambers. Delegates complained that some "miners" were in charge of work in as many as thirty chambers and making from $200 to $600 every two weeks. Such a system had discouraged union membership, made working conditions more difficult, and increased income disparity among miners. David Fowler of the District One executive board interpreted the agreement as preventing the operators from contracting with workers outside of the terms of the agreement, and White stated flatly that "this form of recognition . . . destroyed the subcontractor with his Padrone system."[113] Events would prove White and Fowler to have been either overconfident or dishonest.

John White appeared to be flabbergasted at the lukewarm reaction of quite a few delegates to what he saw as the "great cardinal reform" obtained in the agreement, the eight-hour day.[114] The bituminous mine workers of the Central Competitive Field had achieved it in 1898. Since then the UMWA had encouraged miners across the country to take April 1, the day on which it went into effect, as a holiday. Nevertheless, a number of delegates questioned the actual benefit they would receive. Seldom did most miners work as long as eight hours, much less a full nine-hour day. They left their chambers once they blasted enough coal for their laborer to load for the rest of the day. For some company men, the language of the agreement seemed to indicate that they might receive little or no benefit from the eight-hour day, especially those like the mule drivers, who were expected to walk on their own time to where they began work in the mines.[115]

Those who opposed the agreement called for it to be submitted to a referendum of union members. This had been done in the bituminous region *instead* of calling a ratifying convention, but not in anthracite and never in the union as the *result* of such a convention. President White, who at times seemed to be losing patience with the opponents of the agreement, viewed such a referendum as an abdication of responsibility. The delegates accepted the agreement by a margin of approximately three to one, 581 to 206.[116]

The 1916 agreement contained noteworthy achievements for the UMWA in anthracite. However, what is even more notable for the union's future is the persistent discontent over those issues on which the union's leaders could not wrest concessions from the operators. The lack of payment by weight had infuriated miners practically as long as anthracite coal had been mined. It was a grievance intensely important to the rank-and-file miners of District One, but one that union leaders understandably pursued with little vigor, having failed to make any progress on the issue from the beginning of industrywide negotiations. The lack of the check-off not only decreased union membership, it also made union men especially vulnerable to the pernicious discrimination that bosses had always had so many opportunities to implement, given the complexities of anthracite mining. Obviously its impact on district leaders was not so deeply felt, causing them pragmatically to exchange it for other concessions during collective bargaining. The growth of contracting would become a larger and larger problem, once again providing more occasions for the operation of favoritism, an endemic problem in the capricious anthracite workplace.

The potential for conflict would be greatly heightened as anthracite mine workers, along with so many other Americans, were called on to intensify their labors with the entry of the United States into the First World War. At that time, mine workers realized both an inordinate increase in their bargaining power and a greatly expanded interest by the federal government in their work. Ambitious representatives of the rank and file would use the increased importance of the anthracite industry to demand action on the workers' most deeply felt grievances. Armed with their faith in democracy in the UMWA, these insurgents would find it easier to take charge of the union than to reform the workplace.

10

Insurgency and Democracy, 1917–1925

In 1919, the Children's Bureau of the United States Department of Labor investigated living conditions in Shenandoah and several surrounding towns in the Schuylkill field. The town of Shenandoah was "so hemmed in by mine properties on every side" that it had been unable to expand. Its population density was more than twice that of New York City and three times that of Chicago. Homes were not only crowded, but many had been damaged by mine subsidence. The problem of subsidence had also affected drainage, and even those areas served by sewers faced severe sanitary problems. For most residents there was no collection of garbage, hence it "was often found scattered about the crowded courts." Infant mortality occurred at a rate that was "one of the highest in the country," twice the national average. Almost 60 percent of the boys surveyed had begun work by the age of fifteen, and their tasks in the coal breakers were as dirty and dangerous as they had always been. Not surprisingly, little provision had been made for playgrounds, so children played wherever they could—on streets, on railroad tracks, along trolley tracks, on dumps for garbage and coal refuse, and even in streams full of sewage and drainage from the mines. Finally, as they always had, families who lost fathers in mine accidents faced a terrifying struggle to survive.[1]

Nevertheless, such fundamentally insecure living conditions only placed the families of anthracite mine workers well within the broad range of industrial life in early twentieth-century America. As bleak as life in Shenandoah and the rest of the anthracite region could be, according to the United States Coal Commission it held some distinct advantages over the general isolation that so many bituminous mine workers encountered in numerous company towns. Instead, the vast majority of anthracite mine workers resided in "independent communities" that had "steam and electric railways, good roads, inter-urban telephone connections."[2] The perils that characterized life in Shenandoah were unfortunately much too common, as were the struggles of families for survival across the American industrial landscape. As historian Frank Stricker has noted, a great many industrial workers were left out of the prosperity of the 1920s.[3]

By that decade, the anthracite mine workers had improved their earnings as the underemployment that had dominated their lives in the 1890s gradually abated. From 1916 through 1921, the anthracite mines averaged 273 days, or what practically amounted to full-time work.[4] While wage rates still tended to be somewhat lower than the bituminous industry, anthracite mine workers faced far less underemployment in the early 1920s than their brethren in soft coal. Thus, according to the Coal Commission, they were able to attain a "much higher" standard of living.[5] In comparison to workers in a variety of other industries, anthracite mine workers averaged daily wages higher than some, lower than others. They worked more time than workers in the clothing industry but less than steel workers, where the twelve-hour day was still in force. Overall, the wages of anthracite mine workers were roughly comparable to most industrial occupations.[6]

In 1925, the Coal Commission offered the following evaluation of life in the anthracite fields:

> The earnings of full-time workers . . . certainly permit the essentials of a reasonable standard of living. Those who take full advantage of their opportunities to earn in the various occupations connected with the industry and are not handicapped by serious misfortune need not suffer for shelter, food, clothing, or other decencies and comforts of life, even without supplementary earnings of wife or children.
>
> On the other hand, many of the families of the miners' helpers or laborers have a very uncertain and inadequate income. These families, many of them large, are often in economic distress. . . .
>
> The impression which a fair-minded and sympathetic observer in the anthracite region will gain is of drab and bleak exterior conditions imposed not by lack of earnings or incomes but by the very character of the industry.[7]

However difficult life remained for the men, women, and children who depended on the anthracite coal industry for a living, their material conditions had improved considerably since the struggle for unionization began. In the years following the 1902 strike, anthracite mine workers had a difficult time keeping up with the slowly rising cost of living. However, from 1914 to 1926, they showed the biggest gains in real wages of some fifty-three categories of workers analyzed by economist Paul H. Douglas.[8] Those gains were based on the expanding opportunity for work as well as substantial increases in wage rates obtained during and after the war. However, perhaps the most significant factor in the real wage gains of anthracite mine workers was their dogged determination to maintain wage levels in the 1920s.

The United Mine Workers of America (UMWA) surely played a vital role in this economic progress. Although the increases won by the union fell somewhat short of the peak of the rising cost of living in the summer of 1920, the union recovered gains in real terms as prices fell substantially in the next five years.[9] To prevent wage cuts sought by the operators, the union held out

in 1922 and 1925 for as long as it had in 1902. In 1923, the union even garnered a 10 percent increase after a brief walkout.

The strikes of the 1920s show the solidarity of anthracite mine workers,
but that solidarity was not simply the product of harmony within the union.
As recent immigrant groups had come to dominate the union's ranks in the
1910s, they sought to exercise influence in the union in proportion to their
numbers. Ethnic tensions combined with intractable workplace grievances
and the nation's demand for coal in World War I to nurture insurgent movements in Districts One and Nine. The success of those insurgent movements
demonstrates a product of unionism that may well be of greater significance
than pecuniary gain. Especially by the 1920s, the success of the UMWA, its
openness to immigrant groups, commitment to industrial unionism, and re-
tention of democratic procedures had set it apart from other unions.[10] The
UMWA organized the anthracite industry at the turn of the century not so
much through its own initiative, but by serving as a vehicle that took advantage of workers' militancy. In the 1910s and 1920s, struggles for control of
that vehicle gave mine workers, especially those who had recently come to
America, an opportunity to experience the turmoil and travail of democracy
in a way no nonunion worker could possibly comprehend

"TO DO OUR BIT FOR GOD AND COUNTRY"

As the United States moved toward entering the First World War in 1917, the
anthracite mine workers benefited from the growing shortage of labor and
the anticipated need for coal. By the end of April, just several weeks after the
declaration of war, mine workers received supplemental increases ranging
from 10 percent for miners and their laborers to approximately 20 percent for
company men. In November, miners and laborers obtained additional increases of about 15 to 20 percent, with approximately 20 to 30 percent for
company men.[11] However, these gains did not cause mine workers to show
greater loyalty to their union, and the tightening labor supply undoubtedly
increased turnover at the mines, making it more difficult to keep workers in
the union. Membership in District One fell steadily, declining 14 percent from
an average of more than 28,000 in 1916 to less than 25,000 in the next year.
For 1918, membership averaged slightly less than 18,000, more than 37 percent below the previous year.[12]

The intensity of the insurgent movement in District One had diminished,
but in no way had it disappeared. At the biennial convention in 1917, John T.
Dempsey's hold on the presidency was contested by Eugene McTiernan, who
received slightly more than one-third of the vote and did not contest the
result.[13] The vice-presidency remained in the hands of Joseph Yannis, a man

FIGURE 10.1

Breaker boys playing football in the shadow of the Kingston Coal Company #4 breaker, Kingston, Pennsylvania, 1920 (Courtesy of the Wyoming Historical and Geological Society).

of recent immigrant stock who first won the post in 1913. However, while the vice-presidency remained the one slot on the executive board for recent immigrants, as it had been in the anthracite districts practically since the founding of the union, it was contested with considerable vigor. Yannis had won reelection the first time in 1915 with 40 percent of the vote with the remainder scattered among candidates named Kurowski, Paczkowski, Killowski, Lekarz, and former incumbent Adam Ryscavage. Two years later Yannis took only 38 percent, with the rest garnered by new opponents named Isaacs, Kujawski, Stash, Weiss, Badwak, Gomelko, and Halupka, as well as Stanley Lekarz.[14] Election battles did not only occur in District One. In District Nine, the three officers and the international board member had faced strong challenges in the fall of 1916. President Matthews received 60 percent of the vote in defeating Thomas Butler, and Vice-President John Strambo and International Board Member Martin Nash won by similar margins.[15]

The strenuous demands of work during the war and the gradually accelerating inflation would place considerable stress on those anthracite mine workers who remained in the mines, and those stresses would reignite insurgency. In 1917, the anthracite mines reached their peak production at nearly 100 million tons and would almost equal that figure in 1918. In these years the mines worked a record number of days, 285 and 293 respectively.[16] Record-setting production and the growing shortage of labor led mine workers to look for another supplemental wage increase in 1918 from the United States Fuel Administrator, Harry A. Garfield. He refused the UMWA's request for both anthracite and bituminous miners on August 23, but the union decided to push for an increase for the anthracite men alone. On September 4, Garfield agreed to investigate the cost of living in the anthracite region and to compare wages in anthracite to those in bituminous and other industries.[17]

Mine workers had been mobilizing on their own without sanction from their district leaders. Insurgents had held meetings throughout the summer which, according to the *UMW Journal,* their leaders had declared "illegal and their action null and void."[18] At the beginning of September, delegates from local unions in District Nine had met to demand an increase from Garfield, giving him two weeks to act. On September 7, some 400 delegates from locals in District One followed up on a previous meeting at which they had formulated demands for Garfield. They passed a satirical resolution claiming that, since they were "unable to make a living," they requested "the right to be inducted into the army, where we shall be recognized as willing to do our bit for God and country."[19] They also gave Garfield ten days to grant an increase, cryptically threatening that if he failed to do so, "we will all be soldiers."[20] The first deadline came in the Schuylkill field, and delegates there met on September 15, led by Christ J. Golden, who was opposing James Matthews in that year's race for the district presidency. Without sanction from the district, they declared a walkout to which some 25,000 mine workers in District Nine responded on September 16.[21]

The strike occurred while District Seven was holding its annual convention. That district, which according to its secretary-treasurer "equaled a closed shop organization," showed no sympathy for the walkout. The convention did "not agree that threats and intimidation should be used against the government at this time" and "condemn[ed] any effort . . . to cause suspensions or shutdowns now when our work is needed."[22] Veteran insurgent Enoch Williams and his associates in District One bided their time, displaying no eagerness to join the strike. Garfield responded to the walkout by maintaining that he would not award any increase while the strike continued. Since the walkout occurred at the height of the final Allied offensive against the Germans along the western front, the strikers received vigorous condemnation in the press. At a mass meeting on the third day of the strike, as reports spread that Garfield was likely to recommend an increase, Golden joined with Matthews to urge the men to return to their jobs.[23] That ended the walkout in District Nine and left the insurgents of District One to consider the expiration of their deadline at a meeting on Saturday, September 21. The 450 delegates avoided discussing the strike in Schuylkill. Instead they proclaimed that they "were not pro-Germans or I.W.W.'s or disgruntled obstructionists" and declared their opposition to any strike, pending action by Garfield. They asserted their loyalty to the government and their union, but accused the district's leaders of failing to represent the rank and file.[24]

The anthracite mine workers received their increase after a series of meetings in October between UMWA leaders and operators, who were able to agree on an increase to recommend to Garfield and the government's General Wage Board. The advances, ranging from approximately 15 percent for miners and laborers to 30 percent or more for company men, were termed by the union "the largest single advances in wages ever secured."[25] But this success did noting to quiet insurgency. In District Nine, Christ Golden defeated Matthews for the presidency. In District One, John Dempsey was toppled, not by insurgent action but by his own executive board. On November 6, District Board Member James Gleason called for Dempsey's removal as provided for under the UMWA Constitution on grounds of public intoxication and neglect of duty. Dempsey had five days to respond to such charges, and when he failed to do so the board voted four to two to declare the office vacant. Vice-President Yannis acceded to the presidency, and in January the board appointed Thomas Lowry to replace him as vice-president. Then, pleading ill health, Yannis resigned the presidency to be succeeded by Lowry, and returned to the vice-presidency.[26]

This curious game of musical chairs evoked a strong response from the insurgents. Shortly after Dempsey was removed from office, they had called

FIGURE 10.2
Christ J. Golden, President, UMWA District Nine, 1918–1928 (Originally printed in the memorial booklet for the dedication of the John Mitchell Statue in 1924—Courtesy of the Pennsylvania Historical and Museum Commission, Anthracite Museum Complex, AC 92.50.1).

CHRIS GOLDEN,
President District No. 9, U. M. W. of America

This Page Donated by LOCAL UNION No. 1132, Plymouth, Pa.

for a special convention to elect a new president, but district leaders denied the request, maintaining that the regular convention scheduled for July 1919 was "reasonably close at hand." The insurgents appealed this decision to the International Executive Board, which at first supported them. But the district appealed the International Board's decision, which that board then reversed.[27] The candidates for president of District One were John Dempsey—apparently recovered from his bout with the bottle—and the veteran insurgent, Enoch Williams.

The gathering of District One was stormy from the start. Delegates discussed a variety of issues, calling once again for action on the check-off, which they pointed out the operators had not accepted as part of the 1916 agreement as union leaders had hoped. On another familiar topic, they approved resolutions condemning the operators' dockage and weighing procedures.[28] Arguments arose over the seating of delegates and the action of certain local unions vastly increasing their membership in the months just before the election. When Vice-President Yannis complained about this, a delegate named Marion asked if he had been aware of it in earlier years. When Yannis admitted that he had, Marion asked: "Then how is it that you never raised your voice before this?" You claim you knew all about what you are denouncing now, but you never raised your voice before when you were being nursed by those people."[28] The contentiousness that pervaded the convention prompted the following plea from a veteran delegate named Panek:

> I don't see nothing in this fight to-day. . . . I can see no right to fight delegates for this and that, but only for the right cause of this Organization, fight for the Organization, that's all. It is not right this getting one man mad at another and one bunch here and another bunch there and fighting all the time; that don't help this Convention. We have to stay in one bunch, if the bunch is straight, and if it is not straight we ought to be man enough to say, if you don't be straight you be kicked out. . . . [B]efore you do anything get down and consider the children tomorrow and that we must produce for them and not do harm to the Organization. If we do, then the children be saying: "Papa, where is bread?"[30]

Panek's eloquence had little effect. Concerning the district election, the insurgents tried to push through a resolution which claimed that since "irregularities were perpetrated and . . . the laws of right and justice were abused and trampled upon," the convention should meet in executive session to "hear any violations or irregularities."[31] After a rancorous discussion that led to an abrupt adjournment "amidst some confusion," the resolution was voted down on the following day.[32] A constitutional amendment, in which the Constitution Committee had concurred, directed that any district officer removed for "intoxication . . . shall not be permitted to aspire for office for five years after conviction." Despite protestations by its proponents that the resolution was "aimed at every one and not at any particular person," the resolution's potential impact on candidate Dempsey was obvious and led to its defeat.[33]

The insurgents repeatedly came out on the short end as delegates discussed and eventually accepted the returns reported by the union tellers. Dempsey won with an official count of 8,855 votes, or slightly less than 60 percent, versus Williams's 6,241. John Kolodziejczak, who also on occasion went by the name of Collins, won the vice-presidency with substantial support from many of the same locals that backed Dempsey. He defeated Yannis, Frank Kurowski, John Dworchak, and George Isaacs, sometimes known as Azys. Secretary-Treasurer Mack won by a margin of more than two to one, and, in a bitter battle, incumbent International Board Member Thomas Davis defeated William J. Brennan by a vote similar to that in the Dempsey-Williams race.[34]

The insurgents called attention to affidavits they had testifying that the actual vote of particular locals differed from that reported by the union's tellers. Their opponents took refuge, as Dempsey had in previous disputed elections, in the constitutional provision that prohibited any protest of election returns unless the protest had been lodged within ten days of the voting at the locals. Although the district constitution provided for such a challenge to fraud at the locals, it made no provision for challenging the totals once the locals had sent them to district headquarters. The district tellers' totals had not been revealed until the convention, more than a month after the election. So, in preventing any thorough discussion of the insurgents' charges, the majority could claim it was only adhering to the constitution.[35]

The insurgents did not accept their defeat stoically. Delegate Lewis Davis told the convention:

> I have been in the Organization since 1897, and I want to say that if a man was not a Union man he was not just to himself. . . . Somehow I have come to this Convention starting out with big hopes . . . thinking that the Organization was for the purpose of elevating the principles of the working man to bring him from the gutter as it were, to the highest political level. But it seems I have met with some surprise and I have come to the conclusion that District No. 1 is the crookedest District that I have ever come in contact with (Applause). This Convention to my way of thinking has been one of the foulest proceedings that my imagination could have pictured. . . . I want to say there has been no fair play here and no justice given in this Convention. It seems to be one-sided only and I believe, as a similar assertion was made yesterday,—You are digging your own graves.[36]

Enoch Williams did not mince words either, warning the delegates:

> You will reap what you sow. . . . It is jugglery of votes that has defeated myself and others in District No. 1, and then do you think in the spirit of

fairness and justice and fair play that we are going to stand by the decision of this Convention? Gentlemen, it would be smaller than the most mortal man imaginable if we would not stand up in this Convention and demand our rights. . . .

All I want is this; understand my position in this fight. I am not fighting the fight of Enoch Williams; I am not fighting the fight of Billy Brennan; I am not fighting the fight of George Isaacs; I am in the fight of purity in our Organization, and I am fighting the fight of the rank and file (applause) so that the rank and file of this Organization should have a right to live. I am fighting the fight for a man and his Local Union so he can stand up and oppose the officers of that Union if they are not doing their duty.[37]

Williams and the insurgents did not wait long to make good their threats. As they had on occasion previously, they used workplace grievances to energize the insurgency through a familiar tool, the general grievance committee. In December 1918, soon after John Dempsey was deposed by the executive board, President Joseph Yannis, in an action his predecessor surely would not have taken, urged the presidents of the locals of the Hudson Coal Company, formerly the Delaware and Hudson, to form a general grievance committee.[38] As it brought up grievances with the company and made little headway, the committee allied with the insurgents as the only group that might sanction militant action. At the end of August 1919, less than five weeks after the end of the district convention, workers struck at four mines. They complained of excessive dockage, layoffs, and the company's policy of using mechanical loaders in those places that were easier to mine, leaving the tougher spots for the regular miners.[39] When the general grievance committee met on September 5, it called for all Hudson mines to strike on Monday the 7th. Meanwhile a strike had broken out on September 4 at the Archbald colliery of the Delaware, Lackawanna, and Western (DL & W) over the rate paid to seven miners. This may have served as a pretext for showing support to the Hudson men, because the DL & W general grievance committee, led by Enoch Williams, moved quickly to escalate the Archbald walkout. The general committee of the DL & W endorsed the grievances of the Archbald men and called on its locals to take a strike vote. All of this was done without consulting district headquarters.[40]

When some 12,000 employees of the Hudson Coal Company in Lackawanna County struck on Monday, September 8, President Dempsey had to face the embarrassment of returning from the opening of the UMWA's International Convention in Cleveland. On Tuesday, workers at the DL & W mines in Lackawanna County joined the strike. Although several Hudson mines to the south in Luzerne County had also walked out, DL & W locals there voted to stay at work. Both company and union officials said they would not deal with the grievances while the men were out, and company officials stated that they were "agreeable, and always have been, . . . to tak-[ing] up grievances with the officers of the union." Dempsey stated that "the general committees are usurping the authority vested in the executive board of the union and are setting up a dual organization."[41]

Amidst this spreading turmoil, John Mitchell died in New York City on September 9 at the age of forty-nine. Mitchell's own sense of the significance of his success in anthracite was reflected in his wish to be buried in Scranton. Mine workers across the nation did not work on September 12, the day of his funeral, and delegates attended from a great many anthracite locals.[42] Possibly this event played some role in containing the strike; still, contentious rhetoric continued to flow back and forth. International President John L. Lewis wired his support for Dempsey from the convention and the district executive board gave Dempsey authority to revoke the charters of locals on strike. The district president told the *Scranton Times* that "the general grievance committee has no standing whatsoever and has not the right to frame demands." Concerning any effort to revoke charters, an unnamed member of the DL & W general committee stated that "if Dempsey tries to use that weapon it will be the end of him."[43]

But Dempsey denied any intention of moving against the locals, and district officials instead called the general committees unrepresentative of the many union men who wanted to return to work. The four Hudson locals in Luzerne County that had walked out decided to return after only two days on strike. After hearing speeches by Dempsey and a representative of the Conciliation Board, workers in Olyphant in Lackawanna County agreed to return on Saturday, September 13. By Monday nearly all the Hudson mines had resumed operations, with union officials promising to take the grievances to the Conciliation Board. As the Hudson strike fell apart, the DL & W general committee at first struggled to maintain its walkout, insisting as late as the Saturday deadline that the men would not return. However, the insurgents' lack of confidence may well be reflected by Enoch Williams's denying permission to District Board Member James Gleason and UMWA organizer and onetime fellow insurgent David Fowler to address a mass meeting of DL & W men. On Monday the fifteenth, the DL & W committee agreed that the men should return to work.[44]

These strikes did little to address the grievances of the workers, and in the case of the men of the DL & W, there is substantial doubt whether the grievances that prompted the original walkout at Archbald were in any way sufficient to justify a company-wide strike. But this set of job actions did accomplish a good deal. First, it embarrassed John Dempsey and the district leaders and showed just how little control they had over a large portion of the rank and file. Second, it gave Enoch Williams and the insurgents experience leading a strike that went beyond their own company. In this context, the fact

FIGURE 10.3
John Mitchell Memorial, Scranton, Pennsylvania, dedicated 1924
(photograph by author).

that the walkouts did not resolve the grievances increased the appeal of in-surgency. The general grievance committees had only accepted the inevitable in ending the strikes; union leaders had pushed for the workers to return. Surely, mine workers could expect no thoroughgoing reorganization of the workplace from the Conciliation Board on such basic concerns as dockage and unfair assignment of work. The grievances of the men of the Hudson Coal Company did not differ fundamentally from grievances common long before mechanical loaders had come to the anthracite fields. Such technolog-ical advances only heaped additional complexity upon age-old injustices at the workplace. In the summer of 1920, workplace grievances would combine with accelerating inflation to present the insurgents of District One an un-precedented opportunity to take control of their union.

"UNDER THE GUISE OF TAKING A VACATION"

In March 1919, the anthracite presidents signed the report of the UMWA's Policy Committee, which called for a thirty-hour work week as well as "na-tionalization and democratic management of the coal mines."[45] Only the former was among the demands presented to the anthracite operators when the UMWA opened negotiations in March 1920 to replace the 1916 agree-ment, set to expire at the end of the month. The union's demands included a wage increase of 60 percent, prohibition of "the making of individual agree-ments and contracts in the mining of coal," and full union recognition with the check-off. There were also other basic work reforms long sought by an-thracite mine workers, such as a uniform wage scale, payment by weight in tons of 2,240 pounds, an end to dockage, and a uniform rate of payment for refuse removed in the mining process.[46] Both sides agreed to extend talks be-yond the expiration date, but by May little progress had occurred. The mine workers abandoned the thirty-hour week and lowered their wage demand to 27 percent for miners and approximately 20 percent for company men, the figures bituminous mine workers had received several months before from a presidential commission. The operators had only offered an increase of some 15 percent. Secretary of Labor William B. Wilson, former secretary-treasurer of the UMWA, then joined the negotiations and persuaded the operators to enhance their wage offer slightly. The union's scale committee of anthracite representatives rejected this proposal unanimously. They saw the increase as meager amidst skyrocketing inflation, and they also took little solace in the operators' willingness to sign a contract for the first time officially with the UMWA, but without any closed-shop provision. Finally, the union could not accept the operators' proposal to cap the wages of company men at six dollars a day, which would have resulted in some men not obtaining the full percent-age of the increase or even having to take a wage cut.[47]

Union leaders had no interest in a strike. After declaring a bituminous walkout in November 1919, UMWA President John L. Lewis and other union officials were indicted by the federal government for violating wartime economic controls still in effect because no treaty of peace had yet been signed.[48] President Woodrow Wilson did offer to appoint a commission to arbitrate the demands of the anthracite men, as he had in soft coal. At a tri-district convention at the end of May, Lewis and his vice-president, Philip Murray, recommended that the delegates accept the operators' last offer rather than the President's commission. They based their opposition on a dislike for compulsory arbitration and their belief that no commission would give the anthracite mine workers much more than what Secretary Wilson had been able to wheedle from the operators. Lewis and Murray then left to appear at a hearing in Indianapolis on charges stemming from the bituminous walkout. It is impossible to determine if they might have swayed some delegates had they remained at the convention, but, in their absence, practically no one supported them. District Presidents Kennedy and Golden expressed a strong preference for the commission, while Dempsey, who reportedly favored the operators' offer, failed to attend the convention. Insurgent leader Enoch Williams characterized the operators' proposal as "a damnable proposition." Intensely dissatisfied with it and perhaps anticipating that they would get an increase similar to that of the bituminous men, the delegates endorsed the commission alternative without dissent.[49]

The Anthracite Coal Commission held hearings in Scranton from June 24 to July 20. William L. Connell represented the operators, UMWA International Board Member Neal J. Ferry from District Seven represented the mine workers, and William O. Thompson, president of Ohio State University, represented the public. The union, led by its economist W. Jett Lauck, emphasized the industry's obligation to pay a wage sufficient to provide a decent living for each worker and his family. Attaining such a standard would necessitate an increase substantially larger than the cost of living. UMWA officials also called the Commission's attention to the massive profits anthracite companies had earned in recent years and the rapid rise in coal prices over the last few months. This buttressed the union's assertion that the companies could afford to grant the mine workers' demands without increasing the price of coal. However, the Commission avoided transforming its work into a broad-ranging investigation of the anthracite industry, maintaining that its jurisdiction extended no further than ruling on the specific demands of the UMWA.[50]

Shortly before the Commission finished its deliberations, a new outbreak of militancy occurred in a part of District One that had long posed problems for the union, the mines of the Pennsylvania Coal Company (PCC). For more than a decade these mines, located in and around Pittston, had been domi-

lian immigrants. Some 8,500 mine workers left their jobs on July
over a single grievance—the "contract system," in which compa-
ed over portions of mines to contractors who employed miners and
o work the chambers for a daily wage. Miners complained of con-
paying less than customary rates or charging more than companies
for supplies such as powder. However, the essence of the grievance was
that contractors exercised tyrannical authority over their men in the tradition
of the *padrone* and earned a great deal by doing so. According to a newspaper
report, a contractor could earn as much as $400 to $500 every two weeks,
and "take trips to Italy and live the life of a real money king." While contractors who had "not been in the country more than ten years ha[d] become
immensely wealthy," miners "with vastly more experience in the mining of
coal c[ould] scarcely earn enough to keep their families." As miners had
pointed out regarding contract work as far back as the hearings of the Anthracite Coal Strike Commission, miners working on their own in chambers
had to compete for mine cars with contractors, who commonly received pref-
erential treatment.[51] Reflecting on the strike, Rinaldo Cappellini, one of its
leaders, melodramatically portrayed the depth of the system's corruption:

> [Contractors] were not satisfied to put you in the mines and make you load
> six and seven cars a day for the forty and fifty dollars in two weeks, . . . no,
> they even wanted your dear wife and daughter to play with while you were
> working nights. They wanted your very flesh and blood and they wanted the
> honor of the poor innocent daughter and wife, which has been proven in
> different hotels in Lackawanna and Luzerne counties where they slept.
>
> [I]n the Pittston District you had no organization. Your organization
> was only in existence to this extent that the President of the Local would be
> an assistant foreman; the Secretary of the Local would be a contractor; the
> Vice-president of the Local was a driver boss and the committee all
> politicians.
>
> [A] man would have to go to the foreman and say Mr. Man please give
> me a job,—please,—after giving fifteen or twenty years of his life to the
> company; or go to the contractor and "please, have you got a job for me."
> And their earnings, forty-five or fifty for some, but others sixty or twice as
> much because he stood in with the boss.[52]

The contract system had effectively discouraged union membership. According to one estimate, fewer than 100 of the workers of the PCC belonged
to the union. Two men with rather different goals had begun organizing and
reorganizing workers there some weeks before the strike, D. L. McCue of the
District Executive Board and Enoch Williams. At some point, joining the
union became transformed in the workers' minds into a crusade to eliminate
contracting. The leaders of District One made no immediate effort to encourage the men to return to work, but two UMWA locals at PCC mines in Dun-

more, north of Scranton, where strike leaders had tried to
walkout, passed resolutions opposing it. Those locals noted that
violated the union's agreement and endangered its case before the
Coal Commission. They attributed the strike to an "insidious du
ment," that is, the insurgency.[53]

A meeting on July 23 of a committee of strikers with twelve local priests,
law enforcement officials, and Mayor James J. Kennedy of Pittston showed
that the strike had considerable support from the community. Local newspapers proclaimed neutrality but called on the PCC to deal with grievances, and
a group of clergy even requested that the company abolish the contract system. City police were sympathetic to the strikers, and a detective named Sam
Lucchino investigated charges of contract-related corruption, for which the
PCC had reportedly tried to get him fired. In his youth, Lucchino had been
involved with the "Black Hand," but he had repudiated those ties and had
acquired a reputation for apprehending a great many "criminals among the
foreign speaking element." On the evening of July 21, Lucchino was mur-
dered. His popularity was reflected by the more than 4,000 strikers along
with "what seemed to be the entire Italian population" attending his funeral,
which was reported to be the biggest ever held in Pittston. As he lay near
death, Lucchino had told Police Chief Leo Tierney that a local contractor was
responsible for his shooting. Police arrested two men from Trenton, New Jer-
sey, who they believed were brought to town to eliminate Lucchino.[54]

Although the Pittston strike gradually became fully unified with the insurgent movement, local men held firm control. To maintain close contact
with the rank and file, the strikers' committee, which was the general grievance committee for the PCC, held open meetings every day of the strike.
Their chief spokesmen were Joseph Yannis, former vice-president and—
briefly—president of District One, and two men who exerted greater influence, Alec Campbell and Rinaldo Cappellini. Campbell was the checkweighman at the PCC's #6 mine in Pittston and served as chairman of the
committee. Cappellini had gone to work in the mines at age nine some time
after he had immigrated from Italy, but at age fourteen he lost his right arm
and two fingers on his left hand when a mine car ran over him.[55]

A group of local businessmen, clergy, and representatives of the strikers
met with a superintendent and attorney for the PCC on Monday, July 26. That
meeting resulted in an offer from the PCC to give chambers to miners who
had been working for contractors and deal with other grievances once the
men resumed work, but strike leaders rejected it.[56] Federal agents, who
might have been considering some sort of legal action against the strikers,
urged Cappellini and Campbell to call the men back to work. Cappellini's
response showed the desperation and suspicion of the Pittston strikers: If the

leaders tried to order the men back, they "would be sure we sold them out and we would probably be shot full of bullet holes."[57]

Cappellini headed a delegation that met with PCC officials in New York City on August 3, at which time he handed over affidavits collected by the late Sam Lucchino detailing corruption in contracting. Community leaders began to pressure the strikers to return. Mayor Kennedy suggested a way to end the strike. Workers could accept the guarantee of chambers to all miners who wanted them and then organize thoroughly and refuse to work for contractors. For its part, the company could promise not to discriminate against strikers. The contending parties showed no interest in his proposal. On August 12, the Anthracite Coal Commission and the Board of Conciliation directed the men to go back to work, and the *Scranton Times* agreed. On that same day, workers at the Hudson Coal Company's Laflin mine struck against the contract system there. But Cappellini showed no interest in expanding the PCC walkout, telling the Laflin men that they could help the PCC men most by returning to work to help supply the demand for coal.[58]

According to the United States Bureau of Labor Statistics, during the first six months of 1920, the cost of living had increased more than fifty percent in Scranton.[59] This heightened worker concern over what increase they would receive from the Anthracite Coal Commission, which was drafting its award. Their expectations contributed to insurgent efforts, as did the PCC strike. On August 21 at a meeting of some 4,000 workers, Enoch Williams predicted that every Hudson and DL & W mine would strike too unless the Commission called for elimination of the contract system. He held the PCC responsible for the election of Dempsey and other district officers and, comparing himself to Sam Lucchino, alleged that the company planned some sort of attack on him. Williams called another meeting for the following Saturday, charging that the Commission was holding back its report in the hope of breaking the Pittston strike. On Tuesday the twenty-fourth, in the first episode of large-scale violence since the strike began, sheriff's deputies and state troopers fought with several hundred women who were seeking to discourage the few men who were trying to go to work at the PCC's #6 colliery.[60]

The report of the Anthracite Coal Commission was not officially released until Friday, August 27, but news of its contents had come out two days before, and it was not good for the mine workers. Instead of the 27 percent increase miners in soft coal had obtained from the Bituminous Coal Commission, the majority report of the Anthracite Commission gave only 17 percent. Overall, the increase did not differ substantially from that turned down by the mine workers three months before, although the Commission made no attempt to revive the operators' maximum wage provision for com-

FIGURE 10.4
#6 breaker, Pennsylvania Coal Company, Pittston, Pennsylvania (Courtesy of Hugh Moore Historical Park and Museums—Pennsylvania Coal Company Collection).

pany men. The only workplace concession obtained was compensation for tools lost in mine accidents. The majority report of the Commission refused to abolish the contract system or dockage, although it expressed concern over abuses in these areas. Furthermore, while the operators were directed to recognize the UMWA itself "as party to the agreement" to be formulated along the lines of the Commission's award, that recognition did not include the check-off. Otherwise, the only substantial departure from past agreements was one that both miners and operators had been willing to accept: that it last for only two years.[61]

The insurgents lost little time before taking action. On Saturday, August 28, some 300 insurgent delegates met in Wilkes-Barre. Although the Commission's report had been released, President Wilson had not yet announced his official acceptance of the majority report, to which the UMWA's Neal J. Ferry had issued a vigorous dissent. In a move that showed the mix of nerve and naiveté that characterized the insurgency, the meeting authorized the dispatch of a telegram to President Wilson, signed by Williams, Cappellini, and three other general grievance committee chairmen. They urged the President to reject the majority report before September 1, "otherwise all men will refrain from work."[62] On August 31, the insurgent leaders received the President's response. After urging them to accept the majority report and noting that Ferry had done so in an "honest and manly" way after expressing his dissatisfaction, Wilson added: "If your communication, declaring your intention to refrain from working . . . is intended as a threat you can rest assured that your challenge will be accepted and that the people of the United States will find some substitute fuel to tide them over until the real sentiment of the anthracite mine workers can find expression and they are ready to abide by the obligations they have entered into."[63]

While UMWA officials urged mine workers to accept the award, however unpalatable it might be, District Nine President Golden noted that the men might leave work anyway. Already on August 31, workers had failed to report at mines in each of the districts. On September 1, insurgent delegates from more than half of District One's 125 locals voted at a meeting in Wilkes-Barre to take a "vacation." With federal agents in the city prepared to take action against any "strike," the insurgents, according to the *New York Times,* "displayed a wholesome fear of Federal laws in refusing to talk strike, walkout, tieup, in fact anything but a 'vacation.' "[64] On that same day, the UMWA Scale Committee agreed to accept the award and sign a contract embodying it on the next day in Scranton. By September 3, some 125,000 anthracite mine workers, or 70 percent of the work force, had joined the vacation. Union leaders appealed to President Wilson to urge the operators to meet with them to consider additional concessions beyond the Commission's award, as Wilson had recently requested that operators in the Central Competitive Field do some months after the bituminous award: "The inequalities of the award are so apparent that voluntary uprisings have taken place in opposition and protest in all of the mining districts despite every effort . . . by the officers of the UMWA."[65]

Throughout this tumultuous summer, little had been heard from District One headquarters and President John Dempsey. For several months at least, Dempsey reportedly had been unable to attend to his duties. Perhaps with the hope of combating the insurgents and ending the vacation, the executive board of District One asked Dempsey for his resignation on September 3 and dismissed him the next day when they did not receive it. Enoch Williams proclaimed that, while he was glad to see Dempsey go, the walkout would continue until the workers received an increase equivalent to that of the bituminous men and the elimination of the contract system. Still, relief over Dempsey's departure may help explain why the vacation was least complete in the district where it was declared. By September 4, the walkout was nearly total in Districts Seven and Nine, and in the latter, several hundred pumpmen, firemen, and engineers left their jobs in a show of militancy, thus endangering the mines. Officials from those districts apparently realized the depth of the workers' discontent and took no action to encourage them to return. Meanwhile, perhaps half of the workers of District One were on the job by September 10.[66]

Gradually the vacation strike lost steam. The insurgents had expressed the hope that their walkout would have a positive effect on the President, but it did not. In a telegram to union leaders on September 9, Wilson recalled both his earlier response to the insurgents and the recently concluded world war:

> Notwithstanding the plain warning contained in that telegram, which received wide publicity, the majority of the anthracite coal miners, following the leadership of these men, have refrained from work under the guise of taking a vacation. In doing so they have not deceived any one, not even themselves. When a body of men collectively refrain from working by mutual understanding, however arrived at, it is a strike, no matter what name may be given to it. Our people have fought a great war and made untold sacrifices to insure among other things that a solemn agreement shall not be considered as a mere scrap of paper.[67]

The vacation continued for another week or two in the various parts of the anthracite fields. Momentum toward a resumption was especially strong in District One. On September 16, Enoch Williams decided to abandon the vacation shortly before the union's General Policy Committee of district leaders completed a statement directing the vacationists to go back to work. A gathering of insurgents in Scranton chaired by Williams agreed in advance to accept the recommendations of the Committee.[68] Its statement placed blame for both the walkout and the President's rebuke on the insurgents, "a few unthinking men attempting to usurp the functions of the regularly constituted authorities of the United Mine Workers of America." Still, the Committee scrupulously avoided criticizing the rank and file, noting how hard they had worked in recent years: "The idleness has . . . given the mine workers a well-earned vacation and at the same time manifested their displeasure at the scant measure of justice meted out in the award of the commission."[69]

By September 21, the resumption of work was practically complete in District Seven. In District Nine, the General Mine Committee representing some 10,000 workers in and around Shamokin directed maintenance workers to return to prevent additional damage to the mines. However, they decided that the rest of the workers should stay on strike until operators agreed to take back the maintenance employees who had struck and low-level bosses who had refused to replace them. President Christ Golden took a militant stand in this matter, in part because of his bid for reelection. Workers in Shamokin returned on September 24, but problems persisted, threatening a new walkout.[70] The Conciliation Board resolved the dispute by ruling that all maintenance workers and petty bosses should get their jobs back, but that the UMWA should disavow jurisdiction over any bosses and agree that the strike of the maintenance men was a mistake that would not occur again.[71]

As the vacation strike crumbled in District One, community leaders in Pittston saw an opportunity to settle the strike there. In this endeavor they enlisted the chief of the Pennsylvania Bureau of Mediation and Arbitration, Judge William Tracy. In addressing a mass meeting of strikers on September 9, Tracy called for a committee of five strike leaders to join with a committee from the Greater Pittston Chamber of Commerce to meet with the longtime head of the PCC, W. A. May. At the meeting on the next day, May asked for proof of abuses by contractors, and the workers' committee gave him some affidavits and promised to bring more. At a meeting of the general grievance committee on the eleventh, strike leaders appeared willing to turn negotiations over to the Chamber of Commerce. In words that he probably regretted later, Alec Campbell told the strikers in attendance: "These men are better able to represent you than your leaders here, having better educations and they are able to repudiate any attacks made upon you or your cause."[72]

On Monday, September 13, President John (Collins) Kolodziejczak of District One chaired a meeting at the Pittston State Armory that was billed variously as for the "English-speaking" or "conservative" men. However, a large number of immigrants attended and forced a quick adjournment. When one Tony Mario was invited to translate, he denounced those in charge and urged his fellow Italians to "remain true to Cappellini." Tracy and the Chamber's committee met twice with May and emerged on Friday the seventeenth with his promise to allow Tracy to investigate contracting abuses. Although he believed "there is no such widespread evil as is alleged," the company would cooperate fully with an investigation, which could begin once the men returned to work. This proposal made a favorable impression upon the Chamber's committee, but the strike leaders were highly skeptical.[73]

On Monday, September 20, at a meeting of the general grievance committee, Joseph Yannis told a large crowd of strikers, "We don't want an investigation; we want to abolish the contractors." Such opposition did not deter Tracy and the businessmen. The Chamber's committee called on mine workers to gather that evening to hear May's proposal, and a great many arrived outside the State Armory before the doors were opened. When the committee arrived with Tracy, they summoned mounted state troopers to clear the entrance, even though quite a few police and troopers were already there. Tracy then addressed those assembled outside, inviting all who wanted to hear May's offer to enter, but telling those who didn't to stay out. Reportedly, he made a special appeal to English-speaking and Polish workers. The precise ethnic composition of those who gained admittance to the Armory is uncertain, but Cappellini and Campbell were not allowed in.[74]

Tracy received a rousing welcome from his select audience, and he took full credit for what the press referred to as the "expulsion of the foreign miners." He wanted those assembled to understand that "the law gives a corporation the right of private contract. We cannot deny the right of the PCC to do things that other corporations do." He referred to the company's proposal as "the best possible thing they have to offer." Steve McDonald, veteran leader of the Scranton Central Labor Union, agreed, calling the PCC's offer "the fairest that has come to my notice in the twenty-five years I have been interested in the labor movement." The audience reportedly gave a unanimous endorsement to a motion calling for a return to work, and Tracy promised that those who did so would be fully protected.[75]

The general grievance committee had been outmaneuvered. More mine workers came to work on September 22 than at any time since the beginning of the strike. The committee moved to save face by obtaining procedural changes in the investigation and a promise from May that the company would not interfere with any union local or grievance committee, or with the election of check–docking bosses and checkweighmen. They also received a promise from the Chamber's committee, which had taken the title of "Strike Settlement Committee," to provide continued support to the effort to eliminate abuses in contracting and to help adjust other problems that might arise. No hint of dissatisfaction appeared at a mass meeting on the twenty-third that ratified the general committee's decision to end the strike. Two days later, some 6,000 mine workers paraded to celebrate what appeared to be a dubious victory.[76]

However eager the mine workers of the PCC might have been to get back to making a living, their attitude toward the contract system had not changed. Immediately upon the resumption of work on September 27, numerous disputes arose. Some men complained that the company had failed to carry out its earlier commitment to provide chambers for all miners who wanted them. Even more galling, a number of contractors had been employed directly by the company as section foremen or, as the workers called them, "hustlers" and "pushers." Mine workers also complained of the conspicuous presence of the State Police as they came to work, and the chairman of the Strike Settlement Committee, James A. Joyce, agreed that the company had promised that the troopers would not be there. One Italian member of a grievance committee reported that a boss had greeted his request for a meeting with the superintendent with an ethnic slur. By Wednesday the twenty-ninth, many mine workers were staying away from their jobs, and two mines were almost completely idle. When the company failed to take care of the various problems by Saturday, the general grievance committee called out all mine workers, including essential maintenance personnel.[77]

Such a militant step apparently played no role in the resolution of the dispute, since those maintenance workers who did strike were easily replaced. Instead, momentum toward a resolution came from a most unexpected source—the contractors themselves. On Tuesday, October 5, contractors at the Butler mine offered to resign. The response of the general grievance committee was skeptical, noting that their goal was the abolition of the contracting system. Soon thereafter, contractors at two other mines also offered to quit, and May promised after meeting with Joyce to move the pushers to other posts. For the present at least, contracting was collapsing, and the general grievance committee ordered that the men return on Friday the eighth. Rinaldo Cappellini suggested to the mine workers in attendance that the one way to prevent contracting problems in the future was to join the union. On Saturday, October 9, the *Pittston Gazette* reported that contractors were selling their tools.[78]

The ability of the general committee to snatch a substantial victory from the jaws of a qualified defeat can best be explained by the hate the immigrant workers had for the contracting system. By resuming the strike a little more than one week after declaring an end to it, the general committee merely ratified the determination of the men of the PCC to force change. Although the committee had never called for the resignation of contractors, instead directing its energies toward the company, some strikers might have helped to induce the contractors to quit. In four weeks in August and September 1920, dynamite was set off at the homes of some seven contractors. No one was killed in these incidents, but perhaps that was the point. In any event, even if the dynamiting was more the upshot of personal grudges rather than labor militancy per se, it still confirms the intensity of feeling against contracting.

"WHY SHOULD WE BE CALLED RADICALS OR BOLSHEVIKI OR IWW?"

The vacation strike may not have accomplished the goals Enoch Williams set for it, but more importantly it reflected the strength of the insurgency. John Dempsey was out of the way in District One and the men of the PCC, with their strike concluded successfully, could take over the moribund UMWA locals in and around Pittston. At the end of the vacation strike, the leaders of District One tried to block the insurgents by revoking the charter of Enoch Williams's local for its refusal to open its books to union auditors. Williams successfully appealed the revocation to John L. Lewis, but this controversy gave District One's leaders an excuse to exclude Williams from the ballot as a candidate for secretary-treasurer in district elections in 1921. However, Williams's appeal to the courts succeeded, forcing the district to put him back on the ballot.[79]

Turmoil continued to bubble to the surface at the mines of the PCC. Throughout the fall, the thousands of recent immigrant workers who followed Rinaldo Cappellini, Alec Campbell, and the PCC general grievance committee flocked to local unions. In Local 1581, the insurgents demanded that the duly elected officers step aside. Early in January 1921, workers at the PCC's #14 mine struck, and the general committee threatened to call the men out at all the PCC's mines. In a curious reversal of strategy, the committee suggested that company officials use their influence to persuade the officers to quit. Perhaps gleefully, the PCC noted its October promise not to interfere with local unions. James Joyce of the Strike Settlement Committee had remained closely involved with the general grievance committee, but he could not accept this strike and openly broke with Cappellini. After a stormy meeting of the general committee on Saturday, January 15, the front of Joyce's store, which also served as his home, was dynamited.[80]

Joyce and his daughter were only shaken, not injured, but community outrage was palpable. The Chamber of Commerce, City Council, County Commission, and the general grievance committee offered rewards totaling $5,500 for information leading to the arrest of the perpetrators. Public reaction to the dynamiting combined with the intervention of John L. Lewis to persuade the general committee to give up the strike. On January 16, strike leaders met with Lewis in Wilkes-Barre and accepted his ruling in favor of the local's officers. That did not end the habit of direct action at the mines of the PCC.[81] In mid-June 1921, the general grievance committee took the company's workers out on strike over assorted minor grievances. However, when

FIGURE 10.5

#14 breaker, Pennsylvania Coal Company, Pittston, Pennsylvania (Courtesy of Hugh Moore Historical Park and Museums—Pennsylvania Coal Company Collection).

the District One executive board threatened to revoke the charters of the various locals, the committee ordered an end to the walkout. In the recently held district elections, insurgent leaders Joseph Yannis and John Ruane had triumphed in races for the international executive board and district board respectively. However, if their locals' charters were revoked, they could be prevented from taking office in August after the district convention.[82]

At that convention in July, Enoch Williams defeated longtime Secretary-Treasurer John Mack by a margin of 57 to 37 percent, with three other candidates splitting the remaining votes. Insurgent William J. Brennan won the district presidency by an even larger margin, receiving twice the combined vote of his three opponents. Another veteran insurgent, George Isaacs (Azys), won the vice-presidency over three rivals, including incumbent John (Collins) Kolodziejczak, with 45 percent of the vote. Only one incumbent district board member kept his seat. Williams did not hesitate to lord it over his rivals when they complained about the handling of various procedural matters: "The only trouble here is that certain parties are not getting their own way the same as they have had it in other conventions (applause). No you are now going to have some of the feelings that I have had for years. Take your medicine (loud applause)."[83]

While he did not run for district office in 1921, Rinaldo Cappellini played a prominent role in the convention. In typically fiery fashion, he defended the onetime insurgents against familiar charges: "Why should we be called Radicals or Bolsheviki or I.W.W. when we are only fighting for our rights and for the justice that the country of the Red, White, and Blue gives to all?"[84] His standing among the delegates is evidenced by the invitation extended to him to address the convention after the presidents of Districts Seven and Nine had done so. Outlining his accomplishments against the "slavery" of the contract system in Pittston, he called on his fellow delegates to strengthen the union.

> I believe I have the right to try to drive away slavery as much as I can, and every American citizen who is loyal to the country and not to the almighty dollar should exercise the same rights, because we have an awful work ahead to make this country free and I think it is our duty. . . .
>
> I say to get what is coming to you you have to be organized; you need unity. As I think Brother Kennedy or Golden said there is no use in ridiculing somebody else for if you want to clean house you have to do it from the inside,—and that you have done this time, you have cleaned house from the inside and not from the outside. (Applause).[85]

The victory of the insurgents spurred an increase in membership. Average membership in District One for 1920 was somewhat under 19,000, with the highest figure reached in December, after the vacation strike. For 1921, average membership almost doubled, to just under 36,000.[86] At the same time, convention delegates that year showed their suspicion of authority by voting down a proposed increase in monthly dues from seventy-five cents to one dollar, despite strong support from both incoming and outgoing district officials.[87]

Anthracite mine workers showed the intensity of their solidarity in 1922, when they stayed out for 163 days in a strike they began along with more than 400,000 bituminous men on April 1. The demands of the mine workers were familiarly militant—an increase of 20 percent and the check-off, along with a variety of workplace concessions that had been trotted out consistently since 1900 to little avail. The operators countered with a demand for a reduction in wages of more than 20 percent, pointing to the steady decline in prices since their peak in the summer of 1920. They also sought a provision by which wage levels would be subject to arbitration throughout the contract, for which they suggested a term of five years. The anthracite mine workers, along with their bituminous counterparts, united behind John L. Lewis's policy of ''no backward step.'' Negotiations made no progress and the mine workers waited out an industrial dispute that saw little violence and no attempt to break the strike. Lacking any tentative agreement to submit to a convention, union leaders instead held a referendum in June that overwhelmingly endorsed the walkout. At the end of August, amidst rumors of a possible federal takeover of the mines, Pennsylvania Senators David Reed and George Pepper, with support from President Warren G. Harding, called for an extension of the old contract, pending an investigation of the coal industry by a presidential commission. The operators and the UMWA negotiators accepted their proposal as a basis for ending the strike. The operators, apparently hoping to push again for wage cuts as soon as possible, wanted the contract to last only one year, while the union wanted two. They settled on a term of one-and-a-half years from the expiration of the last contract, or until the end of August 1923.[88]

At the convention called early in September to accept or reject the tentative agreement, District Presidents Brennan, Kennedy, and Golden vigorously endorsed it, as did John L. Lewis. Each of them claimed that the anthracite mine workers had won a noteworthy victory. They assured the delegates that the proposed commission could have nothing more than an advisory role, thus avoiding the binding arbitration that the operators had tried to obtain.[89] In advocating acceptance of the contract, Neal J. Ferry, who had established a reputation for militancy with his ringing dissent to the Anthracite Coal Commission's majority report, appeared chastened by the staunch resistance of the nation's coal operators.

> I remember, my friends, during my career in this organization how I longed to see a national strike, and I figured it out in my own way that this fight could not possibly last above two and a half months, or three at the longest.

> Where is the man here today who would really think that this Anthracite strike is now seven or eight days longer than the great strike of 1902 and not yet over.[90]

However, while most delegates appeared more than ready to return to work, a few veterans of District One's insurgent movement wanted to maintain the strike to obtain the closed shop. Enoch Williams and Rinaldo Cappellini tried to downplay the effects of the lengthy walkout on mine workers and their families. Cappellini deplored that some delegates had claimed "that the mine workers and the children of the Anthracite fields are starving to death. That is not true, and we want to tell the coal companies that it is not true."[91] Williams compared the strike to the recent war.

> Did anybody ever see a battle that sacrifices didn't have to be made? Did anybody ever see a battle that suffering to some extent was not left? Millions of men fighting for a principle over in France were killed, killed fighting for the principle of Democracy. I don't know of one man killed yet in this great industrial conflict that we are in that is of as paramount interest to the mine workers as that was over in France, and not a life lost yet. You are all looking in pretty good shape.[92]

Williams and Cappellini failed to win much support and could not even force a roll-call vote, as the delegates agreed to return to work after five-and-a-half months of idleness.[93] But their quest to continue the strike may have been aimed at a different goal—firmer control of District One. In 1923, Cappellini defeated the incumbent, onetime fellow insurgent William Brennan, with just over 60 percent of the vote to become the district's first elected president of recent immigrant stock. While Williams retained his post by a margin similar to Cappellini's, Joseph Yannis lost his seat on the international executive board to his and Cappellini's former colleague on the PCC's general grievance committee, Alec Campbell. Vice-President Isaacs (Azys) retained his post, but he had sided with Cappellini and Williams in opposing the tentative agreement to end the 1922 strike.[94]

Despite these electoral battles, the district convention of 1923 ran smoothly, without the open and bitter factional fighting that had dominated practically every gathering since 1913. The delegates even agreed to raise dues to one dollar by an unanimous voice vote.[95] The district appeared to be as strong as it had ever been. Possibly because of heightened interest over the election, in 1923 the district attained its highest membership figures since 1913. In addressing the delegates, President Cappellini promised vigorous leadership:

> Now, I am mighty glad this convention has conducted itself in such an orderly and harmonious manner. But don't think for a moment that we don't

know what some locals have done and that we don't know about the corruption and the means that are used. Now, whether I am in two years or more, if I serve you right you will again consider me perhaps, and if I do not you know what to do, but I want the next President, whoever he may be, to get a clean-cut vote from the members of the United Mine Workers of America.[96]

After years as the weakest district in the anthracite fields, District One seemed poised to perfect its organization. District Seven had continued to enjoy what amounted to a closed shop, and District Nine had almost achieved similar status.[97] The union's strength would serve it well in the summer of 1923, as negotiations with the operators proceeded without result toward the August 31 deadline. The prospect of another lengthy strike prompted the Coolidge Administration to use the United States Coal Commission to mediate the dispute. The Commission made no progress, and noted the "mutual distrust" between the parties. Determined to obtain an increase that the operators seemed just as determined to refuse, the union would not accept a renewal of the current contract to 1925. Frustrated by its experience with the Anthracite Coal Commission, it also refused the operators' offer to submit its demands, which closely resembled those of 1922 and 1920, to arbitration. In reporting on its failure to the President, the Commission perceptively went beyond the positions of the parties to explain the source of the gridlock that had come to characterize collective bargaining in anthracite:

> There are inequalities and injustices in the present wage scale, not only in the entire anthracite district, but even in individual localities and mines. . . . [V]ariations in wage rates for the same job are found throughout the anthracite region. . . .
>
> Even with the pieceworkers, or tonnage men, the contract miners and their laborers, the rates paid in different mines can not be directly compared. These differences in tonnage rates may also involve marked inequalities inherited from the more or less haphazard arrangements of rates which prevailed 20 years and more ago.[98]

Overall, the Commission believed that "the renewed agreements have too rigidly retained the practices and conditions of 1902, and have not had adequate flexibility. An industry which is necessarily constantly changing can not tie itself inflexibly to conditions of 20 years ago without hampering the management and working injustice to miners." The Commission added that "no simple method of amending the existing wage scale can reach the desirable result, and direct negotiations to that end seem to be in vain."[99] With the strike deadline rapidly approaching, neither the operators, the union, nor the Administration showed any interest in establishing the "joint committee to make a scientific study of the present wage structure" that the

FIGURE 10.6

Rinaldo Cappellini, President, UMWA District One, 1923–1928 (originally printed in the memorial booklet for the dedication of the John Mitchell Statue in 1924— Courtesy of the Pennsylvania Historical and Museum Commission, Anthracite Musuem Complex, AC 92.50.1).

Compliments of .
LOCAL UNION, No. 484
PROSPECT COLLIERY
Wilkes-Barre, Pa.

RINALDO CAPPELLINI,
President District No. 1, U. M. W. of A.

Commission suggested. Just before the deadline, Pennsylvania Governor Gifford Pinchot offered to mediate the dispute. He suggested a 10 percent wage increase that the operators accepted most grudgingly. Shortly after the mine workers suspended work on September 1, both parties reached an agreement for the next two years, essentially embodying Pinchot's terms. However, contrary to the governor's progressive importunings, the operators passed the wage increase right along to the consumer.[100]

District One built on the successful outcome of the brief 1923 walkout to attain a higher level of organization than ever before. Average membership for 1924 remained at approximately 46,000, as in 1923, and for the first six months of 1925, average membership rose to more than 60,000 men. The total reported for June 1925—84,346—was the largest ever for the district. But its newfound strength made control of District One, which had developed a habitual tendency toward contention and insurgency, especially worth a fight. William Brennan sought to return to the district presidency in 1925, and he did not believe that he got the "clean-cut vote" that Cappellini had promised. Although he was defeated by a margin of almost three to one, he challenged the election returns in one local after another. The accuracy of his charges is less significant than his success in organizing his own faction and the changes that occurred on President Cappellini's slate. The insurgency of 1925 was not simply that of an "out" group against a set of incumbents. While Enoch Williams was easily reelected, two of Cappellini's onetime allies were defeated by substantial margins—International Board Member Alec Campbell (his compatriot from the 1920 Pittston strike) and Vice-President Isaacs (Azys).[101]

Despite the reemergence of factional struggle in District One, in 1925 that district, along with Districts Seven and Nine, displayed the same solidarity that characterized the strike of 1922 in what amounted to a reprise of that conflict. The settlements of 1922 and 1923 had in no way resolved the fundamental tensions in the industry and workers struck again on September 1, 1925. Chastened by the wage increase Pinchot had pushed them to accept, the operators were determined to keep him out of yet another bargaining impasse. As in 1922, the operators wanted wage cuts, and they demanded periodic arbitration of wages on an ongoing basis during the term of the contract. That scheme, which would eliminate any semblance of wage security, held no more interest for the union than it had in 1922. Negotiations broke off on August 3, well before the strike deadline, and did not resume until December 29. When the parties finally agreed in early February 1926 essentially to retain the status quo, they displayed their weariness of struggle by accepting a term of five years. Especially considering the battering the UMWA was absorbing across its onetime bastion, the Central Competitive Field, where one company after another was abandoning the union contract,

John L. Lewis did not exaggerate in labeling the strike of 1925 a significant victory.[102]

"OR I WILL CLEAN THEIR CLOCKS"

The industrial conflicts of 1922 and 1925 reflected not only the intense solidarity of anthracite mine workers but also the determination of the operators to recapture the workers' real wage gains. The struggles of the 1920s, by their very intensity, seemed to foster a kind of siege mentality. Rinaldo Cappellini surely displayed a darker, more threatening visage to his opponents in the union than previous district leaders had shown to him and his fellow insurgents. At the end of the 1925 strike, after praising the rank and file for their loyalty in the longest walkout in the history of anthracite mine workers, Cappellini still had a warning for his opponents. He wanted "the members of District No. 1 who are in the habit of playing the political game" to know that they would "have to give the good members co-operation or I will clean their clocks (Applause and cheers)."[103] Such an attitude could not extinguish opposition in the district, but it did breed measures far different from the "jugglery of votes" on which previous leaders had relied to retain control. By 1928, an insurgent movement had arisen in Cappellini's own local over the same issue that he had ridden out of obscurity, the contract system, which had gradually returned to the mines of the PCC. Several leaders of that insurgency, including Cappellini's onetime ally Alec Campbell, were gunned down in the streets of Pittston. A majority of the district's locals held a special convention without authority from Cappellini and deposed him in favor of William Brennan. With both men claiming to hold the district presidency, John L. Lewis persuaded them to step aside for his choice, longtime member of the district executive board John Boylan.[104]

This turmoil occurred amidst declining production of anthracite and burgeoning underemployment. Both trends accelerated dramatically with the coming of the Great Depression and encouraged more insurgency and violence in the district. In 1933, Cappellini helped found the United Anthracite Miners of Pennsylvania (UAMP), an organization energized by demands for equalizing such opportunity as there was for work among the various collieries. The UAMP dueled with the UMWA for control of the Wyoming field for two years. The engine of insurgency invented in the 1910s, the general grievance committee, loomed large in the struggle. Thomas Maloney, president of the UAMP, had chaired a general committee and the strikes he called led to an intensification of conflict and the creation of the rival union. That movement was brutally repressed by a shaky alliance of the UMWA, governmental authorities, and coal companies. The turmoil ended on Good Friday 1936, when Maloney and his son were killed by a bomb sent through the mail.[105]

The remorseless character of that repression shows that John L. Lewis at least had acquired the coal operators' preoccupation with power rather than legitimacy. His assault on his opponents in the UMWA, beginning almost as soon as he acceded to its presidency, killed the union's venerable tradition of democracy.[106] Men like John Mitchell and John P. White had led the UMWA with great vigor and used a full array of leadership skills, including chiding mine workers paternalistically, to persuade them to endorse their leaders' actions. Yet, however frustrated they became with mine workers' tendencies toward disorder, they did little to threaten the UMWA's decentralized democracy. One UMWA leader who may have thought of doing so, Tom L. Lewis, failed in the attempt.[107] Even John Dempsey felt compelled to exercise his authority, however fraudulently, within a democratic context. Still, it would be much too simple to lay all the blame at the feet of John L. Lewis.

Lewis was by no means the first UMWA leader to have difficulty finding a place for the creative chaos of rank-and-file militancy within the confines of collective bargaining, the only secure haven union officials could see for workers and unions in American life. UMWA officials had traditionally found it difficult to accept rank-and-file militancy on any consistent basis. This was not because they confidently sought dictatorial control, but because they feared the powerful forces arrayed against workers and unions.[108] Democracy in the UMWA could be destroyed in the 1920s only amidst the collapse of both the anthracite and bituminous industries and the union along with them.

The habit of insurgency in the anthracite fields and the democratic spirit that it bred flowed from workplace realities. Miners and their laborers, some 60 percent of the work force, had no confidence in their basis of payment. Such grievances as dockage and the miner's ton continued to bedevil them throughout the period of this study. Workers would demand in vain some semblance of uniformity in wage rates for similar jobs. The many opportunities for favoritism and discrimination that the anthracite workplace offered made the closed shop of critical importance to local union activists and made the UMWA's failure to achieve it all the more galling. Finally, facing the capricious underemployment of the 1930s, mine workers passionately adopted the remedy of equalization of work, but to no avail.

Management viewed such demands as threatening its most basic prerogatives and resisted them vigorously. The men who ran the union knew that to fight for such demands, which were especially difficult to explain to an increasingly concerned public, would imperil the union's survival.[109] Thus, the power of corporate capital placed the workers' most vital concerns in opposition to the institutional, if not the spiritual, welfare of their union. The suspicion and unfairness that the work process generated in anthracite, larded over with the accretion of confusion in each contract after 1903, consequently guaranteed a fertile field for insurgency as well as rank-and-file militancy. Still, as long as the union's survival was assured, the hardships faced by the rank and file could serve as an ironic source of democratic empowerment. The lack of the check-off forced union activists to collect dues directly from workers and gave those workers the opportunity to decide whether or not the union merited their voluntary payment of dues. Similarly, pervasive discontent over workplace injustices goaded many anthracite mine workers into active if often contentious participation in their union.

EPILOGUE

In 1900 and 1902 when the organization commenced to function what did we find back in that early period? Did men have individual liberty? Absolutely not. Did men have political liberty? Not at all. Were the business interests free to function as business interests are known to function in this and other regions? Positively not. And what were the dominating factors that prevented the orderly functioning of the people along their constitutional rights? The anthracite operators in 1900 and 1902 sat on a throne in the anthracite region and autocratically denied not only civil, political and industrial rights of the people, but there have even been cases known in the region where they denied the religious liberty of certain people.

Our organization functioning since 1900 and 1902 up to the present time, has accomplished what? We have at least, if we have done nothing along the lines of economic endeavor, restored liberty to the people of the anthracite region. They are free to work out their own destinies in conformity with the constitution and the laws of the State and the nation, ...[1]

Thomas J. Kennedy, 1922

Anthracite stood above the rest of American industry in real wage gains from 1914 to 1926,[2] but it did not retain that position thereafter. Although 1926 was a reasonably good year of some 244 days of work, production plummeted after the mines satisfied demand left over from the strike of 1925. While more than 84 million tons were mined in 1926, only 69 million were mined in 1930, and in that year the mines averaged only 208 days of work. Still, that year was easily the best of the dismal decade of the thirties. As the industry fell below 200 days of work and even produced fewer than 50 million tons in some years, the number of workers declined too. From some 165,000 in 1926 and 150,000 as late as 1930, the number of workers dropped below 100,000 in 1937. These declines signaled the collapse of the industry that, except for a brief respite during World War II, has proceeded steadily since.[3]

In assessing the impact of unionization on earnings in the anthracite industry, we can only consider it as one of many factors. Most importantly, we

261

must recognize the ultimate reality of mining—that production in the industry necessitates exhausting the supply of the product. More so than in manufacturing pursuits, economic dislocation is an unavoidable fact of life in mining. The United Mine Workers of America (UMWA) deserves a great deal of credit for the gains of the period from 1914 to 1926, but those gains can only be evaluated in the context of a favorable economic climate for the industry, something that the men and women of the anthracite region would never experience again.

Still, the UMWA does deserve credit for something more significant than incremental wage gains. Focusing strictly on the leverage unions can exert over wages belittles workers by assessing their lives solely according to the lowest common economic denominator. By itself, the economic impact of unions on the anthracite industry neither demands nor justifies the foregoing account of the struggle for unionization and the struggles for control of the union that followed. Unionization had a political and cultural significance for workers' lives that can best be displayed by comparing the anthracite fields with a determinedly nonunion industry, steel in the first three-and-a-half decades of the twentieth century. In an address to the 1923 convention of District One, Reverend John J. Curran of Wilkes-Barre compared the anthracite region to Gary, Indiana. A friend of John Mitchell during his first organizing forays in anthracite, Father Curran followed UMWA affairs closely thereafter. The good father did not like what he saw in Gary:

> I want to say to you that two weeks ago I went through the town of Gary, drove through in an automobile. That town does not look like an American town. It did not look like an American town to me. It is dirty, a very dirty, unclean town. It looks like the old town of fifty years ago. . . . Gary is an un-American town and the founder of that town or city is an un-American citizen absolutely.[4]

What Curran may have detected in Gary was the sullenness and fear bred by dictatorial corporate control, the complete absence of the democracy that only unions could bring to an industrial community. John Fitch portrayed a similar atmosphere in his 1912 study, *The Steel Workers.* He described the practically paranoid fear and suspicion that men in the mills in and around Pittsburgh had of discussing anything about their work with an outsider. He also discussed company domination of politics and efforts to control the votes of workers.[5] In his brilliant account of that era of immigrant life in the steel towns of the Monongahela Valley, *Out of This Furnace,* novelist Thomas Bell depicted the impact of this repression. One of his characters, veteran steelworker Mike Dobrejcak, gives the following response to a friend's reprimand over speaking his opinions too freely:

FIGURE Epi.1
John L. Lewis, UMWA President, 1919–1960; Thomas J. Kennedy, President, UMWA District
Seven, 1910–1925, UMWA Secretary-Treasurer, 1925–1947; UMWA Vice-President, 1947–
1960, and UMWA President, 1960–1963; and Reverend John J. Curran.

What are they doing to us? I can remember when people weren't afraid.
Now fear is everywhere, spreading suspicion and bitterness, draining every
man's heart of courage and making honesty a sin against his family's
bread. . . . I can't say what I want, I can't do what I want, I can't even hope
any more that some day things will be better for me.[6]

In the first quarter of the twentieth century, anthracite mine workers did
not come much closer than their nonunion brethren to attaining the visionary
goal of industrial democracy. Throughout the succeeding decades, workers in
a devotedly capitalist America have not done much better. But if we view democracy as a process rather than a result, the accomplishments of anthracite
mine workers through their uneasy relationship with the UMWA are most

substantial, whether in the context of the "open shop" of the turn of the century, the "American plan" of the 1920s, or the antiunion atmosphere of recent days. Perhaps the mere facts of workplace protest, union insurgency, and, more generally, the survival of unions are just as important as the economic gains they have been able to achieve. In the first half of this century, in an industrial workplace dominated increasingly by immigrants and their children, industrial unions offered an alternative, participatory means of "Americanization." Like no other institution, they put an intensely democratic experience within the reach of America's workers.

NOTES

PREFACE

1. David Brody, "The Old Labor History and the New: In Search of an American Working Class," *Labor History* 20 (Winter 1979): 123.

2. John Bodnar, *The Transplanted: A History of Immigrants in Urban America* (Bloomington: Indiana University Press, 1985), 209.

INTRODUCTION

1. The best study of the Mollies is Wayne G. Broehl, Jr., *The Molly Maguires* (Vintage/Chelsea House, 1964). Two works that put the Mollies into a broader context are Harold W. Aurand, *From the Molly Maguires to the United Mine Workers: The Social Ecology of an Industrial Union, 1869–1897* (Philadelphia: Temple University Press, 1971), and Anthony F. C. Wallace, *St. Clair: A Nineteenth-Century Coal Town's Experience with a Disaster-Prone Industry* (Ithaca: Cornell University Press, 1988).

2. The story of the strike is best told by Robert J. Cornell in *The Anthracite Coal Strike of 1902* (Washington: Catholic University of America Press, 1957). Wiebe's contribution, "The Anthracite Strike of 1902: A Record of Confusion," *Mississippi Valley Historical Review* 48 (September 1961): 229–51, is not without flaws, the most important of which is that the strike had more of the elements of a morality play than Wiebe admits.

3. Some historians view insecurity as more of an incubus than a spur to organization. For example, Thomas Dublin sees the Irish immigrants in the Lowell textile mills in the 1850s as not only less economically secure than their native farm-girl predecessors, but also less likely to organize and protest. See *Women at Work: The Transformation of Work and Community Lowell, Massachusetts, 1826–1860* (New York: Columbia University Press, 1979), 198–99. Daniel Walkowitz uses a similar explanation for the lower incidence of protest and unionization among the cotton-mill workers of Cohoes, New York, than among the foundrymen across the river in Troy. See *Worker City, Company Town: Iron and Cotton Worker Protest in Troy and Cohoes, New York, 1855–1884* (Urbana: University of Illinois Press, 1978), 143.

Similarly, a number of historians of industries in which unionization did not occur until the twentieth century have seen difficult working conditions, intermittent work, and low pay as factors that retarded unionization. See David Brody, *Steelworkers in America: The Nonunion Era* (Cambridge: Harvard University Press, 1960; reprint ed., New York: Harper & Row Publishers, Inc., 1969), 96–111; David Alan Corbin, *Life, Work, and Rebellion in the Coal Fields: The Southern West Virginia Miners, 1880–1922* (Urbana: University of Illinois Press, 1981), 31–33; Melvyn Dubofsky, *When Workers Organize: New York City in the Progressive Era* (Amherst: University of Massachusetts Press, 1968), 1–14.

4. On the twin themes of fragmentation and solidarity, see Richard J. Oestreicher, *Solidarity and Fragmentation: Working People and Class Consciousness in Detroit, 1875–1900* (Urbana: University of Illinois Press, 1986), xv–xviii, 166–68, 252–53; and James R. Barrett, *Work and Community in the Jungle: Chicago's Packinghouse Workers, 1894–1922* (Urbana: University of Illinois Press, 1987), 269–80.

5. The anthracite industry's relative lack of technological change distinguishes it in a most significant way from the bituminous coal industry, in which technological change occurred at an intense pace throughout this period. See Keith Dix, *What's a Coal Miner To Do?: The Mechanization of Coal Mining* (Pittsburgh: University of Pittsburgh Press, 1988).

6. On the UMWA's accomplishments in the bituminous industry, see Bruno Ramirez, *When Workers Fight: The Politics of Industrial Relations in the Progressive Era, 1898–1916* (Westport, CT: Greenwood Press, 1978), ch. 1. Ramirez may not be guilty of overstatement in commenting on p. 17 that "few labor events have had as great an impact on the growth of collective bargaining in America as the 1897 bituminous coal miners' strike and the settlement that ensued."

7. Robert Asher compares the UMWA's organizing methods to those of other unions in "Union Nativism and the Immigrant Response," *Labor History* 23 (Summer 1982): 325–48.

8. Jules I. Bogen, *The Anthracite Railroads* (New York: Ronald Press Co., 1927), 54–72, 96–104, 122–39, 161–821, 197–202; Eliot Jones, *The Anthracite Coal Combination in the United States* (Cambridge: Harvard University Press, 1914), 41–97.

9. The concept of a "freedom to control" is thoughtfully developed by Rowland T. Berthoff in "The 'Freedom to Control in American Business History," in *A Festschrift for Frederick B. Artz*, eds. David H. Pinkney and Theodore Ropp (Durham: Duke University Press, 1964), 158–80. Robert H. Wiebe describes the predominantly antiunion attitudes of American businessmen in *Businessmen and Reform: A Study of the Progressive Era* (New York: Quadrangle Books, 1968), 157–78.

10. On the bituminous contract see David Brody, "Labor Relations in American Coal Mining: An Industry Perspective," unpublished paper, 2–4, 12–15. Professor Brody made the helpful suggestion that I consider the impact of the changing competitive picture in anthracite on labor relations, especially in comparison with the bituminous industry.

11. This is a central theme for John Bodnar in "Immigration, Kinship, and the Rise of Working-Class Realism in Industrial America," *Journal of Social History* 14 (Fall 1980): 45–65 and more generally in his book *The Transplanted: A History of Immigrants in Urban America* (Bloomington: Indiana University Press, 1985). Ron Rothbart has thoughtfully expanded upon this emphasis by pointing out that the pragmatic concern of workers for a "family wage" could spur labor militancy as well as discourage it. See " 'Homes Are What Any Strike Is About': Immigrant Labor and the Family Wage," *Journal of Social History* 23 (Winter 1989): 267–84.

For a similar emphasis on industrial workers' goal of security, see David M. Emmons, *The Butte Irish: Class and Ethnicity in an American Mining Town, 1875– 1925* (Urbana: University of Illinois Press, 1989), 1–10, 180–83; Tamara Hareven, *Family Time and Industrial Time: The Relationship between the Family and Work in a New England Industrial Community* (Cambridge: Cambridge University Press, 1982), 359–63; and Jacquelyn D. Hall, James Leloudis, Robert Korstad, Mary Murphy, Lu Ann Jones, and Christopher B. Daly, *Like a Family: The Making of a Southern Cotton Mill World* (Chapel Hill: University of North Carolina Press, 1987), 152.

12. Of course, David Montgomery has developed this concept in *The Fall of the House of Labor: The Workplace, the State, and American Labor Activism, 1865–1925* (Cambridge: Cambridge University Press, 1987), 9–44, and in *Workers' Control in America: Studies in the History of Work, Technology, and Labor Struggles* (Cambridge: Cambridge University Press, 1979), 3–5, 9–31, 91–112. While strikes over work rules may appear most threatening to capitalists as a fundamental attack on their property rights, workers are likely to view such strikes instrumentally, as a way to obtain a fairer deal concerning the particular matter in dispute. Indeed, such walkouts may reflect the "job consciousness" of workers, as discussed by Selig Perlman in *A Theory of the Labor Movement*, reprint ed. (New York: Augustus A. Kelley, Publishers, 1970), 7–8, 169, rather than their potential for revolutionary action.

13. Warren R. Van Tine thoughtfully analyzes how labor leaders' fears for the survival of their unions in dealings with consolidating corporations fostered union centralization at the turn of the century; see *The Making of the Labor Bureaucrat: Union Leadership in the United States, 1870–1920* (Amherst: University of Massachusetts Press, 1973), 66–71.

CHAPTER 1

1. Perry K. Blatz, "Ever-Shifting Ground: Work and Labor Relations in the Anthracite Coal Industry, 1868–1903," Ph.D. dissertation, Princeton University, 1987, 1–21.

2. U.S., Bureau of Census, *Historical Statistics of the United States: Colonial Times to 1970*, 2 parts (Washington: Government Printing Office, 1975), I: 592–93.

3. The estimate for 1880 is from Peter Roberts, *The Anthracite Coal Communities* (New York: The Macmillan Co., 1904), 19. The estimate for 1890 is derived from a census that the Philadelphia and Reading Coal and Iron Company made of its work-

ers, reported in U.S., Department of Labor. *Bulletin of the Department of Labor,* No. 13, "The Anthracite Mine Laborers," by G. O. Virtue (1897): 751. For the 1900 estimate, see Roberts, *Communities,* 19–20; Peter Roberts, *The Anthracite Coal Industry* (New York: The Macmillan Co., 1901), 105; and a nationality survey in Pennsylvania, Secretary of Internal Affairs, *Annual Report,* Part III, *Industrial Statistics* 31 (1903): 431–32.

4. On the Molly Maguires, see Wayne G. Broehl, Jr., *The Molly Maguires* (New York: Vintage/Chelsea House, 1968); Harold W. Aurand, *From the Molly Maguires to the United Mine Workers: The Social Ecology of an Industrial Union, 1869–1897* (Philadelphia: Temple University Press, 1971), 96–114, and Anthony F. C. Wallace, *St. Clair: A Nineteenth-Century Coal Town's Experience with a Disaster-Prone Industry* (Ithaca: Cornell University Press, 1988), 314–66. On ethnic conflict later in the century, see Victor R. Greene, *The Slavic Community on Strike: Immigrant Labor in Pennsylvania Anthracite* (Notre Dame: University of Notre Dame Press, 1968). Differences between old-stock mine workers and eastern and southern Europeans is a major theme in Peter Roberts, *The Anthracite Coal Communities* (New York: Macmillan and Co., Inc., 1904).

5. See Alexander Keyssar, *Out of Work: The First Century of Unemployment in Massachusetts* (Cambridge: Cambridge University Press, 1985), 47–50.

6. These general issues are discussed in three very interesting letters: W. H. Storrs to Samuel Sloan, March 22, August 25, and October 18, 1898, Corporate Records of the Delaware, Lackawanna, and Western Railroad—Coal Department, Lackawanna Historical Society, Scranton, PA; hereafter cited as DL & W Records—Scranton. The overall process is detailed in G. O. Virtue, "The Anthracite Combinations," *Quarterly Journal of Economics* 10 (April 1896): 318–19. Also see Isaac Hourwich, *Immigration and Labor: The Economic Aspects of European Immigration to the United States* (New York: G. P. Putnam's Sons, 1912, reprint ed., Arno Press, Inc., 1969), 432–35.

7. Such a pattern of work can be seen for most of the mine workers of the Lehigh and Wilkes-Barre Coal Company on the company's payrolls for selected months in the 1890s. See Lehigh and Wilkes-Barre Coal Company Payrolls, January 1894, March 1895, and December 1896, Papers of the Lehigh and Wilkes-Barre Coal Company, Wyoming Historical and Geological Society, Wilkes-Barre, PA, hereafter cited as L & W-B Payrolls.

8. Calculated from data presented in Pennsylvania, Secretary of Internal Affairs, *Annual Report,* Part III, *Industrial Statistics* 17 (1889): B4–B15.

9. For some of the numerous examples, see Pennsylvania, Bureau of Mines, *Report of the Bureau of Mines of the Department of Internal Affairs of Pennsylvania—1898* (Harrisburg, PA: William Stanley Ray, State Printer, 1899), 74–75, 102–04, 138, 141–42, 232–35.

10. The figure for manufacturing industries is derived from data in Albert Rees, assisted by Donald P. Jacobs, *Real Wages in Manufacturing: 1890–1914* (Princeton:

Princeton University Press, 1961), 33. The figure for the anthracite industry is calculated from annual data in *Historical Statistics 1:* 592–93.

11. *The World,* New York, February 20, 1890.

12. U.S., Department of the Interior, Census Office, *Report on Mineral Industries in the United States at the Eleventh Census* (Washington: Government Printing Office, 1892), 402, 406.

13. In narrow work, miners at one colliery earned approximately 50 percent more per month than miners in chambers who worked about the same amount of time. See Blatz, "Ever-Shifting Ground," 247–48. For a more detailed description of both narrow work and work in chambers, see *ibid.,* 3–27.

14. *Wilkes-Barre Record,* October 20, 1886.

15. See Roberts, *Industry,* 114–16 and below.

16. On this issue, see Carter Goodrich, *The Miner's Freedom: A Study of the Working Life in a Changing Industry* (Boston: Marshall Jones Co., 1925). For a more detailed picture of the difficulties and complexity involved in close supervision in coal mines, see Hugh Archbald, *The Four-Hour Day in Coal: A Study of the Relation between the Engineering of the Organization of Work and the Discontent among the Workers in the Coal Mines* (New York: H. W. Wilson Co., 1922), 35–52. On systematic and scientific management see Daniel Nelson, *Managers and Workers: Origins of the New Factory System in the United States, 1880–1920* (Madison: University of Wisconsin Press, 1975) and *Frederick W. Taylor and the Rise of Scientific Management* (Madison: University of Wisconsin Press, 1980).

17. Blatz, "Ever-Shifting Ground," 8–21.

18. U.S., Department of the Interior, Bureau of Mines, *Pennsylvania Mining Statutes Annotated,* by J. W. Thompson, Bulletin No. 21 (Washington: Government Printing Office, 1920), 254–56; hereafter cited as Thompson, *Statutes.* Also see Greene, 115 and Alexander Trachtenberg, *The History of Legislation for the Protection of Coal Miners in Pennsylvania* (New York: International Publishers, 1942), 135–37.

19. Tables 1.1 and 1.2 are compiled from data in Pennsylvania, Secretary of Internal Affairs, *Annual Report,* Part III, *Industrial Statistics* 16 (1888), Bvi-Bxvii, B72–B111. For a fuller discussion see Blatz, "Ever-Shifting Ground," 217–21.

20. *Ibid.,* 221.

21. Compiled from data in *Industrial Statistics* 17 (1889): B3, B35–54, B59–B66.

22. See Roberts, *Communities,* 120–22, 124–27; Virtue, "The Anthracite Mine Laborers," 758–59; and *Engineering and Mining Journal* 63 (June 19, 1897): 625; hereafter cited as *E & MJ.*

23. On shifts for miners and their laborers, see L & W-B Payrolls and U.S., Anthracite Coal Strike Commission, "Proceedings of the Anthracite Coal Strike Commission, 1902–1903," 56 vols., 17 (December 11, 1902): 2302–06; 18 (December 19. 1902): 2419–20; 37 (January 19, 1903): 6131–32; 38 (January 20, 1903): 6440, 6454–55; 41 (January 23, 1903): 6906; hereafter cited as "Proceedings." On the common problem of car shortage, see Archbald, 61–63.

24. These calculations are based on data taken from the L & W-B Payrolls. For a fuller presentation of the data, see Blatz, "Ever-Shifting Ground," 241–54.

25. *Ibid.*, 261.

26. See *Industrial Statistics* 16:C2–C14. Although no mine reported wage rates for every job listed, nearly all reported rates for at least fifteen underground jobs and twenty above ground. Some mines reported rates for as many as twenty-five jobs below and thirty on the surface.

27. On classes of jobs held by younger workers see Blatz, "Ever-Shifting Ground," 426, and L & W-B Payrolls.

28. See L & W-B Payrolls and "Proceedings," 1344, 1421–22, 2770.

29. See Table 1.3.

30. *Wilkes-Barre Record*, November 1, 1886.

31. Robert Hunter, *Poverty* (New York: Macmillan and Co., 1904), 52.

32. U.S., Department of Commerce and Labor, Bureau of Labor, *Bulletin of the U.S. Bureau of Labor: Retail Prices 1890 to 1911*, whole no. 105: Part I, 17.

33. See Frank P. Underhill, "Report on Nutrition Investigation: From Data Collected by the Special Committee on Standard of Living," in Robert Coit Chapin, *The Standard of Living Among Workingmen's Families in New York City* (New York: Russell Sage Foundation, 1909), 277–81; Roberts, *Communities*, 101–03, 120–36, 262; Daniel Walkowitz, *Worker City, Company Town: Iron and Cotton-Worker Protest in Troy and Cohoes, New York, 1855–1884* (Urbana: University of Illinois Press, 1978), 263. For a fuller discussion, see Blatz, "Ever-Shifting Ground," 198–203.

34. B. Seebohm Rowntree, *Poverty: A Study of Town Life* (New York: The Macmillan Co., 1902; reprint ed., New York: Howard Fertig, Inc., 1971), 167.

35. U.S. Congress, House, *Testimony Taken by the Select Committee of the House of Representatives to Inquire into the Alleged Violation of the Laws Prohibiting the Importation of Contract Laborers, Paupers, Convicts, and Other Classes*, H. Doc. 572, 50th Cong., 1st sess., 1888, 317–18.

36. *Ibid.*, 204.

37. John Bodnar makes this point in a particularly trenchant manner in "Socialization and Adaptation: Immigrant Families in Scranton, 1880–1900," *Pennsylvania*

History 43 (April 1976): 158–60. He refers to a study by the Pennsylvania Bureau of Industrial Statistics in 1881 of 142 workers' families in which, in every case, the father's earnings were less than half the total earnings of the family. The insufficiency of one breadwinner's earnings to support most working-class families is also depicted in Margaret Byington, *Homestead: The Households of a Mill Town* (New York: Russell Sage Foundation, 1910; reprint ed., Pittsburgh: University Center for International Studies, 1974), 138–44; James R. Barrett, *Work and Community in the Jungle: Chicago's Packinghouse Workers, 1894–1922* (Urbana: University of Illinois Press, 1987), 90–107, and Tamara Hareven, *Family Time and Industrial Time: The Relationship between the Family and Work in a New England Industrial Community* (Cambridge: Cambridge University Press, 1982), 189–217.

38. On the great variety of work for females in the anthracite region see Caroline Golab, "The Impact of the Industrial Experience on the Immigrant Family: The Huddled Masses Reconsidered," in Richard L. Ehrlich, ed., *Immigrants in Industrial America, 1850–1920* (Charlottesville: University Press of Virginia, 1977), 19–27. One hears in the anthracite region reports of grandmothers who worked as slate pickers at least for a while, stuffing their hair into stocking caps.

39. Thompson, *Statutes*, 82, 109–12, 601–05. For commentary on the legislation see Jacqueline Corn, "Protective Legislation for Coal Miners, 1870–1900," in *Dying for Work: Workers' Safety and Health in Twentieth-Century America*, edited by David Rosner and Gerald Markowitz (Bloomington: Indiana University Press, 1989), 71–72, from which the statement on significance is quoted on p. 71; Trachtenberg, 32–35, 41–45; and Wallace, 249–75, 293–313.

40. Thompson, *Statutes*, 605–06.

41. For a fuller discussion of this point, see Blatz, "Ever-Shifting Ground," 275–318.

42. Thompson, *Statutes*, 293–94, 95–96.

43. *Ibid.*, 616–27.

44. This table has been compiled from several sources because, especially for the years before 1891, there is little agreement on the precise number of accidents. The major source is *Report of the Bureau of Mines—1898*, xxx, xlv. That source provides the basic information for the number of employees and number of tons mined for the entire period. However, it does not include nonfatal accidents before 1891, and some of its totals for fatal accidents before 1882 are clearly suspect. Its total for fatal accidents in 1870 is the only one available, but a more accurate total for 1871 can be found in Pennsylvania, *Reports of the Inspectors of Mines of the Anthracite Coal Regions of Pennsylvania for the Year 1876* (Harrisburg, PA: B. F. Meyers, State Printer, 1877), 81. Totals for the next ten years are those compiled by Mine Inspector James Roderick in Pennsylvania, *Reports of the Inspectors of Mines of the Anthracite Coal Regions for the Year 1882* (Harrisburg, PA: Lane S. Hart, State Printer, 1883), 262, which do not differ much from those for the years 1872 through 1876 in *Mine Inspectors' Reports—1876*, 81.

45. Roberts, *Communities*, 271.

46. Frederick L. Hoffman, "Problems of Labor and Life in Anthracite Coal Mining—part IV—Accidents," *E & MJ* 74 (December 13, 1902): 783–84. In this article, Hoffman does not cite statistics for southern states. However, in his "Fatal Accidents in Coal Mining," U.S., Bureau of Labor, *Bulletin of the Bureau of Labor* 21 (September 1910): 452, Hoffman notes higher fatality rates for the period 1899–1908 for West Virginia, Alabama, and Tennessee than for Pennsylvania anthracite.

47. Pennsylvania, *Reports of the Inspectors of Mines of the Anthracite and Bituminous Coal Regions of Pennsylvania for the Year 1889* (Harrisburg, PA: Edwin K. Meyers, State Printer, 1890), 239–43.

48. Roberts, *Communities*, 259–64.

49. *Ibid.*, 266.

50. G. O. Virtue, "The Anthracite Mine Laborers," 769–70; Andrew Roy, *A History of the Coal Miners of the United States* (Columbus, Ohio: J. L. Trauger Printing Co., 1905; reprint ed., Westport, CT: Greenwood Press, 1970), 77.

51. Virtue, "Laborers," 770: Roberts, Communities, 268; Marvin W. Schlegel, *Ruler of the Reading: A Life of Franklin B. Gowen: 1836–1889* (Harrisburg, PA: Archives Publishing Co. of Pennsylvania, Inc., 1947), 63; Andrew Roy, *The Coal Mines* (Cleveland: Robison, Savage & Co., Printers and Stationers, 1876), 248.

52. "Proceedings," 8051–55. This fund was not the very first. The Wilkes-Barre Coal and Iron Company established one in 1869 that lapsed in 1877. For more details on funds, see Blatz, "Ever-Shifting Ground," 91–95. Robert Asher refers to the Reading's fund along with a number of efforts in other industries in "The Limits of Big Business Paternalism: Relief for Injured Workers in the Years before Workmen's Compensation," in Rosner and Markowitz, eds., *Dying for Work*, 19–33. Also see Ray Ginger, "Company-Sponsored Welfare Plans in the Anthracite Industry before 1900," *Bulletin of the Business Historical Society* 27 (June 1953): 112–20.

53. Anthony Bale, "America's First Compensation Crisis: Conflict over the Value and Meaning of Workplace Injuries under the Employers' Liability System," in Rosner and Markowitz, eds., *Dying for Work*, 36.

54. For a fuller discussion, see Blatz, "Ever-Shifting Ground," 282–84.

55. W. R. Storrs to Sloan, October 24, 1889, DL & W Records—Scranton.

56. Sloan to W. R. Storrs, October 25, 1889, Corporate Records of the Delaware, Lackawanna, and Western Railroad, George Arents Research Library, Syracuse University, Syracuse, NY; hereafter cited as DL & W. Records—Syracuse.

57. W. R. Storrs to Sloan, October 26, 1889, DL & W Records—Scranton.

58. Sloan to W. R. Storrs, October 28, 1889, DL & W Records—Syracuse.

59. W. R. Storrs to Sloan, June 25, 1890, DL & W Records—Scranton.

60. W. R. Storrs to Sloan, November 19, 1889, *ibid.* For information on the accident itself, see Pennsylvania, *Reports of the Inspectors of Mines of the Anthracite and Bituminous Coal Regions of Pennsylvania for the Year 1889* (Harrisburg, PA: Edwin K. Meyers, State Printer, 1890), 29.

61. W. R. Storrs to Sloan, October 2, 1890, DL & W Records—Scranton. For information on the accident itself, see Pennsylvania, *Reports of the Inspectors of Mines of the Anthracite and Bituminous Coal Regions of Pennsylvania for the Year 1890* (Harrisburg, PA: Edwin K. Meyers, State Printer, 1891), 30.

62. W. R. Storrs to Sloan, October 18, 1890, *ibid.*

63. Sloan to W. R. Storrs, October 20, 1890, DL & W Records—Syracuse.

64. See Storrs to Sloan, May 6, 1889 (first), and June 25, 1890, DL & W Records—Scranton.

65. Richard Sennett, *Authority* (New York: Alfred A. Knopf, Inc., 1980), 50–83.

CHAPTER 2

1. Quoted in Robert J. Cornell, *The Anthracite Coal Strike of 1902* (Washington: Catholic University of America Press, 1957), 170.

2. William R. Storrs to Samuel Sloan, April 22, 1893, Corporate Records of the Delaware, Lackawanna, and Western Railroad—Coal Department, Lackawanna Historical Society, Scranton, PA; hereafter cited as DL & W Records—Scranton.

3. Rowland T. Berthoff, "The 'Freedom to Control' in American Business History," in *A Festschrift for Frederick B. Artz*, eds. David H. Pinkney and Theodore Ropp (Durham: Duke University Press, 1964), 158–80.

4. Perry K. Blatz, "Ever-Shifting Ground: Work and Labor Relations in the Anthracite Coal Industry, 1868–1903," Ph.D. dissertation, Princeton University, 1987, pp. 50–82; Anthony F. C. Wallace, *St. Clair: A Nineteenth-Century coal Town's Experience with a Disaster-Prone Industry* (Ithaca: Cornell University Press, 1988), 275–313; Harold W. Aurand, *From the Molly Maguires to the United Mine Workers: The Social Ecology of an Industrial Union, 1869–1897* (Philadelphia: Temple University Press, 1971), 65–95; on Gowen, see Marvin W. Schlegel, *Ruler of the Reading: The Life of Franklin B. Gowen, 1836–1889* (Harrisburg, PA: Archives Publishing Co. of Pennsylvania, Inc., 1947), 17–26, 32–37, 62–75.

5. T. V. Powderly, *Thirty Years of Labor* (Columbus, OH: Excelsior Publishing House, 1890), 209; the emphasis is Powderly's.

6. For a fuller account of these strikes, see Blatz, "Ever-Shifting Ground," 87–90; also see Aurand, 110–18, Powderly, 205–219, and the standard source on the 1877

railroad strikes, Robert V. Bruce, *1877: Year of Violence* (Indianapolis: Bobbs-Merrill Company, 1959; paperback reprint, Chicago: Quadrangle Paperbacks, 1979), 296–98.

7. These figures are calculated from data in Jonathan Garlock, comp., *Guide to the Local Assemblies of the Knights of Labor* (Westport, CT: Greenwood Press, 1982), 430–31, 434–49, 460–67, 472–75.

8. Compiled from data in U.S., Commissioner of Labor, *Third Annual Report of the Commissioner of Labor, 1887: Strikes and Lockouts* (Washington: Government Printing Office, 1888), 488–95, 504–07, 532–35.

9. See U.S., Bureau of Labor, *Tenth Annual Report of the Commissioner of Labor, 1894: Strikes and Lockouts* (Washington: Government Printing Office, 1896), 1: 26.

10. *Third Annual Report*, 488–95, 532–35.

11. Aurand, 118–21. For the rise of the Knights across the nation in 1885 and 1886, see Melvyn Dubofsky, *Industrialism and the American Worker, 1865–1920* (Arlington Heights, IL: AHM Publishing Corporation, 1975), 56–57.

12. *Engineering and Mining Journal* 38 (December 6, 1884): 381; 39 (January 24, 1885): 58; (February 7, 1885): 71; (February 14, 1885): 110; hereafter cited as *E & MJ*. Also see *Wilkes-Barre Record*, September 13, 1886; W. H. Tillinghast to S. B. Whiting, August 4, 1888, Papers of the Lehigh and Wilkes-Barre Coal Company, Wyoming Historical and Geological Society, Wilkes-Barre, PA; hereafter cited as L & W-B Papers. The last set of reductions occurred in the Shamokin area in January 1886; see *E & MJ* 42 (October 23, 1886): 297.

13. U.S., Congress, House, Select Committee on Existing Labor Troubles in Pennsylvania, *Labor Troubles in the Anthracite Regions of Pennsylvania, 1887–88*, H. Rept. 4147, 50th Cong., 2nd sess, 1889, 41, 398.

14. *E & MJ* XLII (October 23, 1886): 297; (October 30, 1885): 315; (November 6, 1886): 334; (December 11, 1886): 423. This dispute is called a strike in the issue for November 6 and a lockout in the issue for December 11.

15. Aurand, 121; Victor R. Greene, in *The Slavic Community on Strike: Immigrant Labor in Pennsylvania Anthracite* (Notre Dame: University of Notre Dame Press, 1968), 84; *Labor Troubles*, 398–99.

16. On early corporate domination in the Wyoming field see Blatz, "Ever-Shifting Ground," 56–57. Also see Grace Palladino, *Another Civil War: Labor, Capital, and the State in the Anthracite Regions of Pennsylvania, 1840–1868* (Urbana: University of Illinois Press, 1990), 19, 23–24. On the relative production and employment of the fields, see Blatz, "Ever-Shifting Ground," 57–58, 375. On the determination of leading corporations in the Wyoming field to prevent unionization, see *ibid.*, 55–56, 118–55.

17. *Labor Troubles*, 54–55, 398–99, 475–77, 497; Aurand, 122; Greene, 87–88.

18. *Wilkes-Barre Record*, October 21 and November 4, 1887; Aurand, 125; Greene, 88.

19. *Labor Troubles*, xciii–xciv, cii–cxiv.

20. *Wilkes-Barre Record*, January 11, 1888.

21. *Ibid.*, February 4, 10, and 21, 1888; *New York Times*, February 3, 4, 11, and 21, 1888.

22. Aurand, 129–30; Greene, 101–07; *New York Times*, February 3, 11, 16, and 18, 1888; *Wilkes-Barre Record*, February 13 and 20, 1888.

23. Peter Roberts, *The Anthracite Coal Communities* (New York: The Macmillan Co., 1904), 4, 122–25.

24. C. Pardee Foulke and William G. Foulke, *Calvin Pardee 1841–1923: His Family and His Enterprises* (Philadelphia: The Pardee Company, 1979), 27–30.

25. This is calculated from Pennsylvania, *Reports of the Inspectors of Mines of the Anthracite Coal Regions of Pennsylvania for the Year 1887* (Harrisburg, PA: Edwin K. Meyers, State Printer, 1888). In addition, the coal company begun by Pardee's brother-in-law, George B. Markle, whom Pardee helped to enter the business, mined over 300,000 tons of anthracite in that year. Their relationship is discussed in Foulke and Foulke, 38–39, 92–93.

26. For Pardee's leadership role, see W. H. Tillinghast to J. I. Hollenbeck, June 24, 1887; February 2, 1888; L & W-B Papers. Also see *Wilkes-Barre Record*, September 23, 1887; *Labor Troubles*, 41.

27. *Labor Troubles*, 554–56.

28. W. R. Storrs to Sloan, February 6, 1888, DL & W Records—Scranton.

29. Perry K. Blatz, "Corporate Attitudes Toward Labor Organization: The Controversy Over The Price of Powder in the Lackawanna Valley, 1888–1889," in *Hard Coal, Hard Times: Ethnicity and Labor in the Anthracite Region*, ed. by David L. Salay (Scranton, PA: Anthracite Museum Press, 1984), 40–57.

30. Blatz, "Ever-Shifting Ground," 147–53.

31. The data from which Table 2.2 is compiled are located in *Tenth Annual Report*, 1: 1046–53, 1062–65, 1074–81, 1090–97, 1106–09, 1114–21, 1126–29. For 1889, two walkouts which occurred in Archbald in January are not recorded in the *Tenth Annual Report*. See Pennsylvania, Secretary of Internal Affairs, *Annual Report*, Part III, *Industrial Statistics* 18 (1890): 10C–11C.

In *Conflict and Accommodation: Coal Miners, Steel Workers, and Socialism, 1890–1920* (Westport, CT: Greenwood Press, 1982), 164, Michael Nash presents his compilation of data on strikes in the anthracite industry from the *Tenth Annual Report*. His count of the number of walkouts differs considerably from mine; one possible source of confusion could be found in the *Report's* listing of strikes by locality for the entire coal industry, rather than grouping anthracite and bituminous separately.

32. *Tenth Annual Report,* 1:23.

33. *Ibid.,* 1:1050–53, 1114–17, 1126–29.

34. *Ibid.,* 1:1046–49, 1062–65, 1118–21, 1126–29.

35. *Ibid.,* 1:26.

36. These thirty-nine do not include strikes of less than one day in duration. See *Ibid.,* 1:10. Also, the *Report* counted lockouts separately and listed one in the anthracite industry during this period. See *Ibid.,* 1: 1346–49. In only one of the strikes in the anthracite industry did the walkout affect more than one "establishment," and only two put more than 1,000 employees out of work. See *Ibid.,* 1: 1046–49, 1116–19.

37. *United Mine Workers Journal,* August 27, 1891; hereafter cited as *UMWJ.* While the *UMWJ* made no mention of it, the first UMWA local in anthracite apparently organized in 1890. In the John Mitchell Papers at the end of 1902, there is a list of locals in anthracite from 1890 through 1902, and Local 4751 from Ashland is the only one listed before 1894. See "Number of Local Unions Reporting Each Year Since Formation—U.M.W. of A. in the Anthracite Field," John Mitchell Papers (microfilm edition), Catholic University of America, Washington; hereafter cited as Mitchell Papers (microfilm).

38. *UMWJ,* March 2, 1893.

39. *Ibid.,* May 23, 1893.

40. Concerning the bituminous strike of 1894, see *UMWJ,* April 19–August 9, 1894, and Jeremy Brecher, *Strike!* (Boston: South End Press, 1972), 69–76.

41. *UMWJ,* August 23, 1894.

42. *Ibid.,* October 18 and November 8, 1894.

43. *Ibid.,* November 8, 1894.

44. *Ibid.,* December 20, 1894; see *UMWJ,* December 27, 1894, for reference to minimum initiation fee.

45. *Ibid.,* February 21, 1895. Districts were entitled to "one vote for 100 members or less, and an additional vote for each 100 members or majority fraction thereof." See *UMWJ,* January 10, 1895.

46. *Ibid.,* January 17, 1895.

47. *Ibid.,* May 16, 1895.

48. *Ibid.,* May 2, 1895.

49. Peter Roberts, *The Anthracite Coal Industry* (New York: The Macmillan Co., 1901), 212, 222–27; the quotation can be found on p. 212.

50. *Ibid.*, July 18, 1895.

51. *Ibid.*, August 8, 1895.

52. *Ibid.*, August 22, 1895.

53. *Ibid.*, September 5, 1895.

54. *Ibid.*, October 3, 1895.

55. *Ibid.*

56. *E & MJ* LXI(March 7, 1896): 238; (April 11, 1896): 358.

57. *Ibid.*, LX(October 5, 1895): 331.

58. *UMWJ*, February 20, 1896.

59. *Ibid.*, March 26, 1896.

60. *Ibid.*, April 23, 1896.

61. *Ibid.*, October 1, 1896.

62. *Ibid.*, January 21, 1897.

63. *Ibid.*, February 7, 1895.

64. *Ibid.*, July 18, 1895.

65. For sliding scale rates, see *E & MJ* LXI(April 11, 1896): 358.

66. *UMWJ*, August 23, 1894.

67. *Ibid.*, August 15, 1895.

68. See *Wilkes-Barre News-Dealer,* quoted in *UMWJ*, September 3, 1891.

69. *UMWJ*, July 18, 1895.

70. *Ibid.*, October 22, 1896.

71. *Ibid.*, November 5, 1896.

72. *Ibid.*, December 3, 1896.

73. Fahy mentions his legislative work in Fahy to John Mitchell, March 4, 1897, Mitchell Papers (microfilm).

74. U.S., Department of the Interior, Bureau of Mines, *Pennsylvania Mining Statutes Annotated*, by J. W. Thompson, Bulletin No. 21 (Washington: Government Printing Office, 1920), 366; hereafter cited as Thompson, *Statutes.*

75. *Wilkes-Barre Record of the Times,* August 31, 1897.

76. *UMWJ,* December 3, 1896, June 17, 1897; also see John Mitchell's testimony in U.S., Industrial Commission, *Reports of the Industrial Commission,* vol. 12, *Report of the Industrial Commission on the Relations of Capital and Labor Employed in the Mining Industry* (Washington: Government Printing Office, 1901), 52.

77. *UMWJ,* July 1, 1897.

78. The revision required applicants for miners' certificates to "answer intelligently and correctly at least twelve questions in the English language pertaining to the requirements of a practical miner." Thompson, *Statutes,* 257–58. Greene, 115, states that the provision was enacted as part of the first version of the miners' certificate law in 1889. Cf. Thompson, *Statutes,* 254–56.

79. Thompson, *Statutes,* 5–8.

80. *UMWJ,* February 14 and March 14, 1895; December 5, 1896.

CHAPTER 3

1. Peter Roberts, *The Anthracite Coal Industry* (New York: The Macmillan Co., 1901), 20–22, 155.

2. The impact of the company store is described in Roberts, *Industry,* 131. Company housing's impact is described in Peter Roberts, *The Anthracite Coal Communities* (New York: The Macmillan Co., 1904), 122–23. The impact of the company doctor is described in U.S., Congress, House, Select Committee on Existing Labor Troubles in Pennsylvania, *Labor Troubles in the Anthracite Regions of Pennsylvania, 1887–88,* H. Report #4147, 50th Cong., 2nd sess., 1889, 481–82, 487, 559–60, 597.

3. *Wilkes-Barre Record of the Times,* August 17 and 20, 1897; Victor R. Greene, *The Slavic Community on Strike: Immigrant Labor in Pennsylvania Anthracite* (Notre Dame: University of Notre Dame Press, 1968), 129–30; Michael Novak, *The Guns of Lattimer: The True Story of a Massacre and a Trial, August 1897-March 1898* (New York: Basic Books, Inc., Publishers, 1978), 18–20.

4. William H. Storrs to Samuel Sloan, August 19, 1897, Corporate Records of the Delaware, Lackawanna and Western Railroad—Coal Department, Lackawanna Historical Society, Scranton, PA; hereafter cited as DL & W Records—Scranton.

5. *Wilkes-Barre Record of the Times,* August 20, 1897; Novak, 25–26.

6. *Wilkes-Barre Union-Leader,* August 20, 1897.

7. *Wilkes-Barre Record of the Times,* August 20 and 24, 1897; Greene, 130–31; Novak, 52–56.

8. *Wilkes-Barre Record of the Times,* August 31, 1897; Novak, 62–66.

9. *Wilkes-Barre Record of the Times,* August 31, 1897. Ironically, on the day after the strike began at Coleraine, Judge Acheson of the United States Circuit Court declared the wage tax on unnaturalized aliens to be unconstitutional.

10. *Ibid.,* September 3, 1897; Greene, 131–32; Novak, 67–75. The differing composition of the work forces at Milnesville and Coleraine can be seen in Pennsylvania, Bureau of Mines, *Report of the Bureau of Mines of the Department of Internal Affairs of Pennsylvania—1897* (Harrisburg, PA: William Stanley Ray, State Printer, 1898), 147.

11. *Wilkes-Barre Record of the Times,* September 10, 1897; Novak, 77–90.

12. Novak, 90–92.

13. *Wilkes-Barre Record of the Times,* September 10, 1897; Novak, 81–82, 92–105.

14. *Engineering and Mining Journal* 64 (September 11, 1897): 318; hereafter cited as *E & MJ.*

15. Novak, 103.

16. *Ibid.,* 95–96; U.S., Department of State, *Papers Relating to the Foreign Relations of the United States with the Annual Message of the President, Transmitted to the Congress, December 5, 1898* (Washington: Government Printing Office, 1961), 51, 54. These two sources disagree concerning when the workers at Harwood commenced their strike. According to Novak, Fahy organized the local on the afternoon of the seventh, after the strike had begun.

17. *Wilkes-Barre Record of the Times,* September 10, 1897; Novak, 98–100.

18. Novak, 109–34.

19. Aside from the increases granted by Van Wickle and the L & W-B, few other operators granted either wage increases or changes in work rules. There is no evidence of concessions at some of the collieries where workers struck, and at others the only concessions were promises of increased freedom for workers with regard to the company store, company doctor, or company housing—concessions Van Wickle's employees and those of the L & W-B also obtained. The only evidence I have found of an increase in wages other than those for Van Wickle's workers and those of the L & W-B is Novak's mention on p. 174 of an increase of 10 percent for some workers at Harwood. However, I found no reference to this in the newspapers, and the *Wilkes-Barre Union-Leader* reported on September 24 that the number of workers at Harwood had been growing gradually. This indicates that the workers were reluctant to return, an unlikely occurrence if they had received a substantial increase.

The Lehigh Valley Coal Company and the Mt. Carmel Coal Company (which operated the Silver Brook colliery near Audenried) did nothing more than to promise their employees greater freedom regarding the company store, company doctor, and company housing. See U.S., Industrial Commission, *Reports of the Industrial Com-*

mission, vol. 12, *Report of the Industrial Commission on the Relations of Capital and Labor Employed in the Mining Industry* (Washington: Government Printing Office, 1901), 42; *The World*, New York, September 25, 1897; *Wilkes-Barre Record of the Times*, September 24, 1897. At collieries where "compulsion" in dealing with the company store was a grievance, the precise issue involved may not have been formal company rules requiring that workers deal with the store, but certain informal arrangements that rewarded those who did so with favors. For example, Van Wickle's superintendent, Roderick, admitted the possibility of informal pressure on workers to deal with the company store. See Novak, 66.

20. *Wilkes-Barre Record of the Times*, September 14 and 24, 1897. For a list of the collieries on strike as of September 15, see *E & MJ* 64 (September 18, 1897): 348.

Perhaps the most militant act of the days during which the strikes subsided was the burning of the Evans breaker, operated by Van Wickle. Both the state mine inspector and a newspaper reporter believed that the breaker had been burned deliberately. See Pennsylvania, *Report of the Bureau of Mines—1897*, 132; *Wilkes-Barre Record of the Times*, September 24, 1897. Also, it is interesting to note how quickly militancy subsided at the collieries of G. B. Markle and Company, located several miles to the east of Lattimer. On September 13, a committee of workers presented a list of thirteen demands to the company, ranging from raises for most workers to an end to compulsion in dealing with the company store. The committee gave the company ten days to respond and the company did so on September 22 without agreeing to any. However, Markle's workers never went on strike, and did not even request local arbitration, which the company offered. See U. S., Anthracite Coal Strike Commission, *Report to the President on the Anthracite Coal Strike of May–October, 1902* (Washington: Government Printing Office, 1903), 144–45.

21. This spontaneity is discussed by Greene, 130–36, 148–49, and by Novak, 16–21, 63–69, 77–80, 172–78.

22. The confusion of the settlements at various companies is exemplified by the L & W-B, where workers were reportedly prepared to resume work on Tuesday, September 14, after their committee reached an agreement with Lawall on the previous Saturday. However, they did not return until Monday, September 20, at rates which, while they generally exceeded those paid when the strike began, were in some cases still below those in effect prior to Jones's reforms. The final obstacle to a settlement seemed to be the committee's demand for raises for the underground workers who, of course, had not initiated the strike. Eventually, the committee agreed to arbitrate the issue. Two representatives of the workers would meet with two representatives of the company to choose a fifth person, and these five would gather data from nearby collieries to be used in arriving at rates for underground miners. *Wilkes-Barre Record of the Times*, September 14 and 24, 1897. Cf. listing of rates before and after Jones's reforms, *Wilkes-Barre Union-Leader*, August 20, 1897.

On p. 177, Novak states that, as part of the settlement at the L & W-B's mines, "Gomer Jones was replaced" as superintendent of the company's Honey Brook division. Although *Wilkes-Barre Record of the Times*, September 21, 1897, quotes an unnamed source as stating that Jones "will be fired," there is no evidence that this actually occurred. Pennsylvania, Bureau of Mines, *Report of the Bureau of Mines of the Department of Internal Affairs of Pennsylvania—1898*, 153, 189 lists Jones as the superintendent for the Honey Brook mines, and *Wilkes-Barre Record of the Times*, November 14, 1899, reports Jones's dismissal on that date, more than two years after the Lattimer massacre.

23. Quoted in *UMWJ*, September 30, 1897, without any reference to the original source.

24. *Philadelphia Press*, September 17, 1897, quoted in *UMWJ*, November 18, 1897. For other references to Fahy's conservatism during the Lattimer strikes, see *Hazleton Standard*, September 17, 1897, and *Hazleton Plain-Speaker*, September 23, 1897, quoted in *UMWJ*, October 18, 1897.

25. *UMWJ*, January 13 and February 3, 1898.

26. *Ibid.*, February 17, 1898.

27. *Ibid.*, May 12, 1898.

28. For the terms of the agreement in the Central Competitive Field, see *UMWJ*, February 3, 1898. Also see Bruno Ramirez, *When Workers Fight: The Politics of Industrial Relations in the Progressive Era, 1898–1916* (Westport, CT: Greenwood Press, 1978), ch. 1; and Joseph M. Gowaskie, "From Conflict to Cooperation: John Mitchell and the Bituminous Coal Operators, 1898–1908," *The Historian* 38 (August 1976): 669–88.

29. *Ibid.*, March 31, 1898.

30. *Ibid.*

31. John Fahy to Michael Ratchford, March 26, 1898, John Mitchell Papers microfilm edition, Catholic University of America, Washington; hereafter cited as Mitchell Papers (microfilm).

32. *UMWJ*, July 14 and 21, 1898.

33. *Ibid.*, October 6, 1898. Of course, 1898 was a horrendous year for the anthracite industry, one in which breakers averaged only 152 days of work. See U.S., Bureau of Census, *Historical Statistics of the United States: Colonial Times to 1970*, 2 parts (Washington: Government Printing Office, 1975), 1:592–93.

34. *Ibid.*, June 2, 1898.

35. *Ibid.*, June 2, 23, and July 14, 1898.

36. *Ibid.*, May 5 and 19, 1898.

37. *Ibid.*, July 28, 1898.

38. *Ibid.*, August 18, 1898.

39. *Ibid.*, September 15 and October 6, 1898.

40. *Ibid.*, October 13, 1898.

41. *Ibid.*, December 15, 1898.

42. As a preliminary step to such negotiations, District Seven in May 1898 decided to send blank forms to each local "to get the exact price paid for all kinds of work at the different collieries and also what is charged for mine supplies." See *UMWJ*, May 11, 1898.

43. *Ibid.*, December 15, 1898.

44. *Ibid.*, March 23, 1899. In *The Slavic Community on Strike*, Victor Greene gives John Fahy considerable credit for the UMWA's early success in anthracite. However, he fails to examine Fahy's role in 1898, when the union's bright prospects were not realized. Additional light can be shed upon "Mine Worker's" oblique criticism of Fahy by a letter written in August 1899 by then former UMWA president, Michael Ratchford, to union president John Mitchell. Ratchford recalled speaking with Fahy shortly after the national convention of January 1898, at which time Ratchford "learned from him that he was indifferent (to say the least) about returning to the anthracite region." Ratchford offered him work for national headquarters, but only if he would resign the presidency of District One. Fahy neither refused nor accepted this offer, and Ratchford, who saw him several times that year in Ohio, extended the offer again on a number of occasions. Meanwhile, Ratchford received several inquiries from the anthracite region asking "when Mr. Fahy would return and in some cases I was demanded to send him there or send his resignation." However, Ratchford had no power, under the national and district constitutions, to force Fahy to resign. Apparently Fahy spent most of 1898 with his sister who was bedridden at her home in New Straitsville, Ohio. When Ratchford wired Fahy in July 1898 to tell him he should either return to the anthracite region or resign his presidency and go to work for national headquarters, Fahy replied that matters in the anthracite region did not require his attention. See Michael Ratchford to John Mitchell, August 21, 1899, Mitchell Papers (microfilm).

45. *Wilkes-Barre Record*, December 7, 1896.

46. *Ibid.*, December 7 and 8, 1896.

47. *Ibid.*, December 7, 1896.

48. *Ibid.*, December 8, 1896.

49. W. H. Storrs to Sloan, September 15, 1897, DL & W Records—Scranton.

50. W. H. Storrs to Sloan, October 15, 1897, *ibid.*

51. W. H. Storrs to Sloan, October 18, 1897, *ibid.*

52. W. H. Storrs to Sloan, date illegible, located in letterbook in either late June or early July in 1898, *ibid.* This walkout may well be explained by the fact that, gen-

erally, drivers were required not only to harness their mules and have them ready when the miners began work, but they also had to unhitch the mules and give them water at the end of the day. Drivers might well view this as overtime, since they had to work more time than the regular day; however, management maintained that those tasks had traditionally been performed by drivers. A onetime mine worker describes these duties in Bruno Leganowski interview by W. K. Brown and J. D. Mercier, June 1972, tape recording, Eckley Oral History Project, Pennsylvania Historical and Museum Commission, Harrisburg, PA.

53. *Scranton Republican,* June 3 and 5, 1899.

54. W. H. Storrs to Sloan, February 3, 1899, DL & W Records—Scranton.

55. *UMWJ,* April 27, 1899.

56. *Ibid.,* February 23, 1899.

57. *Ibid.,* April 13, 1899.

58. *Ibid.* For Fahy, see Novak, 55–56; *UMWJ,* September 15, 1898. Nationality locals persisted for decades in anthracite. See *UMWJ,* December 20, 1906; April 7, 1910; April 10, 1913; September 2, 1915; and January 6, 1916.

59. *UMWJ,* June 1, 1899.

60. Charles J. Thain to W. C. Pearce, July 23, 1899; George Hartlein to W. C. Pearce, July 24, 1899; James Dorsett to John Mitchell, July 29, 1899, Mitchell Papers (microfilm).

61. John Fahy to John Mitchell, July 31, August 2 and 18, 1899; John Mitchell to John Fahy, August 8, 1899, *ibid.*

62. John Mitchell to T. W. Davis, August 31, 1899, *ibid.;* Joseph Michael Gowaskie, "John Mitchell: A Study in Leadership," Ph.D. dissertation, Catholic University of America, 1968, 48–53.

63. U.S., Congress, Joint Committee on Printing, *Biographical Directory of the American Congress, 1774–1971,* S. Doc. 92–98, 92nd Cong., 2nd sess. (Washington: United States Government Printing Office, 1971), 1471. Also, Nicholls is listed among those passing the examination in Pennsylvania, *Report of the Bureau of Mines—1897,* 108. The *Biographical Directory* states that he "was appointed superintendent of mines" at some time soon after passing the examination. However, I have found no evidence to confirm this.

64. Roger J. Howell, Scranton, PA, interview by the author, December 1979, tape recording in possession of author.

65. *Wilkes-Barre Record,* June 29, 1899.

66. *Ibid.*

67. A mine inspector condemned this apparently common practice in Pennsylvania, *Reports of the Inspectors of Mines of the Anthracite and Bituminous Coal Regions of Pennsylvania for the Year 1890* (Harrisburg, PA; Edwin K. Meyers, State Printer, 1891), 208.

68. *Wilkes-Barre Record,* June 29, 1899.

69. On the far greater incidence of accidents due to falls over accidents from explosions, see Pennsylvania, *Reports of the Inspectors of Mines of the Anthracite and Bituminous Coal Regions for the Year 1888* (Harrisburg, PA: Edwin K. Meyers, State Printer, 1889), 4, 97; Pennsylvania, *Reports of the Inspectors of Mines of the Anthracite and Bituminous Coal Regions of Pennsylvania for the Year 1889* (Harrisburg, PA: Edwin K. Meyers, State Printer, 1890), 119, 205; and Pennsylvania, *Report of the Bureau of Mines—1897,* 4–5. On the increased likelihood of accidents from falls as safety lamps were used, see Perry K. Blatz, ''Ever-Shifting Ground: Work and Labor Relations in the Anthracite Coal Industry, 1868–1903,'' Ph.D. dissertation, Princeton University, 1987, 298–301.

Keith Dix contrasts the relative lack of interest by government and the mining industry in preventing accidents due to falls with the extensive effort they devoted to preventing mine explosions. See *Work Relations in the Coal Industry: The Hand-Loading Era, 1880–1930* (Morgantown: Institute for Labor Studies, West Virginia University, 1977), 67–104.

70. *Wilkes-Barre Record,* July 1, 1899.

71. *Ibid.,* June 30, 1899.

72. *Ibid.,* July 4, 6, and 7, 1899.

73. *Ibid.,* July 11, 1899; *E & MJ* 68 (July 15, 1899): 78.

74. References to walkouts at other mines in *Wilkes-Barre Record,* July 4, 6, and 7, 1899 contain no specific mention of UMWA activity at those mines.

75. *UMWJ,* July 27, 1899; *E & MJ* 68 (July 22, 1899): 108; *Wilkes-Barre Record,* August 11, 1899. The quotation is from the *Wilkes-Barre Record.*

76. *Wilkes-Barre Record,* July 28, 1899.

77. *UMWJ,* August 17, 1899. The workers of William A. remained militant after the strike had been settled. On Saturday, September 2, workers there walked out to protest the discharge of a worker whom management had fired for alleged incompetence. The workers returned on Monday; there was no report of whether or not the company reinstated the discharged worker. See *Wilkes-Barre Record of the Times,* September 5, 1899.

78. *Ibid.,* August 24, 1899; *E & MJ* 68 (August 5, 1899): 168, (August 19, 1899): 228.

79. *UMWJ,* August 24, 1899.

80. *Ibid.*, October 5, 1899; *E & MJ* 68 (October 14, 1899): 468.

81. *Wilkes-Barre Record,* July 26, 1899.

82. "Proceedings," 1130–31; 2425.

83. *Ibid.*, 2250–52.

84. *Ibid.*, 2391.

85. *Ibid.*, 2250–52.

86. *Ibid.*, 1762–63, 2391. William Mates, an employee of the L & W-B, stated that after the strike of 1900, that company decided to require eight inches of topping at the foot of the shaft. The company's miners wanted the cars to be examined for topping in the chambers instead of at the foot of the shaft, but the company refused. "Proceedings," 2422.

87. *Ibid.*, 1388–89.

88. *Wilkes-Barre Record,* July 26 and August 1, 1899; *Wilkes-Barre Record of the Times,* August 8, 1899. Nicholls and Miller both signed the final agreement with the SCC as members of the employees' committee. See "Schedule of Prices and Wages Agreed Upon by the Management and Superintendent of the Susquehanna Coal Company and Committee of Employees," December 11, 1899, Mitchell Papers (microfilm); hereafter cited as "Schedule."

89. *Wilkes-Barre Record of the Times,* August 8, 1899.

90. *Ibid.*

91. *Ibid.*, August 29, 1899.

92. *Ibid.*, September 5, 1899.

93. *E & MJ* 68 (October 7, 1899): 438.

94. *UMWJ,* October 26 and November 23, 1899.

95. *Wilkes-Barre Record of the Times,* October 6, 1899.

96. *UMWJ,* October 26, 1899.

97. Benjamin James to W. C. Scott, September 30, 1899, Mitchell Papers (microfilm).

98. John Fahy to John Mitchell, December 3, 1899, *ibid.*

99. Benjamin James to John Mitchell, October 3, 1899, *ibid.*

100. *Wilkes-Barre Record of the Times,* October 6, 1899.

101. *Ibid.*, October 3, 1899; *UMWJ,* November 2, 1899.

102. *Ibid.*, October 26, 1899.

103. *Wilkes-Barre Record of the Times*, October 24, 1899.

104. *Ibid.*, October 31, 1899; *UMWJ*, November 2, 1899.

105. *Wilkes-Barre Record of the Times*, November 24, 1899. Apparently the engineers and pumpmen, whose primary task was to keep the collieries from flooding, had been called out on strike originally. However, not all of them had walked out and the company had replaced those who did. See *Wilkes-Barre Record of the Times*, December 5, 1899.

106. *Ibid.*, November 24, 1899; *UMWJ*, November 30, 1899. The extent to which UMWA leaders were involved in this episode is unclear; however, Nicholls stated that he attended the meeting on November 20 at which the women decided to act.

107. *UMWJ*, November 30, 1899.

108. *Wilkes-Barre Record of the Times*, November 24 and December 8, 1899.

109. *Ibid.*, November 24, 1899.

110. *Ibid.*, December 5 and 12, 1899.

111. *Ibid.*, December 15, 1899; "Schedule," Mitchell Papers (microfilm). The document contained no reference to the UMWA, so, regardless of the union's intimate involvement in the strike, the company could maintain that it had in no way recognized the union.

112. *UMWJ*, December 14, 1899.

113. "Schedule," Mitchell Papers (microfilm); *Wilkes-Barre Record of the Times*, December 15, 1899.

114. *UMWJ*, November 2, 1899.

CHAPTER 4

1. *United Mine Workers Journal*, January 18, 1900; hereafter cited as *UMWJ*. For the three districts, UMWA membership totaled 8,993, with 1,467 in District Nine and only 341 in District Seven.

2. Joseph M. Gowaskie, "From Conflict to Cooperation: John Mitchell and the Bituminous Coal Operators, 1898–1908," *The Historian* 38 (August 1976): 677–83.

3. Cf. *Ibid.*, 670–72, 675–76, and Eliot Jones, *The Anthracite Coal Combination in the United States* (Cambridge: Harvard University Press, 1914), 40–97.

4. *UMWJ*, January 11, 1900.

5. Truesdale to Loomis, January 2, 1900. Corporate Records of the Delaware, Lackawanna and Western Railroad, George Arents Research Library, Syracuse University, Syracuse, NY; hereafter cited as DL & W Records—Syracuse.

6. *Scranton Times,* January 9 and 18, 1900. When District One reconvened on January 18, two committees, one from Luzerne County and one from Lackawanna County, were selected to try to arrange meetings with operators. If those committees did not succeed, the district executive board would then apply to President Mitchell for permission to strike. See United Mine Workers of America, *Proceedings of the Convention of District #1, United Mine Workers of America, January 14–16, 1901, Edwardsville, Pa.* (n.p., n.d.), 10–11.

Four superintendents responsible for some 40 percent of the Wyoming field's production insisted they would have nothing to do with the UMWA. See *Scranton Times,* January 23, 1900.

7. United Mine Workers of America, Executive Board Minutes, February 3, 1900, John Mitchell Papers (microfilm edition), Catholic University of America, Washington; hereafter cited as Mitchell Papers (microfilm).

8. *Ibid.,* February 3 and 5, 1900. In outlining a course of action for the union in anthracite Mitchell accurately predicted the future. During the meeting of February 3, Mitchell stated: "I have advised the men to continue the work of organization until we could bring about a conference of all the districts. I have favored a joint conference of officers and delegates of the three districts there, and that they inaugurate a general movement for better conditions, and if they fail, that [a] strike be inaugurated at the proper time. I believe that strike sentiment often carries unorganized men with it, and if we get everybody working together, I believe it is possible to inaugurate a strike that will sweep the district. If everything else fails, I believe we could win by that method."

9. This table is based on information in Perry K. Blatz, "Ever-Shifting Ground: Work and Labor Relations in the Anthracite Coal Industry, 1868–1903," Ph.D. dissertation, Princeton University, 1987, 416–27. In general, the strikes were traced in local newspapers, the *UMWJ,* and the *Engineering and Mining Journal,* hereafter cited as *E & MJ.* Also, some fifteen other strikes for which only a limited amount of information could be found are referred to in Blatz, "Ever-Shifting Ground," 416–27.

10. *Wilkes-Barre Record of the Times,* May 11 and 25, 1900; *Wilkes-Barre News Dealer,* May 25, 1900; *UMWJ,* May 24, 1900; and *E & MJ* 69 (May 12, 1900): 569.

11. *Scranton Times,* June 6, 1900.

12. *Ibid.,* July 30 and August 4, 1900.

13. U.S., Anthracite Coal Strike Commission, "Proceedings of the Anthracite Coal Strike Commission, 1902–1903," 56 vols., 30 (January 10, 1903): 4757; see also *Scranton Times,* July 25, 1900.

14. *Ibid.,* June 8 and 9, and July 20, 1900.

15. *Ibid.,* July 20, 23, 24, 25, and 26, 1900.

16. *Ibid.,* July 27 and 30, August 2 and 4, 1900.

17. *UMWJ*, March 29, 1900.

18. *Ibid.*, April 19, 1900.

19. *Ibid.*, June 21, 1900.

20. Thomas D. Nicholls to John Mitchell, June 9, 1900, Mitchell Papers (microfilm). In this letter, Nicholls states that only two of the strikes then in progress in the district had been authorized. One of these was probably the strike against the Butler Mine Company; see *Wilkes-Barre Record of the Times*, April 20, 1900. Also, I found no evidence of efforts by companies to provoke local strikes. Nicholls's and Thain's remarks may well display their pique over the workers' failure to obtain the union's permission before engaging in strike action.

21. *Ibid.*, May 3, 1900. Also see March 29, 1900.

22. *Ibid.*, May 10, 1900. On Fahy's absence, also see *ibid.*, March 29, 1900.

23. *Ibid.*, May 24, 1900.

24. *Ibid.*, May 31, 1900.

25. *Ibid.*, June 21, 1900.

26. *Ibid.*, June 28, 1900. In the *Slavic Community on Strike: Immigrant Labor in Pennsylvania Anthracite* (Notre Dame: University of Notre Dame Press, 1968), 159, Victor R. Greene states that "in 1900 District Nine was as strongly situated as was Wyoming District One." While District Nine claimed fifty-five locals as of the middle of the year, District One began the year with sixty-three, and continued to organize throughout the year. Also, the relative lack of militancy in District Nine as compared to District One casts further doubt on Greene's assertion.

27. Benjamin James to Thomas Duffy, June 28, 1900, Mitchell Papers (microfilm).

28. John Fahy to John Mitchell, July 1, 1900, *ibid.*

29. *Ibid.* Apparently Mitchell repeated former UMWA President Ratchford's offer of trading the district presidency for a post on the national union payroll as an organizer. In this letter, Fahy responded to Mitchell's offer by stating that he would not become an organizer, although doing so would be the better course for him financially. He added that he knew of no one who would accept the district presidency "under the existing poor financial circumstances of this district."

30. United Mine Workers of America, *Proceedings of the Fifth Quarterly Convention, District One, United Mine Workers of America, Pittston, Pa., July 9–10, 1900*, Mitchell Papers (microfilm).

31. John Fahy to John Mitchell, July 15, 1900, and Call for Convention, July 17, 1900, *ibid.*

32. *UMWJ,* March 15, 1900; see also *Scranton Times,* February 26, 1900.

33. Truesdale to Loomis, April 16, 1900, DL & W Records—Syracuse.

34. Truesdale to Loomis, April 11, 1900, *ibid.*

35. Truesdale to Loomis, August 3, 1900, *ibid.*

36. *Scranton Times,* July 31, 1900; see also *UMWJ,* August 16, 1900, and *E & MJ* 70 (August 4, 1900): 139.

37. *Scranton Times,* August 11, 1900; see also *E & MJ* 70 (August 18, 1900): 200.

38. Pennsylvania, Bureau of Mines, *Report of the Bureau of Mines of the Department of Internal Affairs of Pennsylvania—1900* (Harrisburg, PA: William Stanley Ray, State Printer, 1901), 47, 98, reports 8,310 DL & W employees in the second and third mine inspection districts, which were the districts closest to Scranton.

39. *Scranton Times,* August 11 and 23, 1900. The DL & W had conducted a similar sort of canvass in 1889; see chapter 2.

40. *Ibid.,* August 23 and September 7, 1900. In "The Company Union Movement, 1900–37: A Re-examination," *Business History Review* 56 (Autumn 1982): 335–57, Daniel Nelson pays little attention to company unions which were little more than company puppets, as the Lackawanna Union so clearly was. Nevertheless, from the evidence presented by Nelson, which contains no mention of the Lackawanna Union, the DL & W's effort may well be regarded as pioneering. For the strike call, see *UMWJ,* September 13, 1900.

41. J. P. Gallagher, John T. Dempsey, and George Hartline [*sic*] to the Operators of the Anthracite Coal Fields of Pennsylvania, August 16, 1900, Mitchell Papers (microfilm).

42. *Scranton Times,* August 29, 1900; also see *E & MJ* 70 (September 1, 1900): 259.

43. Peter Roberts, *The Anthracite Coal Industry* (New York: The Macmillan Co., 1901), 129–51; Peter Roberts, *The Anthracite Coal Communities* (New York: The Macmillan Co., 1904); 122–23.

44. U.S., Department of the Interior, Bureau of Mines, *Pennsylvania Mining Statutes Annotated,* by J. W. Thompson, Bulletin No. 21 (Washington: Government Printing Office, 1920), 395–99.

45. U.S., Industrial Commission, *Reports of the Industrial Commission,* vol. 12, *Report of the Industrial Commission on the Relations of Labor and Capital Employed in the Mining Industry* (Washington: Government Printing Office, 1901), 143, 652. For instances of companies ignoring the law before it was overturned, see W. R. Storrs to Samuel Sloan, June 6, 8, 13, and 27, and August 17, 1891; Corporate

Records of the Delaware, Lackawanna, and Western Railroad—Coal Department, Lackawanna Historical Society, Scranton, PA.

46. Tables 1.3 and 1.4 show that the largest proportion of company men averaged less than $1.50, and that most of these were slate pickers. Most of the rest of the company men averaged more than $1.50 per day, but less than $1.75, and thus they fell into the group slated for the next largest increase.

47. J. P. Gallagher, John T. Dempsey, and George Hartline [*sic*] to the Operators of the Anthracite Coal Fields of Pennsylvania, August 16, 1900, Mitchell Papers (microfilm). The D & H stated that its dockage for 1899 "amounted to less than 3 per cent, namely 2.79 per cent of the coal mined." See "Statement of the Delaware and Hudson Company Showing Position of the Operators, September 1900," in U.S., Department of Labor, *Bulletin of the Department of Labor*, "Report to the President on the Anthracite Coal Strike," by Carroll D. Wright (November 1902): 1168; hereafter cited as Wright's report.

48. *Ibid.*, 1168.

49. See Perry K. Blatz, "Corporate Attitudes Toward Labor Organization: The Controversy Over the Price of Powder in the Lackawanna Valley, 1888–1889," in *Hard Coal, Hard Times,* ed. by David L. Salay (Scranton, PA: Anthracite Museum Press, 1984), 40–57. The UMWA reported that prices for powder at mines controlled by the Pennsylvania Railroad in the western portion of the Schuylkill field were slightly higher than those charged by the P & R. See *UMWJ*, March 29, April 5 and 12, 1900.

50. J. P. Gallagher, John T. Dempsey, and George Hartline [*sic*] to the Operators of the Anthracite Coal Fields of Pennsylvania, August 16, 1900, Mitchell Papers (microfilm).

51. Wright's report, 1169.

52. *Ibid.*

53. *E & MJ* 44 (December 3, 1897): 413. After the strike of 1875, operators in the Schuylkill field paid set rates to outside laborers and only paid underground workers according to the sliding scale. However, in the Lehigh field it seems that outside laborers were paid according to the scale. See U.S., Congress, House, Select Committee on Existing Labor Troubles in Pennsylvania, *Labor Troubles in the Anthracite Regions of Pennsylvania, 1887–88,* H. Rept. 4147, 50th Cong., 2d sess., 1889, 39, 467–77.

54. Wright's report, 1173.

55. J. P. Gallagher, John T. Dempsey and George Hartline [*sic*] to the Operators of the Anthracite Coal Fields of Pennsylvania, August 16, 1900, Mitchell Papers (microfilm).

56. Wright's report, 1171.

57. The UMWA did not formulate a wage scale for company men, and this omission may well show their relative lack of influence and lack of participation in the union.

58. Robert J. Cornell, *The Anthracite Coal Strike of 1902* (Washington: Catholic University of America Press, 1957), 43–46; Robert H. Wiebe, "The Anthracite Strike of 1902: A Record of Confusion," *Mississippi Valley Historical Review* 48 (September 1961): 236; *UMWJ*, August 30 and September 13, 1900. Hanna did succeed in arranging for G. M. Cummings, a vice-president of the Erie Railroad, to meet informally with Mitchell, but no substantive negotiations took place. See Cornell, 45.

59. Truesdale to Loomis, September 7, 1900; DL & W Records—Syracuse.

60. Truesdale to Loomis, September 13, 1900, *ibid.*

61. Cornell, 46–47.

62. Truesdale to Loomis, September 20, 1900, DL & W records—Syracuse.

63. U.S., Anthracite Coal Strike Commission, *Report to the President on the Anthracite Coal Strike of May–October 1902* (Washington: Government Printing Office, 1903), 144–45, 164.

64. *Ibid.*, 161–62.

65. *Ibid.*, 161–62; see also Cornell, 52–53.

66. Greene, 168; Cornell, 48; *The World* (New York), September 22 and 23, 1900. Greene, 165–70, gives an excellent description of the turmoil which occurred in Shenandoah during the first week of the strike.

67. *The World* (New York), September 23, 1900; Cornell, 47.

68. Cornell, 47–48; *The World* (New York), September 20, 25, and 29, and October 2, 1900.

69. Donald Sayenga, "The Untryed Business: An Appreciation of White and Hazard," *Proceedings of the Canal History and Technology Symposium* 2 (1983): 105–14.

70. Minutes of the Meetings of the Board of Mangers, October 1, 1900, Corporate Records of the Lehigh Coal and Navigation Company, Pennsylvania Historical and Museum Commission, Harrisburg, PA; hereafter cited as LC & N Records. Lance E. Metz, Program Director and Historian at the Center for Canal History and Technology, Easton, PA, kindly permitted me to examine the microfilm edition of the LC & N Records at the Center.

71. *The World* (New York), October 17 and 19, 1900; Minutes of the Meetings of the Board of Managers, November 5, 1900, LC & N Records, states that the mob totaled 5,000. Also see E. C. Morris to W. C. Scott, October 19, 1900, Mitchell Papers (microfilm—misdated 1904).

72. Minutes of the Meetings of the Board of Managers, November 5, 1900, LC & N Records.

73. *Tamaqua Evening Courier,* November 9, 1900, in Minutes of the Meetings of the Board of Managers, LC & N Records. For further information concerning the LC & N's beneficial fund, see Blatz, "Ever-Shifting Ground," 94–95.

74. Cornell, 53–56.

75. *Ibid.,* 46–47, 56–57; *UMWJ,* October 4, 1900. The executive board of District One issued a statement on October 1 rejecting the operators' offer as a basis for settlement. The board pointed out that, since miners commonly were paid for certain tasks at rates decided upon only after completion of the task, a nominal advance of 10 percent would have no effect "on about one-eighth" of the work performed by miners. As it had since the Nanticoke strike of the previous year, the district continued to call for "a fixed price on all kinds of work." In its statement, the board also mentioned other demands not addressed in the notices, such as those for semimonthly pay, checkweighmen, and payment by weight in tons of 2,240 pounds. According to the board: "The diversity of condition and the intricacies of the various questions at issue make it an impossibility to settle the vexed questions except by a joint conference of miners and operators, or by a board of arbitration." See *ibid.*

76. *The World* (New York), October 1, 1900.

77. *UMWJ,* October 4, 1900.

78. Cornell, 57; *UMWJ,* October 11, 1900.

79. *Ibid.,* October 18, 1900.

80. Truesdale to Loomis, October 15, 1900, DL & W Records—Syracuse.

81. *UMWJ,* October 18, 1900; Cornell, 58.

82. Truesdale to J. S. Harris, October 18, 1900, DL & W Records—Syracuse.

83. Truesdale to Loomis, October 18, 1900, *ibid.*

84. *New York Herald,* October 24, 1900; *New York Tribune,* October 25, 1900.

85. Truesdale to Loomis, October 24, 1900 DL & W Records—Syracuse.

86. "Minutes of a Meeting," October 24, 1900, Mitchell Papers (microfilm).

87. *UMWJ,* November 1, 1900.

88. *New York Times,* October 27, 1900; *UMWJ,* November 1 and 8, 1900.

89. United Mine Workers of America, *Proceedings of the Joint Convention of Districts One, Seven, and Nine, United Mine Workers of America, Hazleton, Pa., August 27–30, 1901* (Shamokin, PA: The News Publishing Co., 1901), 8. Also see *UMWJ,* October 31, 1901. Mitchell Day was celebrated as recently as 1953; see Carl

Corlsen, *Buried Black Treasure: The Story of Pennsylvania Anthracite* (Bethlehem, PA: The Author, 1953), 91

In his evaluation of the strike at the UMWA's national convention in January 1901, Mitchell stated: "In order that you may fully understand the timidity and reluctance with which we entered upon this conflict it is but fair that you should know that of the 142,500 mine workers employed in the anthracite fields, less than 8,000 were members in good standing of our organization." See *UMWJ*, January 24, 1901. If the union actually had so few members, Mitchell and his fellow UMWA leaders deserve most of the credit for the strike's success. However, the three anthracite districts had a total membership in good standing of 8,993 at the close of 1899 (see *UMWJ*, January 18, 1900), and it is most unlikely that membership declined during the ensuing eight-and-a-half months of intensive organizing. Also, in January 1901, Thomas Nicholls reported that District One's membership at the preceding district convention in July 1900 stood at 10,000; see *Proceedings of the Convention of District One, January 1901* (n.p., n.d.), 9.

90. *UMWJ*, November 29, 1900, urged the mine workers in a front-page headline "To Conscientiously Fulfill Their Part of the Contract." This usage occurred frequently thereafter in the *UMWJ*.

CHAPTER 5

1. Truesdale to Loomis, November 2, 1900, Corporate Records of the Delaware, Lackawanna, and Western Railroad, George Arents Research Library, Syracuse University, Syracuse, N.Y.; hereafter cited as DL & W Records—Syracuse.

2. *United Mine Workers Journal*, November 29, 1900; hereafter cited as *UMWJ*.

3. According to Thain, the D & H, DL & W, and LV allowed check–docking bosses. See *UMWJ*, November 29, 1900. However, representatives of each of these companies testified before the Anthracite Coal Strike Commission that they did not have check–docking bosses. See U.S., Anthracite Coal Strike Commission, "Proceedings of the Anthracite Coal Strike Commission, 1902–1903," 56 vols., 30 (January 10, 1903): 4773, 36 (January 17, 1903): 6016, 39 (January 21, 1903): 6499; hereafter cited as "Proceedings." Still, Charles C. Rose, superintendent of the D & H, stated that most docking bosses belonged to the union in spite of the company's wishes, and William J. Richards, superintendent of the L & W-B, also testified that his company's docking bosses belonged to the union. See "Proceedings," 4733, 6767. According to testimony in the "Proceedings," only one of the leading companies, the Temple Iron Company, instituted check–docking bosses after the strike of 1900. See 6386, 6405.

4. *UMWJ*, November 29, 1900.

5. *Ibid.*, see also *Engineering and Mining Journal* 70 (November 3, 1900): 530; hereafter cited as *E & MJ*.

6. *UMWJ*, November 8, 1900. James's views may have reflected his sixteen years of experience in bituminous mining, in which the miner generally loaded his

own coal. For James's career, see U.S. Industrial Commission, *Reports of the Industrial Commission*, vol. XII: *Report of the Industrial Commission on the Relations and Conditions of Capital and Labor Employed in the Mining Industry* (Washington: Government Printing Office, 1901), 138. James was soon ousted from the UMWA hierarchy after he lobbied against a bill, favored by the union, that increased the number of mine inspectors and lowered their salary. See "Statement by Alfred B. Garner," John Mitchell Papers (microfilm edition), Catholic University of America, Washington; hereafter cited as Mitchell Papers (microfilm); United Mine Workers of America, *Proceedings of the Convention of District One, United Mine Workers of America, April 8–11, 1901, Olyphant, Pa.*, (Scranton, PA: Sanders Printing Co., 1901), 14–15. For some time James had been viewed as a rival to Mitchell and other UMWA leaders. See Mother Jones to Mitchell, November 30, 1900; Frederick Dilcher to Mitchell, December 17 and 26, 1900; Mitchell to Thomas Nicholls, January 4, 1901; and Mitchell to Benjamin James, June 17, 1901, all in the Mitchell Papers (microfilm).

For bituminous miners generally working as partners, without laborers, see John Brophy, *A Miner's Life*, ed. John O. O. Hall (Madison: University of Wisconsin Press, 1964), 43–49; Keith Dix, *Work Relations in the Coal Industry: The Hand Loading Era, 1880–1930* (Morgantown: West Virginia University Press, 1977), 8–14; and John Mitchell's testimony, "Proceedings," 566.

7. *UMWJ*, December 20, 1900.

8. *E & MJ* 70 (December 22, 1900): 740.

9. *UMWJ*, February 28, 1901.

10. United Mine Workers of America, *Proceedings of the Semi-Annual Convention of District One, United Mine Workers of America, January 13–17, 1902, Wilkes-Barre, Pa.* (Scranton, PA: Sanders Printing Co., 1902), 57–58.

11. United Mine Workers of America, *Proceedings of the Convention of District One, United Mine Workers of America, January 14–16, 1901, Edwardsville, Pa.* (n.p., n.d.), 26–28; *UMWJ*, December 20, 1900. See also *UMWJ*, January 3, 1901, *E & MJ* 70 (December 20, 1900): 740; and a retrospective account by one of the grievance committee members, Edward Blackledge, in *UMWJ*, May 12 and 26, June 2 and 9, 1910.

12. *Proceedings of the Convention of District One, January 1901*, 18.

13. *UMWJ*, January 3, 1901.

14. *Ibid.*, January 10, 1901.

15. *Ibid.*, December 20, 1900; *E & MJ* 70 (December 20, 1900): 740.

16. *E & MJ* 70 (December 20, 1900): 740.

17. *UMWJ*, February 7, 1901.

18. *E & MJ* 71 (January 26, 1901): 129.

19. *UMWJ*, February 14, 1901.

20. *Ibid.*, January 17, 1901.

21. *Ibid.*, January 24, 1901.

22. Truesdale to Chappell, February 5, 1901, DL & W Records—Syracuse.

23. Robert J. Cornell, *The Anthracite Coal Strike of 1902* (Washington: Catholic University of America Press, 1957), 61–64.

24. Mitchell to Fairley, March 13, 1901, Mitchell Papers (microfilm).

25. Mitchell to Ryan, March 19, 1901; Easley to Mitchell, n.d., *ibid.;* see also Cornell, 64–65.

26. *Ibid.*, 65–66; Mitchell to Hanna, March 20, 1901, Mitchell Papers (microfilm).

27. Mitchell to Ryan, March 21, 1901, *ibid.* In this letter, Mitchell informed Ryan: "I think that it would be perfectly safe for you to take up as much stock as you desire with full assurance that there will be no suspension, although we will go to the very verge of strike before giving up." The stock which Ryan planned to buy is not specified.

28. Cornell, 66–67. The process by which the Morgan interests took control of most of the anthracite railroads is described in Eliot Jones, *The Anthracite Coal Combination in the United States* (Cambridge: Harvard University Press, 1914), 48–84. See also Jules I. Bogen, *The Anthracite Railroads* (New York: Ronald Press Co., 1927), 65–72, 102–03, 131–35, 178–81, and Cornell, 33–36. For the Erie's holdings see Jones, 82–84.

29. Mitchell to William B. Wilson, March 26, 1901, Mitchell Papers (microfilm), quoted in Cornell, 67.

30. *UMWJ*, November 29 and December 20, 1900.

31. Mitchell to Wilson, March 26, 1901, Mitchell Papers (microfilm).

32. Cornell, 67–68.

33. Elizabeth C. Morris to Wilson, March 30, 1901, Mitchell Papers (microfilm).

34. "To the Miners and Mine Workers of the Anthracite Region," March 29, 1901, *ibid.*

35. Mitchell to Wilson, March 26, 1901, *ibid.*

36. See Joseph M. Gowaskie, "From Conflict to Cooperation: John Mitchell and the Bituminous Coal Operators, 1898–1908," *The Historian* 38 (August 1976): 677–80.

37. Warren R. Van Tine discusses the concern for security that characterized many labor leaders at the turn of the century in *The Making of the Labor Bureaucrat: Union Leadership in the United States, 1870–1920* (Amherst: University of Massachusetts Press, 1973), 68–72.

38. *Proceedings of the Convention of District One, April 1901*, 10–11.

39. *UMWJ*, May 2, 1901. The strike was first mentioned in *UMWJ*, April 18, 1901.

40. Elizabeth C. Morris to Mitchell, May 23, 1901, Mitchell Papers (microfilm).

41. *UMWJ*, June 13, 1901.

42. *Ibid.*, June 27, 1901.

43. Gerrity to Mitchell, July 7, 1901, Mitchell Papers (microfilm).

44. *UMWJ*, July 25, 1901; *Proceedings of the Semi-Annual Convention of District One, January 1902*, 12–14. In his report to that convention, Thomas Nicholls estimated that the firemen's strike idled 60 percent of the district's workers.

45. *UMWJ*, July 25, 1901.

46. Price to Mitchell, July 18, 1901, Mitchell Papers (microfilm).

47. *UMWJ*, August 1, 1901.

48. *Ibid.*, August 22, 1901. The firemen's abortive strike surely played a role in the adoption by the American Federation of Labor, at its December 1901 convention in Scranton, of the "Scranton Declaration" on craft autonomy. While endorsing that principle, it allowed for exceptions for "some few industries" isolated "from thickly populated centers." This exception, intended specifically for coal mining, had strong support from John Mitchell. The UMWA would be permitted to retain jurisdiction over that relatively small number of workers, like the firemen, that other crafts could claim. The anthracite fields, of course, were among the least isolated of coal-mining areas. On the declaration, see Philip Taft, *The A.F. of L. in the Time of Gompers* (New York: Harper & Brothers, Publishers, 1957), 194–98.

49. *Ibid.*, August 1, 1901.

50. *Ibid.*

51. Cornell, 70.

52. United Mine Workers of America, *Proceedings of the Convention of District One, July 8–12, 1901, Scranton, Pa.* (Scranton: Sanders Printing Co., 1901), 8; *UMWJ*, April 25, 1901.

53. *E & MJ* 71 (April 13, 1901): 473.

54. "Proceedings," 5774–75.

55. *Proceedings of the Convention of District One, July 1901*, 8.

56. *UMWJ*, July 11, 1901.

57. *Ibid.*, August 15, 1901.

58. "Proceedings," 6409–10, 6457.

59. *Ibid.*, 4937–38, 5461–62.

60. *Ibid.*, 4919–22, 4951–58.

61. *Ibid.*, 5492.

62. *Ibid.*, 5412–15.

63. *Ibid.*, 5021.

64. *Ibid.*, 4974–5020.

65. *Ibid.*, 5775.

66. *Ibid.*, 6950–52.

67. *Ibid.*, 7037–38.

68. *Ibid.*, 6911–13, 6922.

69. *Ibid.*, 5773–74.

70. *Ibid.*, 4027–29.

71. *Ibid.*, 6768. Other incidents occurred between young mine workers and their supervisors after the strike of 1902. John Veith, superintendent of the P & R, told the Anthracite Coal Strike Commission that his company experienced "several cases . . . where boys refused to perform their duty . . . and when they were dismissed for disobeying, nobody else would take their places." See *ibid.*, 7871.

72. *Ibid.*, 6951–52.

73. *Ibid.*, 7058.

74. *Ibid.*, 6147.

75. *New York Times*, October 4, 1902.

76. United Mine Workers of America, Executive Board Minutes, August 13, 1901, Mitchell Papers (microfilm). Francis H. Nichols, in "Children of the Coal Shadow," *McClure's Magazine* 15 (February 1902): 441, reported that workers under sixteen years of age paid dues ranging from ten to twenty-five cents according to their income.

77. Executive Board Minutes, August 13, 1901, Mitchell Papers (microfilm).

78. Cornell, 69; Mitchell to Wilson, March 26, 1901, Mitchell Papers (microfilm).

79. George F. Baer to W. J. Richards, W. H. Truesdale, Alfred Walter, R. C. Luther, and T. P. Fowler, May 22, 1901; the quotation is from the letter to Richards, general superintendent of the L & W-B. Reading Railroad Papers, Hagley Library, Wilmington, DE; hereafter cited as Reading Papers. For Baer's appointment as president of the Reading Companies, see *New York Times*, April 1 and 4, 1901.

80. Nicholls, Duffy, and Fahy to Mitchell, August 11, 1901, Mitchell Papers (microfilm).

81. *UMWJ*, August 22, 1901.

82. United Mine Workers of America, *Proceedings of the Joint Convention of Districts One, Seven, and Nine, United Mine Workers of America, August 27–30, 1901, Hazleton, Pa.* (Shamokin, PA: The News Publishing Co., 1901), 3–5. For Baer's denial, see U.S., Department of Labor, *Bulletin of the Department of Labor,* No. 43, "Report to the President on the Anthracite Coal Strike," by Carroll D. Wright (November 1902): 1205; hereafter cited as Wright's report.

83. *Proceedings of the Joint Convention of Districts One, Seven, and Nine, August 1901,* 3.

84. *UMWJ*, September 5, 1901.

85. Cornell, 71–72; Mitchell to Hanna, September 6, 1901, Mitchell Papers (microfilm).

86. Cornell, 72; Mitchell to Wilson, September 26, 1901, Mitchell Papers (microfilm). Of course, Underwood was lying. George F. Baer wrote to a number of his colleagues that Thomas "had virtually acted for all of us." See Baer memorandum, September 23, 1901, Reading Papers.

87. See *ibid;* also Baer to W. H. Truesdale, October 3, 1901, and Baer to Underwood, October 4, 1901; Reading Papers. Underwood's willingness to meet with the union leaders moved Baer to state that Underwood "lacks the wisdom and judgment essential in the conduct of a great railway system." See Baer memorandum.

88. Mitchell to Easley, October 18, 1901, Mitchell Papers (microfilm).

89. Cornell, 72–73, 81–83. J. P. Morgan's associates continued to act as intermediaries in the effort to arrange a meeting between the UMWA and the operators. On October 7, 1901, Mitchell wrote John Fahy that Easley had learned that a Morgan partner named Ream would set up a conference soon. Apparently nothing came of this initiative. See Mitchell to Fahy, October 7, 1901, Mitchell Papers (microfilm).

90. *E & MJ* 72 (October 12, 1901): 473; McKay to Mitchell, September 25 and October 1, 1901, and Mitchell to McKay, October 2, 1901, Mitchell Papers (microfilm).

91. *Proceedings of the Semi-Annual Convention of District One, January 1902,* 16–17.

92. Nicholls to Mitchell, November 5 and 20, 1901, Mitchell Papers (microfilm); *E & MJ* 72 (December 14, 1901): 801.

93. "Proceedings," 4025–39, 6587–90; Nicholls to Mitchell, November 5, 1901, Mitchell Papers (microfilm).

94. *UMWJ,* November 7 and 14, 1901; Nicholls to Mitchell, November 5 and 20, 1901, and Mitchell to Nicholls, November 7, 1901, Mitchell Papers (microfilm). Gilbert Jones, assistant mine superintendent for Temple, discusses the episode in "Proceedings," 6461–63.

95. Truesdale to Loomis, November 7, 1901, DL & W Records—Syracuse.

96. Truesdale to Baer, November 11, 1901, *ibid.*

97. Truesdale to Loomis, December 21, 1901, DL & W Records, Syracuse. Truesdale failed to mention that John Mitchell had joined the Industrial Department's executive committee of twelve employers, twelve labor representatives, and twelve public representatives. See Cornell, 81.

98. Truesdale to Loomis, December 21, 1901, DL & W Records—Syracuse.

99. Lecture delivered at Franklin and Marshall College, January 16, 1902, by George F. Baer, president of the board of trustees, Mitchell Papers (microfilm).

100. *Ibid.*

101. *Ibid.*

102. *Ibid.*

103. Baer to E. B. Thomas, October 23, 1901, Reading Papers.

CHAPTER 6

1. United Mine Workers of America, *Minutes of the Thirteenth Annual Convention of the United Mine Workers of America January 20–29, 1902, Indianapolis, Ind.* (Indianapolis: Hollenbeck Press, 1902), 65. For the total number of employees, see U.S., Anthracite Coal Strike Commission, *Report to the President on the Anthracite Coal Strike of May–October 1902* (Washington: Government Printing Office, 1903), 29. According to United Mine Workers of America, *Proceedings of the Semi-Annual Convention of District One, United Mine Workers of America, January 13–17, 1902, Wilkes-Barre, Pa.* (Scranton, PA: Sanders Printing Co., 1902), 20, boys were counted as half members.

2. *Minutes of the Thirteenth Annual Convention, January 1902,* 65.

3. *Ibid.,* 18–19. Union leaders had advocated such a policy for quite some time. See United Mine Workers of America, *Proceedings of the Convention of District One,*

United Mine Workers of America, January 14–16, 1901, Edwardsville, Pa (n.p., n.d.), 25; *United Mine Workers Journal,* August 15, 1901; hereafter cited as *UMWJ.* Organizer C. S. Pottier wrote Mitchell in July 1901, that "Brothers mostly composed of foreign element was allways opposed to colliery locals, but at present they realize that we can much easyer transact business in colliery locals." See Pottier to Mitchell, July 16, 1901, John Mitchell Papers (microfilm edition), Catholic University of America, Washington, DC; hereafter cited as Mitchell Papers (microfilm).

4. *UMWJ,* January 23, 1902.

5. *Ibid.,* January 16, 1902.

6. For District Seven's fee, see *ibid.,* January 16, 1902; for District Nine's interest in raising its fee, see Fahy's statement, *ibid.,* December 5, 1901. the report on District Nine's convention made no reference to any action on this matter. See *ibid.,* December 26, 1901.

7. *Ibid.,* December 5, 1901. The report on the district convention included no information concerning action on this issue; see *ibid.,* December 26, 1901.

8. *UMWJ,* January 23, 1902; Robert J. Cornell, *The Anthracite Coal Strike of 1902* (Washington: Catholic University of America Press, 1957), 74.

9. *UMWJ,* January 30, 1902; Cornell, 74–75.

10. *UMWJ,* February 27, 1902.

11. *Ibid.,* February 20, 1902; R. A. Phillips, E. E. Loomis's successor as mining superintendent for the DL & W, testified in U.S., Anthracite Coal Strike Commission, "Proceedings of the Anthracite Coal Strike Commission, 1902–1903," 56 vols., 36 (January 17, 1903): 6061–62, hereafter cited as "Proceedings;" that the check-in system had been in place for approximately a year and a half.

12. U.S., Department of Labor, *Bulletin of the Department of Labor,* No. 43, "Report to the President on the Anthracite Coal Strike," by Carroll D. Wright (November 1902): 1200–02; hereafter cited as Wright's report.

13. Truesdale to Loomis, January 17, 1902, Corporate Records of the Delaware, Lackawanna, and Western Railroad, George Arents Research Library, Syracuse University, Syracuse, NY; hereafter cited as DL & W Records—Syracuse.

14. Truesdale to Loomis, February 1, 1902, *ibid.*

15. *Ibid.*

16. *Ibid.*

17. "Proceedings," 6086–87; Wright's report, 1199.

18. "Proceedings," 6086–87; Wright's report, 1199.

19. *Engineering and Mining Journal* 73 (April 12, 1902): 533, (April 19, 1902): 565; hereafter cited as *E & MJ; UMWJ,* March 6 and 20, 1902. The quotation is from Loomis's report in Wright's report, 1199.

20. *UMWJ,* March 6 and 13, 1902.

21. Mitchell, Nicholls, Duffy, and Fahy to Thomas, February 13, 1902, Mitchell Papers (microfilm).

22. Thomas to Mitchell, Nicholls, Duffy, and Fahy, February 20, 1902, in *Report to the President on the Anthracite Coal Strike of May-October 1902,* 219–21. Cf. Cornell, 75–78.

23. Cornell, 75–78. For the texts of the letters, see *Report to the President on the Anthracite Coal Strike of May-October 1902,* 217–23.

24. United Mine Workers of America, *Proceedings of the Joint Convention of Districts One, Seven, and Nine, United Mine Workers of America, March 18–24, 1902, Shamokin, Pa.* (Shamokin, PA: Ashland Record, 1902), 16–20. These resolutions apparently were not mandatory; I have found no evidence that the walkout against the DL & W spread to other collieries or that one began at the mines of the D & H.

25. *Ibid.,* 28–29. See also "Resolution Introduced by Mr. Nicholls, March 22, 1902," Mitchell Papers (microfilm).

26. *Proceedings of the Joint Convention of Districts One, Seven, and Nine, March 1902,* 29–30.

27. "President Mitchell, to the Convention of the Three Anthracite Districts, at the session of Saturday, March 22, 1902," Mitchell Papers (microfilm).

28. *Ibid.*

29. *Ibid.*

30. *Proceedings of the Joint Convention of Districts One, Seven, and Nine, March 1902,* 32–33.

31. Cornell, 81–83.

32. *Ibid.,* 83–84; *Proceedings of the Joint Convention of Districts One, Seven, and Nine, March 1902,* 25–27. With regard to the demands, cf. Cornell, 80. In contrast to the numerous specific demands of 1900, several of which were directed solely toward regional grievances, this list was more concise and sufficiently general to appeal to all segments of the workforce. Cf. chapter 4.

33. "Report of President John Mitchell, to the Delegates of Districts One, Seven, and Nine, United Mine Workers of America, Grand Opera House, Hazleton, Pa., May 15, 1902," Mitchell Papers (microfilm); Cornell, 81–87.

34. *Ibid.*, 81, 86.

35. *Ibid.*, 87–88; statement by Mitchell, May 3, 1902, Mitchell Papers (microfilm).

36. "Minutes of Meetings of the Joint Executive Boards of the Three Anthracite Districts, held in Carpenters' Hall, Scranton—May 7th to 10th, 1902;" John Mitchell, Thomas Nicholls, John Dempsey, Thomas Duffy, J. P. Gallagher, John Fahy, and George Hartlein to the Anthracite Mine Workers, May 9, 1902, Mitchell Papers (microfilm).

37. *New York Herald,* May 13–15, 1902.

38. United Mine Workers of America, "Minutes of the Joint Convention of Districts One, Seven, and Nine, United Mine Workers of America, May 14–16, 1902, Hazleton, Pa.," p. 47, Michael J. Kosik Collection, Fred Lewis Pattee Library, Pennsylvania State University Park, PA; hereafter cited as Kosik Collection.

39. *Ibid.*, 56.

40. "Address of President John Mitchell, Stating His Position on What Course the Convention Should Follow Regarding the Calling of a Strike. Delivered to the Joint Convention of Districts One, Seven, and Nine, United Mine Workers of America, Grand Opera House, Hazleton, Pa., May 15, 1902," Mitchell Papers (microfilm).

41. "Minutes of the Joint Convention of Districts One, Seven, and Nine, May 1902," 29, Kosik Collection.

42. *Ibid.*, 68.

43. *Ibid.*, 77.

44. *Ibid.*, 80.

45. *Ibid.*, 57.

46. *Ibid.*, 58.

47. *Ibid.*, 102.

48. George Baer to E. B. Thomas and W. H. Truesdale, May 2, 1902, Reading Railroad Papers, Hagley Library, Wilmington, DE.

49. George W. Perkins to J. P. Morgan, George W. Perkins Papers, Columbia University Library, New York, NY.

50. "Proceedings," 7103; Cornell, 98–99.

51. Cornell, 98–99. Nevertheless, Peter Roberts estimated that 80 percent of the engineers, pumpmen, and firemen joined the walkout. See Roberts, "The Anthracite Conflict," *Yale Review* 11 (November 1902): 298.

52. Cornell, 105, 110.

53. Wright's report, 1148.

54. *Ibid.*, 1154.

55. *Ibid.*, 1165.

56. *Ibid.*, 1166.

57. U.S. Anthracite Coal Strike Commission, *Report to the President on the Anthracite Coal Strike of May–October 1902* (Washington: Government Printing Office, 1903), 61–62.

58. Wright's report, 1166–67.

59. Cornell, 111–13; Joseph Michael Gowaskie, "John Mitchell: A Study in Leadership," Ph.D. dissertation, Catholic University of America, 1968, 91–92, 151–53, 164–65.

60. Cornell, 93, 100–02, 113–16.

61. Gowaskie, "John Mitchell: A Study in Leadership," 171.

62. "Report of Special Convention of the United Mine Workers of America, Called to Consider the Strike in the Anthracite Field, Indianapolis, Indiana, July 17–19, 1902," 1, Mitchell Papers (microfilm).

63. *Ibid.*, 11.

64. *Ibid.*, 6–22.

65. *Ibid.*, 18, 22–23.

66. *Ibid.*, 33–34.

67. *Ibid.*, 40–42.

68. *Ibid.*, 29–76, 95; see also Cornell, 116–18. David Alan Corbin, in *Life, Work, and Rebellion in the Coal Fields: The Southern West Virginia Miners, 1880–1922* (Urbana: University of Illinois Press, 1981), 48, exhibits considerable confusion concerning the West Virginia bituminous strike of 1902 and its relationship to the anthracite strike. Corbin claims "that Mitchell opposed carrying the 1902 anthracite (hard coal) strike into West Virginia. . . . Contrary to the desires of their president, the delegates to the 1902 convention favored a general sympathetic strike and wanted it to include West Virginia. . . . Consequently, the delegates overruled Mitchell and ordered the West Virginia miners to cease work." While Mitchell opposed a "general sympathetic strike," he strongly supported a walkout in West Virginia, which had begun on June 7 as a result of a meeting on May 23 of district and national officers who had been authorized by an earlier district convention to declare a strike.

Robert H. Wiebe, in "The Anthracite Strike of 1902: A Record of Confusion," *Mississippi Valley Historical Review* 48 (September 1961): 231–35, 239–40 and Sheldon H. Harris, in "Letters from West Virginia: Management's Version of the 1902

Coal Strike," *Labor History* 10 (Spring 1969): 232, maintain that the UMWA failed to provide aid to striking mine workers in West Virginia and abandoned them to focus the union's efforts on anthracite. However, Joseph M. Gowaskie, in "John Mitchell: A Study in Leadership," 144–46, shows that the union provided considerable support for the West Virginia strikers. Overall, Gowaskie's chapter on West Virginia, 117–46, is far superior to either Corbin's, Harris's or Wiebe's treatment.

69. Cornell, 117–22.

70. *E & MJ* 73 (May 24, 1902): 743, (June 7, 1902): 813, (June 21, 1902): 875, (June 28, 1902): 910, and 74 (July 12, 1902): 62. For a discussion of washeries, see Peter Roberts, *The Anthracite Coal Industry* (New York: The Macmillan Co., 1901), 223–27.

71. *E & MJ* 74 (August 9, 1902): 198, (September 6, 1902): 324, and (September 20, 1902): 390; Roberts, "Anthracite Conflict," 298; Victor R. Greene, *The Slavic Community on Strike: Immigrant Labor in Pennsylvania Anthracite* (South Bend: University of Notre Dame Press, 1968), 188–89. Interestingly, Mitchell believed that the strike could have been lost in the days shortly after the special convention in Indianapolis. Newspapers stated that all strikers would receive substantial sums for relief, and these stories generated considerable disaffection when such sums were not available. However, union leaders were able to defuse the situation. See Cornell, 119–21.

72. Greene, 183–92; Cornell, 152–54.

73. Cornell, 123–27, 131–42. See also William H. Truesdale to R. M. Olyphant, August 22 and 25, 1902, DL & W Records—Syracuse.

74. Truesdale to W. J. Burke, September 5, 1902, *ibid.*

75. Cornell, 163–72.

76. Wiebe, "Anthracite Strike," 244.

77. *E & MJ* 74 (September 27, 1902): 427, (October 4, 1902): 464, and (October 11, 1902): 499. Wiebe, in "Anthracite Strike," 244, erroneously states that " a fuel crisis occurred in the East because the cities succumbed to a panic which public officials and retailers exacerbated." Although public officials may well have heightened public concern over the crisis, that crisis was indeed genuine, at least over the short term, due to the railroads' difficulty in supplying cars to carry bituminous.

78. *E & MJ* 74 (October 4, 1902): 437.

79. For the concern displayed by several of those officials, see Cornell, 173–77.

80. *UMWJ*, October 9, 1902.

81. *Ibid.*, October 2, 1902. At the hearings held by the Anthracite Coal Strike Commission, John Earley and P. F. O'Hora, both presidents of locals at mines operated by the Pennsylvania Coal Company, confirmed Nicholls's statement. They

testified that Grimes had tried to bribe them and other union officials. See "Proceedings," 2113, 2157.

82. Cornell, 174–83.

83. *Ibid.*, 184. See also *New York World,* October 4, 1902.

84. Cornell, 184.

85. *New York Times,* October 4, 1902. See also Cornell, 184.

86. *New York Times,* October 4, 1902.

87. *Ibid.*

88. *New York World,* October 4, 1902; Cornell, 186–87.

89. Cornell, 187–200; Roberts, "Anthracite Conflict," 300–01.

90. Cornell, 201–22.

91. *Ibid.*, 223–25.

92. *Ibid.*, 225–35; *UMWJ,* October 23, 1902. The Commission's members were Brigadier General John M. Wilson, retired from the Corps of Engineers; E. W. Parker, chief statistician of the Coal Division of the United States Geological Survey; George Gray, former U.S. Senator from Delaware and judge of the Third Circuit Court; Thomas H. Watkins, former managing partner of Simpson and Watkins Coal Company, which had been absorbed by the Temple Iron Company; Bishop John L. Spalding of Peoria, Illinois; and Roosevelt's "sociologist," E. E. Clark, Grand Chief of the Order of Railway Conductors. Carroll D. Wright served as the Commission's recorder.

In a letter written on October 22 and also in his *Autobiography,* Roosevelt gave considerable emphasis to a plan he had formulated to seize the mines with federal troops and operate them while a commission deliberated. However, Cornell has carefully shown that this plan, even if it was conceived during the final stages of Root's negotiations, had no discernible impact upon them. See Cornell, 210–17.

93. Cornell, 163–64, 187–90; Gowaskie, "John Mitchell: A Study in Leadership," 189; Bruno Ramirez, *When Workers Fight: The Politics of Industrial Relations in the Progressive Era, 1898–1916* (Westport, CT: Greenwood Press, 1978), 40–41; Wiebe, "Anthracite Strike," 240.

94. More than $400,000 was given from outside of the UMWA. Cornell skillfully summarizes the aid effort; see 117–22. Robert Asher notes Mitchell's concern for fairness in "Union Nativism and the Immigrant Response," *Labor History* 23 (Summer 1982): 344.

The extent of the fund amazed William H. Truesdale of the DL & W. He commented that the information the companies had received "as to the financial resources of the United Mine Workers Association was entirely erroneous." He added: "The figures given also prove what I have said all along, that it was a most remarkable feature of the strike, namely that a fund larger than has ever been previously raised in the history of the world for any such purpose was turned over to these people who were wholly without responsibility and disbursed without supervision or check by the parties who contributed toward the fund or anyone in their interest, to see that it was honestly and properly applied to the objects to which donated." See Truesdale to T. P. Fowler, January 23, 1903, DL & W Records—Syracuse.

95. For example, Lawrence Twardoski continued to work as a miner during the strike. His twenty-eight ducks were killed and his cow was stolen. When Twardoski found the cow she was nearly dead, having been tied so tightly to a tree that she could not lower her head to graze. "Proceedings," 4453–54.

CHAPTER 7

1. George F. Baer told the Commission at its opening session that the operators could not "consent to Mr. Mitchell's appearing here as the representative and as the president of that organization [UMWA]. So far as he appears here to represent any of the miners in the anthracite region that are in our employ we have no objection." Mitchell accepted this status and added, "I appear here as the representative of the anthracite coal mine workers." See U.S., Anthracite Coal Strike Commission, *Report to the President on the Anthracite Coal Strike of May–October 1902,* (Washington: Government Printing Office, 1903), 60–61.

During the Commission's opening sessions, attorneys who represented some 2,000 "nonunion mine workers" gained the Commission's approval to join the proceedings as well. However, the testimony elicited on their behalf focused on alleged acts of intimidation by strikers against those who continued to work, rather than on working conditions. See Robert J. Cornell, *The Anthracite Coal Strike of 1902* (Washington: Catholic University of America Press, 1957), 240–41.

2. *Report to the President on the Anthracite Coal Strike of May–October 1902,* 39–41. These demands differed in several interesting respects from those formulated in March at the convention in Shamokin. That convention called for an eight-hour day rather than a 20 percent decrease in hours. While this would make no difference to most company men, for whom the ten-hour day was standard, it would potentially have some impact for those who worked a twelve-hour day. Also, at Shamokin the union called for a 23 percent increase in rates for contract miners, but only where coal could not be weighed. Where it was possible to weigh coal, the convention apparently thought that an increase to sixty cents per ton would suffice. Finally, the delegates at Shamokin demanded a "minimum day-wage scale," which is not mentioned in the demands presented to the Anthracite Coal Strike Commission. See United Mine Workers of America, *Proceedings of the Joint Convention of Districts One, Seven, and Nine, United Mine Workers of America, Shamokin, Pennsylvania, March 18–24, 1902* (Ashland, PA: Ashland Record, 1902), 25–27.

The "nonunion mine workers" presented demands that differed somewhat from those of the union. While the nonunion men called for an increase of 20 percent on rates paid to contract miners and for the weighing of coal, they also demanded an increase of 20 percent for those paid a set wage rather than a reduction in hours, since they insisted upon " a right to work as many hours" as they chose. They also decried the possibility of an agreement between the UMWA and the operators and demanded that the UMWA cease annoying them and their families. For the full text of their demands, see *Report to the President on the Anthracite Coal Strike of May–October 1902*, 94–96.

3. Peter Roberts, "The Anthracite Conflict," *Yale Review* 11 (November 1902): 303 and Peter Roberts, *The Anthracite Coal Industry* (New York: The Macmillan Co., 1901), 119. See also chapter 1 and U.S., Anthracite Coal Strike Commission, "Proceedings of the Anthracite Coal Strike Commission, 1902–1903," 56 vols., 39 (January 21, 1903): 6577–81, 45 (January 28, 1903): 7685–91; hereafter cited as "Proceedings."

4. Roberts, "Anthracite Conflict," 303, and Roberts, *Industry*, 120; "Proceedings," 4721, 5327.

5. Roberts, "Anthracite Conflict," 303. For the amount of coal produced by the fields, compare the totals for anthracite inspection districts one through four (Wyoming) and five through eight (Lehigh and Schuylkill) in Pennsylvania, Bureau of Mines, *Report of the Bureau of Mines of the Department of Internal Affairs of Pennsylvania—1900* (Harrisburg, PA: William Stanley Ray, State Printer, 1901), 5, 32, 68, 105, 155, 203, 233, 254. For annual shipments from each field, see *Report to the President on the Anthracite Coal Strike of May–October 1902*, 20.

6. *Proceedings of the Joint Convention of Districts One, Seven, and Nine, March 1902*, 26.

7. "Proceedings," 6566–67.

8. *Ibid.*, 1718–23, 1734.

9. *Ibid.*, 2231–37, 2248–49, 2253–54, 2308–10.

10. By August 1902, Phillips had become superintendent while his predecessor, E. E. Loomis, had become a vice-president of the DL & W. See W. H. Truesdale to Phillips, August 20, 1902, Corporate Records of the Delaware, Lackawanna, and Western Railroad, George Arents Research Library, Syracuse University, Syracuse, NY; hereafter cited as DL & W Records—Syracuse.

11. "Proceedings," 6165–72.

12. *Report to the President on the Anthracite Coal Strike of May–October 1902*, 70–71, 195–96.

13. *Ibid.*, 71.

14. "Proceedings," 6988–89, 7683–84, 8961. In *The Anthracite Coal Industry*, 114–15, Peter Roberts stated that companies would fix prices for new veins by supplying tools and powder to two of the best miners for them to begin work in a vein. At the end of one month, the foreman would measure their production and set mining rates so that miners with similar skills could earn approximately $2.50 per day.

15. A more blatant effort to increase the size of mine cars appears to have taken place at the St. Clair Coal Company, located in Schuylkill County. On August 28, 1899, its president reported to the board of directors that the company planned to make all of its cars "a uniform size and style." On December 8, he reported that although he had feared the possibility of trouble from the men due to the company's "enlarging" its cars, none had occurred. See minutes of the meetings of the board of directors, Minute Book #1, St. Clair Coal Company Papers, Hagley Library, Wilmington, DE.

16. *Proceedings of the Joint Convention of Districts One, Seven, and Nine, March 1902,* 26.

17. Roberts, "The Anthracite Conflict," 303; "Proceedings," 2164, 2329, 4777, 5248; *Report to the President on the Anthracite Coal Strike of May–October 1902,* 23–24.

18. "Proceedings," 2164, 2329.

19. *Ibid.,* 2172.

20. *Ibid.,* 2329, 2334, 5371–72.

21. *Ibid.,* 5371–72.

22. *Ibid.,* 4721–22.

23. *Ibid.,* 4777.

24. *Ibid.,* 5248, 5327.

25. *Ibid.,* 5257, 5330–35.

26. *Ibid.,* 5226, 7172.

27. *Ibid.,* 17, 7172.

28. An attorney for the PCC admitted this; see *ibid.,* 5226.

29. *Report to the President on the Anthracite Coal Strike of May–October 1902,* 59.

30. "Proceedings," 1131–32, 5248.

31. *Ibid.,* 5248.

32. *Ibid.,* 4773, 5250, 5760, 6016, 6623; cf. pp. 6386, 6405.

33. *Ibid.,* 6600–01.

34. *Ibid.,* 1954.

35. *Ibid.,* 7059.

36. *Ibid.,* 6766, 6881.

37. *Ibid.*, 5249.

38. *Ibid.*, 2913–15.

39. *Ibid.*, 6498, 6502.

40. *Ibid.*, 2424.

41. *Ibid.*, 1283.

42. *Ibid.*, 1296.

43. *Ibid.*, 1298.

44. *Ibid.*, 1765–66.

45. *Ibid.*, 2377–86.

46. *Ibid.*, 1115–16, 1126.

47. *Ibid.*, 6015, 6401.

48. *Ibid.*, 5398.

49. *Ibid.*, 7033.

50. *Ibid.*, 5314.

51. Albert C. Leisenring, superintendent of the Upper Lehigh Coal Company, told the Commission that "it would be impossible to ask the miner to thoroughly clean the coal before loading," although he did believe that miners could do a better job of cleaning their coal. See *ibid.*, 7582.

52. *Report to the President on the Anthracite Coal Strike of May–October 1902*, 177.

53. *Ibid.*

54. *Ibid.*, 178.

55. *Ibid.*

56. Calculated from data in *ibid.*, 199 and in U.S., Department of Commerce and Labor, Bureau of Labor, *Bulletin of the U.S. Bureau of Labor: Retail Prices 1890 to 1911*, Whole No. 105: Part 1 (Washington: Government Printing Office, 1912), 17.

57. *Ibid.*, 179.

58. *Ibid.*, 180.

59. *Ibid.*, 179.

60. "Proceedings," 8083.

61. *Ibid.*, 8109. The high level of transiency shown by miners at Indian Ridge contrasts sharply with the considerable persistence shown by workers at Wanamie colliery discussed in chapter 1. However, miner's laborers at Wanamie persisted at a far lower rate, and this should be considered in any comparison, since miners in the Schuylkill field, where Indian Ridge and the other mines of the P & R were located, generally worked without laborers, as partners. Furthermore, the phenomenon of "floating" may well have been much less prevalent among non-miners.

62. *Ibid.*, 8038.

63. Peter Roberts, *The Anthracite Coal Communities* (New York: The Macmillan Co., 1904), 33.

64. For average hours per breaker start, see *Report to the President on the Anthracite Coal Strike of May–October 1902*, 189–91.

65. "Proceedings," 4795.

66. *Ibid.*, 5368.

67. *Ibid.*, 6059–64. In his report on the strike, Carroll D. Wright included a refutation of the mine workers' demands by E. E. Loomis, Phillips's predecessor. In his statement, Loomis listed the hours worked from January 16 through January 31, 1902 by some seventy-seven of the DL & W's miners "selected at random" from the company's mines. According to Loomis, these miners averaged only five hours of work per day. See U.S., Department of Labor, *Bulletin of the Department of Labor*, No. 43, "Report to the President on the Anthracite Coal Strike," by Carroll D. Wright (November 1902): 1187–1202.

68. "Proceedings," 5768, 5771.

69. *Ibid.*, 5769.

70. *Ibid.*, 1926–27.

71. *Ibid.*, 1144.

72. *Ibid.*, 1145.

73. With regard to miners leaving work on their own see Carter Goodrich, *The Miner's Freedom: A Study of the Working Life in a Changing Industry* (Boston: Marshall Jones Co., 1925), 64, and Hugh Archbald, *The Four-Hour Day in Coal: A Study of the Relation Between the Engineering of the Organization of Work and the Discontent Among the Workers in the Coal Mines* (New York: H. W. Wilson Co., 1922), 63.

74. "Proceedings," 3214–15, 5338–41. After W. A. May of the PCC and HCI, under cross-examination, stated that the miner could work longer and either "help the laborer load" or "straighten up his place," May had the following exchange with Clarence Darrow:

Q. [Darrow] How long has it been since the laborer loaded the coal and the miner cut it?

A. [May] As long as I can remember.

Q. Of course the boss could go in and help load it if he wanted to?

A. Yes, sir.

Q. Or the General Superintendent?

A. Yes, sir.

Q. According to my idea that would be the way to do it, but this world is divided up into castes and we have to stand by it. . . .

See pp. 5338–39.

75. *Ibid.*, 3210.

76. *Ibid.*, 5525. See also p. 5770.

77. *Ibid.*, 3288.

78. *Ibid.*, 1505, 1523.

79. *Ibid.*, 6547.

80. *Ibid.*, 8918–19.

81. *Ibid.*, 8928.

82. *Ibid.*, 4792.

83. Although the UMWA did not demand an increase in wages for company men, nevertheless the earnings of many company men could only be characterized as barely adequate at best. In a number of positions which were not generally filled by youths, workers often averaged less than $400 in earnings. See data on the earnings of laborers, footmen, headmen, and teamsters, among others, for several companies in *Report to the President on the Anthracite Coal Strike of May–October 1902*, 182–86.

84. *Ibid.*, 189–91.

85. "Proceedings," 6583–84.

86. *Ibid.*, 1344, 1421–22, 2770.

87. *Ibid.*, 1404–28.

88. *Ibid.*, 1425.

89. *Ibid.*, 1429–48.

90. *Ibid.*, 1345.

91. *Ibid.*, 2770–73.

92. *Ibid.*, 3042–43.

93. *Ibid.*, 6298.

94. *Ibid.*, 6336.

95. *Ibid.*, 6354–58.

96. *Ibid.*, 6408.

97. *Ibid.*, 6355.

98. *Ibid.*, 7874–75.

99. *Ibid.*, 7940.

100. For example, see *David Montgomery, Beyond Equality: Labor and the Radical Republicans, 1862–1872* (New York: Alfred A. Knopf, Inc. 1967; paperback ed., New York: Vintage Books, 1972), 231–49.

101. *Report to the President on the Anthracite Coal Strike of May–October 1902*, 53–56. The Commission also awarded a retroactive increase of 10 percent for almost all company men on their earnings from November 1, 1902, to April 1, 1903, when the cut in hours would go into effect.

In its award to workers in positions which were manned continuously, the Commission apparently paid close attention to the amount of exertion required in each job. Engineers who hoisted water would have to do so continually, whether or not the breaker was in operation. John Veith, mining superintendent for the P & R, discussed the hoisting of water at several of that company's collieries, where tanks of approximately 2,400 gallons were hoisted about sixty times an hour. See "Proceedings," 7877. Any of these engineers who had worked an eight-hour day before the strike would receive an increase of 10 percent.

Similarly, the firemen had to keep the boilers going for both the day and night shifts. In contrast, engineers who hoisted men and coal alternated between the arduous day shift and the less-taxing night shift. With regard to pumpmen, the Commission may also have believed their work to be somewhat easier than that of the engineers who hoisted water or the firemen. Still, the Commission concluded that both the pumpmen and the engineers who hoisted men and coal deserved at least one day off per week.

102. *Report to the President on the Anthracite Coal Strike of May–October 1902*, 51.

103. *Ibid.*, 50.

104. *Ibid.*, 46, 50–51.

105. *Ibid.*, 60, 68–69. Operators were required to permit the employment of check–docking bosses and/or checkweighmen at any colliery where requested by a majority of the contract miners. The miners would have to pay any such workers, whose wages could be deducted by the operator from the earnings of the miners if a

majority of them so desired. Interpretation of this clause generated considerable controversy; see chapter 8.

106. *Ibid.*, 57.

107. *Ibid.*, 59.

108. *Ibid.*, 59–60. Sixty cents per ton had been a goal for the UMWA since 1900, when the union's statement of grievances included the following: "The rate per legal ton paid to miners being about 42 cents when compared with bituminous coal, namely 60 cents per ton and upward, shows the injustice of the price paid for anthracite which sells for so much more in the markets." See J. P. Gallagher, John T. Dempsey, and George Hartline [*sic*] to the Operators of the Anthracite Coal Fields of Pennsylvania, August 16, 1900, John Mitchell Papers, microfilm edition, Catholic University of America, Washington, DC.

109. Samuel D. Warriner of the LV showed some interest in a uniform method of payment for miners and regularizing the multitude of wage rates that mine workers received. For his thoughtful testimony, see "Proceedings," 6577–80; 6626.

110. "Proceedings," 4918–38, 5031–32, 5045–46, 5053–54, 5058–60, 5441–46, 5457–62, 6039, 6424–25, 6544–46, 8528–31, 8548–50, 8552–53, 8647–48. George Gray, chairman of the Commission, was not at all persuaded by the companies' charges; see *ibid.*, 7647. The United States Bureau of Labor reached a similar conclusion in its report, *Regulation and Restriction of Output* (Washington: Government Printing Office, 1904), 510–29.

111. *Report to the President on the Anthracite Coal Strike of May–October 1902*, 70.

112. *Ibid.*, 79. Neither the workers' representatives, the operators' representatives, nor the Commission devoted much attention to the miner's laborers. Counsel for the UMWA called only six to testify, as compared to some eighty miners. See "Proceedings," *passim*. Accountants for two companies that paid laborers directly told the Commission that it was practically impossible to trace individual miner's laborers through the payrolls to calculate their earnings. See *ibid.*, 5826, 6531. For those companies that kept no track of laborers, the contending parties spent a considerable amount of time arguing over the average percentage of miners' gross earnings that laborers earned. However, this discussion was directed toward compiling data on miners' earnings, not those of their laborers. See *ibid.*, 3189–90, 4810–11, 5649–50, 5655, 8824–25, 8832–45; *Report to the President on the Anthracite Coal Strike of May–October 1902*, 175–76.

113. See Edgar Sydenstricker, "The Settlement of Disputes Under Agreements in the Anthracite Industry," *Journal of Political Economy* 24 (March 1916): 279; Anthracite Board of Conciliation, *Work of the Board of Conciliation Appointed by the Anthracite Coal Strike Commission for Three Years Ending March 31, 1906* (Wilkes-Barre, PA: Record Press, 1908), 16–17.

114. *Ibid.*, 71–72.

115. *Report to the President on the Anthracite Coal Strike of May–October 1902*, 79.

116. *Ibid.* 67–68.

CHAPTER 8

1. Robert J. Cornell, *The Anthracite Coal Strike of 1902* (Washington: Catholic University of America Press, 1957), 257.

2. *Pittsburgh Post*, March 22, 1903. Anticipating the settlement, Mitchell informed a close friend that "inside information indicates that we shall get a substantial increase in wages and on the whole shall win our fight." See Mitchell to H. N. Taylor, March 11, 1903, John Mitchell Papers (microfilm edition), Catholic University of America, Washington; hereafter cited as Mitchell Papers (microfilm).

3. *New York Times*, March 22, 1903.

4. William H. Truesdale to Everett Warren, March 21, 1903, Corporate Records of the Delaware, Lackawanna, and Western Railroad, George Arents Research Library, Syracuse University, Syracuse, NY, hereafter cited as DL & W Records—Syracuse.

5. Robert Asher, "Union Nativism and the Immigrant Response," *Labor History* 23 (Summer 1982): 341–45.

6. On the issue of rank-and-file apathy in turn-of-the-century labor organizations, see Warren R. Van Tine, *The Making of the Labor Bureaucrat, Union Leadership in the United States, 1870–1920* (Amherst: University of Massachusetts Press, 1973), 90–94.

7. For example, see *Mount Carmel Item*, March 21, 1903; *Scranton Times*, March 21, 1903; *Mahanoy City Daily American*, March 21, 1903; *Hazleton Daily Standard*, April 2, 1903. For DeSilva's statement, see *Hazleton Daily Standard*, March 23, 1903. Clippings for this period from these papers among others are in the John Mitchell Papers, Catholic University of America, Washington—hereafter cited as Mitchell Papers—but are not included in the microfilm edition of the Mitchell Papers.

8. For brief references to dissatisfaction, see *Mahanoy City Daily American*, March 23, 1903; *Hazleton Daily Standard*, March 24 and April 2, 1903; Dettrey is quoted in the *Daily American;* his statement on the elimination of strikes is reported in the *Daily Standard*, March 23, 1903; clippings located in Mitchell Papers.

9. See *Hazleton Daily Standard*, March 23, 1903 (where Nicholls is quoted), *Wilkes-Barre Record*, March 24, 1903, clippings located in Mitchell Papers; and *New York Times*, March 22 and 24, 1903. Joe Gowaskie offers a more negative assessment

of the workers' reaction in "John Mitchell and the Anthracite Mine Workers: Leadership Conservatism and Rank-and-File Militancy," *Labor History* 27 (Winter 1985–86): 54–57.

10. *United Mine Workers Journal,* March 26, 1903; hereafter cited as *UMWJ.* Of course, similar hopes for the supposed inevitability of "contractual relations" had arisen after the 1900 settlement and were vigorously pursued by John Mitchell up to the beginning of the 1902 strike. Even during the Commission's hearings he had sought on two occasions to conclude an agreement with the operators. However, these efforts met with the opposition of several if by no means all of the railroad presidents. See Cornell, 242–47.

11. For example, see *Shamokin Daily Dispatch,* April 3, 1903, *Pittston Gazette,* April 6, 1903, *Philadelphia Record,* April 6, 1903, and *Philadelphia North American,* April 3, 5, and 9, 1903, clippings located in Mitchell Papers; also see Gowaskie, "Rank-and-File Militancy," 57–60.

12. *New York Times,* April 21 and 22, 1903; *UMWJ,* April 23 and 30, 1903; Anthracite Board of Conciliation, *Work of the Board of Conciliation Appointed by the Anthracite Coal Strike Commission for Three Years Ending March 31, 1906,* (Wilkes-Barre, Pa: Record Press, 1908) 47–77. Also see *Philadelphia North American,* April 9 and 11, 1903; *Philadelphia Record,* April 21 and 23, 1903; and *Philadelphia Public Ledger,* April 21, 1903; clippings located in Mitchell Papers. Also see Gowaskie, "Rank and File Militancy," 57–60.

13. See minutes of meeting of the Executive boards of Districts 1, 7, and 9, Wilkes-Barre, April 21–22, 1903, Mitchell Papers (microfilm).

14. George F. Baer to Thomas D. Nicholls, W. H. Dettrey, and John Fahy, May 13, 1903, *ibid.*

15. *UMWJ,* June 4, 11, and 18, 1903; United Mine Workers of America, *Proceedings of the Joint Convention of Districts 1, 7, and 9, United Mine Workers of America, June 15–16, 1903,* (Ashland, PA: Ashland Record, 1903), 10–14. Also see *Philadelphia Public Ledger,* June 14, 1903; *Philadelphia North American,* June 15, 1903; *Philadelphia Record,* June 16, 1903; *Pittston Gazette,* June 15, 1903, *Scranton Truth,* June 16, 1903, and *Scranton Times,* June 17, 1903; clippings located in Mitchell Papers. Also see Gowaskie, "Rank-and-File Militancy," 61–62. A great deal of pro-strike talk occurred at the convention. However, before the convention the operators had come in for a good deal of public criticism, even from business interests, and Mitchell had received assurance, discussed in the newspapers, that the operators would accept the convention's appointment of representatives to the Board. See *Philadelphia North American,* June 4, 8, 9, and 15, 1903; *Wall Street Journal,* June 4, 1903; *Scranton Truth,* June 4, 1903; *Wilkes-Barre Leader,* June 4, 1903; clippings located in Mitchell Papers.

16. *UMWJ,* May 28, July 30, and August 6, 1903.

17. *Ibid.,* July 2 and August 6, 1903.

18. Irving Bernstein, ''Arbitration,'' in *Industrial Conflict*, ed. by Arthur Kornhauser, Robert Dubin, and Arthur M. Ross (New York: McGraw-Hill Book Company, 1954), 304–07, 312.

19. *Work of the Board Ending March 31, 1906*, 73.

20. U.S., Anthracite Coal Strike Commission, *Report to the President on the Anthracite Coal Strike of May–October 1902* (Washington: Government Printing Office, 1903), 56.

21. *Work of the Board Ending March 31, 1906*, 47–77. I have found no mention by the union of any attempts to restore the ten-hour day; for example see United Mine Workers of America, ''Proceedings of the Tri-District Convention, Districts One, Seven, and Nine, United Mine Workers of America, Shamokin, Pennsylvania, December 14–16, 1905,'' Michael J. Kosik Collection, Fred Lewis Pattee Library, Pennsylvania State University, University Park, PA; hereafter cited as Kosik Collection, and United Mine Workers of America, *Proceedings of the Special Convention of Districts One, Seven, and Nine, United Mine Workers of America, Scranton, Pennsylvania, May 3–5, 1906* (Scranton, PA: Scranton, Truth Print, 1906).

22. Truesdale to Baer, April 7, 1903; also see Truesdale to Baer, April 9, 1903; DL & W Records—Syracuse.

23. *Work of the Board Ending March 31, 1906*, 40–47, 93–96, 102–03; *UMWJ*, May 5, 1904.

24. *Work of the Board Ending March 31, 1906*, 219–47; United Mine Workers of America, *Proceedings of the Sixth Annual Convention of District No. 1, United Mine Workers of America, Pittston, Pennsylvania, July 11–16, 1904* (Scranton, PA: Sanders Printing Co., 1904), 17–21; *UMWJ*, July 7, 1904; Gowaskie, ''Rank-and-File Militancy,'' 65–66.

25. *Proceedings of the Sixth Annual Convention of District No. 1, July 1904*, 17.

26. *Ibid.*, 17–21, 78; E. C. Morris to John Mitchell, July 14 and July 18, 1904, Mitchell Papers (microfilm); *UMWJ*, October 6, 1904; *Work of the Board Ending March 31, 1906*, 219–47; Gowaskie, ''Rank-and-File Militancy,'' 65–66. Interestingly, some locals had trouble mobilizing to hire a checkweighman. One month after Gray's decision, John Fallon, national executive board member from District One, criticized locals ''for not taking advantage'' of the decision. See *UMWJ*, October 27, 1904. During negotiations in 1906, the operators claimed that miners had appointed checkers ''only at a few of the collieries; at all the others they have not thought it worth while to incur this expense.'' See George F. Baer et al to John Mitchell et al., March 9, 1906, reprinted in *Minutes of Joint Conferences of Anthracite Mine Operators and Mine Workers with Correspondence Connected Therewith, February, March, April and May 1906*, 47, Mitchell Papers (microfilm); hereafter cited as *Minutes of Joint Conferences*.

27. *Work of the Board Ending March 31, 1906, passim*. For example, in the grievances of Jacob Ball, Charles H. Jones, and Charles Doorley against the P & R, ''*Resolved*, That inasmuch as the complainants are now employed the grievances be

withdrawn" or in grievances 22, 43, 75, 76, 77, 78, 79, and 81, *"Resolved,* That the Board of Conciliation recommend, inasmuch as the operators at Summit Branch Colliery at Williamstown and at Short Mountain Colliery at Lykens have offered to provide employment as opportunity offers . . . that these men be given preference over other men for such positions as they are capable of filling." See *Ibid.,* 150, 153.

28. *Ibid.,* 103–08.

29. *Ibid.,* 8–13, 17–23, 103–08, 215–19. In a case decided in April 1904, Wright decided that he could not sustain a grievance filed by a president of a local union suspended for one month for posting notices in violation of company rules. While Wright apparently believed the company official who stated he didn't even know that the worker was a union member, still he called the suspension "altogether too severe" and thus "a violation of the real spirit of the award." See 215–19.

30. *UMWJ,* September 17, 1903; also see September 10 and 24, 1903.

31. *Work of the Board Ending March 31, 1906,* 179–82, 255–59.

32. *Ibid.,* 186–89.

33. *Ibid.,* 118–25, 197–99.

34. *Ibid.,* 299–300.

35. *Ibid.,* 290–92.

36. *Ibid., passim.* The intention of District One officials to avoid the Board is reported in a *Scranton Tribune* article reprinted in *UMWJ,* September 21, 1905.

37. United Mine Workers of America, *Proceedings of the Fifteenth Annual Convention of the United Mine Workers of America Held in the City of Indianapolis, Indiana, January 18 to 27, 1904, Inclusive* (Indianapolis: Cheltenham Press, 1904), 24.

38. *UMWJ,* May 19, 1904. McEnaney succeeded Thomas Nicholls in 1909 (see chapter 9).

39. *Ibid.,* August 31, 1905.

40. *Ibid.,* November 23, 1905.

41. *Work of the Board Ending March 31, 1906,* 334.

42. For Kudlich's meeting with Dettrey, see *UMWJ,* September 15, 1904. For Kudlich's detailed responses, see Kudlich to Condy Gallagher and Patrick Carr, April 3, 1903; Kudlich to Mc Geehan, et al, September 30, 1903, Anthracite Museum-Eckley Miners' Village, Pennsylvania Historical and Museum Commission, Eckley, Pennsylvania. Also see *UMWJ,* October 15, 1903.

43. A variety of problems persisted there through 1905; for example see *UMWJ,* November 10, 1904; March 2, May 25, June 8, and August 31, 1905.

44. *Ibid.*, May 18, 1905.

45. *Ibid.*, April 20, 1905.

46. United Mine Workers of America, *Proceedings of the Seventh Annual Convention of District No. 1, United Mine Workers of America, Dunmore, Pennsylvania, July 17–22, 1905* (Scranton, PA: Sanders Printing Co., 1905), 40–41; *UMWJ*, May 25 and June 1, 1904.

47. *UMWJ*, September 7, 1905; *Scranton Truth*, August 14–30, 1905.

48. E. C. Morris to John M. Sutton, March 6, 1903, Mitchell Papers (microfilm).

49. For Ryscavage's April report, see E. C. Morris to John Mitchell, April 13, 1903, *ibid.*

50. *UMWJ*, November 5, 1903; also see *ibid.*, November 12, 1903.

51. *Ibid.*, February 25, 1904.

52. *Proceedings of Sixth Annual Convention of District No. 1, 1904*, 5–6. For accounts of various rallies, see *UMWJ*, November 12 and December 17, 1903; January 14, February 18, April 7, May 19 and 26, June 30, October 27, and November 3, 1904.

53. *Ibid.*, July 7, 1904.

54. Reprinted in *ibid.*, January 26, 1905.

55. United Mine Workers of America, *Minutes of the Thirteenth Annual Convention of the United Mine Workers of America, Held at Indianapolis, Indiana, January 20–29, 1902* (Indianapolis: Hollenbeck Press, 1902), 65; United Mine Workers of America, *Minutes of the Sixteenth Annual Convention of the United Mine Workers of America Held in Tomlinson Hall, Indianapolis, Indiana, January 16–23, 1905* (Indianapolis: Cheltenham Press, 1905), 8. The highest figure for membership that I've found after the 1902 strike is for November 1903, in which a total of 62,148 mine workers were recorded in good standing, with 36,987 in District One, 8,049 in District Seven, and 17,112 in District Nine. Month-by-month data is available from that point, and the anthracite districts did not reach that figure again until October and November 1905 (see below). See Mitchell Papers (microfilm). Of course, figures were based on the per capita tax sent to district and national headquarters, and as John Mitchell told the 1904 national convention: "No inconsiderable number of our local unions fail or refuse to report capitation tax to the National or district offices upon the full numbers of members paying to them." See *UMWA, Fifteenth Annual Convention—1904*, 29.

56. See *ibid.*, 36–38.

57. See Gowaskie, "Rank-and-File Militancy."

58. United Mine Workers of America, *Proceedings of the Fifth Annual Convention of District No. 1, United Mine Workers of America, Plymouth, Pennsylvania, July 13–18, 1903,* 79.

59. *Proceedings of the Fifth Annual Convention of District No. 1, 1903,* 79, 95–96; also see UMWA, *Fifteenth Annual Convention—1904,* 199.

60. *Ibid.,* 138.

61. See cards marked "Notes relating to the various Districts, 1903–1905," Mitchell Papers.

62. United Mine Workers of America, *Minutes of the Fourteenth Annual Convention of the United Mine Workers of America Held in the City of Indianapolis, Indiana, January 19 to 27, 1903, Inclusive* (Indianapolis: Hollenbeck Press, 1903), 501.

63. For sympathetic statement see John Mitchell to John P. Reese, February 9, 1903, Mitchell Papers (microfilm). On the rivalry between Mitchell and Lewis, see Elsie Glück, *John Mitchell, Miner: Labor's Bargain with the Gilded Age* (New York: John Day Company, 1929; reprint ed., New York: Greenwood Press, 1969), 50–54, 84–85.

64. The most comprehensive account of the union in these years can be found in Maier B. Fox, *United We Stand: The United Mine Workers of America 1890–1990* (Washington, DC: United Mine Workers of America, 1990), 40–81; on the increase, also see United Mine Workers of America, *Proceedings of Sessions of the National Convention of United Mine Workers of America, Held March 5th and 7th, Indianapolis, Indiana* (n.p., n.d.), 15, Mitchell Papers (microfilm).

65. Jane Addams, "The Present Crisis in Trade-Union Morals," *North American Review* 179 (August 1904): 178.

66. Elmer Dover to John Mitchell, February 15, 1904, Mitchell Papers (microfilm).

67. J. P. Reese to John Mitchell, February 17, 1904, *ibid.; UMWJ,* February 25, 1904. Glück, 161–62.

68. On Parry and the NAM see Robert H. Wiebe, *Businessmen and Reform: A Study of the Progressive Movement* (Chicago: Quadrangle Books, 1962), 25–31, 167–71. On the NCF, see Marguerite Green, *The National Civic Federation and the American Labor Movement 1900–1925* (Washington: Catholic University of America Press, 1956), *passim;* Philip Taft, *The A.F. of L. in the Time of Gompers* (New York: Harper & Brothers, Publishers, 1957), 225–31. On the rivalry between the two see Green, 90–132; Wiebe, 31, 159–71, and David Montgomery, *The Fall of the House of Labor: The Workplace, The State, and Labor Activism, 1865–1925* (New York: Cambridge University Press, 1987), 272–75.

69. On the centrality of Hanna's role in the NCF and the significance of the 1902 anthracite strike as a turning point, see Green, 39–60, 104–07.

70. Ralph M. Easley to John Mitchell, February 8, 1904, Mitchell Papers (microfilm).

71. John Mitchell, Tom L. Lewis, and William B. Wilson to the Members of the Local Unions of the United Mine Workers of America, March 9, 1904, *ibid.*

72. *Proceedings of the National Convention of United Mine Workers of America, Held March 5th and 7th,* 16, *ibid.*

73. Mat Charlton, James Pritchard, and William Fitzsimmons to John Mitchell, March 25, 1904, *ibid.*

74. *Proceedings of the National Convention Held March 5th and 7th,* 15, *ibid.*

75. UMWA, *Fourteenth Annual Convention—1903,* 483.

76. Mitchell, Lewis, and Wilson to UMWA members, March 9, 1904, *ibid.*

77. United Mine Workers of America, *Minutes of the Sixteenth Annual Convention of the United Mine Workers of America, Held at Indianapolis, Indiana, January 16 to 23, 1905* (Indianapolis: Cheltenham Press, 1905), 11–18, *ibid.* For the socialist reaction see John H. M. Laslett, *Labor and the Left: A Study of Socialist and Radical Influences in the American Labor Movement, 1881–1924* (New York: Basic Books, 1970), 204–05, 208–09; Nick Salvatore, *Eugene V. Debs: Citizen and Socialist* (Urbana: University of Illinois Press, 1982), 209–10; Raúl Calderón-Jemio, "John Mitchell and the UMW," unpublished seminar paper, University of Connecticut, 1986. For the end of those strikes, see United Mine Workers of America, *Minutes of the Seventeenth Annual Convention of the United Mine Workers of America, Held at Indianapolis, Indiana, January 16 to 24, 1906* (Indianapolis: Cheltenham Press, 1906), 38; United Mine Workers of America, *Minutes of the Eighteenth Annual Convention of the United Mine Workers of America, Held at Indianapolis, Indiana, January 15 to 22, 1907* (Indianapolis: Cheltenham Press, 1907), 38. Debs's views on the Commission's award are referred to scathingly in *UMWJ,* May 12 and June 2, 1904.

78. UMWA, *Sixteenth Annual Convention—1905,* 9. Reverend John J. Curran, a Wilkes-Barre priest who had strongly supported Mitchell and the UMWA in the 1902 strike, encouraged Mitchell's critical view of the anthracite mine workers. He wrote Mitchell that he had accurately placed "the blame of wrong doing . . . in the ranks of the local unions." Curran found it "positively sickening to see those ungrateful brutes who were lifted up out of the sink of despair and hopelessness, now dead to all sense of past favors and forgetful of all that has been done for them." He warned Mitchell that were he to visit the anthracite region soon, he might "receive only a half-hearted welcome from the majority of the miners," but added that as the expiration of the Commission's award approached, "the men will bestir themselves and respond to your appeals as in times gone by." See Curran to Mitchell, January 16, 1905, Mitchell Papers (microfilm). On Curran, see Cornell, 114–15, 158–59.

79. See list placed at end of July, end of August, and end of December 1905, Mitchell Papers (microfilm).

80. Speech at Old Forge, June 20, 1905, *ibid.*

81. *Ibid.*

82. *Ibid.*

83. For meeting plans, Mitchell to J. J. Curran, January 16, 1905; February 23, 1905; August 4, 1905, Mitchell Papers (microfilm); on attendance, see list placed at end of 1905, *ibid.*

84. *Pottsville Chronicle,* September 11, 1905, located in Mitchell Papers. For other reports of the reception Mitchell received in various anthracite towns, see *Scranton Tribune,* June 5, 1905; *Wilkes-Barre Times,* August 14 and 15, 1905; *Wilkes-Barre News,* August 19, 1905; *Philadelphia Record,* October 29, 1905; located in Mitchell Papers.

85. Mitchell to W. D. Ryan, August 26, 1905, Mitchell Papers (microfilm).

86. Mitchell to Ralph Easley, September 11, 1905, *ibid.*

87. See membership figures, Mitchell Papers (microfilm). Cf. discussion of Mitchell's tour and figures in Gowaskie, "Rank-and-File Militancy," 71–73.

88. For a reference to District One's dispensation, see United Mine Workers of America, *Proceedings of the Eighth Annual Convention of District No. 1, July 16–21, 1906, Carbondale, Pennsylvania* (Scranton, PA: Sanders Printing Co., 1906), 33.

89. See Louis N. Hammerling to John Mitchell, April 27, 1905; Mitchell to Hammerling, May 5, 1905; Hammerling to E. C. Morris, May 17, 1905; Mitchell to Hammerling, May 25, 1905 (two telegrams); Hammerling to Mitchell, May 25, 1905. In the Mitchell Papers, there is a partial document dated June 8 which refers to the mine workers' willingness to accept a renewal of the award of the Coal Strike Commission, to be accomplished through the Conciliation Board. It bears no signature, but the name "(Mr. Hammerling)" is marked beneath. Louis N. Hammerling was an immigrant newspaperman and business promoter who cultivated close ties with Mitchell and Republican politicians. See James O. Morris, "The Acquisitive Spirit of John Mitchell, UMW President (1899–1908)," *Labor History* 20(Winter 1979): 27. Hammerling helped to arrange the meeting with Connell, and that document raises the likely possibility that Mitchell and Connell may have discussed renewal of the award. See "(Mr. Hammerling)", June 8, 1905.

90. Mitchell to H. N. Taylor, September 4, 1905; also see Mitchell to Taylor, August 28, 1905, *ibid.*

91. Easley to Mitchell, September 8, 1905, *ibid.* In 1901, Underwood had been more willing to deal with the UMWA than his fellow railroad executives; see chapter 6.

92. Mitchell to Easley, September 11, 1905, Mitchell Papers (microfilm).

93. Easley to Mitchell, December 12, 1905, *ibid.*

94. David Willcox, "Present Conditions in the Anthracite Coal Industry," *North American Review* 181 (August 1905): 227–28. On August 1, Easley mentioned the article in a telegram to Mitchell; Mitchell's secretary responded that he had taken a copy to his speaking engagement at Nanticoke. See Easley to Mitchell, August 1, 1905; E. C. Morris to Easley, August 1, 1905, Mitchell Papers (microfilm).

95. Neill to Mitchell, December 13, 1905, *ibid.*

96. "Proceedings of the Tri-District Convention—December 1905," 29–30, Kosik Collection.

97. *Ibid.*, 93–94.

98. *Ibid.*, 95–96.

99. *Ibid.*, 96.

100. *Ibid.*, 97–98.

101. *Ibid.*, 99, 102.

102. *Ibid.*, 98–99, 101–02.

103. *Ibid.*, 102–03.

104. *Ibid.*, 105.

105. Of the twenty settled by the umpire in the Board's first three years, only four were sustained or partially sustained. See *Work of the Board Ending March 31, 1906*, 335.

106. "Proceedings of the Tri-District Convention—Shamokin, 1905," Kosik Collection, 99–100.

107. *Ibid.*, 109.

108. *Ibid.*, 110–11.

109. *Ibid.*, 52.

110. *Ibid.*, 83–91.

111. *Ibid.*, 91–92.

112. For quotation see John Mitchell to Charles P. Neill, December 20, 1905; also see Mitchell to George F. Baer, December 20, 1905, Mitchell Papers (microfilm).

113. Mitchell to Baer, December 20, 1905, *ibid.*

114. George F. Baer to Mitchell, December 22, 1905, *ibid.*

115. UMWA, *Seventeenth Annual Convention—1906*, 247–51.

116. United Mine Workers of America, Executive Board Minutes, March 15, 1906, 173–76; United Mine Workers of America, *Minutes of the Special Convention of the United Mine Workers of America, March 15–30, 1906, Indianapolis, Indiana* (Indianapolis: Cheltenham Press, 1906), 12–14; *Pittsburgh Post,* May 2, 1906; Glück, 184–96.

117. *Minutes of Joint Conferences,* 2–5.

118. *Ibid.,* 5–7.

119. *Ibid.,* 8–12.

120. Cornell, 81–88.

121. Mitchell to Baer, February 27, 1906, reprinted in *Minutes of Joint Conferences,* 13–30.

122. Baer to Mitchell, February 28, 1906, reprinted in *ibid.,* 31.

123. Mitchell to Baer, March 1, 1906, reprinted in *ibid.,* 31–33.

124. Baer et al. to Mitchell et al., reprinted in *Minutes of Joint Conferences,* 34–52.

125. UMWA, *Minutes of the Special Convention—March 1906,* 58–102; for number in favor, see statement by Mitchell in UMWA, *Eighteenth Annual Convention—1907,* 275; for number of those opposed, see *Pittsburgh Post,* March 31, 1906;

126. Mitchell to Baer, March 17, 1960, in *Minutes of Joint Conferences,* 52–54.

127. Baer to Mitchell, March 20, 1906, in *ibid.,* 55–57.

128. *Pittsburgh Post,* March 30 and 31, 1906.

129. Mitchell to Baer, March 29, 1906, Mitchell Papers (microfilm). Cf. Gowaskie, ''Rank and File Militancy,'' 77.

130. *Pittsburgh Post,* March 30, 1906.

131. *UMWJ,* April 5, 12, and 19, 1906.

132. *Minutes of the Joint Conferences,* 58–63.

133. *Ibid.,* 63.

134. *Ibid.,* 63–79.

135. *Ibid.,* 64–65.

136. *Ibid.,* 85.

137. *Ibid.,* 85.

138. *Ibid.,* 85–86.

139. *Ibid.*, 88–91.

140. *Ibid.*, 94–95.

141. *Ibid.*, 97–99.

142. *Ibid.*, 100–02.

143. For example, see *Pittsburgh Post*, March 19, April 6, and April 11, 1906.

144. *Minutes of the Joint Conferences*, 103–09.

145. *Ibid.*, 122–25.

146. *Ibid.*, 124–30.

147. *Ibid.*, 131–36.

148. This, of course, reflects the operators' emphasis, not Roosevelt's. See George F. Baer et al. to Mitchell et al., April 17, 1906, in *Minutes of the Joint Conferences*, 139; cf. *Report to the President on the Anthracite Coal Strike of May–October 1902* (Washington: Government Printing Office, 1903), 14.

149. Baer et al. to Mitchell et al., April 17, 1906, in *Minutes of the Joint Conferences*, 137–40.

150. *Pittsburgh Post*, April 25, 1906.

151. Mitchell et al. to Baer et al., April 26, 1906, in *Minutes of the Joint Conferences*, 141–45.

152. *Pittsburgh Post*, April 27, 1906.

153. George F. Baer et al. to Mitchell et al., April 27, 1906, in *Minutes of the Joint Conferences*, 145–51.

154. *Pittsburgh Post*, April 30–May 4, 1906.

155. *Proceedings of the Special Convention of Districts One, Seven, and Nine—May 1906*, 78–79.

156. *Pittsburgh Post*, May 5, 1906.

157. Notes, probably taken by Mitchell himself, written on a copy of a printed report of the committee's negotiations presented to the Tri-District convention, May 1906, Mitchell Papers. Also see Notes of the meetings of the general committee, May 4, 1906, J. P. Gallagher, secretary, included in UMWA, Executive Board Minutes, following 175, Mitchell Papers (microfilm).

158. Cf. Gowaskie, "Rank and File Militancy," 80.

159. *Proceedings of the Special Convention of Districts One, Seven, and Nine—May 1906*, 82.

160. *Ibid.*, 84–85.

161. *Minutes of the Joint Conferences*, 153–64.

162. *Ibid.*, 164, 171.

163. *Proceedings of the Special Convention of Districts One, Seven, and Nine—May 1906*, 99–103.

164. *Ibid.*, 107–08. On the eagerness of some workers to return and plans by the companies to try to resume operations, see Peter O'Donnell to J. J. Curran, May 2, 1906, Mitchell Papers (microfilm).

165. *Pittsburgh Post*, May 10, 1906.

166. *Ibid.*, March 31, 1906.

167. *Ibid.*, May 4–6, 1906; *New York Times*, May 8 and 9, 1906. On the immigrants' discontent, also see George Hartlein to John Mitchell, May 11, 1906, Mitchell Papers (microfilm).

168. UMWA, *Eighteenth Annual Convention—1907*, 37; UMWA, Executive Board Minutes, July 30, 1906, 215, Mitchell Papers (microfilm).

169. *UMWJ*, May 10, 1906.

170. United Mine Workers of America, *Proceedings of the Ninth Annual Convention of District No. 1, United Mine Workers of America, July 15–20, 1907, Wilkes-Barre, Pennsylvania* (Scranton, PA: Sanders Printing Co., 1907), 11. Vice-President T. L. Lewis noted the reluctance of anthracite mine workers to pay the assessment; see *UMWJ*, December 13, 1906. On the assessment, see UMWA, Executive Board Minutes, July 30, 1906, 215, Mitchell Papers (microfilm).

171. See monthly membership figures, Mitchell Papers (microfilm).

CHAPTER 9

1. United Mine Workers of America, *Proceedings of the Nineteenth Annual Convention of the United Mine Workers of America Held in the City of Indianapolis, Indiana, January 21 to February 3, inclusive, 1908* (Indianapolis: Cheltenham Press, 1908), 56.

2. The 53 percent figure is calculated from data compiled by the Pennsylvania Department of Mines reported in *United Mine Workers Journal*, March 7, 1912; hereafter cited as *UMWJ*. This calculation excludes nearly 5,000 workers reported as ''Austrian,'' who might have been of eastern or southern European ethnicity but born in the Austro-Hungarian Empire. The figure for 1900 is from Peter Roberts, *The Anthracite Coal Industry* (New York: The Macmillan Co., 1901), 105.

3. United Mine Workers of America, *Proceedings of the Eighth Annual Convention of District No. 1, United Mine Workers of America, July 16–21, 1906, Carbon-*

dale, Pennsylvania (Scranton, PA: Sanders Printing Co., 1906), 54. Several less drastic proposals along the same lines were also introduced but not adopted. See *ibid.*, 71–75.

4. United Mine Workers of America, *Proceedings of the Ninth Annual Convention of District No. 1, United Mine Workers of America, July 15–20, 1907, Wilkes-Barre, Pennsylvania* (Scranton, PA: Sanders Printing Co., 1907), 12.

5. Thomas B. Cochran and Herman P. Miller, compilers, *Smull's Legislative Hand Book and Manual of the State of Pennsylvania—1907* (Harrisburg, PA: Harrisburg Publishing Co., State Printer, 1907), 473.

6. For the AFL's effort in this area, see Philip Taft, *The A.F. of L. in the Time of Gompers* (New York: Harper & Brothers, Publishers, 1957), 295–97. The other leader elected to Congress was William B. Wilson, UMWA Secretary-Treasurer, also of Pennsylvania. The president of District Seven, William Dettrey, ran for Congress on the Socialist ticket in 1906 but was defeated. The *UMWJ*, November 8, 1906, blamed his defeat on a lack of support from the Socialists.

7. United Mine Workers of America, *Minutes of the Eighteenth Annual Convention of the United Mine Workers of America, Held at Indianapolis, Indiana, January 15 to 22, 1907* (Indianapolis: Cheltenham Press, 1907), 31.

8. *UMWJ*, April 25 and May 2, 1907.

9. UMWA, Executive Board Minutes, June 28, 1907, p. 28, Mitchell Papers (microfilm).

10. UMWA, *Nineteenth Annual Convention—1908*, 29.

11. Thomas D. Nicholls et al. to the Officers and Members of Local Unions in Districts 1, 7, and 9, August 22, 1907, Mitchell Papers (microfilm); UMWJ, August 22 and September 5, 1907. United Mine Workers of America, *Proceedings of the Tenth Annual Convention of District No. 1, United Mine Workers of America, July 20–25, 1908, Scranton, Pennsylvania* (Scranton, PA: Sanders Printing Co., 1908), 13–14.

12. UMWA, *Nineteenth Annual Convention—1908*, 26–27; *Proceedings of the Tenth Annual Convention of District No. 1, July 1908*, 13–14.

13. UMWA, *Nineteenth Annual Convention—1908*, 29.

14. *UMWJ*, February 22, March 8, June 14, August 2, and September 6, 1906; *Proceedings of the Eighth Annual Convention of District No. 1, July 1906*, 46; *Proceedings of the Ninth Annual Convention of District No. 1, July 1907*, 34. For the union's role in other disputes, see *UMWJ*, August 9, 1906, and March 28, 1907.

15. *UMWJ*, November 19, 1908; for similar action by the union, also see August 15, 1907.

16. For example, see *ibid.*, September 27, 1906.

17. Board of Conciliation, *Compilation of Grievances for Three Years Beginning April 1st, 1906, and Ending March 31, 1909* (Wilkes-Barre, PA: Record Print, 1909), 36–50, first quotation from 41, second from 50. Also see *UMWJ*, January 9 and 16, October 1, 1908.

18. *UMWJ*, October 1, 1908. For problems in collecting dues, also see *ibid.*, December 6, 1906. Most collecting had apparently been done at the meeting of the union local, which was obviously easy for "dues dodgers" to avoid.

19. See days worked in various years, U.S., Bureau of Census, *Historical Statistics of the United States: Colonial Times to 1970*, 2 parts (Washington: Government Printing Office, 1975), I: 592–93.

20. *UMWJ*, July 30, August 20 and 27, and September 3, 1908.

21. For membership figures, see *ibid.*, January 21, 1909; for dispensations, see *ibid.*, July 9 and December 17, 1908.

22. United Mine Workers of America, *Proceedings of Joint Convention of Districts Nos. 1, 7, and 9, United Mine Workers of America, Scranton, Pennsylvania, October 12–15, 1908* (Scranton: Sanders Printing Co., 1908), 21.

23. *UMWJ*, April 23, 1908.

24. For election results, see *UMWJ*, February 11, 1909. For Hartlein's attitude toward Fahy, see Hartlein to John Mitchell, August 14, 1903, Mitchell Papers (microfilm). For Nicholls's resignation, see *Scranton Times*, January 20 and February 19, 1909, and *UMWJ*, March 4, 1909. He left Congress upon completion of his second term. See *ibid.*, March 31, 1910.

25. United Mine Workers of America, *Proceedings of Joint Convention of Districts Nos. 1, 7, and 9, United Mine Workers of America, Scranton, Pennsylvania, March 23–24, 1909* (Scranton, PA: Sanders Printing Co., 1909), 20–21.

26. *Proceedings of Joint Convention of Districts 1, 7, and 9—March 1909*, 28–30.

27. *Proceedings of the Tenth Annual Convention of District No. 1—July 1909*, 14–16. As an interesting precursor to the 1912 agreement, which called for the establishment of colliery grievance committees, committees "of employees directly interested" were given a role in considering grievances before referral to the Conciliation Board.

28. William J. Walsh, *The United Mine Workers of America as Economic and Social Force in the Anthracite Territory* (Washington: Catholic University of America Press, 1931), 129.

29. *UMWJ*, June 3, 1909.

30. *Ibid.*, November 11, 1909.

31. *Ibid.*, November 28, 1907; September 17 and October 1, 1908.

32. *Ibid.*, June 3, 1909.

33. United Mine Workers of America, *Proceedings of the Twelfth Annual Convention of District No. 1, United Mine Workers of America, July 18–23, 1910, Scranton, Pennsylvania* (Scranton: Sanders Printing Co., 1910), 10. As an example of the problems local unions faced, L.U. 1495 at #9 colliery in Pittston "was practically dead" as the result of the company closing the mine to rebuild the breaker. See *UMWJ*, June 2, 1910.

34. Patrick M. Lynch, "Pennsylvania Anthracite: A Forgotten IWW Venture, 1906–1916," M.A. thesis, Bloomsburg State College, Bloomsburg, PA, October 1974, 11–13, 30–32.

35. *Scranton Times*, May 3, 1910.

36. *Ibid.*, May 17, 19, 20, 23, and 24, 1910; also see *UMWJ*, May 26 and June 2, 1910.

37. *Scranton Times*, May 25, 1910.

38. *Ibid.*, May 24, 26, 28, and 30, 1910; also see *UMWJ*, June 2, 1910.

39. *Ibid.*, May 28 and 30, June 1–3, 1910. Two of the mines that joined the strike toward the end, the Consolidated and the Butler, were owned by the Hillside Coal and Iron Company which, like the PCC, was a subsidiary of the Erie Railroad. See *Proceedings of the Twelfth Annual Convention of District No. 1, July 1910*, 15; *Scranton Times*, June 1 and July 1, 1910.

40. *Scranton Times*, June 6–9, 1910.

41. *UMWJ*, June 16, 1910. While Lynch notes that the IWW had five locals in anthracite in 1910, all in the vicinity of the PCC's mines, he adds that the IWW itself claimed no direct role in the strike. See Lynch, 32–33.

42. *Scranton Times*, June 30 and July 1, 1910; *UMWJ*, July 7, 1910; *Proceedings of the Twelfth Annual Convention of District #1, July 1910, 11–15*.

43. *Scranton Times*, June 21, 1910.

44. *UMWJ*, July 7, 1910.

45. *Ibid.*, August 18–26, 1910; also see *UMWJ*, August 25 and September 8, 1910. After several altercations with state troopers, some twenty-one immigrant strikers were arrested and charged with rioting, but Memolo paid the fines of several and had several others released to his custody while they arranged bail.

46. *UMWJ*, September 1 and 15, 1910; *Scranton Times*, August 22, 1910.

47. *Scranton Times,* September 1, 1910.

48. For membership figures, see *UMWJ,* January 18, 1912; for locals abandoned see *ibid.,* January 26, 1911.

49. *UMWJ,* March 2, 9, and 30, 1910; also see Elsie Glück, *John Mitchell, Miner: Labor's Bargain with the Gilded Age* (New York: John Day Company, 1929; reprint ed., New York: Greenwood Press, 1969), 232–39 and John H. M. Laslett, *Labor and the Left: A Study of Socialist and Radical Influences in the American Labor Movement, 1881–1924* (New York: Basic Books, 1970), 214–16. After considering possibly leaving the union, Mitchell resigned his post at the NCF. He did not attend the convention.

50. United Mine Workers of America, *Proceedings of Joint Convention of Districts Nos. 1, 7, and 9, United Mine Workers of America, Pottsville, Pennsylvania, October 31–November 3, 1911* (Shenandoah, PA: Herald Print, 1911), 34–35;

51. See *UMWJ,* February 20, 1913.

52. *UMWJ,* January 18, 1912.

53. U.S., Bureau of the Census, *Historical Statistics of the United States: Colonial Times to 1970* (Washington: Government Printing Office, 1975), 1:592–93.

54. United Mine Workers of America, *Proceedings of the Fourteenth Annual Convention of District No. 1, United Mine Workers of America, Scranton, Pennsylvania, July 15–20, 1912* (Scranton: Sanders Printing Co., 1912), 14–33; *Scranton Times,* April 1–25, 1912; *UMWJ,* March 21 and 28, April 4, 11, and 18, 1912; also see *Negotiations of Anthracite Coal Operators and Anthracite Mine Workers—Addresses of International President, John P. White and International Statistician, William Green* (Indianapolis: Cheltenham-Aetna Press, 1912), 3–29 and Walsh, 130–31.

55. See *Scranton Times,* April 29–May 11, 1912; *Negotiations, 1912,* 43, 64–66.

56. *Negotiations—1912,* 46–47.

57. *Ibid.,* 46, 51.

58. *Ibid.,* 36–37.

59. *Walsh,* 158–59.

60. For membership figures, see *UMWJ,* February 20, 1913; for number of meetings, see *ibid.,* August 29, 1912.

61. *Ibid.,* August 8, 1912.

62. *UMWJ,* August 28, 1913 and February 26, 1914. Also on button strikes, see Edgar Sydenstricker, "The Settlement of Disputes Under Agreements in the Anthracite Industry," *Journal of Political Economy* 24 (March 1916): 270.

63. Kennedy led the district for the next fifteen years and then played a major role in the international union, as secretary-treasurer from 1925 to 1947, vice-president from 1947 to 1960, and president from 1960 to 1962. See Gary M. Fink, ed., *Biographical Dictionary of American Labor*, rev. ed. (Westport, CT: Greenwood Press, 1984), 334–35.

64. *UMWJ*, October 3, 1912. Reportedly locals in the valley refused to allow workers to join for two dollars, as a dispensation would have permitted, but instead required that they pay ten dollars.

65. *Ibid.*, August 17, September 7 and 14, 1910.

66. *Ibid.*, August 29, 1912 and September 2, 1915.

67. *Ibid.*, October 17, 1912.

68. *Ibid.*, August 1, 1912.

69. *Ibid.*, April 24 and June 19, 1912.

70. *Ibid.*, July 29, 1913.

71. This occurred in November 1912 and May, August, and November 1913. See *ibid.*, February 20, 1913 and January 22, 1914.

72. *Ibid.*, December 26, 1912.

73. See Sydenstricker, 258–59. While general grievance committees were common only in the Wyoming field, according to Sydenstricker, the Schuylkill field had a general committee that had representatives from grievance committees throughout the entire field. Two resolutions were submitted to the Tri-District Convention of 1915 urging that the Conciliation Board be replaced with a grievance procedure based on the general grievance committee. One of these resolutions was from several locals in District One, the other from a local in Mahanoy City in District Nine. See United Mine Workers of America, *Proceedings of Joint Convention of Districts Nos. 1, 7, and 9, United Mine Workers of America, Wilkes-Barre, Pa., September 7th to 10th, 1915* (Wilkes-Barre: Gornik Print, 1915), 103–05, 144–45.

74. *Scranton Times*, February 1 and 3, 1913.

75. *UMWJ*, March 27, 1913. On Holton's candidacies, see election returns, unpaginated at back in United Mine Workers of America, *Proceedings of the Fifteenth Annual Convention of District No. 1, United Mine Workers of America, July 21–26, 1913, Wilkes-Barre, Pennsylvania* (Scranton: Sanders Printing Co., 1913) and United Mine Workers of America, *Proceedings of the Sixteenth Consecutive and First Biennial Convention of District No. 1, United Mine Workers of America, July 19–24, 1915* (Scranton: Sanders Printing Co., 1915).

76. United Mine Workers of America, *Proceedings of the Thirteenth Annual Convention of District No. 1, United Mine Workers of America, Wilkes-Barre, Pennsylvania, July 17–22, 1911* (Scranton: Sanders Printing Co., 1911), 43.

77. United Mine Workers of America, *Proceedings of the Fourteenth Annual Convention of District No. 1, United Mine Workers of America, Scranton, Pennsylvania, July 15–20, 1912* (Scranton: Sanders Printing Co., 1912), 61.

78. *Proceedings of the Fifteenth Annual Convention of District No. 1, July 1913,* 161.

79. *Ibid.,* 197.

80. *Ibid.,* 163–64.

81. *Ibid.,* 169–70.

82. *Ibid.,* 22.

83. *Scranton Times,* July 28, 1914.

84. *Ibid.,* July 21 and 28, 1914.

85. *Ibid.,* July 29–30, 1914; *UMWJ,* August 6, 1914.

86. *Scranton Times,* July 31, 1914.

87. *UMWJ,* August 6, 1914.

88. *Ibid.,* October 23, 1913 and February 5, 1914.

89. See *Proceedings of the Sixteenth Consecutive and First Biennial Convention of District No. 1, July 1915,* passim.

90. See election returns, unpaginated at back in *Proceedings of the Fifteenth Annual Convention of District No. 1, July 1913* and *Proceedings of the Sixteenth Consecutive and First Biennial Convention of District No. 1, July 1915.* Fowler's quotation is on p. 167.

91. *UMWJ,* January 21, 1915 and February 4 and 11, 1915.

92. *Ibid.,* February 4, 1915; also see December 10, 1914.

93. *Ibid.,* January 22, 1914.

94. *Proceedings of the Sixteenth Consecutive and First Biennial Convention of District No. 1, July 1915,* 57.

95. *Ibid.,* September 9, 1915.

96. United Mine Workers of America, *Report of Proceedings of the Seventeenth Consecutive and Second Biennial Convention of District No. 1, United Mine Workers of America, Wilkes-Barre, Pennsylvania, July 16–21, 1917* (Scranton: Sanders Printing Co., 1917), 57.

97. *Proceedings of the Sixteenth Consecutive and First Biennial Convention of District No. 1, July 1915,* 136–37.

98. *Ibid.*, 99–100, also see pp. 98–99, 101–03.

99. For District Nine figures, see *UMWJ*, October 26, 1916; on District Seven, see *ibid.*, September 2, 1915.

100. *Proceedings of Joint Convention of Districts Nos. 1, 7, and 9*, pp. 54–55; *UMWJ*, September 16, 1915. On machine mining, the *Wilkes-Barre Record*, April 5, 1916, reported during negotiations in 1916 that only 1500 out of the 80 million tons of anthracite mined annually were mined by machine. Anna Rochester states in *Labor and Coal* (New York: International Publishers, 1931), 108–11, that less than 2 percent of anthracite was cut by machine by the end of the 1920s, and "considerably less than 5 percent" was loaded by machine. Of course, the slow pace of technological change in anthracite stands in stark contrast to the rapid change occurring in bituminous mining during these years. See Keith Dix, *What's a Coal Miner to Do?: The Mechanization of Coal Mining* (Pittsburgh: University of Pittsburgh Press, 1988).

101. *Ibid.*, October 21, 1915.

102. *Historical Statistics*, 1:592–93.

103. Patrick M. Lynch, "Pennsylvania Anthracite: A Forgotten IWW Venture, 1906–1916," M.A. thesis, Bloomsburg State College, October 1974, 60–61, 151–55. Also on the Greenwood strike, see *Wilkes-Barre Record*, February 23, 25, and 26, March 9 and 10, 1916.

104. *UMWJ*, April 6, 1916. Patrick Lynch estimates the total number of adherents of the IWW in anthracite at five to ten thousand; see Lynch, 97. I believe that this could be a reasonable estimate of those who might have held IWW sympathies at one time or another, but I doubt that number of anthracite mine workers gave the Wobblies ongoing support. What is clear is that the insurgent movement in District One carefully kept its distance from the IWW, and that the *Wilkes-Barre Record*, at least, showed little interest in the IWW in February, March, April, and May 1916. On April 6, a reporter for the *Record* noted rumors of IWW organizing but stated that "leaders of the mine workers' organization regard the 'Ettor Movement' . . . as too insignificant to be recognized as a factor in the present negotiations."

105. *UMWJ*, March 2–May 4, 1916; *Wilkes-Barre Record*, March 3–May 1, 1916.

106. *Ibid.*, May 2, 1916.

107. "Proceedings of Tri-District Convention Districts Nos. 1, 7, and 9, United Mine Workers of America, Pottsville, Pennsylvania, May 2–4, 1916," 47, Michael J. Kosik Collection, Fred Lewis Pattee Library, Pennsylvania State University, University Park, PA; hereafter cited as Kosik Collection.

108. *Ibid.*, 90–95.

109. *Ibid.*, 52.

110. *Ibid.,* 61–62.

111. *Ibid.,* 58. For similar sentiments expressed by other delegates, see pp. 57 and 69.

112. *Ibid.,* 61.

113. For White's quotation, see *ibid.,* 70, for Fowler's comments, see pp. 56–57; for further discussion, see pp. 103–05.

114. *Ibid.,* 32, 128–29, 132 (for quotation), and 160.

115. For miners, see *ibid.,* 126, 150; for drivers, see pp. 127, 139–42. As the new agreement was being implemented, at a number of collieries drivers were given a starting time before the official opening time. Some who proceeded to arrive at work late were told they could not work that day, and this led to a number of brief strikes. See *Wilkes-Barre Record,* May 10 and 11, 1916.

116. For referendum discussion, see "Proceedings of Tri-District Convention, Pottsville, 1916," 187–91, 197–99, 226, Kosik Collection; for vote total, see *ibid.,* 253.

CHAPTER 10

1. U.S., Department of Labor, Children's Bureau, *Child Labor and the Welfare of Children in an Anthracite Coal-Mining District* (Washington: Government Printing Office, 1922), *passim.*

2. Marie L. Obenauer, "Living Conditions Among Coal Mine Workers of the United States," *Annals of the American Academy of Political and Social Science* 111 (January 1924): 13–23; see p. 22 for quotation.

3. Frank Stricker, "Affluence for Whom?—Another Look at Prosperity and the Working Classes in the 1920s," *Labor History* 24 (Winter 1983): 5–33.

4. Edward Eyre Hunt, F. G. Tryon, and Joseph H. Willits, eds., *What the Coal Commission Found: An Authoritative Summary by the Staff* (Baltimore: Williams & Wilkins Company, 1925), 312.

5. *Ibid.,* 300.

6. Horace B. Drury, "Wages in the Coal Industry as Compared with Wages in Other Industries (With Special Reference to the Anthracite Situation)," *Annals of the American Academy of Political and Social Science* 111 (January 1924): 314–43. For a recent work which comes to a similar conclusion regarding the bituminous industry, see Price Fishback, *Soft Coal, Hard Choices: The Economic Welfare of Bituminous Coal Miners, 1890–1930* (New York: Oxford University Press, 1992).

7. United States Coal Commission, *Report* (Washington: Government Printing Office, 1925) 1:34.

8. Paul H. Douglas, *Real Wages in the United States, 1890–1926*, reprint edition (New York: Augustus M. Kelley, Publishers, 1966), 648, 653; also see pp. 343–57, 19–64.

9. For fluctuations in the cost of living see *ibid.*, 19–64.

10. Melvyn Dubofsky and Warren Van Tine characterize the UMWA in this era "as a decentralized institution in which effective administrative authority existed at the district level." See Dubofsky and Van Tine, *John L. Lewis: A Biography*, abridged edition (Urbana: University of Illinois Press, 1986), 86.

11. *United Mine Workers Journal*, May 3, 1917, hereafter cited as *UMWJ;* and Hunt, Tryon, and Willits, *Coal Commission*, 307.

12. For membership figures, see United Mine Workers of America, *Report of Proceedings of the Seventeenth Consecutive and Second Biennial Convention of District No. 1, United Mine Workers of America, Wilkes-Barre, Pennsylvania, July 16–21, 1917* (Scranton, PA: Sanders Printing Co., 1917), 57; and United Mine Workers of America, *Report of Proceedings of the Eighteenth Consecutive and Third Biennial Convention of District No. 1, United Mine Workers of America, Scranton, Pennsylvania, Commencing July 21, 1919* (Scranton: Sanders Printing Co., 1919), 52.

13. Nevertheless, after a closer and more bitter campaign in 1919 in which he was not a candidate, McTiernan told that convention: "I will tell you right now that I was elected to be President of this District." See *Proceedings of the Eighteenth Consecutive and Third Biennial Convention of District No. 1, July 1919*, 277.

14. See election returns, unpaginated at back of *Proceedings of the Sixteenth Consecutive and First Biennial Convention of District No. 1, July 1915* and *Proceedings of the Seventeenth Consecutive and Second Biennial Convention of District No. 1, July 1917*.

15. *UMWJ*, October 26, 1916.

16. United States, Bureau of the Census, *Historical Statistics of the United States: Colonial Times to 1970* (Washington: Government Printing Office, 1925), 1:592–93.

17. *Proceedings of the Eighteenth Consecutive and Third Biennial Convention of District No. 1, July 1919*, 33–35; Maier B. Fox, *United We Stand: The United Mine Workers of America, 1890–1990* (Washington: United Mine Workers of America, 1990), 181–86.

18. *UMWJ*, October 1, 1918.

19. *New York Times*, September 9, 1918. Maier Fox maintains that the federal government had prohibited miners from enlisting; see Fox, 185. This seems most unlikely; see *New York Times*, July 8 and August 12, 1918. There is no mention of such a prohibition in President Wilson's plea for increased production of coal, dated August 9 and printed in the *Times* on August 12.

20. *Wilkes-Barre Record,* September 9–10, 1918; the September 16 issue refers to the earlier meeting in District Nine.

21. *Ibid.,* September 16 and 17, 1918.

22. *Ibid.,* September 17, 1918; also see *UMWJ,* October 1, 1918. The candidacy of District Seven President Thomas Kennedy for the International Vice-Presidency against appointed incumbent John L. Lewis might have provided a special incentive for District Seven to take a strong stand against insurgency. Kennedy was defeated by a margin of more than two-to-one. See *ibid.,* February 15, 1919.

23. *Wilkes-Barre Record,* September 19–20, 1918. The *UMWJ* accused "I.W.W. extremists" of inciting the strike, but the local newspaper made no mention of any. Several Wobblies from the Pittston area had been picked up by federal agents in June 1917 and were sentenced in September 1918. See *Wilkes-Barre Record,* September 2, 1918 and *UMWJ,* October 1, 1918.

24. *Wilkes-Barre Record,* September 23, 1918.

25. *Proceedings of the Eighteenth Consecutive and Third Biennial Convention of District No. 1, July 1919,* 36–40, for quotation, see p. 40. The advance is very complex and detailed, and the percentage figures offered above are only estimates. For a useful table describing anthracite increases, see Hunt, Tryon, and Willits, *Coal Commission,* 306–07.

26. *Proceedings of the Eighteenth Consecutive and Third Biennial Convention of District No. 1, July 1919,* 67–68. A brief mention of Dempsey's neglect of duty can be found in United Mine Workers of America, *Proceedings of the Joint Convention of Districts Nos. 1, 7 and 9, United Mine Workers of America, Wilkes-Barre, Pennsylvania, September 7–10, 1915* (Wilkes-Barre: Gornik Print, 1915), 190–91. Two delegates asked why Dempsey had not attended the convention. The convention chair, Thomas J. Kennedy of District Seven, then asked the delegates if they really cared "to wash out the dirty linen of District No. 1?"
While this can qualify as little more than speculation, Yannis's return to the vice-presidency could possibly reflect the reluctance of other district leaders to have a man of recent immigrant stock in the district's top post.

27. *Proceedings of the Eighteenth Consecutive and Third Biennial Convention of District No. 1, July 1919,* 124–25.

28. *Ibid.,* 183–84, 206–07.

29. *Ibid.,* 172–73. Also see pp. 21 and 76.

30. *Ibid.,* 171.

31. *Ibid.,* 185–86.

32. *Ibid.,* 186–203; see p. 196 for quotation.

33. *Ibid.*, 211–15; see p. 211 for resolution, p. 213 for quotation.

34. *Ibid.*, see election returns, unpaginated at back.

35. *Ibid.*, 246–91. Those charges took a variety of forms. For example, the returns of locals which totaled more votes than their paid-up membership were void according to the constitution. However, insurgents claimed that in some cases totals were changed for pro-insurgent locals so that their entire vote could be tossed out. See *ibid.*, pp. 271–76. The votes of eleven locals were rejected because of "overvoting." *Ibid.*, see election returns, unpaginated at back.

36. *Ibid.*, 317.

37. *Ibid.*, 258–59.

38. *Ibid.*, 69.

39. *Scranton Times*, September 2, 1919.

40. *Ibid.*, September 5 and 6, 1919.

41. *Ibid.*, September 8 and 9, 1919; quotations are from September 9. Also see *New York Times*, September 8 and 9, 1919.

42. *Scranton Times*, September 10 and 12, 1919; *New York Times*, September 12, 1919.

43. *Scranton Times*, September 10, 1919.

44. *Ibid.*, September 11–16, 1919; *New York Times*, September 12 and 16, 1919.

45. *Proceedings of the Eighteenth Consecutive and Third Biennial Convention of District No. 1, July 1919*, 124.

46. United Mine Workers of America, *Proceedings of the Tri-District Convention of Districts Nos. 1, 7 and 9, United Mine Workers of America, Wilkes-Barre, Pennsylvania, August 19–23, 1919* (Scranton, PA: Sanders Printing Co., 1919), 123–24; and Harold Kenneth Kanarek, "Progressivism in Crisis: The United Mine Workers and the Anthracite Coal Industry During the 1920s," Ph.D. dissertation, University of Virginia, 1972, 38–39.

47. United Mine Workers of America, *Proceedings of the Tri-District Convention Comprising District One, Seven and Nine, United Mine Workers of America, Wilkes-Barre, Pennsylvania, May 24–27, 1920* (Scranton, PA: Sanders Printing Co., 1920), 9–17, 31–36; and Kanarek, 38–39.

48. Dubofsky and Van Tine, 43–45.

49. *Proceedings of the Tri-District Convention Comprising District One, Seven and Nine, Wilkes-Barre, Pennsylvania, May 24–27, 1920*, 11–13, 31–44, 65–74, 111–21, 129 (for Williams's quotation), and 160–61. For Dempsey's position, see

UMWJ, June 1, 1920. Also see Kanarek, 38–41; and United Mine Workers of America, *Report of Proceedings of the Nineteenth Successive and Fourth Biennial Convention of District No. 1, United Mine Workers of America, Wilkes-Barre, Pennsylvania, Commencing July 18, 1921* (Scranton, PA: Sanders Printing Co., 1921), 20–24. On the 1920 Bituminous Coal Commission, see Dubofsky and Van Tine, 45–48.

50. Kanarek, "Progressivism in Crisis," 41–61.

51. *Scranton Times*, July 15, 16, 20 and August 2, 1920. For further information on the contract system, which continued to generate disputes in and around Pittston for many years, see Ben M. Selekman, "Miners and Murder: What Lies Back of the Labor Feud in Anthracite," *Survey Graphic* 60 (May 1928): 151–55, 192–93.

52. *Proceedings of the Nineteenth Successive and Fourth Biennial Convention of District No. 1, July 1921*, 156–57.

53. *Scranton Times*, July 16, 19, 20, 23, 24, and 27, 1920. A UMWA local in Pittston which probably had enrolled only a small minority of workers at its mine also condemned the strike; see *ibid.*, July 21, 1920.

54. *Ibid.*, July 21, 23, 24, and August 10, 1920.

55. *Ibid.*, July 16–August 2, 1920; *Pittston Gazette*, August 2–7, 1920. On Cappellini and Campbell, see Selekman, "Miners and Murder," 151; and United Mine Workers of America, *Record of Proceedings of the Tri-District Convention of Districts Nos. 1, 7 and 9, United Mine Workers of America, Scranton, Pennsylvania, June 26–29, 1923* (Shenandoah, PA: Herald Print, 1923), 191.

56. *Scranton Times*, July 26, 27, and August 2, 1920. On August 17, the *Times* reported on two other cases in past years in which murders had occurred over problems with the contract system.

57. *Ibid.*, July 28, 1920.

58. *Ibid.*, August 4, 5, 12, 16, 1920.

59. *Ibid.*, August 12, 1920.

60. *Ibid.*, August 21 and 24, 1920; *Pittston Gazette*, August 24, 1920.

61. For text of award, see *UMWJ*, September 15, 1920. Also see *Scranton Times*, August 25–27, 1920. For the text of Secretary Wilson's offer, see *Proceedings of the Nineteenth Successive and Fourth Biennial Convention of District No. 1, July 1921*, 21–22.

62. *Scranton Times*, August 30, 1920; *New York Times*, August 30, 1920.

63. *Pittston Gazette*, August 31, 1920. President Wilson's response was drafted by Secretary of Labor William B. Wilson. See Arthur S. Link, ed., *The Papers of Woodrow Wilson* (Princeton: Princeton University Press, 1992), 66:75–77.

64. *New York Times,* September 2, 1920; see also September 1 and *Scranton Times,* August 31, 1920.

65. *New York Times,* September 4, 1920; also see September 3. Wilson had made such requests to operators in the Central Competitive Field in the months following the award of the Bituminous Coal Commission. See *Pittston Gazette,* September 4, 1920.

66. On Dempsey's dismissal, see *Pittston Gazette,* September 4 and 6, 1920; on the progress of the strike, see *ibid.,* September 4, 8, 10, 11, 1920 and *New York Times,* September 2–10, 1920.

67. *New York Times,* September 11, 1920. Secretary of Labor W. B. Wilson also drafted this statement for the President; see Link, ed., *Wilson Papers,* 66:104–08.

68. *Pittston Gazette,* September 12–16, 1920; *New York Times,* September 12–16, 1920. Williams claimed that all Lackawanna County locals were represented at the insurgents' meeting, but according to the press, it was mainly attended by locals from the DL & W. See *Pittston Gazette,* September 16, 1920.

69. For text of statement, see *UMWJ,* October 1, 1920; also see *New York Times,* September 17, 1920.

70. *New York Times,* September 18–23, 1920; *Pittston Gazette,* September 14, 15, and 20–23, 1920; October 5 and 6, 1920.

71. *UMWJ,* November 1, 1920.

72. *Pittston Gazette,* September 9–11, 1920; for quotation, see September 11.

73. *Ibid.,* September 13–18, 1920.

74. *Ibid.,* September 20–21, 1920.

75. *Ibid.,* September 21, 1920.

76. *Ibid.,* September 22–25, 1920.

77. *Ibid.,* September 27–October 2, October 4, 1920.

78. *Ibid.,* October 4–9, 1920.

79. *Pittston Gazette,* September 25, 1920, June 21, 1920; *Proceedings of the Nineteenth Successive and Fourth Biennial Convention of District No. 1, July 1921,* 64.

80. *Pittston Gazette,* January 8–17, 1920.

81. *Ibid.,* January 17–20, 1920. Immediately after the settlement of that walkout, workers at the Butler colliery struck over the employment of four former "hustlers." The general committee threatened again to call a company-wide strike, and the

PCC threatened to close the mine indefinitely. The dispute was resolved when the "hustlers" agreed to join the union. See *ibid.*, January 21–28, 1921.

82. *Ibid.*, June 17–29, 1921. Shortly after this strike was settled, some workers at the Ewen colliery struck briefly over the company's employment of a former contractor. See *ibid.*, July 2, 1921.

83. *Proceedings of the Nineteenth Successive and Fourth Biennial Convention of District No. 1, July 1921*, 116. For election returns, see *ibid.*, unpaginated.

84. *Ibid.*, 119.

85. *Ibid.*, 157.

86. For membership figures, see *Proceedings of the Nineteenth Successive and Fourth Biennial Convention of District No. 1, July 1921*, 64–65 and United Mine Workers of America, *Report of Proceedings of the Twentieth Successive and Fifth Biennial Convention of District No. 1, United Mine Workers of America, Wilkes-Barre, Pennsylvania, July 16th to 21st inclusive, 1923* (Scranton, PA: Commercial Printing Company, 1923), 130.

87. *Proceedings of the Nineteenth Successive and Fourth Biennial Convention of District No. 1, July 1921*, 258–72.

88. United Mine Workers of America, *Record of Proceedings of the Tri-District Convention of Districts Nos. 1, 7 and 9, United Mine Workers of America, Wilkes-Barre, Pennsylvania, September 6–9, 1922* (n.p., n.d.), 46–93 and Harold K. Kanarek, "The Pennsylvania Anthracite Strike of 1922," *Pennsylvania Magazine of History and Biography* 99 (April 1975): 207–25. For the demands, see United Mine Workers of America, *Proceedings of the Tri-District Convention of Districts Nos. 1, 7 and 9, United Mine Workers of America, Shamokin, Pennsylvania, January 17–20, 1922* (Coaldale, PA: Panther Creek News Print, 1922), 167–69.

89. *Record of Proceedings of the Tri-District Convention of Districts Nos. 1, 7 and 9, Wilkes-Barre, Pennsylvania, September 6–9, 1922*, 76–117, 205–14.

90. *Ibid.*, 197.

91. *Ibid.*, 219.

92. *Ibid.*, 183–84.

93. *Ibid.*, 241–42.

94. *Proceedings of the Twentieth Successive and Fifth Biennial Convention of District No. 1, July 1923*, election returns, unpaginated at back.

95. *Ibid.*, 239.

96. *Ibid.*, 248; for membership figures see p. 130 and United Mine Workers of America, *Report of Proceedings of the Twenty-First Consecutive and Sixth Biennial*

Convention of District No. 1, United Mine Workers of America, Wilkes-Barre, Pennsylvania, July 20–25, 1925 (Scranton, PA: Commercial Printing Company, 1925), 126.

97. Coal Commission, *Report*, 1:99. For the 1923 demands and discussion of them, see *Record of Proceedings of the Tri-District Convention of Districts Nos. 1, 7 and 9, June 26–29, 1923*, 167–231.

98. Coal Commission, *Report*, 1:143. For the Commission's account of its role in the negotiations, see 139–45.

99. *Ibid.*, 143–44.

100. Robert H. Zieger, "Pinchot and Coolidge: The Politics of the 1923 Anthracite Crisis," *Journal of American History* 52 (December 1965): 565–81; United Mine Workers of America, *Proceedings of the Re-convened Tri-District Convention, Districts Nos. 1, 7 and 9, United Mine Workers of America, Scranton, Pennsylvania, September 17, 1923* (Scranton: Sanders Printing Co., 1923), 22–38. For the Commission's suggestion, see Coal Commission, *Report*, 1:144–45.

101. *Proceedings of the Twenty-First Consecutive and Sixth Biennial Convention of District No. 1, July 1925*, 14–17, 42–51, 126, 154–77, 188–203, and election returns, unpaginated at back.

102. United Mine Workers of America, *Proceedings of the Tri-District Convention of Districts Numbers 1, 7 and 9, United Mine Workers of America, Scranton, Pennsylvania, February 16, 1926* (n.p.: Mahanoy Press, 1926), 35–55, 92–99; Harold K. Kanarek, "Disaster for Hard Coal: The Anthracite Strike of 1925–26," *Labor History* 15(Winter 1974): 44–62; Walsh, 141–46; and Douglas Keith Monroe, "A Decade of Turmoil: John L. Lewis and the Anthracite Miners, 1926–1936," Ph.D. dissertation, Georgetown University, 1976, 34–46. On the union's collapse in the Central Competitive Field, see Dubofsky and Van Tine, 100–08.

103. *Proceedings of the Tri-District Convention of Districts Numbers 1, 7 and 9, February 16, 1926*, 83–84.

104. On Cappellini's troubles in Pittston and the murder of Campbell, see Selekman, "Miners and Murder." On his ouster, see Monroe, "Decade of Turmoil," 81–91.

105. On the UAMP, see Monroe, "Decade of Turmoil," 182 ff. Interestingly, Monroe labels the once indefatigable insurgent Enoch Williams, who retained his post as district secretary-treasurer through the 1930s, as "a long-time [John L.] Lewis friend and dedicated loyalist." See p. 254. John Bodnar offers a fascinating oral-history account of workers' struggles in the Wyoming field in the 1930s in *Anthracite People: Families, Unions and Work* (Harrisburg, PA: Pennsylvania Historical and Museum Commission, 1983). Perhaps the ultimate expression of rank-and-file rebellion in anthracite is a strike that began at the end of 1942 in which some 20,000 mine workers walked off their jobs to protest a substantial increase in UMWA dues. See

J. R. Sperry, "Rebellion Within the Ranks: Pennsylvania Anthracite, John L. Lewis, and the Coal Strikes of 1943," *Pennsylvania History* 40 (July 1973): 293–312.

106. Dubofsky and Van Tine, 86–99.

107. Fox, 126–35.

108. Lorin Lee Cary makes a similar point concerning opposition to militancy in the early days of the Congress of Industrial Organizations. See "Institutionalized Conservatism in the Early CIO: Adolph Germer, A Case Study," *Labor History* 13(Fall 1972): 475–504.

109. This theme is common to other places and other times. Peter N. Stearns comments on the failure of European unions at the turn of the century to deal effectively with workplace issues in *Lives of Labor: Work in a Maturing Industrial Society* (New York: Holmes and Meier, 1975), 322–25. David Brody discusses the intensity of management's concern for its "right to manage" after World War II and the response of union leaders in "The Uses of Power I; Industrial Battleground," in *Workers in Industrial America: Essays in the Twentieth Century Struggle* (New York: Oxford University Press, 1980), 173–214.

EPILOGUE

1. United Mine Workers of America, *Proceedings of the Tri-District Convention of Districts Nos. 1, 7 and 9, United Mine Workers of America, Held at Shamokin, Pennsylvania, January 17–20, 1922* (Coaldale, PA: Panther Creek News Print, 1922), 10.

2. Paul H. Douglas, *Real Wages in the United States, 1890–1926*, reprint edition (New York: Augustus M. Kelley, Publishers, 1966), 653.

3. United States, Bureau of the Census, *Historical Statistics of the United States: Colonial Times to 1970* (Washington: Government Printing Office, 1975), 1:592.
   The decline of the anthracite industry is a topic that surely deserves more extensive study than it has received. For a brief impressionistic overview, see Donald L. Miller and Richard E. Sharpless, *The Kingdom of Coal: Work, Enterprise, and Ethnic Communities in the Mine Fields* (Philadelphia: University of Pennsylvania Press, 1985), 286–324.

4. United Mine Workers of America, *Report of Proceedings of the Twentieth Successive and Fifth Biennial Convention of District No. 1, United Mine Workers of America, Wilkes-Barre, Pennsylvania, July 16th to 21st inclusive, 1923* (Scranton, PA: Commercial Printing Company, 1923), 9.

5. John Fitch, *The Steel Workers* (Pittsburgh: University of Pittsburgh Press, 1989), 214–20, 229–31.

6. Thomas Bell, *Out of This Furnace* (Pittsburgh: University of Pittsburgh Press, 1976), 194–95.

SELECT BIBLIOGRAPHY

I. PRIMARY SOURCES

A. Manuscript and oral history collections

Detroit, MI. Wayne State University. Walter P. Reuther Library. Archives of Labor and Urban Affairs. Papers of Edward J. Falkowski.

Harrisburg, PA. Pennsylvania Historical and Museum Commission. Corporate Records of the Lehigh Coal and Navigation Company (microfilm edition).

————. Eckley Oral History Project. Tape Recordings.

————. Scranton Oral History Project. Tape Recordings.

Interviews conducted by the author (tape recordings in possession of author).

————. Howell, Roger J. Scranton, PA. December 9, 1979, and March 27, 1980.

————. Milner, E. Stewart. Dunmore, PA. June 16, 1980.

————. Seliga, Joseph and Seliga, Michael. Hazleton, PA. December 10, 1980.

New York, NY. Columbia University Library. Papers of George W. Perkins.

New York, NY. New York Public Library. Papers of the National Civic Federation.

Pottsville, PA. Historical Society of Schuylkill County. Payroll Collection.

Scranton, PA. Lackawanna Historical Society. Corporate Records of the Coal Department—Delaware, Lackawanna, and Western Railroad.

Syracuse, NY. Syracuse University. George Arents Research Library. Corporate Records of the Delaware, Lackawanna, and Western Railroad.

University Park, PA. Pennsylvania State University. Fred Lewis Pattee Library. Historical Collections and Labor Archives. Michael J. Kosik Collection.

Washington, DC. Catholic University of America. John Mitchell Papers.

————. John Mitchell Papers (microfilm edition).

343

Weatherly, PA. Eckley Miners' Village, Anthracite Museum Complex. Edgar Kudlich Papers.

Wilkes-Barre, PA. Wyoming Historical and Geological Society. Papers of the Lehigh and Wilkes-Barre Coal Company.

————.Papers of the Parrish Coal Company.

Wilmington, DE. Hagley Library. St. Clair Coal Company Papers.

————. Reading Railroad Papers.

B. Government hearings and reports

Anthracite Board of Conciliation. *Work of the Board of Conciliation Appointed by the Anthracite Coal Strike Commission for Three Years Ending March 31, 1906.* Wilkes-Barre, PA: Record Press, 1908.

Board of Conciliation. *Compilation of Grievances for Three Years Beginning April 1st, 1906, and Ending March 31st, 1909.* Wilkes-Barre, PA: Record Print, 1909.

Massachusetts. Bureau of Statistics of Labor. *Labor Bulletin of the Commonwealth of Massachusetts.* No. 32 (July 1904).

Massachusetts. Bureau of Statistics of Labor. *Labor Bulletin of the Commonwealth of Massachusetts.* No. 34 (December 1904).

Pennsylvania. Bureau of Mines. *Report of the Bureau of Mines of the Department of Internal Affairs of Pennsylvania, 1897–1903.* Harrisburg, PA: William Stanley Ray, State Printer, 1898–1904.

————. Commission to Investigate the Waste of Coal Mining. *Report of Commission Appointed to Investigate the Waste of Coal Mining with the View to the Utilizing of the Waste.* Philadelphia: Allen, Lane, and Scott's Printing House, 1893

————. *Reports of the Inspectors of Mines of the Anthracite Coal Regions of Pennsylvania, 1876–1887.* Harrisburg, PA: B. F. Meyers, State Printer, 1877–1878; Lane S. Hart, State Printer, 1879–1885; Edwin K. Meyers, State Printer, 1886–1888.

————. *Reports of the Inspectors of Mines of the Anthracite and Bituminous Coal Regions of Pennsylvania, 1888–1892.* Harrisburg, PA: Edwin K. Meyers, State Printer, 1889–1893.

————. *Reports of the Inspectors of Coal Mines of Pennsylvania, 1893–1896.* Harrisburg, PA: Clarence M. Busch, State Printer, 1894–1897.

————. Secretary of Internal Affairs. *Annual Report.* Part III: *Industrial Statistics.* VIII–XXXI (1878–1903).

U.S. Anthracite Coal Strike Commission. "Proceedings of the Anthracite Coal Strike Commission, 1902–1903." 56 vols. (microfilm edition).

————. *Report to the President on the Anthracite Coal Strike of May–October, 1902.* Washington: Government Printing Office, 1903.

U.S. Bureau of Labor. *Regulation and Restriction of Output.* Washington: Government Printing Office, 1904.

————. *Tenth Annual Report of the Commissioner of Labor, 1894: Strikes and Lockouts.* 2 vols. Washington: Government Printing Office, 1896.

U.S. Coal Commission. *Report of the United States Coal Commission.* 5 parts. Washington: Government Printing Office, 1925.

U.S. Commissioner of Labor. *Third Annual Report of the Commissioner of Labor, 1887: Strikes and Lockouts.* Washington: Government Printing Office, 1888.

U.S. Congress. House. Select Committee on Existing Labor Troubles in Pennsylvania. *Labor Troubles in the Anthracite Regions of Pennsylvania, 1887–88.* H. Rept. 4147, 50th Cong., 2nd sess., 1889.

————. House. *Testimony taken by the Select Committee of the House of Representatives to Inquire into the Alleged Violation of the Laws Prohibiting the Importation of Contract Laborers, Paupers, Convicts, and Other Classes.* H. Doc. 572, 50th Cong., 1st sess., 1888.

————. Senate. *Report on Conditions of Employment in the Iron and Steel Industry in the United States.* 3 vols. S. Doc. 110, 62nd Cong., 1st sess., 1911.

U.S. Department of Commerce and Labor. *Bulletin of the U.S. Bureau of Labor: Retail Prices 1890 to 1911.* Whole No. 105, Part I. Washington: Government Printing Office, 1912.

————. *Bulletin of the U.S. Bureau of Labor: Retail Prices 1890 to 1911.* Whole No. 105, Part II. Washington: Government Printing Office, 1912.

U.S. Department of Labor. *Bulletin of the Department of Labor.* "Report to the President on the Anthracite Coal Strike," by Carroll D. Wright. No. 43. Washington: Government Printing Office, 1902.

————. Children's Bureau. *Child Labor and the Welfare of Children in an Anthracite Coal-Mining District.* Washington: Government Printing Office, 1922.

U.S. Department of State. *Papers Relating to the Foreign Relations of the United States with the Annual Message of the President, Transmitted to the Congress, December 5, 1898.* Washington: Government Printing Office, 1901.

U. S. Department of the Interior. Bureau of Mines. *Pennsylvania Mining Statutes Annotated,* by J. W. Thompson. Bulletin No. 21. Washington: Government Printing Office, 1920.

———. Census Office. *Compendium of the Eleventh Census: 1890.* 3 parts. Washington: Government Printing Office, 1894.

———. Census Office. *Report on Mineral Industries in the United States at the Eleventh Census: 1890.* Washington: Government Printing Office, 1892.

———. United States Geological Survey. *Twenty-Second Annual Report of the United States Geological Survey to the Secretary of the Interior 1900–1901. Part III. Coal, Oil, Cement.* Washington: Government Printing Office, 1902.

U.S. Industrial Commission. *Reports of the Industrial Commission.* Volume XII. *Report of the Industrial Commission on the Relations of Capital and Labor Employed in the Mining Industry.* Washington: Government Printing Office, 1901.

C. Newspapers and periodicals

Engineering and Mining Journal. Volumes 38–74 (1884–1902).

Monthly Labor Review. Volumes 2–21 (1916–1925).

New York Herald—1900, 1902.

New York Times—1888, 1902–1903, 1906, 1916, 1918, 1919, 1920, and 1921.

New York Tribune—1900.

Pittsburgh Post—1903, 1906.

Pittston Gazette—1920–1921.

Scranton Republican—1889, 1899.

Scranton Times—1900, 1904–1906, 1910, 1912–1914, 1919–1920.

The World, New York—1890, 1897, 1900, 1902.

United Mine Workers' Journal—1891–1920.

Wilkes-Barre Record—1886–1900, 1916–1918.

Wilkes-Barre Record of the Times—1886–1900.

Wilkes-Barre Union Leader—1897.

D. Published Convention Proceedings, United Mine Workers of America

District One Convention Proceedings, 1900–1925. Fred Lewis Pattee Library, Pennsylvania State University, University Park, PA.

National Convention Proceedings, 1900–1908. John Mitchell Papers (microfilm edition).

Tri-District Convention Proceedings, Districts One, Seven, and Nine, *1915, 1919, 1920, 1922, 1923, 1925, and 1926.* Fred Lewis Pattee Library, Pennsylvania State University, University Park, PA.

II. SECONDARY SOURCES AND OTHER WORKS

A. Works contemporaneous to the period of this study

Addams, Jane. "The Present Crisis in Trade-Union Morals." *North American Review* 179 (August 1904): 178–93.

Archbald, Hugh. *The Four-Hour Day in Coal: A Study of the Relation between the Engineering of the Organization of Work and the Discontent among the Workers in the Coal Mines.* New York: H. W. Wilson Co., 1922.

Chance, Henry Martyn. *Report on the Mining Methods and Appliances used in the Anthracite Coal Fields.* Vol. AC. *Second Geological Survey of Pennsylvania.* Harrisburg, PA: Board of Commissioners for the Second Geological Survey, 1883.

Chapin, Robert Coit. *The Standard of Living Among Workingmen's Families in New York City.* New York: Russell Sage Foundation, 1909.

Coal and Metal Miners' Pocketbook of Principles, Rules, Formulas, and Tables. 9th ed. Scranton, PA: International Textbook Co., 1904.

Crew, H. H. *History of Scranton, Pennsylvania.* Dayton, OH: United Brethren Publishing House, 1891.

Drury, Horace B. "Wages in the Coal Industry as Compared with Wages in Other Industries (With Special Reference to the Anthracite Situation)." *Annals of the American Academy of Political and Social Science* 111 (January 1924): 314–43.

Fitch, John. *The Steel Workers.* Reprint edition. Pittsburgh: University of Pittsburgh Press, 1989.

Hambridge, Jay. "An Artist's Impression of the Colliery Region." *Century Magazine* 55 (April 1898): 822–28.

Harris, Joseph S. "The Beneficial Fund of the Lehigh Coal and Navigation Company." *Transactions of the American Institute of Mining Engineers* 12 (February 1884): 587–607.

Harrison, Shelby M. "Nine Years of the Anthracite Conciliation Board." *The Survey* 28 (April 20, 1912): 150.

Hitchcock, Frederick L. *History of Scranton and Its People.* 2 vols. New York: Lewis Historical Publishing Co., 1914.

Hoffman, Frederick L. "Problems of Labor and Life in Anthracite Coal Mining." *Engineering and Mining Journal* 74. (November 22, December 6, December 13, and December 20, 1902): 675–76, 746–47, 783–84, 811–12.

Hourwich, Isaac A. *Immigration and Labor: The Economic Aspects of European Immigration to the United States.* New York: G. P. Putnam's Sons, 1912. Reprint edition. New York: Arno Press, Inc., 1969.

Hunt, Edward Eyre; Tryon, F. G.; and Willits, Joseph H. *What the Coal Commission Found: An Authoritative Summary by the Staff.* Baltimore: Williams and Wilkins Company, 1925.

Hunter, Robert. *Poverty.* New York: Macmillan and Co., 1904.

Jones, Chester Lloyd. *The Economic History of the Anthracite-Tidewater Canals.* Publications of the University of Pennsylvania. Series in Political Economy and Public Law, No. 22. Philadelphia: John C. Winston, Co., 1908.

Jones, Eliot. *The Anthracite Coal Combination in the United States.* Cambridge: Harvard University Press, 1914.

Maguire, John. "Early Pennsylvania Coal Mine Legislation." *Publications of the Historical Society of Schuylkill County* 4 (1912–14): 337–40.

More, Louise Boland. *Wage-Earners' Budgets: A Study of Standards and Cost of Living in New York City.* New York: Henry Holt and Company, 1907.

Nichols, Francis H. "Children of the Coal Shadow." *McClure's Magazine* 15, February 1903, pp. 435–44.

Obenauer, Marie L. "Living Conditions Among Coal Mine Workers of the United States." *Annals of the American Academy of Political and Social Science* 111 (January 1924): 13–23.

Patterson, Joseph F. "After the W.B.A." *Publications of the Historical Society of Schuylkill County* 4 (1912–14): 168–84.

———. "Old W.B.A. Days." *Publications of the Historical Society of Schuylkill County* 2 (1907–1910): 355–84.

———. "Reminiscences of John Maguire after Fifty Years of Mining." *Publications of the Historical Society of Schuylkill County* 4 (1912–14): 305–36.

Philadelphia and Reading Railroad Company. *Report of the President and Managers of the Philadelphia and Reading Railroad Company for the Year Ending November 30, 1888, together with the Report of the Philadelphia and Reading Coal and Iron Company.* Philadelphia: Dando Printing and Publishing Company, 1889.

Platt, Franklin. *A Special Report to the Legislature upon the Causes, Kinds and Amount of Waste in Mining Anthracite.* Vol. A2. *Second Geological Survey of Pennsylvania.* Harrisburg, PA: Board of Commissioners of the Second Geological Survey, 1881.

Powderly, T. V. *Thirty Years of Labor: 1859 to 1889*. Columbus, OH: Excelsior Publishing House, 1890.

Roberts, Peter. *The Anthracite Coal Communities*. New York: The Macmillan Co., 1904.

————. *The Anthracite Coal Industry*. New York: The Macmillan Co., 1901.

————. "The Anthracite Conflict." *Yale Review* 11 (November 1902): 298.

Rood, Henry Edward. "A Polyglot Community." *Century Magazine* 55 (April 1898): 809–21.

Rowntree, B. Seebohm. *Poverty: A Study of Town Life*. Reprint edition. New York: Howard Fertig, Inc., 1971.

Roy, Andrew. *A History of the Coal Miners of the United States*. Reprint edition. Westport, CT: Greenwood Press, 1970.

————. *The Coal Mines*. Cleveland, OH: Robison, Savage & Co., Printers and Stationers, 1876.

Sydenstricker, Edgar. "The Settlement of Disputes Under Agreements in the Anthracite Industry." *Journal of Political Economy* 24 (March 1916): 254–83.

Virtue, G. O. "The Anthracite Combinations." *Quarterly Journal of Economics* 10 (April 1896): 296–323.

————. "The Anthracite Mine Laborers." *Bulletin of the Department of Labor* 13 (November 1897): 728–74.

Warne, Frank Julian. "The Anthracite Coal Strike." *Annals of the American Academy of Political and Social Science* 17 (January 1901): 15–52.

Weeks, Joseph D. "Report of Joseph D. Weeks on Industrial Arbitration and Conciliation." In Massachusetts. Bureau of Statistics of Labor. *Twelfth Annual Report*. Boston: Rand, Avery, and Co., Printers to the Commonwealth, 1881, pp. 3–75.

Wetherill, J. Price. "How Anthracite Coal is Mined." In Platt, Franklin. *A Special Report to the Legislature upon the Causes, Kinds and Amount of Waste in Mining Anthracite*. Vol. A2. Second Geological Survey of Pennsylvania. Harrisburg, PA: Board of Commissioners for the Second Geological Survey, 1881.

Willcox, David. "Present Conditions in the Anthracite Coal Industry." *North American Review* 181 (August 1905): 216–28.

B. More recent works

Asher, Robert. "Union Nativism and the Immigrant Response." *Labor History* 23 (Summer 1982): 325–48.

——. "The Limits of Big Business Paternalism: Relief for Injured Workers in the Years before Workmen's Compensation." In *Dying for Work: Workers' Safety and Health in Twentieth-Century America*, pp. 19–33. Edited by David Rosner and Gerald Markowitz. Bloomington: Indiana University Press, 1987.

Aurand, Harold W. "The Anthracite Miner: An Occupational Analysis." *Pennsylvania Magazine of History and Biography* 104 (October 1980): 462–73.

——. " 'Do Your Duty!': Editorial Response to the Anthracite Strike of 1902." In *Hard Coal, Hard Times: Ethnicity and Labor in the Anthracite Region*, pp. 153–64. Edited by David L. Salay. Scranton, PA: Anthracite Museum Press, 1984.

——. *From the Molly Maguires to the United Mine Workers: The Social Ecology of an Industrial Union, 1869–1897*. Philadelphia: Temple University Press, 1971.

Barrett, James R. *Work and Community in the Jungle: Chicago's Packinghouse Workers, 1894–1922*. Urbana: University of Illinois Press, 1987.

Bell, Thomas. *Out of This Furnace*. Reprint edition. Pittsburgh: University of Pittsburgh Press, 1976.

Bernstein, Irving, "Arbitration." In *Industrial Conflict*, pp. 301–15. Edited by Arthur Kornhauser, Robert Dubin, and Arthur M. Ross. New York: McGraw-Hill Book Company, 1954.

Berthoff, Rowland T. "The 'Freedom to Control' in American Business History." In *A Festschrift for Frederick B. Artz*, pp. 158–80. Edited by David H. Pinkney and Theodore Ropp. Durham: Duke University Press, 1964.

——. "The Social Order of the Anthracite Region, 1825–1902." *Pennsylvania Magazine of History and Biography* 89 (July 1965): 261–91.

Blatz, Perry K. "The All-too-Youthful Proletarians: Breaker Boys of the Anthracite Coal Region in the Early 1900s." *Pennsylvania Heritage* 7 (Winter 1981): 13–17.

——. "Corporate Attitudes toward Labor Organization: The Controversy over the Price of Powder in the Lackawanna Valley, 1888–1889." In *Hard Coal, Hard Times: Ethnicity and Labor in the Anthracite Region*, pp. 40–57. Edited by David L. Salay. Scranton, PA: Anthracite Museum Press, 1984.

——. "Local Leadership and Local Militancy: The Nanticoke Strike of 1899 and the Roots of Unionization in the Northern Anthracite Fields." *Pennsylvania History* 58 (October 1991): 278–97.

——. " 'Our Present Deplorable Condition': The UMW Tries to Organize the Anthracite Region in the 1890s." In *The Early Coal Miner*, pp. 101–13. Edited by Dennis F. Brestensky. Uniontown: Pennsylvania State University, Fayette Campus, 1991.

————. "Ever-Shifting Ground: Work and Labor Relations in the Anthracite Coal Industry, 1868–1903." Ph.D. Dissertation, Princeton University, 1987.

Bodnar, John. *Anthracite People: Families, Unions and Work.* Harrisburg: Pennsylvania Historical and Museum Commission, 1983.

————. "The Family Economy and Labor Protest in Industrial America: Hard Coal Miners in the 1930s." In *Hard Coal, Hard Times: Ethnicity and Labor in the Anthracite Region,* pp. 78–99. Edited by David L. Salay. Scranton, PA: Anthracite Museum Press, 1984.

————. *Immigration and Industrialization: Ethnicity in an American Mill Town, 1870–1940.* Pittsburgh: University of Pittsburgh Press, 1977.

————. "Immigration, Kinship, and the Rise of Working-Class Realism in Industrial America." *Journal of Social History* 14 (Fall 1980): 45–65.

————. "Immigration and Modernization: The Case of Slavic Peasants in Industrial America." *Journal of Social History* 10 (Fall 1976): 44–71.

————. "Socialization and Adaptation: Immigrant Families in Scranton, 1880–1900." *Pennsylvania History* 43 (April 1976): 154–72.

————. *The Transplanted: A History of Immigrants in Urban America.* Bloomington: Indiana University Press, 1985.

Bogen, Jules I. *The Anthracite Railroads.* New York: Ronald Press Co., 1927.

Brecher, Jeremy. *Strike!* Boston: South End Press, 1972.

Brody, David. "The Old Labor History and the New: In Search of an American Working Class." *Labor History* 20 (Winter 1979): 111–26.

————. *Steelworkers in America: The Nonunion Era.* Reprint edition. New York: Harper & Row, 1969.

————. *Workers in Industrial America: Essays in the Twentieth Century Struggle.* New York: Oxford University Press, 1980.

————. "Labor Relations in American Coal Mining: An Industry Perspective." Unpublished paper.

Broehl, Wayne G., Jr. *The Molly Maguires.* New York: Vintage/Chelsea House, 1964.

Brophy, John. *A Miner's Life.* Edited by John O. O. Hall. Madison: University of Wisconsin Press, 1964.

Bruce, Robert V. *1877: Year of Violence.* Chicago: Quadrangle Paperbacks, 1970.

Buder, Stanley. *Pullman: An Experiment in Industrial Order and Community Planning, 1880–1930.* New York: Oxford University Press, 1967.

Calderón-Jemio, Raúl. "John Mitchell and the United Mine Workers." Unpublished seminar paper, University of Connecticut, 1986.

Campbell, Stuart William. "Businessmen and Anthracite: Aspects of Change in the Late Nineteenth Century Anthracite Industry." Ph.D. Dissertation, University of Delaware, 1978.

Cary, Lorin Lee. "Institutionalized Conservatism in the Early CIO: Adolph Germer, A Case Study." *Labor History* 13 (Fall 1972): 475–504.

Coleman, J. Walter, *The Molly Maguire Riots: Industrial Conflict in the Pennsylvania Coal Region*. Richmond, VA: Garrett and Massie, 1936.

Conway, Alan, ed. *The Welsh in America: Letters from the Immigrants*. Minneapolis: University of Minnesota Press, 1961.

Corbin, David Alan. *Life, Work, and Rebellion in the Coal Fields: The Southern West Virginia Miners, 1880–1922*. Urbana: University of Illinois Press, 1981.

Corlsen, Carl. *Buried Black Treasure: The Story of Pennsylvania Anthracite*. Bethlehem, PA: By the Author, 1953.

Corn, Jacqueline. "Protective Legislation for Coal Miners, 1870–1900: Response to Safety and Health Hazards." In *Dying for Work: Workers' Safety and Health in Twentieth-Century America*, pp. 67–82. Edited by David Rosner and Gerald Markowitz. Bloomington: Indiana University Press, 1987.

Cornell, Robert J. *The Anthracite Coal Strike of 1902*. Washington: Catholic University of America Press, 1957.

Dix, Keith. *Work Relations in the Coal Industry: The Hand-Loading Era, 1880–1930*. Morgantown: Institute for Labor Studies, West Virginia University, 1977.

———. *What's a Coal Miner to Do?: The Mechanization of Coal Mining*. Pittsburgh: University of Pittsburgh Press, 1988.

Douglas, Paul H. *Real Wages in the United States, 1890–1926*. Reprint edition. New York: Augustus M. Kelley, Publishers, 1966.

Douglass, Dave. "The Durham Pitman." In *Miners, Quarrymen, and Saltworkers*, pp. 207–95. Edited by Raphael Samuel. London: Routledge & Kegan Paul, 1977.

Dublin, Thomas. *Women at Work: The Transformation of Work and Community in Lowell, Massachusetts, 1826–1860*. New York: Columbia University Press, 1979.

Dubofsky, Melvyn. *Industrialism and the American Worker, 1865–1920*. Arlington Heights, IL: AHM Publishing Corporation, 1975.

————. *When Workers Organize: New York City in the Progressive Era*. Amherst: University of Massachusetts Press, 1968.

Dubofsky, Melvyn, and Van Tine, Warren. *John L. Lewis: A Biography*. New York: Quadrangle/The New York Times Book Co., 1977.

Eavenson, Howard M. *The First Century and a Quarter of American Coal Industry*. Pittsburgh: Privately Printed, 1947.

Emmons, David M. *The Butte Irish: Class and Ethnicity in an American Mining Town, 1875–1925*. Urbana: University of Illinois Press, 1989.

Fishback, Price. *Soft Coal, Hard Choices: The Economic Welfare of Bituminous Coal Miners, 1890–1930*. New York: Oxford University Press, 1992.

Fisher, Waldo E. "Anthracite." In *How Collective Bargaining Works: A Survey of Experience in Leading American Industries*, pp. 280–317. Edited by Harry A. Millis and Natalie Pannes. New York: Twentieth Century Fund, 1942.

Foulke, C. Pardee and Foulke, William G. *Calvin Pardee 1841–1923: His Family and His Enterprises*. Philadelphia: The Pardee Company, 1979.

Fox, Maier, B. *United We Stand: The United Mine Workers of America 1890–1990*. Washington: United Mine Workers of America, 1990.

Garlock, Jonathan, compiler. *Guide to the Local Assemblies of the Knights of Labor*. Westport, CT: Greenwood Press, 1982.

Ginger, Ray. "Company-Sponsored Welfare Plans in the Anthracite Industry before 1900." *Bulletin of the Business Historical Society* 37 (June 1953): 112–20.

Glück, Elsie. *John Mitchell, Miner: Labor's Bargain with the Gilded Age*. Reprint edition. New York: Greenwood Press, 1969.

Golab, Caroline. *Immigrant Destinations*. Philadelphia: Temple University Press, 1977.

————. "The Impact of the Industrial Experience on the Immigrant Family: The Huddled Masses Reconsidered." In *Immigrants in Industrial America*, pp. 1–32. Edited by Richard L. Ehrlich. Charlottesville: University Press of Virginia, 1977.

Goodrich, Carter. *The Miner's Freedom: A Study of the Working Life in a Changing Industry*. Boston: Marshall Jones Co., 1925.

Gouldner, Alvin W. *Patterns of Industrial Bureaucracy: A Case Study of Modern Factory Administration*. New York: The Free Press, 1954.

————. *Wildcat Strike*. Yellow Springs, OH: Antioch Press, 1954.

Gowaskie, Joseph M. "From Conflict to Cooperation: John Mitchell and the Bituminous Coal Operators, 1898–1908." *The Historian* 38 (August 1976): 669–88.

————. "John Mitchell and the Anthracite Mine Workers: Leadership Conservatism and Rank-and-File Militancy." *Labor History* 27 (Winter 1985–86): 54–83.

————. "John Mitchell: A Study in Leadership." Ph.D. Dissertation, Catholic University of America, 1968.

Green, Marguerite. *The National Civic Federation and the American Labor Movement 1900–1925*. Washington: Catholic University of America Press, 1956.

Greene, Victor R. *The Slavic Community on Strike: Immigrant Labor in Pennsylvania Anthracite*. Notre Dame: University of Notre Dame Press, 1968.

Gutman, Herbert G. *Work, Culture, and Society in Industrializing America: Essays in American Working-Class and Social History*. New York: Vintage Books, 1977.

Hall, Jacquelyn D.; Leloudis, James; Korstad, Robert; Murphy, Mary; Jones, Lu Ann; and Daly, Christopher B. *Like a Family: The Making of a Southern Cotton Mill World*. Chapel Hill: University of North Carolina Press, 1987.

Hareven, Tamara K. *Family Time and Industrial Time: The Relationship between the Family and Work in a New England Industrial Community*. Cambridge: Cambridge University Press, 1982.

Harris, Sheldon H. "Letters from West Virginia: Management's Version of the 1902 Coal Strike." *Labor History* 10 (Spring 1969): 228–40.

Hobsbawm, E. J. *Primitive Rebels: Studies in Archaic Forms of Social Movement in the 19th and 20th Centuries*. Reprint edition. New York: W. W. Norton & Co., 1965.

Hodas, Daniel. *The Business Career of Moses Taylor*. New York: New York University Press, 1976.

Hoffman, John N. *Girard Estate Coal Lands in Pennsylvania, 1801–1884*. Smithsonian Studies in History and Technology, No. 15. Washington: Smithsonian Institution Press, 1972.

Hudson Coal Company. *The Story of Anthracite*. New York: Hudson Coal Company, 1932.

Kanarek, Harold K. "Disaster for Hard Coal: The Anthracite Strike of 1925–1926." *Labor History* 15 (Winter 1974): 44–62.

————. "The Pennsylvania Anthracite Strike of 1922." *Pennsylvania Magazine of History and Biography* 93 (April 1975): 207–25.

————. "Progressivism in Crisis: The United Mine Workers and the Anthracite Coal Industry During the 1920s" Ph.D. Dissertation, University of Virginia, 1972.

Korson, George. *Black Rock: Mining Folklore of the Pennsylvania Dutch*. Baltimore: The Johns Hopkins Press, 1960.

———— . *Minstrels of the Mine Patch: Songs and Stories of the Anthracite Industry.* Philadelphia: University of Pennsylvania Press, 1938.

Laslett, John H. M. *Labor and the Left: A Study of Socialist and Radical Influences in the American Labor Movement, 1881–1924.* New York: Basic Books, 1970.

Lester, Richard A. *As Unions Mature: An Analysis of the Evolution of American Unionism.* Princeton: Princeton University Press, 1958.

Licht, Walter, *Working for the Railroad: The Organization of Work in the Nineteenth Century.* Princeton: Princeton University Press, 1983.

Lichtenstein, Nelson. *Labor's War at Home: The CIO in World War II.* Cambridge: Cambridge University Press, 1982.

Link, Arthur S., editor. *The Papers of Woodrow Wilson.* Volume 66, August 2–December 23, 1920. Princeton: Princeton University Press, 1992.

Long, Clarence D. *Wages and Earnings in the United States, 1860–1890.* Princeton: Princeton University Press, 1960.

Lüdtke, Alf. "Organizational Order or *Eigensinn?* Workers' Privacy and Workers' Politics in Imperial Germany." In *Rites of Power: Symbolism, Ritual, and Politics Since the Middle Ages,* pp. 303–33. Edited by Sean Wilentz. Philadelphia: University of Pennsylvania Press, 1985.

———— . "Cash, Coffee-Breaks, Horseplay: *Eigensinn* and Politics among Factory Workers in Germany circa 1900." In *Confrontation, Class Consciousness, and the Labor Process: Studies in Proletarian Class Formation,* pp. 65–95. Edited by M. Hanagan and C. Stephenson. New York: Greenwood Press, 1986.

Lynch, Patrick M. "Pennsylvania Anthracite: A Forgotten IWW Venture." M.A. Thesis, Bloomsburg State College, 1974.

Montgomery, David. *Beyond Equality: Labor and the Radical Republicans, 1862–1872.* New York: Alfred A. Knopf, 1967. Paperback edition New York: Vintage Books, 1972.

———— . *Workers' Control in America: Studies in the History of Work, Technology, and Labor Struggles.* Cambridge: Cambridge University Press, 1979.

———— . *The Fall of the House of Labor: The Workplace, the State, and American Labor Activism, 1865–1925.* Cambridge: Cambridge University Press, 1987.

Morris, James O. "The Acquisitive Spirit of John Mitchell, UMW President (1899–1908). *Labor History* 20 (Winter 1979): 5–43.

Mumford, John K. *Anthracite.* New York: Industries Publishing Co., 1925.

Nash, Michael. *Conflict and Accommodation: Coal Miners, Steel Workers, and Socialism, 1890–1920.* Westport, CT: Greenwood Press, 1982.

Nelson, Daniel. "The Company Union Movement, 1900–37: A Reexamination." *Business History Review* 56 (Autumn 1982): 335–57.

———. *Frederick Winslow Taylor and the Rise of Scientific Management*. Madison: University of Wisconsin Press, 1980.

———. *Managers and Workers: Origins of the New Factory System in the United States, 1880–1920*. Madison: University of Wisconsin Press, 1975.

———. *American Rubber Workers and Organized Labor, 1900–1941*. Princeton: Princeton University Press, 1988.

Novak, Michael. *The Guns of Lattimer: The True Story of a Massacre and a Trial, August 1897–March 1898*. New York: Basic Books, Inc., Publishers, 1978.

Oestreicher, Richard J. *Solidarity and Fragmentation: Working People and Class Consciousness in Detroit, 1875–1900*. Urbana: University of Illinois Press, 1986.

Palladino, Grace. *Another Civil War: Labor, Capital, and the State in the Anthracite Regions of Pennsylvania, 1840–68*. Urbana: University of Illinois Press, 1990.

Perlman, Selig. *A Theory of the Labor Movement*. Reprint edition. New York: Augustus M. Kelley, Publishers, 1970.

Powell, H. Benjamin. "The Pennsylvania Anthracite Industry, 1769–1976," *Pennsylvania History* 46 (January 1980): 3–27.

Ramirez, Bruno. *When Workers Fight: The Politics of Industrial Relations in the Progressive Era, 1898–1916*. Westport, CT: Greenwood Press, 1978.

Rees, Albert, assisted by Jacobs, Donald P. *Real Wages in Manufacturing: 1890–1914*. Princeton: Princeton University Press, 1961.

Rodgers, Daniel T. "Tradition, Modernity, and the American Industrial Worker." *Journal of Interdisciplinary History* 7 (Spring 1977): 655–81.

Rochester, Anna. *Labor and Coal*. New York: International Publishers, 1931.

Rothbart, Ron. " 'Homes Are What Any Strike Is About': Immigrant Labor and the Family Wage," *Journal of Social History* 23 (Winter 1989): 267–84.

Salvatore, Nick. *Eugene V. Debs: Citizen and Socialist*. Urbana: University of Illinois Press, 1982.

Sayenga, Donald. "The Untryed Business: An Appreciation of White and Hazard." *Proceedings of the Canal History and Technology Symposium* 2 (1983): 105–14.

Schatz, Ronald W. *The Electrical Workers: A History of Labor at General Electric and Westinghouse*. Urbana: University of Illinois Press, 1983.

Schlegel, Marvin W. *Ruler of the Reading: The Life of Franklin B. Gowen, 1836–1889*. Harrisburg, PA: Archives Publishing Co. of Pennsylvania, Inc., 1947.

Seltzer, Curtis. *Fire in the Hole: Miners and Managers in the American Coal Industry.* Lexington: University Press of Kentucky, 1985.

Sennett, Richard. *Authority.* New York: Alfred A. Knopf, 1980.

Sperry, J. R. "Rebellion Within the Ranks: Pennsylvania Anthracite, John L. Lewis, and the Coal Strikes of 1943," *Pennsylvania History* 40 (July 1973): 293–312.

Stearns, Peter N. *Lives of Labor: Work in a Maturing Industrial Society.* New York: Holmes and Meier, 1975.

Stevenson, George E. *Reflections of an Anthracite Engineer.* Scranton, PA: By the author, 1931.

Taft, Philip. *The A.F. of L. in the time of Gompers.* New York: Harper & Brothers, Publishers, 1957.

Taylor, Philip. *The Distant Magnet: European Emigration to the U.S.A.* New York: Harper & Row Publishers, 1971.

Temin, Peter. *Iron and Steel in Nineteenth-Century North America: An Economic Inquiry.* Cambridge: M.I.T. Press, 1964.

Thompson, E. P. "Time, Work-Discipline, and Industrial Capitalism." *Past and Present* 38 (1967): 56–97.

Trachtenberg, Alexander. *The History of Legislation for the Protection of Coal Miners in Pennsylvania, 1824–1915.* New York: International Publishers, 1942.

Valletta, Clement. " 'To Battle for Our Ideas': Community Ethic and Anthracite Labor, 1920–1940." *Pennsylvania History* 58 (October 1991): 311–29.

Van Tine, Warren R. *The Making of the Labor Bureaucrat: Union Leadership in the United States, 1870–1920.* Amherst: University of Massachusetts Press, 1973.

Walkowitz, Daniel. *Worker City—Company Town: Iron and Cotton-Worker Protest in Troy and Cohoes, New York, 1855–1884.* Urbana: University of Illinois Press, 1978.

Wallace, Anthony F. C. "The Ventilation of Coal Mines." In *The Social Context of Innovation.* Princeton: Princeton University Press, 1982.

———. *St. Clair: A Nineteenth-Century Coal Town's Experience with a Disaster-Prone Industry.* Ithaca: Cornell University Press, 1988.

Walsh, William J. *The United Mine Workers of America as Economic and Social Force in the Anthracite Territory.* Washington: Catholic University of America Press, 1931.

Wiebe, Robert H. "The Anthracite Strike of 1902: A Record of Confusion." *Mississippi Valley Historical Review* 48 (September 1961): 229–51.

———. *Businessmen and Reform: A Study of the Progressive Movement.* Chicago: Quadrangle Books, 1962.

Wyman, Mark. *Hard Rock Epic: Western Miners and the Industrial Revolution, 1860–1910.* Berkeley: University of California Press, 1979.

Yearley, C. K., Jr. *Enterprise and Anthracite: Economics and Democracy in Schuylkill County, 1820–1875.* Baltimore: The Johns Hopkins Press, 1961.

Zieger, Robert H. "Pinchot and Coolidge: The Politics of the 1923 Anthracite Crisis." *Journal of American History* 52 (December 1965): 565–81.

INDEX

Accidents: examples, 22, 32; insurance and aid for victims, 32–35, 272n; statistics, 29–32
Addams, Jane: 182–83
Allen, William: 111, 158
Amalgamated Association of Miners and Laborers: 39, 41
American Federation of Labor: 117–18, 207, 296n
Anthracite Coal Commission (1920): 240, 243–45, 254, 255
Anthracite Coal Strike Commission (1902–03): award and findings, 7–8, 166–69, 172–73, 174–75, 177, 182, 312n; hearings, 141–66; labor's assessment, 171, 173, 185, 193; members of, 306n; operators' assessment, 171, 188, 195; renewal of, 205, 210, 215, workers' demands, 142, 152, 161, 306n; mentioned, 112, 140, 184, 198–99, 202, 207, 216, 241
Atwell, William: 161
Aulsbach, Jackson: 163

Baer, George F.: and negotiations—1906, 188, 192, 193; and negotiations—1912; opposition to UMWA, 113–15, 118–20; strike of 1902, 1, 37, 127–28, 131, 137–38, 298n, 305n; mentioned, 171, 175, 186, 216
Bell, Thomas: 262–63
Berthoff, Rowland: 37
Black Diamond Coal Company: 111–12, 151
Board of Conciliation: 1903–1912, 175–78, 179, 198–99, 208–09, 213, 218;

post-1912, 237, 243, 247; establishment, 168–69, 171, 173–74, worker discontent over, 172, 190–91, 193–94; mentioned, 181, 239
Boylan, John: 258
Brennan, William J.: defeated for District One presidency, 235, 254, 257; wins presidency, 252; mentioned, 236, 253, 258,
Bryden, Alexander: 146–47, 151, 157
Butler, Thomas: 231

Campbell, Alec: murder of, 258; mentioned, 242, 250, 254, 257
Cappellini, Rinaldo: and labor turmoil 1919–21, 241–43, 245, 248–49, 250; president of District One, 254, 257, 258; mentioned, 252
Carbondale, PA: 9, 66, 76, 112, 151
Carne, William: 201
Check-docking boss: and Coal Strike Commission award, 166, 176–77, 312–13n; and local labor disputes, 77, 100–01, 179, 214; mentioned, 148, 224, 293n
Check-off: as UMWA demand, 194, 216–17, 234, 253; failure to obtain in anthracite, 171, 181–82, 205, 215, 217–18, 222–26, 239; mentioned, 260
Child labor: extent, 12, 227; militancy, 44–45, 56, 81–83, 100, 109–13, 116, 297n; work and earnings, 20; mentioned, 34
Clark, E. E.: 305n

359